WARSHIP
VOLUME IX

Edited by Andrew Lambert

Conway Maritime Press

Naval Institute Press

WARSHIP Volume IX

Managing Editor Robert Gardiner
Editor Andrew Lambert
Art Editor Mark Stevens

Frontispiece
Daring, the first ship to carry the 4.5in
Mk VI twin mounting (as described in John
Campbell's 'British Naval Guns' series). The
ship is pictured off Malta in December 1953.

CPL

Published in the UK by
Conway Maritime Press Limited
24 Bride Lane
Fleet Street
London EC4Y 8DR

**Published and distributed in the
United States of America and Canada by**
the Naval Institute Press
Annapolis Maryland 21402

Library of Congress Catalog Card No 78-55455
UK ISBN 0 85177 403 2
USA ISBN 0-87021-984-7

Manufactured in the United Kingdom

Contents

editorial

As *Warship* enters its ninth year it is my pleasure to announce that I have taken over from Randal Gray as editor of this well established journal. Over the past year Randal has more than maintained the high standards set by his predecessors, and I am sure that you will all join me in thanking him for his excellent temporary stewardship.

Those who recall the previous issue will be aware of my interest in the transitional period of the mid-nineteenth century. More generally, however, I am interested in the interaction between naval policy, technology and design during the last two centuries.

In the forthcoming quartet of issues there will be no basic change from the established formula of *Warship*. The articles will be of the usual high standard, many of them being produced by authors already well known to regular readers. This said, it would be well to remember that the health of any journal depends upon its contributors. New authors are always welcome to send articles, photo features and A's & A's to the *Warship* offices.

In this issue D K Brown begins another instalment of his series 'Attack and Defence' with a detailed study of the pre-1914 trials and the influence they had on design in the period leading up to Jutland. In this respect it is highly topical to consider the trial firings of a Sea Eagle air-to-surface missile and Tigerfish torpedoes at the 'County' class guided missile destroyer *Devonshire* that took place last year. The pre-1914 trials revealed most of the defects that were shown in such high relief at Jutland; was this the case before 1982? I must say that it appears doubtful, and it has been suggested that the Falklands campaign forced the Royal Navy to relearn many of the lessons of the 1939–45 period. The *Sheffield* gave a graphic demonstration of the fragility of modern warships; quite simply, they are not designed to withstand damage. The *Devonshire*, by contrast, belonged to the usual class of trials target – obsolescent, inert and expendable. For all that, she proved far tougher than the more modern ships of the fleet, as her sister the *Glamorgan*, along with the *Rothesay* class frigates, had already demonstrated in 1982. As for the trials of 1983 there is a hint of the publicity stunt about them, not only for the new Sea Eagle, but also for the unproven Tigerfish torpedo.

Hans Lengerer's three-part article on the Japanese aircraft carriers *Junyo* and *Hiyo* illustrates the perennial obstacle to international attempts at effective arms limitation: cheating. Lord Chatfield had predicted this while attending the Washington Conference in 1921. The Japanese were to become the masters of the clandestine. Only they thought of building fleet aircraft carriers as merchant ships in order to increase the number available shortly after the outbreak of war. The development of this policy makes fascinating reading. Other nations considered such designs, including Great Britain, but none went so far as to sacrifice warship qualities in order to add numbers to a fleet supposedly limited by a treaty signed by a free and willing nation.

Andrew Lambert

The *Devonshire* taken through the periscope of the nuclear submarine *Swiftsure*. The damage caused on 16–17 July 1984 amidships by the Sea Eagle, and in the flight deck area by the Tigerfish torpedo are graphically illustrated.   *MoD*

Maestrale class weapons and sensors

by Stefano Cioglia

The *Grecale* commissioning at La Spezia Naval Arsenal on 5
January 1983.

The bridge of the *Grecale* with SMA MM/SPS-702 radar on
the foremast and Selenia RAN-10S (MM/SPS-774) on the
short after mast. Note the drawing of the winds on the side of
the bridge, this class all being named after breezes.

1 The octuple launcher for the Aspide missiles of the Selenia
   Albatross Mk 2 system on board the *Maestrale*.

2 The triple tube launcher for Mk 46 or A-244 AEW torpedoes
   and the Breda-Bofors 40mm/70 twin mounting on the
   starboard side of *Maestrale*.

2

1 The *Libeccio*'s radar outfit and secondary guns.

2 The new compact launcher for the Otomat Mk 2 Teseo surface-to-surface missile aboard the *Libeccio*.

3 The *Euro* during her launching ceremony at Riva Trigoso Muggiano Naval Yard on 25 March 1983.

4 Another view of the bridge of *Euro*.

3

4

The sterns of *Euro*, on the right, and *Espero* under construction.

The Japanese aircraft carriers Junyo and Hiyo

by Hans Lengerer and Tomoko Rehm-Takahara

AIRCRAFT CARRIER BUILDING IN JAPAN 1920–1936 AND THE REASONS FOR THE USE OF CONVERTED AUXILIARY AIRCRAFT CARRIERS
Drawing from their experiences with the seaplane carrier *Wakamiya Maru* as well as the actions of the British seaplane carriers and aircraft carriers converted from merchant ships and warships, the Imperial Japanese Navy (IJN) early on perceived the importance of the aircraft carrier for actions within the large areas of the Pacific Ocean. In 1919 the keel of the *Hosho* was laid down. This ship was conceived, designed and built exclusively for using aircraft with wheels and became the first true aircraft carrier in the world, completed some time earlier than the British *Hermes*. The building of the *Hosho* was part of the 8-6 Fleet Completion Programme of 1918.

In the following programme, the 8-8 Fleet Replenishment Programme of 1920, two aircraft carriers were included with a normal displacement of 12,500 tons each. Besides the nucleus of the 8-8 Fleet – 8 new (less than 8 years in service) battleships and 8 new battle-cruisers – the IJN intended to put into service 3 aircraft carriers of about 34,500 tons normal displacement before the Washington Disarmament Conference. When this conference opened in November 1921 the proposal of the United Stated sought to limit aircraft carrier tonnage to 80,000 tons standard displacement for the USA and Great Britain (= 5 ships) and to 48,000 tons for Japan (= 3 ships). The Japanese delegation objected, but they failed to receive the desired parity, although they pressured the other delegations into accepting their wish for three aircraft carriers of 27,000 tons each (= 81,000 tons). Article VII of the Treaty of Washington, therefore, fixed the total tonnage of aircraft carriers for Japan at 81,000 tons (82,296 metric tons), and for the USA and Great Britain at 135,000 tons each (137,160 metric tons). In Chapter 2 part 4 of the Treaty the aircraft carrier was defined as a ship of more than 10,000 tons standard displacement determined for the special and exclusive purpose of carrying aircraft and built in a manner than aircraft could land and take off from it. The maximum displacement for a ship was limited to 27,000 tons in Article IX. Nevertheless permission was granted to build two aircraft carriers of 33,000 tons each within the scope of the total displacement. Besides these limitations there were a number of restrictions concerning armament, armour, bulges etc which we need not mention here.

At this time the IJN wanted the *Hosho* (not included in the Treaty of Washington because her standard displacement was less than 10,000 tons) and three ships of 27,000 tons each. In the revised fleet replenishment programme, *ie* the modified motion for fiscal year 1923, the planning of 3 aircraft carriers of about 34,500 tons standard displacement was altered to the same number of ships but displacing about 63,000 tons. The *Shokaku* and the other still-unnamed ship from the 8-8 Fleet Replenishment Programme were stricken. Instead of them the battlecruisers *Amagi* and *Akagi* were to be converted into aircraft carriers of 27,000 standard displacement each. In order to reach the goal of 81,000 tons another aircraft carrier (CV) would be built later.

The principles of the defence policy of Japan were altered for the second time in 1923. The Imperial Defence Committee decided that the minimum strength for the defence of Japan was to be 9 battleships, 3 aircraft carriers, 40 cruisers, 144 destroyers, 70 submarines and some aircraft groups counted as first line-ships.

In the Auxiliary Replenishment Programme of 1924 the building of one aircraft carrier (CV) of 27,000 tons and three aircraft supply ships *(Kokuhokyukan)* of 10,000 tons each were proposed, but the execution of the programme would have needed more than 900 million Yen and therefore could not be realised. Instead of these ships the building of the CVL *Ryujo* was allowed in the New Shipbuilding Replenishment Programme of 1927. The ship was classified as a seaplane carrier *(Suijokibokan)*, probably as a replacement for the *Wakamiya*, in this programme, the enormous reduction of the displacement continued with the following carriers based on the new policy of the IJN. According to the latest thinking the USA had continued to be their primary hypothetical foe and the ratio of Japanese CVs was to be kept equal to that of the USN. The decision was made in view of the vulnerability of CVs to battle damage and it was feared that with one well-placed bomb or torpedo the ship could be put out of action. For this reason quantity rather than quality was given first consideration. Because the Washington Treaty allowed a total tonnage of 135,000 tons for the USA while that for Japan was reduced to 81,000 tons, the displacement of the single ship had to be drastically reduced in order to reach the goal of numerical parity. At this time the

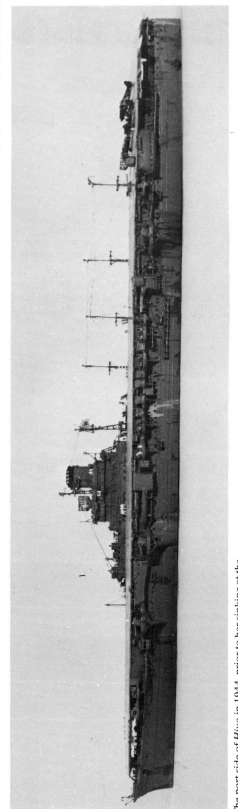

The port side of *Hiyo* in 1944, prior to her sinking at the Battle of the Marianas. This and all other photographs of models are of two superb 1/1200 scale models built by Michael Wünschmann.
Jurgen Peters

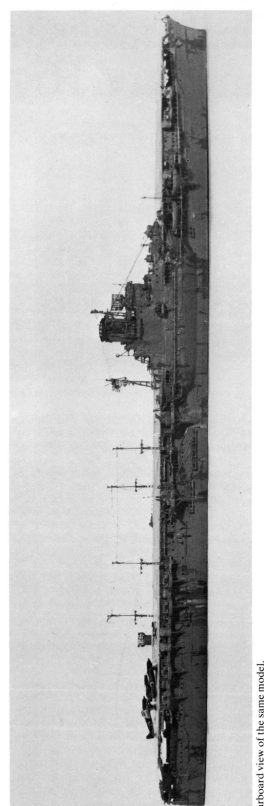

Starboard view of the same model.
Jurgen Peters

leaders of the IJN believed that a ship of 8000 tons displacement could be operated as fleet carrier. This was also why the IJN proposed to include carriers of less than 10,000 tons in the London Treaty. A short review of the development of the CV shows that this was not true and the IJN acted without foresight. But in those years the building of a fleet of cruisers with flight decks was discussed in the USA and the IJN tried to cope with this situation by building the smallest possible operative CV. As a matter of fact the number of carriers grew to four during the life of the Washington Treaty but since only CVs which displaced 27,000 tons were intended for the defence of Japan the IJN therefore considered only three to come within the treaty limitations of 81,000 tons.

In the first London Treaty (1930) the definition of the CV was altered to bring ships of less than 10,000 tons within the restrictions, as proposed by the IJN. This treaty was a result of the failure of the Washington Treaty to limit the number of lesser naval vessels (other than BBs, BCs, CVs). The treaty stipulated only that they were not to exceed 10,000 tons standard displacement, but no undertaking was given about the number that might be built. Consequently, every country sought to make up the deficiency in capital ships by building heavy cruisers ('Treaty Cruisers'), light cruisers, destroyers and submarines. In order to prevent the increase in these categories it was decided to limit them also at the London Conference of 1930.

Under this treaty Japan was allocated the following ratios to American and British strength: CAs 60 per cent, CLs and DDs 70 per cent, SSs parity, so that the overall fighting strength of the IJN was kept to a ratio of 70 per cent. This treaty was received with the most profound dissatisfaction by the IJN and it was the main reason for the adoption of the plan by which, on the outbreak of war, merchant vessels would be rapidly converted – and in particular the large passenger liners would be prepared for conversion into CVs – to make up for the shortage of warships.

At this time the IJN possessed or was building four CVs: the *Hosho* of 7470 tons; the *Akagi* and *Kaga* of 26,900 tons each; and the *Ryujo* of 7100 tons. Also in existence was the *Wakamiya*, rated as an aircraft carrier (*Kokubokan*) on April 1920 despite the fact that she was a seaplane carrier (*Suijokibokan*). This was the result of a new proposal for the augmentation of naval vessels necessary for the defence of Japan that had been submitted by the Deputy Chief of the Naval General Staff, Vice-Admiral Kichisaburo Nomura, in March 1928. He was concurrently the Chief of the Committee for Armament Restrictions and his plan foresaw four CVs in the first line strength.

Because *Hosho* and *Wakamiya* had already been laid down before 12 November 1921 and could be replaced without regard to their age (Article VIII Washington Treaty and Article 9 London Treaty) the total tonnage of CVs so far constructed was 60,900 tons according to the treaties. Subtracting this amount from the total tonnage, 20,100 tons were left for new construction. The problem for the IJN was to build within this limit about equal the number of CVs possessed by the USN and at

the same time to take care not to challenge the USN by ambitious shipbuilding programmes.

In accordance with this policy, the First Naval Armament Replenishment Programme of 1930 included one carrier of only 9800 tons displacement, but in the final draft of the programme this carrier was cancelled.

With the next great proposal, the Second Naval Armament Replenishment Programme of 1934, two CVs displacing 10,050 tons each were built. These were the *Soryu* and *Hiryu*, temporarily known as aircraft carriers nos 1 and 2 respectively and being again the Japanese reply to the flight-deck cruisers which it was rumoured the USN would build. Displacing about twice the tonnage of the *Ryujo* these carriers became the first modern operative CVs of the IJN. Adding their tonnage (20,100 tons) to the tonnage of the CVs already in commission, the total tonnage allowed by the treaties was achieved. Having now no further legal opportunity to build CVs, the IJN included auxiliary naval vessels in this programme that were built with the intention of being converted into aircraft carriers within three months.

On 29 December 1934 Japan submitted notification of the abrogation of the Washington Treaty. It was felt that the naval ratio that had been adopted both in the Washington and London treaties was unreasonable and would not guarantee the security of Japan. At the Naval Disarmament Conference, held in London in December 1935, the USA and Great Britain disagreed with Japan's proposals and refused parity. The Japanese delegation withdrew from the conference on 15 January 1936. Thus, with the expiration of both the Washington and London treaties, Japan was no longer committed to any treaty obligations with the USA and Great Britain.

The principles of Japanese defence policy were altered for the third and last time before the end of World War II, on 3 June 1936. The nucleus of the first line fleet was to consist of 12 BBs, 10 CVs, 28 CAs and CLs, 13 flotilla leaders, 96 DDs, 70 SSs and 65 naval aircraft groups. After intensive research for the Second Naval Limitation Conference it had been discovered that Japan did not have the facilities, material or finance to compete with the USA in naval armament and especially with regard to the number of BBs. Therefore it was decided to construct the two largest and most effective BBs in the world. As for CVs the IJN wanted to avoid numerical inferiority so kept to its policy of keeping the ratio of the Japanese CVs equal to, if not greater than, that of the USA. If it was not possible to balance the USN in the number of CVs or if the USN planned to increase in CVs and the Japanese plan to maintain parity with the USN could not be realised with regular CVs, first class merchant ships would be requisitioned and converted into CVs in order to obtain this goal.

Reviewing the Japanese CV building policy during the period of the Naval Limitation Treaties we can see that the total tonnage of 81,000 tons was obtained (in fact the total tonnage was exceeded because the CVs had a higher than declared standard displacement). In view of the vulnerability of the CV the IJN decided to retain parity with the number of CVs built by the USN. Because on the one hand the total tonnage of CVs was

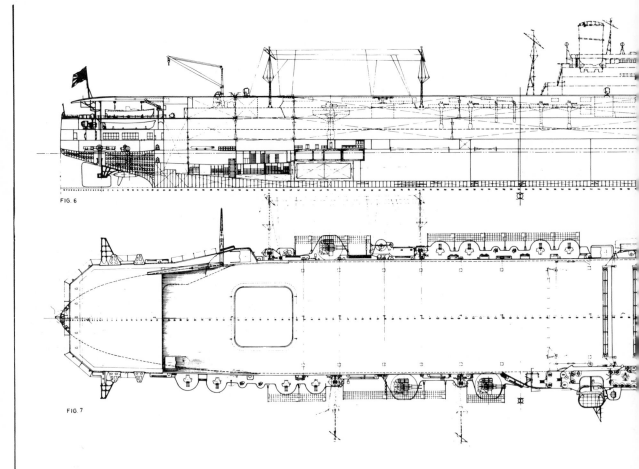

FIG. 6

FIG. 7

The *Hiyo* class as designed; note the already significant anti-aircraft battery.

Drawn by Michael Wünschmann

subject to strict limitations during the period of the treaties and on the other hand it had been found that Japan's shipbuilding industry could not compete with the USA in naval armaments, the solution was to build ships that did not come under the treaty limitations but could easily be converted into CVs in time of war. It was natural to fall back upon already proven solutions because the conversions of the RN during World War I were the first step in the development of CV, and many other merchant ships saw action as auxiliaries. The conversion of the Cunard liner *Campania* especially had demonstrated the use of this type of ship as an aircraft carrier.

The IJN therefore decided:

1) to subsidise the building of merchant ships that could be converted into auxiliaries on the outbreak of war.
2) auxiliary naval vessels not subject to the treaties but designed and constructed so that they could be converted into CVs within three months (submarine depot ships – designed as fast fleet oilers – *Tsurugizaki* and *Takasaki*, submarine depot ship *Taigei*, seaplane carriers *Chitose* and *Chiyoda*).
3) to subsidise the building of large, fast passenger liners that could be operated as liners in time of peace but speedily converted into auxiliary aircraft carriers in time of war (in fact the ships later were classified as regular aircraft carriers).

In the following section the building of the subsidised ships will be dealt with at some length.

DEVELOPMENT OF JAPANESE MERCHANT SHIPPING AND ITS CAUSES

When the Sino-Japanese War began in 1894 the Japanese merchant fleet amounted only 160,000 tons, but this figure had nearly doubled when it ended. Ten years later, during the Russo-Japanese War, Japanese shipping increased from about 650,000 tons to nearly one million. This ships were used to carry military supplies and troops to the mainland, and they were, in most cases, old foreign vessels purchased at low prices, because Japanese shipbuilding capacity was very small and technical ability lagged behind. A further ten years later

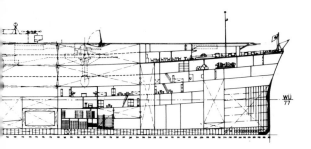

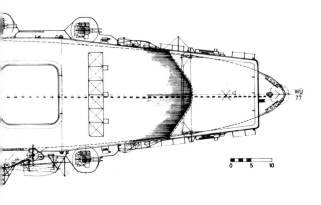

maintaining Japanese interests and rights on the continent of Asia. For these, it was essential to keep shipping free at all times for the movement of troops and military supplies in an emergency. Examples of this policy can be found in all the wars mentioned in this section. For transportation, medium and large type cargo and passenger ships were most suitable and the Government assisted with their cost. The large passenger liners on the services to North America and Europe not only represented the policy of advancing Japanese merchant shipping standards to meet the challenge of first class liners built by the United States, Britain, and France, but also played an essential part in national defence strategy.

After World War I the development of the aeroplane proceeded rapidly and all nations recognised the value of the new weapon. One consequence was that the part to be played by aircraft carriers in any future conflict was seen to take on greater significance. At the same time a number of fundamentally difficult problems hindered plans to increase the numbers of this new type of ship. During the period of the Naval Limitation Treaties the number of aircraft carriers in commission was subjected to strict control. The example of *Akagi* and *Kaga*[3] clearly demonstrates also that apart from the great expenditure necessary to maintain aircraft carriers it was constantly necessary to carry out improvements and conversions in order to adapt them to the frequent and rapid changes that were taking place in aircraft design and performance. It was therefore decided to construct large superior class liners which could be readily converted to aircraft carriers in time of war. The first examples of this policy were the passenger liners of the *Asama Maru* class.

On the eve of the Showa Era (from 1926 on) the IJN demanded a speed of 20kts or more and a displacement of 15,000 tons or more as the prerequisite for the conversion of a liner into an auxiliary aircraft carrier. The *Asama Maru* class was designed to meet the requirements, measuring 16,975 tons and having a speed of 20.7kts. The building of these ships (*Asama Maru, Tatsuta,* and *Titibu Maru,* which later became the *Kamakura Maru*) was subsidised by the Ministry of Transportation, and in designing the ships the constructors were obliged to provide for their conversion into an auxiliary aircraft carrier within three months. Having been commissioned between September 1929 and March 1930, the ships operated as modern high-performance vessels (all fitted with diesel engines) on the San Francisco service. When the Greater East Asia War (the Japanese name for World War II) broke out in December 1941 the IJN wanted to convert this class into aircraft carriers but there was a great number of other, and more modern, ships to be converted and the shipyards had no capacity left during the first year of the war. Therefore, all these ships were sunk before the Navy's request could be realised.

It might be of interest to add that during conversion their diesel engines were to be replaced by destroyer turbines and that this was the result of a study ordered immediately after the sinking of four Japanese aircraft carriers at the battle for Midway.

World War I began and Japan, in accordance with the Anglo-Japanese Alliance, declared war on Germany and became one of the victorious nations. At the beginning of this war the merchant fleet comprised 1,770,000 tons and reached 3,350,000 tons in 1921.[1] Once more it had nearly doubled its tonnage at the outbreak of the war.

This progress had been made possible by the development of the shipbuilding industry. After the Russo-Japanese War, mainly as a result of the major expansion of naval armaments, the equipment and technical ability of the Japanese shipyards made a remarkable leap forward and continued to advance.[2] Besides the influence of naval expansion the other major factors were the two laws concerning the encouragement of shipbuilding and shipping that had been passed by the Diet in 1896. Under the first, owners who ordered ships from domestic yards received building subsidies, while the second granted operating subsidies only for vessels built in Japan.

In reviewing the development of Japanese merchant shipping another major factor that compelled the spectacular advance of Japanese shipping must not be forgotten – the national defence strategy, *ie* the policy of

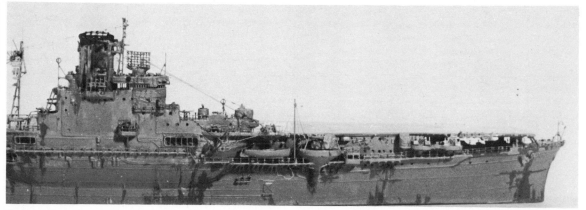

Starboard bow close up, clearly showing the merchant hull form.

Jurgen Peters

A few years after the design of these ships, in 1933, the IJN again wanted the buliding of superior passenger liners for the North America service that should have a speed of 24kts and be capable of being converted ito auxiliary aircraft carriers. Planning and research was done in close cooperation with the Japan Mail Steamship Company (Nippon Yusen Kaisha – NYK) and the Osaka Merchant Ship Company (Osaka Shosen Kaisha – OSK) but these were not built because of financial constraints.

In 1935, the NYK projected the construction of three combined cargo/passenger ships for the European service. The IJN again took part at the design stage and planned a speed of 24kts but the same reasons as mentioned previously withheld the permission for subsidies and the ships were not built. The failure to build more clandestine auxiliary aircraft carriers came in the middle of the 'scrap-and-build' policy in the first phase of the Shipping Improvement Programme that began in October 1932.

After the end of World War I the extreme wartime prosperity had suddenly reversed and businesses crashed disastrously. British and American shipping returned to oriental waters and moreover, the large number of cargo ships which had been hastily built in Japan during wartime were now to a great extent unwanted. By the late 1920s, trade with China had dropped to a low level, the Wall Street crash in September 1929 had caused financial panic and the Japanese economy was cast into a profound depression. As the depression had deepened and widened, the 'Manchurian Incident' took place in September 1931. In the critical situation, defensive measures on the Asian mainland and the Pacific Ocean became a matter of urgent necessity. As one consequence the import of materials and equipment for military expansion increased sharply, but among the ships that had been hurriedly built during World War I there were many of low speed and poor overall performance and it was impossible to operate

them with any commercial advantage in the fierce competition that then prevailed in the international shipping market. At Kobe and other commercial ports one hundred or more ships were laid up idle, their total tonnage being about 320,000 tons. Observing this, the planning staffs (the first departments of the Naval and Army General Staff) concluded that sea transportation capacity was far below what would be needed in the event of war to serve both expeditionary forces to the mainland and defence operations in the Pacific area.

They therefore strongly advocated the replacement of obsolescent merchant vessels with a more efficient fleet, that is the above mentioned 'scrap-and-build' policy. As part of this subsidy programme some military requirements were established. In all merchant ships of 4000 gross tons and over, capable of a minimum speed of 13.5 knots structural elements necessary for their eventual conversion for military use were to be provided. These elements consisted principally of structural foundations for the installation of guns, two to six per ship and ranging in calibre from 12cm to 20cm[4]. For security reasons, elements of ship construction were not specified in writing, but were mutually agreed and varied in design and scope largely in accordance with the initiative of the shipbuilder. A moderate, but considerable degree of control, however, was exercised by the Government through its prerogative to approve plans.

In the meantime the course of international events had taken a turn for the worse. Many countries denounced the new state of Manchukuo as being nothing but a puppet government and the League of Nations at Geneva refused to recognise it. Because it became impossible to expect anything other than dispute and criticism, Japan had decided to leave that body in 1933. In 1934, Japan, after due warning, denounced the Washington Treaty and in 1936 the (Second) London Naval Limitation Conference failed. In October an Anti-Comintern Pact was signed by Japan and Germany. Diplomatic relations between Japan and China went from crisis to crisis until in July 1937 they were finally shattered by war. Hostilities spread to Tientsin, Shanghai, Nankin, Canton, and Hankow, until the whole of China was ablaze, and the war took on the appearance of a long-term conflict.

Following the expiration of the Washington and London Naval Limitation Treaties on 31 December 1936 each country launched a new naval shipbuilding programme. As a second line of defence, special attention was given to the strengthening of merchant fleets. Because of the United States in particular put in hand the construction of large modern merchant vessels, Japan enacted a law to provide subsidies for superior type vessels. Of the 12 large passenger liners built under the first phase of this programme, no less than 5 ships were designed to meet the requirements of the IJN for conversion into an auxiliary aircraft carrier.

In 1937 the *Nitta Maru* class (*Nitta Maru, Kasuga Maru, Yawata Maru*; 17,000 tons, 21 knots) intended for NYK's European service were subsidised. One year later the *Argentina Maru* class (*Argentina Maru, Brazil Maru*; 13,000 tons, 21 knots) destined for OSK's South America, East Coast service, followed[5]. These ships were structurally designed to be converted into aircraft carriers; they did, however, not embrace any visible military characteristics, such as offset funnels, special elevators, gun supports, or flight decks. *Brazil Maru* sank before conversion; the other ships were converted shortly before and after the outbreak of the war, *Kasuga Maru* becoming the CVE *Taiyo*, *Yawata Maru* the CVE *Unyo*, *Nitta Maru* the CVE *Chuyo*, and *Argentina Maru* the CVE *Kaiyo*.

The bridge of *Junyo*, taken postwar.
Author's collection

In order to enter into competition with the Dollar Line, the Canadian Pacific Line,[6] and the *Scharnhorst*[7] of the North German Lloyd, NYK planned as early as 1936 to build two super passenger liners for service between Japan and the west coasts of the United States and Canada. An important factor for this plan had also been the decision of the International Olympic Games Committee to hold the summer games of the 1940 Olympics in Tokyo.

It was not possible to build large luxury liners without subsidies. As we have seen earlier, the building of passenger liners according to the requirements of the IJN by NYK and OSK failed in 1933 and again in 1935. The Ministry of the Navy (*Kaigunsho*) therefore had a special interest in both ships and laid two designs before the Ministry of Transportation (*Teishinsho*) . One design showed a liner 219.5m (720ft) long and with a speed of 24 knots while the other one covered a ship only 200m (656ft) long but having the same speed. If the ships were built according to these designs the Government would pay all costs, but in the end, neither of the designs was submitted to the Diet.

In 1937 the Ministry of Transportation suggested two ships whose building costs should amount to 24 million Yen each, 80 per cent of which would be subsidized by the Government. Regarding displacement and speed they were similar to the designs of the Ministry of the Navy. Negotiations with the Ministry of Finance (*Okurasho*) failed because it wanted to pay only 50 per cent. The Ministry of the Navy intervened and finally the

Overhead view showing the flight deck arrangements, the canted funnel and the lack of catapults.
Jurgen Peters.

Starboard view of *Junyo* in 1945 showing the modifications projected during her repair after battle damage in 1944.
Jurgen Peters

negotiating parties agreed to a compromise with the Government taking over 60 per cent of the building costs. In 1938 the Large Size Superior Ships Construction Programme passed the Diet. It consisted of only two ships, the subjects of this article.

A review of the development of the Japanese merchant shipping shows that after the struggle for technical improvement and expansion more and more ships were designed and constructed so that they could be easily converted into auxiliary war vessels. To build these ships, the Government initiated a number of subsidy programmes and all ships built with subsidies could be requisitioned and converted into auxiliaries (*Tokusetsu kansen*). This measure was formalised into the War Armament Preparation Programme (*Shusshi Junbi Keikaku*) and the IJN's plan was to strengthen the fleet with good ships in time of war. All ships were built during peacetime as clandestine units of the navy. When war began a great number of merchant ships had already been requisitioned, the Army having 519 ships, (2,161,000 tons) and Navy 482 ships (1,740,000 tons). Fast mercantile oil tankers formed the main strength of the fleet train[8], and other merchant ships were converted into auxiliary cruisers (merchant raiders), auxiliary seaplane carriers, auxiliary gunboats, auxiliary patrol boats, auxiliary minesweepers and minelayers etc. Superior passenger liners should have been converted into auxiliary aircraft carriers but as we have seen out of the 10 ships especially designed and constructed for this purpose 4 were sunk before conversion, 4 were converted into CVEs and only 2 acted as fleet carriers: the ships built under the Large Size Superior Ship Construction Programme and described in detail below.

BUILDING OF KASHIWARA MARU AND IZUMO MARU

The minimum requirements of the IJN for a possible conversion into an auxiliary aircraft carrier and NYK's preliminary specification at the time of the negotiations are given in Table 1 for sake of comparison. As well as these requirements the ships had to be so designed and constructed that they could be converted into auxiliary aircraft carriers within 3 months. Details about structure, arrangement etc were also laid down.

Looking at the table we can see some differences between the ideas of the NYK and the requirements of the IJN. For this reason the Ministry of Transportation, the Ministry of the Navy and the Naval Technical Department (*Kaigun Kansei Honbu*) participated in the design.

As for structural and arrangement details the IJN required

1) Double hull.[9]
2) Extra tank capacity for fuel oil (the location of the fuel oil tanks outside the boiler rooms served as additional protection to the double hull in this area).
3) Provisions for the installation of extra longitudinal and transverse bulkheads.
4) Separation of the turbine rooms by a longitudinal bulkhead at the centreline of the ship (the navy took the more difficult fitting out of these spaces into account).

5) Strengthened main deck.
6) Extra height between decks.
7) Arrangement of the superstructure and passenger accommodation that speedily allowed the installation of elevators and hangars.
8) Additional space for the installation of electric cables etc needed for operations as aircraft carriers.
9) Fitting of a bulbous bow (this was used for the first time in Japanese merchant ships).
10) Installation of gasoline tanks for the operation of the aircraft before and behind the machinery spaces.

Notwithstanding these provisions required for conversion into an aircraft carrier no gun supports or outboard funnels were included in the design.

The IJN wanted a maximum speed of 26kts or, if that were too difficult, at least 25.5kts. From the standpoint of economy, however, a maximum speed of 24kts was considered to be the limit. As a compromise the turbines and main boilers were designed to develop 56,250shp for a maximum speed of 25.5kts, but could develop only 80 per cent of their maximum performance during use as passenger liners, thus giving the ships a full speed of 24kts. The increased performance of the boilers and turbines resulted in the employment of high pressure high temperature watertube boilers with a steam pressure of 40 bar and a steam temperature of 420° Celsius. Until the end of the war no other ship had such boilers and there are no other examples of the use of these boilers in warships of the IJN.

The final column of Table 1 shows the changes and additional parameters that were decided during the initial discussions. *Kashiwara Maru* and *Izumo Maru* would have become the largest passenger liners of the Japanese merchant fleet. The other ships, planned to be converted into auxiliary aircraft carriers, the *Asama Maru* class, the *Nitta Maru* class, and the *Argentina Maru* class, could not be compared with them.

The first deck continued from bow to stern was the main deck. Below it there were the upper deck, first deck, third deck, fourth deck and hold. Above it there was the superstructure consisting of the bridge deck, promenade deck and the boat deck.

On the eve of 1939 the NYK ordered one ship each from Mitsubishi Heavy Industries Ltd and Kawasaki Shipbuilding Ltd. The keel of the *Kashiwara Maru* (building number 900) was laid down on building slip no 3 of the Nagasaki yard of Mitsubishi on 20 March 1939. Eight months later, on 30 November 1939, Kawasaki started building *Izumo Maru* (building number 660) on building slip no 4 in their yard at Kobe (three days before, the aircraft carrier *Zuikaku* was launched there).

Japan's leading naval architect, Technical Vice-Admiral Yazura Hiraga acted as advisor to Mitsubishi Heavy Industries Ltd during the construction of *Kashiwara Maru*. Under his guidance this class was designed as Japan's largest and most modern luxury passenger liners taking the German *Bremen* as a model. The lines of their hulls followed those of the German ship, and because they were such large ships no precedent could be found in Japan prior to their building, so special steel was used for longitudinal strength mem-

The stern of *Junyo* with details of the deck edge sponsons.

Jurgen Peters

Junyo at Sasebo on 28 May 1946; although stripped of all her armament the shields fitted for the rocket guns are visible between the positions they would have occupied ahead of the bridge.

Author's collection

TABLE 1: COMPARISON OF IJN REQUIREMENTS AND NYK PROPOSAL WITH FINAL DESIGN

	IJN requirement	NYK specification	Final design
Designed displacement (tons)			
Full load	–	–	31,915
Empty	–	–	21,500
Deadweight	–	–	10,415
Capacity (gross tons)	26,500 – 27,000	26,500	27,700
Volume of loading area			
(cubic metres)	–	–	5,824
Length (metres)	–	205	206
Length oa (metres)	210	–	–
Beam (metres)	25	26	26.70
Depth – promenade deck to			
waterline (metres)	–	14.80	13.90
Draught (metres)			
Full load	–	–	9.175
Empty	–	–	6.705
Maximum speed (knots)	26 – 25.5	24	25.5
Speed on one engine (knots)	19	–	24
Cruising speed (knots)	19	–	24
Engine power (shp)			
Maximum	60,000	56,250	56,250
Cruising speed	48,000	45,000	45,000
Machinery	–	2 turbines	2 turbines
Boilers	–	–	6 Mitusbishi
Shafts	–	2	2
Passengers	–	–	220 first class, 120 second, 550 third, 890 total
Passengers and crew	–	1317	–

bers. The bulbous bow and the boilers previously mentioned were also something new for Japanese merchant shipbuilding. The equipment of the *Izumo Maru* was equal to that of the *Kashiwara Maru* and until October 1941 the building of both ships went according to plan.

To be continued

NOTES

[1] In 1918, by the time of the Armistice, the figure had risen to 2,300,000 tons but taking into account building in progress at this date the final figure in 1921 is more realistic to explain the advances during World War I.

[2] Except for the naval dockyards, ordinary shipyards built naval as well as merchant vessels because technique, facilities and workmanship did not differ greatly and therefore was possible to introduce new methods and to lower costs by coordinating work on both kinds of ships.

[3] See *Warship* 22–24.

[4] Supports intended for guns of 15cm or larger nearly always were cylindrical in form. For smaller guns and in instance of acute shortages, double channels, forming a built-up 'H' column were used. In practice the number of guns actually installed at the time of military commission was less than the number provided for in the original design – due primarily to a shortage of guns usually not more than two guns per ship were installed.

[5] It might be of interest to add that the programme also included the OSK ships *Hokoku Maru, Aikoku Maru,* and *Gokoku Maru* (10,500 tons, 20 knots, for Africa service) of which the first and second mentioned were famous as auxiliary cruisers (merchant raiders. *Awa Maru* (and their sister ship *Mishima Maru*; NYK, 10,500 tons, 20 knots, Australian service), whose sinking while acting as a Red Cross ship by an American submarine still produces headlines, was also part of this programme.

[6] The *President Coolidge* and the *President Hoover* of the Dollar Line as well as the *Empress of Japan* of the Canadian Pacific Line had also been rivals of the first Japanese passenger liners that could be converted into auxiliary aircraft carriers int ime of war: the *Asama Maru, Tatsuta Maru,* and *Kamakura Maru.*

[7] This ship became later the fifth Japanese CVE, the *Shinyo*.

[8] During the Taisho Era (1912–1926) the IJN used its own ships for transporting fuel oil and used mercantile oil tankers as reserve only. During the Showa Era (starting in 1926) the building of oil tankers, except those for special purposes (*ie* ships that could be easily converted into midget submarine mother ships and other types of naval vessels) was stopped and the guiding rules altered. Mercantile oil tankers were now to be used as supply ships for the fleet. For building large and fast oil tankers owners received subsidies from the Government. This took place before the Subsidy Laws described in this article came into force.

[9] With rare exceptions, the design of merchant ships included no special provisions for making them more capable of withstanding battle damage. The first exceptions were six army transports (four 7,000 gross tons, 18kt ships and two 4,500-ton 14kt ships) built between 1932 and 1936, followed by the *Kashiwara Maru* and *Izumo Maru*, which were built with double hulls and fitted with special angle irons so that extra bulkheads could be installed at the time of conversion (see also note 3).

warship wings

No 10
The Buccaneer
by Roger Chesneau

An S Mk 2 prepares to depart from *Eagle*, 1971. Elevons and flaps are 'down' and elevators 'up' and nosewheel raised to aid take-off whilst the aircraft is held back on the catapult.

Fleet Air Arm Museum

We turn for this issue to an aircraft so advanced in concept at the time of its design that it is, thirty years later, still in service and, indeed, likely to remain so for a long time yet, simply because its qualities are still totally relevant to modern air warfare.

In the early 1950s, the emergence of the Soviet Navy as a potent surface force began to cause some apprehension in Admiralty corridors, especially the commissioning of the new *Sverdlov* class cruisers: memories of the consternation caused by German pocket battleships were still fresh in the mind – and of these ships there were merely a handful by comparison. These were still the times when a specific piece of hardware could be afforded in order to counter a specific threat, with no compromise needed to work all sorts of other missions into an airframe, and Specification NA 39 (June 1952) was issued requesting designs for a carrier-based aircraft

Two Royal Navy Buccaneer S Mk 2s in a low-level formation flypast, October 1978. Note the prominent bulge along the rear fuselage – the most obvious manifestation of the 'area rule' principle.

HMS Ark Royal

that could fly fast, far and very low (beneath the sweep of hostile radar beams) out to a large enemy surface ship, destroy it, and return to base. Conceived in an era when high-altitude bombing – out of AA gun/missile range but hardly of radar range – was all the rage, the specification proved to be particularly far-sighted.

NA 39 eventually emerged as the Blackburn Buccaneer. Early production aircrat were powered – or, more accurately, underpowered – by de Havilland Gyron Junior turbojets, and the type, designated S Mk 1, began to enter service in early 1961; the definitive version, S Mk 2, appeared in mid-1965, having solved the problem by means of Spey turbofans which produced about 50 per cent more thrust and imparted not only considerably more 'poke' but also greatly enhanced range at cruise ratings, owing to their fuel efficiency.

Some of the clues to the Buccaneer's longevity have already been hinted at. Low-altitude penetration is very much a concern of the present; fuel economy is equally relevant since the oil price explosion of the early 1970s; and high speed at what amounts to zero altitude makes the same sorts of basic demands on designers today as it did thirty years ago. First, it requires an incredibly strong airframe, and with components such as wing panels machined from solid metal the Buccaneer certainly has that. Second, there is very little point in producing an aircraft that can fly supersonic at low level when this is

A view of an RAF S Mk 2 (XV Sqn), showing the aircraft's 'slipper' tank; CBLS practice bomb dispensers are carried on the outboard pylons.

Richard L Ward

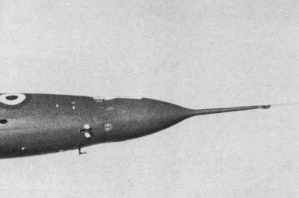

likely to require afterburning and thus double, treble or even quadruple fuel consumption and dramatically reduce range. Furthermore, air density and turbulence at low altitudes are apt to give an incredibly uncomfortable ride; features like computer-controlled wing sweep (*à la* Tornado) can overcome this, but only at vast technological complexity and huge financial cost. From the point of view of evading defences, supersonic speed makes not much difference: it is not much easier to stop an intruder coming in at 100ft at Mach 0.9 than at Mach 1.1.

Buccaneer's high, low-level speed is produced not only through the power of its engines. A significant factor is very clever aerodynamics, proving that 1950s thinking on the subject, though regarded as unfashionable and in some quarters, is not wholly to be cast aside. During the 1960s and 1970s, and indeed to some extent today, aircraft potency was frequently assessed in terms of its speed and of the number of weapons pylons beneath the wing. Aircraft A, which could make Mach 2 and had 16 bombs and half a dozen missiles strung across its span, was automatically superior to Aircraft B, which made only Mach 0.9 and had no pylons; the fact that Aircraft A could only be driven flat out for six minutes before it ran out of fuel and in any case had its top speed cut by 65 per cent when all those impressive weapons were hung on was conveniently overlooked – and the glossy sales brochures naturally did not stress the point. The Buccaneer philosophy was to throw out as many drag-inducing encumbrances as possible: its smooth contours were emphasised by the application of 'area

S Mk 2 XK527 demonstrates four pre-production Martel ASMs. This missile, an Anglo-French venture, was produced in two versions, radar homing and TV-guided. The outline of the Buccaneer's unique rotary bomb bay is also visible, as is the semi-recessed arrestor hook.

British Aerospace

rule' – bulging parts of the fuselage when sudden losses of cross-sectional area would otherwise cause turbulence, particularly immediately abaft the wing and tailfin. For the same reason, a unique rotating bomb bay, capable of accommodating 4000lb of weapons, was provided. Even when external carriage was accepted, a specially designed 'slipper' tank, faired into the wing rather than slung baldly on a pylon, was devised.

Designed as a carrier-based bomber, the Buccaneer showed the usual naval features: folding wings for improved stowage (together with a split-airbrake tail cone and folding nose radome, which of course have other functions as well); a rugged undercarriage; and catapult strop attachment points and a tail hook. More innovative was the boundary layer system. In order to provide the wings with maximum lift when manoeuvring near to the parent carrier, supplementary movable surfaces such as slats and full-span flaps were rejected in favour of a system of minute slits along the leading edges of the wing and tailplane. Air bled off from the main powerplants and transferred via ducts was ejected at high speed through these slits; the air passing over the wing was thereby rendered less dense than during normal flight, with the result that additional lift was generated, cutting stalling speed by some 15kts.

The wing fold mechanisms of an RAF Buccaneer reveals also the circular ducts either side which deliver air associated with the boundary layer system. The store on the inboard pylon is a Pave Spike target designator, associated with the delivery of laser-guided bombs.

Linewrights Ltd

With the phasing out of the Royal Navy's fleet carriers in the late 1970s, Buccaneers were transferred to RAF control, joining new-built aircraft already operating with that service in the overland strike and shore-based anti-shipping roles. The former mission has now been handed over to Tornado, but RAF Lossiemouth still flies Martel-equipped Buccaneers. With the new Sea Eagle ASM due to become operational next year and, perhaps, updated avionics and ECM fits in the offing, the RAF clearly has no intention of giving up its SME 2S, even though fatigue problems have reduced the numbers. The Buccaneer is still a highly potent weapon, and, although now back on land, it still fulfills the function for which it was originally designed. *Plus ça change* – with good reason!

BUCCANEER S Mk 2 SPECIFICATION

Overall length	63ft 5in
Span	44ft
Max height	16ft 3in
Wing area	514.7ft²
Engines	Two Rolls-Royce Spey Mk 101 turbofans, 11,100lb thrust each
Max speed	In excess of 600kts at 200ft
Range	In excess of 2000nm
Tactical radius	In excess of 500nm
Weight	62,000lb max take-off
Weapons	(RN service) nuclear or conventional weapons up to 4000lb in bomb bay; bombs, ASMs or rocket pods on four pylons, 3000lb each

ATTACK AND DEFENCE
by D K Brown RCNC

No 5

Prior to World War I

In the first decade of the twentieth century a considerable number of trials were carried out using obsolete warships to test fire control, projectiles and protection. These trials were backed up by tests on shore against replicas of different parts of ships. As a result of these trials the RN had a very good idea of the value and effect of different types of projectile and the type of protection needed against them. With one or two exceptions, all the important lessons were recorded before the war started though time and resources were inadequate to correct some deficiencies. There should have been few surprises in war.

TRIALS SHIPS

Ship	Date	Purpose of Trial
Belleisle	1900–03	Various
Scorpion	1901	Long range firing by *Crescent* (beached)
Riddesdale	1905–06	Underwater protection
Landrail	1906	Fire control
Hero	1907	Fire control and effect of shell fire
Skate	1906	Anti torpedo craft gun fire
Ferret	1909–11	
Edinburgh	1909–10	Effect of shell fire
Empress of India	1913	Firing practice
Zebra	?	Explosion in fuel oil tanks
A1 (submarine)	1911–12	Diving shell
A3 (submarine)	1911–12	

From the material aspects, the trials on the *Edinburgh* were by far the most important.

TYPES OF PROJECTILE

Armour piercing (AP). Some older guns used uncapped projectiles with a burster of about 2–3 per cent of the total weight. When such a shell struck a hard-faced plate both the shell and the plate were distorted. The plate would dish over a diameter about three times that of the shell, distributing the impact over a considerable area of the plate. The nose of the shell would be driven back tending to split the body of the projectile.

The hard face thus acted by commencing the destruction of the projectile and the plate 'receives the blow of a disintegrated mass instead of the penetrating thrust of a carefully designed tool'[1]. If the plate was unable to resist the blow, a cone-shaped piece would be punched out with a maximum diameter of about three times that of the shell.

By the use of a cap, the stress of the impact was distributed over the head of the shell instead of being concentrated on the point but even the soft cap loaded the plate, reducing its power of resistance. In this way initial damage to the projectile was avoided and the point would penetrate the hard surface layer and continue to bore through the rest of the plate. If the projectile had enough energy it would drill a hole of roughly its own diameter. Since less energy was required to perforate than to punch, capped shell would pierce much thicker armour than the older uncapped shells.

Armour piercing shells were originally powder-filled because the impact would often detonate an HE filling. However the capped projectiles had a less severe impact and it was found that a lyddite (picric acid) filling would usually withstand the jolt without premature detonation and most later shells were so filled. About 2½ per cent of the weight of a modern capped shell is burster charge.

From each batch of 400 shells, two were tested, one with inert filling being fired through armour, and one recovered intact to show that it had withstood the strain of firing.

Common pointed capped. The advantage of a soft cap applied to common shell as well and the later versions with a nose radius equal to four times the calibre (4crh) were almost as good at penetrating armour as APC. The common shell carried a much larger burster, some

9 per cent of the total weight, and broke into very large splinters which were capable of causing severe damage.

Lyddite shell. This had a very large, high explosive burster and, as will be seen, caused very severe damage over a wide area both by blast and from the myriad of tiny splinters.

EFFECTS OF DIFFERENT TYPES OF SHELL

Armour piercing capped. At close range, 6000–8000yds, these shells would penetrate KC armour of thicknesses equal to their own calibre when the impact was normal, *ie* axis of the shell perpendicular to the plate. By 12,000yds penetration would have fallen to about ⅔–¾ calibre. Performance when striking at an angle was poor. 'These shells seldom penetrate even medium armour unbroken if striking obliquely, and in the case of APC-filled HE this marked tendency to break up lessens materially the chance of obtaining the detonation of these shells actually clear of, and behind armour, under service conditions.'[1] They would usually burst with a low order explosion (not detonate) in passing through the plate.

An APC-filled HE striking armour normally with just sufficent velocity to perforate unbroken would usually detonate about three quarters of the way through the plate causing considerable damage. Powder-filled APC would usually detonate a few feet behind the armour. On the other hand, HE-filled APC had a much better effect against lightly armoured structure as they detonated with many large fragments. Powder-filled HE often failed to fragment as the fuze blew out, venting much of the force of the explosion. For example, 13.5in AP shell detonates 5–18ft behind 4in KC armour.

It is clear that British armour piercing shells were seriously defective and that this was known well before the war. The development of long range firing made these defects more serious as oblique impact was almost certain.

Capped common shell. These were unlikely to penetrate the main armour but would go through 3–4in KC and burst some feet behind with heavy splinter damage.

Lyddite shell. The Royal Navy had been much impressed with the damage caused by big HE shells both in the trials against *Belleisle*, described later, and in the Russo-Japanese War. Lyddite shell bursting in the unarmoured parts of a ship would rupture decks and bulkheads nearby so opening up large areas of the ship to flooding or to fire. The splinters were small and travelled considerable distances causing much damage to electric cables in particular. Lyddite gave off large clouds of black smoke when it burst and this would obscure the vision of gunlayers on the stricken ship.

Quite thin armour would keep out lyddite HE shell; for example, 4in KC would keep out 12in or even 13.5in Lyddite at 6,000 yards. For this reason, the RN retained their upper belts and extensions fore and aft of the main belt. The 'all or nothing' system used on USS *Nevada* seems to have been unwise since so much of the essential services of the ship was unprotected from the devastating effects of HE shell.

The 1915 Gunnery Manual recommended the use of lyddite or common shell against battleships at ranges at which APC would fail to penetrate. By implication, this would seem to be at ranges over about 12,000 yards.

ARMOUR[2]

Warrior and her immediate successors had wrought iron armour. Initially this was 4½in thick, the thickest which could then be produced but this was soon increased. Compound armour, with a hard steel face plate, hammer welded to a tough iron back, was used during the 1880s but all steel armour was introduced for *Barfleur, Centurion* and *Renown*. Such armour was more than a match for Palliser shot but when forged steel armour piercing shot came into use further improvement in armour was needed.

This improvement was achieved by the Harvey process in which the face of the armour was first 'carburised' or 'cemented' by increasing the carbon content of the first inch of thickness. This was then hardened by heating and sudden chilling. Krupp then introduced various alloying elements and a more elaborate procedure for heat treatment. Various slight changes were then made by British firms and modern British ships in World War I had armour which was at least as good as the German and probably a little better[3] These advances in armour protection can be summarised by the following thicknesses:

9in Krupp	is equivalent to
11¾in Harvey	is equivalent to
18¾in all steel	is equivalent to
18¾in compound	is equivalent to
23½in wrought iron.	

These figures refer to uncapped projectiles and no comparison is available for resistance to capped shell.

The latest British armour at the outbreak of war was a steel alloy with about 3½–4 per cent nickel, 1½–2 per cent chromium and small percentages of carbon, manganese and molybdenum.

Pieces were taken from each plate for mechanical and chemical tests and the hardness of the face was measured after all the treatment had been completed. In addition, a fully-treated plate was tested in actual firing trials from time to time. Plates of 4in thickness and above were tested unbacked and supported along two sides only. Thinner plates were supported on substantial wood backing. For tests up to 5in plate CPC shell were used and for thicker plates APC. In both cases the shells were filled with salt. Several rounds were fired into each plate at specified striking velocities and compared with the performance of a 'standard' plate. In practice, performance varied considerably and occasionally a bad batch was rejected.

The tough back of KC armour did not require the thick timber backing used behind wrought iron and compound armour though, occasionally, wood packing strips were used. The back was soft enough for holes to be drilled and tapped to accept the securing bolts after manufacture was complete. The design of the bolting arrangements to secure the armour was a complicated business as the bolt holes were bound to weaken the plate while insufficient bolting could allow the plates to fall off under impact. Once hardened, the face could not be cut with any tools and any fitting adjustment had to be

A stern view of the battleship *Edinburgh* while part of the
Mediterranean Fleet, 1887–94.

CPL

Belleisle during her period of active service.
CPL

made by grinding.

Some tests of spaced armour were made in which a thin, decapping plate was followed by an air space before the shell, without its cap, met the hardened plate in the rear. No benefits were found in any of a long series of trials.

Special steel, containing vanadium or molybdenum, was used for roofs of gun turrets. It was envisaged that shells would strike at a very shallow angle, say 20°, and the aim was to use a protective plate which would dish considerably without tearing.

The purpose of armour decks was said to be to keep out:[1]
(a) fragments and blast of AP shell which perforate the vertical armour and burst inside the ship;
(b) pieces of side armour and structure driven in by a shell;
(c) descending shell which gets over the top of the vertical armour;
(d) fragments of shell which burst on the upperworks.

Two protective decks were thought to be necessary, one at the upper edge of the armour and one at the lower edge. The material used for protective decks in later ships was a high tensile steel containing silicon. This material would stretch under load as much as would mild steel and was much cheaper than the KNC or nickel steel used in ships up to the *Orion* class.

Rather limited evidence at Jutland suggests that the deck protection was adequate. On surviving ships only one splinter penetrated the protective decks even though many were heavily damaged. On the other hand,

the deck thickness in both British and German ships was inadequate to keep out plunging shells and this may have contributed to the loss of the British battlecruisers.

In many ships, coal bunkers were an important part of the protection and, during tests made about 1885, it was found that 2ft of coal was equivalent to 1in of steel. Shell fire was unlikely to set fire to coal. The older, deck-protected cruisers relied to a considerable extent on the coal carried at the level of the waterline to preserve their stability after damage. Coal would restrict both the amount of water entering and limit the 'free surface' effect.

To be continued

References
1 The Gunnery Manual 1915. Royal Navy.
2 D K Brown RCNC. Limits to Growth. British Battleship Design 1840–1904. 500 years of Nautical Science. National Maritime Museum 1981.
3 S V Goodall RCNC. The ex-German battleship *Baden*. Trans. INA 1921.

PART TWO

GRAF ZEPPELIN

by M J Whitley

CONSTRUCTION AND FATE

The contract for the hull of 'B' was placed with Germania Werft at Kiel, on 11 February 1935 with 'A' being ordered from Deutsche Werke later on 16 November 1935 on which date a separate contract for 'B's machinery was placed. German practice at the time was to keep the ship's name secret until the launching ceremony and as a result, at the time of their keel-laying, they were known only as 'A' and 'B' respectively. Two further units, 'C' and 'D', figured in forward planning for future fleet build-up but remained pipe dreams. 'C' would have been built by Germania and 'D' by Deutsch Werke from April 1941 for completion in July 1944. The estimated cost of the carrier programme was 264 million Reichsmark spread over the period 1935 to 1942.

As it happened due to slipway availability, 'B' was the first to be laid down, on 30 September 1936, as yard No 555 with 'A' following on 28 December 1936 (yard No 252) but construction of the latter made better progress subsequently. The main reason for this was yard capacity, for in this period of intense rearmament, shipyards, steel mills, foundries and factories were all over-loaded with orders, and programmes were being continually put back. Even before the carriers were laid down, doubts about holding their scheduled completion dates ('A' 1 April 1939 and 'B' 15 November 1939) were being expressed in Staff circles. While both yards had in hand a heavy cruiser and four or five destroyers each, Germania had, in addition, six 'F' boats and was more heavily engaged in the U-boat programme than Deutsche Werke. Already, their destroyer programme had been seriously delayed with construction times going out to almost four years, whilst Deutsche Werke was building the same ships in just over two years. Progress on 'B' was dependent on cruiser 'J' (later *Prinz Eugen*) whose construction had been delayed three months by the late completion of shore trials of her machinery and she continued to absorb manpower badly needed on 'B'. In fact, Germania were forced to inform OKM that 'B' could not be completed until eleven months after the *Prinz Eugen* left the yard. 'A' too was in trouble at Deutsch Werke as unforeseen difficulties in the detailed construction of such a new type of vessel, combined with the late delivery of her turbines from Brown-Boverie led to a 10½-month slip in her completion date. Further slippage occurred as a result of the continuing alterations to *Blücher*, fitting out in the same yard and occupy-

ing resources needed on the new carrier.

By early 1938, a shortage of welders forced a halt on the construction of 'B' after about 500 tonnes had been worked into the hull and by autumn when the figure had risen to 1300 tonnes, the *Algemeinesmarineamt* (General Naval Office) was already suggesting to Raeder that the ship should be suspended and avoid committing a further 1500 tonnes of material assembled but not yet worked in. It would appear that already the *Algemeinesmarineamt* were having considerable doubts as to the whole carrier programme in its present form. It was suggested that the design as it stood was not suitable for Atlantic employment on the grounds that the machinery was suspect, (possibly a reference to high pressure steam propulsion), and could not be rectified or modified in 'B'. Yet the Atlantic was the very place she was meant to operate! Furthermore, the role of the carrier was to secure Germany's maritime lines of communication in conjunction with battleship groups but it was not possible to build sufficient numbers of the size of 'A' on cost grounds alone, so the construction of larger numbers of smaller carriers would appear to suit Germany's requirements more fully. In fact, it was reported that the Development Office had made such a sketch design based upon 10,000 tonnes with fewer aircraft and the ability to catapult aircraft direct from the hangar. For a moment however, no action was taken on the proposal but work continued on a very lethargic basis.

After almost two years on the ways, 'A' was ready for launching at Deutsche Werke in December 1938. On 8 December the new ship was named *Graf Zeppelin* by the Gräfin Hells von Branesten-Zeppelin, daughter of the famous airship designer, and finally went afloat in the presence of Hitler and Goering bedecked with swastika flags and bunting to be towed to the fitting out quay by the diminutive harbour tugs *Emil* and *Auguste* and their consorts. Here work continued both internally and externally with the funnel, mast and superstructure being erected. Unfortunately, for the *Kriegsmarine* however, war clouds were gathering over Europe – four years ahead of schedule! The consequence of the actual outbreak of war in 1939 was that the impressive 'Z' plan fell into ruins with work only proceding on those ships which could be completed within a short space of time and while work continued on *Graf Zeppelin*, her unfortunate sister 'B' had all work stopped on 19 September 1939 when she had been completed up to the armoured

The *Graf Zeppelin* at Stettin in 1942.

deck. After lying rusting on the slip for a few months, the incomplete hull was broken up from February 1940, some five months before her planned launching date. In October 1939, Hitler agreed that as well as the smaller ships, the completion of five large units under construction could be continued – *Bismarck, Tirpitz, Seydlitz, Prinz Eugen* and *Graf Zeppelin* but for *Seydlitz*, and particularly the aircraft carrier, the invasion of Norway in April 1940 finally sounded their death knell. The acquisition of such a large coastline to defend absorbed huge numbers of men, weapons and small craft, much of which was purloined from other uses, so that during the course of one of his regular conferences with the Führer on 29 April 1940, Admiral Raeder himself proposed halting construction of the carrier. The ship could have been commissioned by the end of 1940 but she would be without guns for a further ten months and her fire control equipment had been seriously delayed by the sale of equipment to Russia under the German–Soviet Agreement. Her heavy flak had been diverted for other purposes whilst the 15cm guns had been sent to Norway for coastal defence. Thus the ship would not be usable after trials until the end of 1941.

At a further conference at Obersaltzburg in July Hitler acknowledged the usefulness of aircraft carriers and saw the necessity for a 'flight-deck cruiser' as well as the resumption and completion of *Graf Zeppelin*. After this conference, the construction office suggested an 'M' type cruiser equipped to carry 14 aircraft with a sacrifice

in speed and gun power, but such ideas were a nonsense – why start a half-baked new project from scratch when an almost complete vessel of the true carrier type was already available? It is probable that this idea was merely the necessary response to a demand from the Führer and made with no intention of carrying it out, but the idea was resurrected some two years later.

All work on the ship stopped and on 12 July 1940 she left Kiel in tow for the port of Gotenhafen in East Prussia. Escorted by the old minesweeper *Nautilus*, the two had reached Sassnitz by the 18th, where two twin 3.7cm guns were fitted before moving on to her final destination. Here the ship lay until mid-1941, when Hitler's invasion of Russia caused the OKM to consider moving her in case of Soviet air attacks. The date of the invasion was set for 22 June 1941 and on the 16th, the OKM ordered Gruppe (nord) to have the ship out of Gotenhafen by the 19th at the latest. Flag Officer (Minelayers) was to provide an escort. Since it had earlier been decided not to move the carrier, this late change of plan was unwelcome to Vice-Admiral Schmundt (Flag Officer, Cruisers) who was in sea-going command of the Naval side of 'Barbarossa'. In the run-up to 'Barbarossa', his most important tasks were the laying of defensive minefields, particularly across the central Baltic between Memel and Oland ('Wartburg') and the only tugs available were two already allocated as salvage tugs to this operation. These two vessels, *Danzig* and *Albert Forster*, left Gotenhafen with *Graf Zeppelin* in tow at midday on 19 June and by early afternoon on the 21st reported the carrier safely secured in Stettin. Later in the year, after the threat of Soviet attack had disappeared with the advance of the German army into Russia, *Graf Zeppelin* returned to Gotenhafen once again.

Here, used only as a floating warehouse, she remained until early 1942, when a decision was made to recommence construction in the light of the usefulness of carriers in the sea war. The design was modified, giving her a slightly different appearance. In particular, a large funnel cap and tower mast structure wrere to be added, the searchlights removed, and 'vierling' 2cm to replace the single weapons and radar was to be installed. Apart from these cosmetic changes, it had been found after calculation, that when fully loaded and equipped for service, the ship would have had a list of $4\frac{1}{2}°$, which could only be compensated by the selective consumption of oil fuel over a period of 100 hours. As this was obviously excessive, it was decided to add bulges to the hull, compensating for the list by using thicker plate on the port bulge and incorporating some 300 tonnes of solid fixed ballast. This addition of bulges would also improve seaworthiness and range for they were divided horizontally to form two separate fuel bunkers, increasing bunkerage to 6740 tonnes.

This move from Gotenhafen back to Kiel for resumption of work was codenamed 'Zander', under the command of Fregatten Kapitän Remler from Kiel dockyard. The naval arsenal at Gotenhafen was ordered to arm the carrier with six twin 3.7cm, six 2cm 'vierlings' and instal four searchlights for self-defence. Anti-submarine escort was to be provided by the minesweepers *M 37*, *M 3* and *M 14* together with boats of the 3rd VP flotilla, six boats from the UAS (*Damme, Stolpe, Spree, Pregel, Nogat* and *Brake*) and an air escort from Bd F Gr 1/196. The transfer was to commence on 26 November 1942, using the tugs *Eisbär, Cappella* and *Passat*. By the evening of the 25th, the carrier was ready to move but the following day, weather conditions had deteriorated with high winds preventing the tow from leaving Hela Bay. After anchoring east of Hela, the convoy finally sailed again on the 30th and passing westwards, the incomplete carrier anchored in Heinkendorfer Bay off Kiel in fog, during the evening of 3 December. *Graf Zeppelin* was put into floating dock for the necessary alterations to be made.

LATER PROJECTS

In August 1942 Raeder had informed Hitler of SKL's opinion (SKL = *Seekriegsleitung* or Naval War Staff) that the centrepiece of a construction programme for a future fleet should be the building of aircraft carriers. However, building of battleships was not yet to be abandoned and, in deference to the Führer's wishes, the gun calibre question was to be re-examined. Later in the year, SKL produced a treatise upon the use of aircraft carriers with the fleet in which it concluded that a battleship hybrid equipped to operate aircraft was undesirable, as the aircraft fittings would incur serious penalties in the battleship featues. If aircraft carriers were to accompany battleships in a task force, then the classic roles of shipboard catapult aircraft (reconnaissance,

anti-submarine and fighter) could be assumed by the escorting carriers and ship-board catapult provision be dispensed with. If, on the other hand, carriers could not be built in sufficient numbers, then it would be necessary to allocate space and equipment for 6–8 aircraft on capital ships (ie twice the capacity of *Tirpitz*).

Although the battleship/cruiser hybrid was not favoured, an aircraft-carrying cruiser was a recurring theme in the Tirpitzüfer, the main contention being its description and construction as either a 'cruiser with aircraft fitment' or 'aircraft carrier with adequate armament'. It was certainly considered possible to build a cruiser/carrier, the problems in accommodating the flight deck being solved by detailed attention to the catapult and arrestor arrangements. Such a ship would have the speed and armament of a cruiser and be able to utilise these features, together with her armour and aircraft complement in the scout, flak protection, convoy escort and mercantile warfare roles. The existence of such a design would not, in the opinion of the SKL, be the death-knell of the true aircraft carrier, whose main role was seen in the context of the battleship task force.

In fact, the SKL envisaged two roles for carriers, whose size was dependent upon tactical considerations. Paralleling the role of the cruiser/carrier was a small aircraft carrier of about 15,000 tonnes – a size which the Construction Office believed would permit series construction. This would have a high speed, good radius of action, be armed with 12cm guns but carry only a reduced number of aircraft, although sufficient for the tasks proposed. The second type was a large carrier which was seen as indispensible for operations with the Fleet. A ratio of small-to-large types of 5:1 was proposed. Raeder who liked the possibilities of the cruiser-carrier, ordered an investigation of its merits. These thoughts no doubt led to the designs to be described shortly.

Despite the resumption of work on *Graf Zeppelin*, the *Quartier-Meisteramt* of the SKL still had considerable misgivings as to the suitability of the design and in the course of a memorandum in 1942 on the subject of a build-up of the fleet after the war, saw the need for a complete re-casting of the basic design. This would feature dual purpose 12.7cm guns, have radius of action similar to that of the battleships, with a cruiser's speed and good sea-keeping properties for Atlantic deployment. (This may have been the design specification, code-named 'Lilienthal', which featured in the 1943 war games at the *Kriegsakademie*. It envisaged a 58,000 tonne vessel armed with twenty 12.7cm DP guns, able to carry 100 aircraft and incorporated a 100mm armoured flight deck.) Also envisaged was a 'flight-deck cruiser' which was to be an aircraft carrier with good armament and not merely a cruiser with a flight deck. This ship was intended for mercantile warfare, carrying 12 general purpose and 9 fighter aircraft – its main armament. Up to 1943, sketch designs had been prepared for four flight-deck cruisers (*Flugdeckkreuzer*) of between 10,000 and 40,000 tonnes, with heavy cruiser type guns, two aircraft carriers of normal type of 30,000 and 30,000 tonnes, simple escort type carriers and a flying boat tender. This was in addition to the conversions of

Seydlitz and various liners.

The design for a 'Grosseflugzeugkreuzer' (project AI & AII) envisaged a 40,000-tonne ship with a three-shaft 210,000hp machinery installation and capable of 34kts. This incorporated a hangar 160m long and could accommodate 12 fighters and 16 bombers. A gun armament of 4–20.3cm, 16–15cm and 16–10.5cm was provided, with the 15cm still being shipped in casements. Armouring was fairly extensive, totalling 9000 tonnes with a 150mm main belt and 60–100mm armoured deck. A variation of this project was a modification as a true aircraft carrier with the 20.3cm guns being omitted and a consequent increase in the aircraft capacity. The hangar length was increased to 210m, allowing the operation of 26 bombers and 12 fighters. The dimensions, engines and hull were to be identical to the 'Grossflugzeugkreuzer' but with the omission of the heavy guns, the weight breakdowns were differently arranged. This design was referred to as the 'Grosseflugzeugtrager'.

An even larger project was the 'Atlantikflugzeugkreuzer' (projects AIII & AIV) which displaced about 70,000 tonnes, carried 38 aircraft and was armed with four or six 28cm (11in) guns! With armoured deck and flight deck up to 150mm thick and a waterline belt of 250mm this was indeed a heavily protected vessel. Once again a modification of the sketch design was a true aircraft carrier layout, which, by the omission of the 28cm guns, allowed the aircraft complement to rise to 38 bombers and 12 fighters.

At the other end of the scale, sketch designs were prepared for three small flight-deck cruisers, designs EIV, EV and EVI which varied between 12,750 tonnes and 22,200 tonnes full load displacement. Protection varied between light cruiser and heavy cruiser standards and the main armament comprised 15cm guns. Aircraft complements varied between 10 and 25. Two sketches were also prepared for flying boat tenders (*Flugboot-träger*). These two projects, IG and IE envisaged ships of 13,000 tonnes or 36,500 tonnes able to carry seven or ten Bv138 flying boats. Finally, in March 1944 a meeting was called to discuss the conversion of freighters into auxiliary carriers, presumably on the same lines as the British 'MAC' ships. It was suggested that a 3,000-tonne ship could be equipped to operate 2–3 fighters and the 9,000-tonne 'Hansa' standard ship, 5 or 6. there was no great enthusiasm for the project however, and nothing came of it.

None of the projects described above (and detailed more fully in the tables) ever progressed beyond the preliminary paperwork stage and were merely 'quantified ideas'. At the time that they were being formulated, the likelihood of their reaching fruition was gone for ever and, like many other of the design staffs ideas after 1941, they remained grandiose pipe dreams.

FINAL CANCELLATION

In the meantime however, events far to the north of Norway were developing into a situation which was to have a direct effect upon the rusty and incomplete carrier sitting in dock over 1200 miles to the south. The event in question was operation 'Regenbögen', the attack of *Lützow* and *Admiral Hipper* upon the convoy JW 51B bound for Russia. As a result of the disastrous failure of the German ships to destroy the convoy, Hitler ordered all the Fleet's big ships to be scrapped and although the new C-in-C, Admiral Dönitz, managed to avoid the execution of most of the order, the completion of an aircraft carrier for which there would be no capital ship or cruiser support made no sense. Once again, on 30 January 1943, work stopped aboard the *Graf Zeppelin*. Some makeshift work continued until March to prepare the ship for yet another move for Admiral von Conrady at OKM had ordered her back to the east. Deutsche Werke at Kiel estimated that the ship would be ready for towing out by 15 April and OKM requested a suitable berth be prepared at Pillau. The codename for the tow this time was 'Zugvogel' and the ship would be part of the Naval Salvage & Service Command, towing commander Kapitän zu See Ritschel. The flak weapons and searchlights were re-installed and two barrage balloons added for good measure. Anti-submarine and air escort was also provided. Towing speed was to be 6kts using tugs *Eisbär*, *Norder*, *Taifun* and *Passat*. 'Zugvogel' sailed late in the afternoon of 20 April and arrived in Swinemünde on the 23rd before finally being berthed at Stettin. Her transfer further east to Pillau was cancelled in the face of opposition, particularly from the U-boat command, because a berth in Pillau could not have been provided without seriously disrupting existing berthing arrangements for U-boats and minelayers.

Polish underground members promptly reported her arrival to British intelligence and on 23 June photographic reconnaissance aircraft confirmed her presence moored to a wharf on the Parnitz river, opposite Grosskraftwerk near the Danzig-Parnitz canal, some two miles east of Stettin. Allied naval intelligence had been interested in the ship's progress and whereabouts since 1940 and reports from both British and French sources had often suggested that her completion was imminent. In June 1942 the British had believed her to be nearing completion and anticipated sea trials in three weeks but full operational capability not for at least a further three months. Almost eight months later, her arrival at Kiel had led to new reports of her impending entry into service when it was believed that she might become operational in June 1943. However, the ship's arrival in Stettin and her condition, as revealed by PR photographs as well as underground reports, now suggested the truth – her construction had been abandoned. British naval intelligence reports dated 29 June 1943 acknowledged this, speculating that the reason could have been due to lack of materials, shortage of manpower, major breakdown of machinery or other unknown cause.

Graf Zeppelin remained in Stettin, forlorn and abandoned until 1945, when, in the face of the Russian advance, a decision had to be made as to her future. Since the top priorities for the fleet were U-boats and minesweepers, there was only one answer – it was not worthwhile moving her. Thus, on 25 April 1945, almost exactly two years after arrival in the port, the still incomplete carrier was scuttled in shallow waters, her machin-

TABLE 4: AIRCRAFT CARRIERS

	Graf Zeppelin	Grosseflugzeugträger (Grosseflugzeugkreuzer) Projekt AI & AII	Atlantikflugzeugträger (Atlantikflugzeugkreuzer) Projekt AIII & AIV
Dimensions (m)	250×27×8.5	250×32×8.75	280×38×11 (×11.5)
Displacement 40%	27,500t	36,000t	61,500t (65,500t)
Displacement 75%	29,500t	38,000t	65,500t (69,000t)
Displacment 100%	31,000t	40,000t	67,500t (71,500t)
Hangar width	2×16m	1×21m	1×26m
Hangar length	160m	210m (160m)	250m (190m)
Horsepower	4×50,000	3×70,000	4×70,000
Speed at 75% disp	34½kts	34kts	34kts
Endurance	6500nm	18,000nm	20,000nm
Hull wt	10,750t	12,500 (11,500)t	20,000 (21,500)t
Armour wt	5000t	9000t	21,000 (21,500)t
Engines	5250t	6500t	9000t
Guns & aircraft	2500t	2500 (3500)t	3500 (5500)t
Equipment	1000t	1500t	3000t
Fuel	6000t	7000t	10,000t
Reserve	500t	1000t	1000t
Full load	31,000t	40,000 (40,000)t	67,500 (71,500)t
Heavy guns	Nil	Nil (4–20.3cm)	Nil (4 or 6–28cm)
Medium guns	16–15cm	16–15cm	16–15cm
Flak	12–10.5cm, 20–3.7cm	16–10.5cm, 20–3.7cm	16–10.5cm, 20–3.7cm
Armour			
Upper/flight deck	20mm	50–20mm	50 (50/150)mm
Armoured deck	60mm	60–100mm	150 (150/50)mm
WL belt	100mm	150mm	250mm
Side belt	20mm	50mm	50 (50/150)mm
Casemates	20mm	150mm	150mm
Torpedo bulkhead	20mm	45mm	50mm
Hangars	20mm	20mm	50mm
Aircraft			
Bombers	28	26 (16)	38 (26)
Fighters	10	12 (12)	12 (12)

ery wrecked and the town abandoned.

After the German surrender, the Allied Tripartite Commission divided the remaining warships of the former *Kriegsmarine* between the victors and made provision for unserviceable vessels to be scrapped. The provisions were scrupulously observed by the British and Americans but were largely ignored by the Soviets. *Graf Zeppelin*, being a category 'C' ship (*ie* damaged or scuttled) should, under the terms of the commission, have been destroyed or sunk in deep water by 15 August 1946, but this was not done and local pilots reported in the middle of 1947, that she had been raised (possibly by March 1946) and would soon be loaded with captured equipment for towing back to Russia. She is believed to have sailed from Swinemünde on 14 August 1947.

The subsequent fate of the incomplete ship is still, thirty-seven years later, something of a mystery. Various authors and naval historians have put forward differing views as to the end of this enigmatic vessel. The ship was removed from Swinemünde, for she was not scrapped there. Certain sources allege her arrival in, and later breaking up at, Leningrad but there is no positive proof that she ever arrived in the port and the docking of such a large and unusual ship would surely have been noticed by Western intelligence. Thus since *Graf Zeppelin* sailed from Swinemünde but never arrived in Leningrad, the obvious inference is that she was lost at sea. Lenton records her fate as being mined north of Rügen on 15 August 1947, a date which accords well with her reported sailing date but unfortunately the position does not. Rügen cannot be said to be on a passage route between Swinemünde and Leningrad, for it lies well to the west of Swinemünde. A more likely answer it that the ship was lost either to a mine or due to stress of weather somewhere to the north, probably in the Gulf of Finland, where minefields remained in abundance and any surface wreckage would not be visible to prying Western eyes. Under tow, with no power supplies and only a small passage crew, the salvaged hull would be in a low damage control condition and, as a result, very vulnerable to weather or explosion damage.

POST MORTEM

The unhappy story of the *Graf Zeppelin* reflects the uncertainty and indecision within *Kriegsmarine* circles during the 1930s as to the future role of the Fleet itself. There were two main schools of thought, those who were battleship protagonists and those who ardently favoured the build up of the U-boat force. Under the command of Admiral Raeder, the battleship faction held sway, at least until the very end of that decade but even with the emphasis on the surface fleet, there was little recognition of the role of the aircraft carrier. This was partly due to inexperience with the type but it has to be admitted that its true potential did not come to be realised until 1940 with the attack on Taranto even within those navies experienced in carrier operation. Inside the North Sea operational area, carriers were not strictly necessary, nor were they of much advantage in the Baltic. The Atlantic, however, was a different matter but here such operations as were contemplated were of a cruiser warfare nature with independent operation of 'Panzers-

TABLE 5: SMALL FLIGHT-DECK CRUISERS

	Entwurf E IV	*Entwurf E V*	*Entwurf E VI*
Dimensions (m)	190×19	212×21.3	240×26.5
Type displacement	10,500t	15,550t	19,500t
40% displacement	11,400t	17,000t	21,300t
75% displacement	12,200t	18,250t	22,200t
100% displacement	12,750t	19,150t	23,100t
Hangar width	13m	15m	17.5m
Hangar length	94m	104m	120m
Maximum hp	120,000 steam + diesel	180,000 steam + diesel	180,000 diesel
Speed at 40% disp.	c34kts	c35.5kts	c34kts
Speed at 75% disp.	33.5kts	34.9kts	c33.5kts
Endurance at 19kts	9000nm	12,000nm	12,000nm
Endurance at 12kts	21,000nm	28,000nm	28,000nm
Guns	4–15cm (2×2), 8–8.8cm (4×2), 12–3.7cm (6×2), 8–2cm (2×4)	8–15cm (4×2), 10–8.8cm (5×2), 12–3.7cm (6×2), 12–2cm (3×4)	8–15cm (4×2), 12–8.8cm (6×2), 12–3.7cm (6×2), 12–2cm (3×4)
Armour	As light cruiser: 50mm WL belt, no splinter protection to hangar	60mm WL belt, 20mm deck, torpedo bulkhead 17mm, splinter protection to hangar	As heavy cruiser
Aircraft	7 fighters + 3 Stuka (or 10 fighters)	8 fighters + 10 Stuka	9 Bf109 + 16 Ju87 (or 19 Bf109)

One of the last views ever taken of the ship, Swinemünde 26 June 1947.

chiffe' and light cruisers. The use of an aircraft carrier in a task force was not initially envisaged.

In the 1930s, war planning was based on the possibilities of France, Poland or Russia being the likely opponents in any future conflict, of which only France

had an aircraft carrier. As this ship, *Béarn*, was of dubious effectiveness, it was probably considered that in the Atlantic, the threat of air attack could be discounted outside land-based aircraft range and that the ship's own catapult flights would provide adequate reconnaissance information. Then, with the growing likelihood of Britain becoming a future enemy and the intention of operating groups of ships as raiding forces in the Atlantic, the requirement for air cover became more pressing. The equipment of the Fleet Air Arm may have been obsolete but there could be no discounting the threat of its torpedo bomber force. Thus the *Kriegsmarine* began its carrier programme but with little priority and scant consideration in most of the plans for the build-up of the fleet.

Things did not progress smoothly even after the two ships had been ordered because of the chronic overloading of industrial capacity in 1937–1939. Then, when war was certain, it was only possible to complete a few of the large surface ships – those which could be operational by 1941 at the latest, in the expectation of a short war. The resources allocated to the remainder were all diverted to more pressing needs, to the detriment of the carrier programme. This left the capital ships without any air cover at all, the dangers of which did not become apparent until the *Bismarck* sortie when it would not be unreasonable to suggest that had *Graf Zeppelin* been present, her Bf109 fighters would have prevented the Swordfish torpedoes from ever reaching the battleship and the sortie might not have ended so abruptly

When it was decided to resume the completion of *Graf Zeppelin* in 1942 after the demonstrations of the type's success at Taranto, Pearl Harbor and the Indian Ocean,

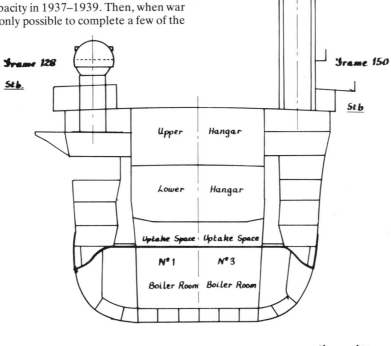

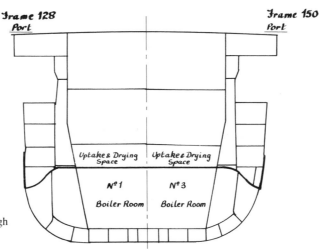

A series of frame sections through *Graf Zeppelin* (see also p36). *Author's drawings*

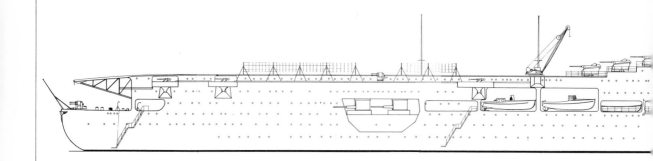

Frame 214,8

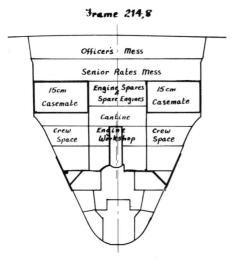

Officer's Mess

Senior Rates Mess

| 15cm Casemate | Engine Spares & Spare Engines | 15cm Casemate |

Canteen

| Crew Space | Engine Workshop | Crew Space |

Frame 185,35

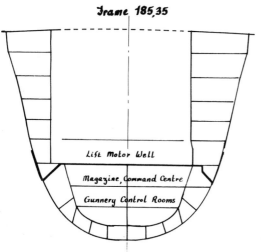

Lift Motor Well

Magazine, Command Centre

Gunnery Control Rooms

Frame 40·6   50·65

Port   Stb

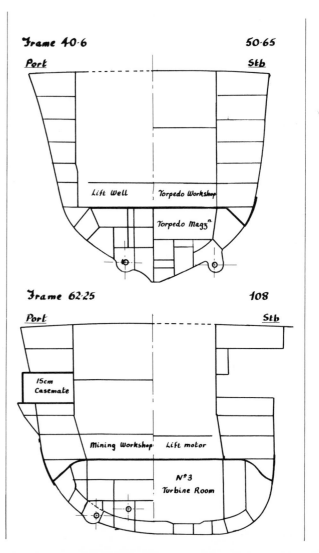

Lift Well   Torpedo Workshop

Torpedo Mag^n

Frame 62·25   108

Port   Stb

15cm Casemate

Mining Workshop   Lift motor

N° 3 Turbine Room

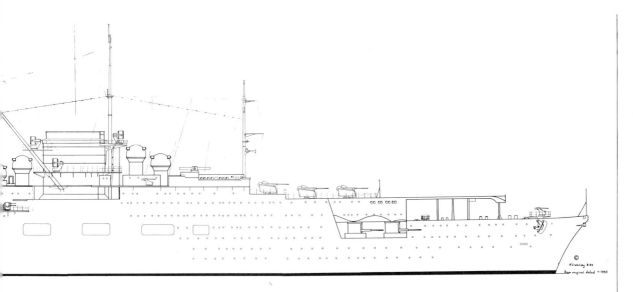

the *Kriegsmarine*'s requirement for the ship no longer actually existed for, apart from the independent Atlantic deployment of 'Panzerschiffe' planned for 1942/43 no further Atlantic sorties were envisaged. The capital ships just did not exist to form a homogenous raiding squadron and the abortive action in the Barents Sea in December 1942 finally killed all ideas of useful employment of an aircraft carrier. Thus, *Graf Zeppelin* was once again put into a backwater and all the plans, projects and schemes for further carriers were rendered unrealistic under the strategic conditions now prevailing. Like so many other projects, military, air force and naval, it was defeated by the attempts to produce far too many ship types on a limited industrial base in too short a length of time. Contrary to general belief, despite the inter-service squabbles, the *Luftwaffe* had produced the aircraft; it was the *Kriegsmarine*'s lack of clearcut policy for surface ships which led to the carrier's failure to achieve operational status.

TABLE 6: FLUGBOOTTRÄGER

	Entwurf IG	*Entwurf IE*
Displacement	13,000t	36,000t
Horsepower	64,000	240,000
Shafts	3	4
Speed at 75% load	28½/29½kts	34½kts
Endurance	18,000nm	30,000nm
Armour		
Torpedo bulkhead		
space	4m	4m
Torpedo bulkhead	45mm	45mm
Deck	45mm	50mm (150mm magazines & engine room)
Side	60mm	250mm (max)
Guns	8–10.5cm, 8–3.7cm	4–15cm, 20–3.7cm, 24–2cm
Aircraft	5 Bv138	8 Bv138
+ Reserve aircraft	2 Bv138	2 Bv138

Note: All foregoing data tables taken from *Hauptamt Kriegschiffbau* KIIIM 2840/42.

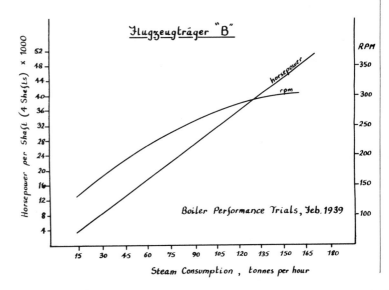

Elevation of *Graf Zeppelin*.
Author's drawings

The origins of Russian and Soviet MTBs

by René Greger

For the Soviet Union, 1977 marked not only the anniversary of the war against Turkey a century earlier, but also the centenary of the first wartime engagement between a torpedo launch and a warship. The Russians could justifiably claim that it was their boats which first earned the title 'mosquitoes of the sea'. In the USSR these boats are considered to be the direct ancestors of the fast rocket and torpedo boats which are so numerous today.

In 1877 a total of six spar torpedo boats were operating in the Danube delta against a powerful detachment of the Turkish Fleet that had been stationed there. Two of them, *Shutka* and *Mina*, were of iron construction, the remainder wooden. The four wooden boats used their spar torpedoes to sink the Turkish monitor *Seifi* on 27 May 1877; but the two iron boats had an even more significant part to play before the crossing of the Danube by the Russian Army. They repeatedly attacked the Turkish Fleet, and, although they did not sink any of them, forced the Turks to retire. During June 1877 *Shutka* in particular was very successful in these operations.

Shutka, a Thornycroft-built steam cutter on the Danube in June 1877.

Author's collection

One of the unsuccessful Nixon motor torpedo boats.
Author's collection

In the meantime the first experiments were being carried out with Whitehead torpedoes carried on steam launches, under the initiative of Captain, later Admiral, Makarov. One ship was fitted with a tube under the keel, the *Chesma*. On the night of 26 January 1878 she sank the Turkish guardship *Intibah* in the Black Sea off Batumi; this was the first successful combat use of a Whitehead torpedo against a warship. During this period the Russian Navy showed a preference for very small torpedo boats, and produced a series of such vessels designated 'minononski' (torpedo cutters); standard torpedo boats were designated 'minononscy'.

THE RUSSO-JAPANESE WAR

In the Russo-Japanese War of 1904–5 the small boats were again called into service. In besieged Port Arthur four steam launches from armoured ships were equipped with a torpedo and they operated in the outer roadstead against Japanese torpedo boats and minesweepers. According to Russian information the launch from the battleship *Pobieda* sank a Japanese torpedo boat during these operations. In the final phase of the conflict, on 5 September 1905, the first attack by a torpedo-equipped motor boat against an enemy ship took place off Vladivostock. This was not a specially designed boat, but only a large rowing boat into which a

petrol engine and two temporary torpedo launching systems had been installed.

The Russian Navy did however possess true motor torpedo boats at this time, having, as is well known, purchased motor boats as well as submarines in the USA after the outbreak of war. The motor boats were built by the firm of Lewis Nixon in Perth, New Jersey, which had tried in vain to interest the American Navy in their designs. The 27m boat, powered by two 300hp petrol engines, attained a speed of 25 knots on trials before a Russian Navy Commission in December 1904. Although she was not carrying military equipment at the time, this boat was accepted and the American firm were given orders for the supply of engines and components for 9 more vessels. These 10 boats were assembled by the spring of 1906 at Sebastopol, and were transported to Kronstadt in the same year. They served in the Baltic Fleet as Minonoski Nos 1–10 until 1912, during which time their inferior petrol engines were replaced by diesel engines. Up to that time all the boats carried one 47mm Hotchkiss QF gun, one or two machine guns and one, rotating, torpedo launcher on deck. With this equipment they were only capable of 18kts which was insufficient for their intended role. After conversion in 1912 most of the boats were transferred to harbour duties, and only one boat, designated

In the early years after the Civil War this photograph was
claimed to show one of the first projects of the famous
designer A N Tupolev. In fact it is one of the US-built motor
boats delivered to the Tsarist Navy in 1916–17 with a painted
naval flag introduced in 1923. There was no MTB carrying the
designation ANT-2.

Author's collection

SK-1 (*ie* patrol boat No 1) was employed in the First
World War (reports that this vessel also served in the
Second World War are incorrect).

The Tsarist Navy did not manage to bring any of its
own projects for motor torpedo boats to fruition. Two
plans were drawn up by the Baltic Fleet for arming fast
motor boats with torpedo launching systems (based on
the Italian MAS boats), but they were not approved,
and the conversion of a ship's motor boat, which had
already been commenced, was cancelled. There have
been many reports in Western naval literature of a conversion of a fast submarine hunter and patrol boat,
SK-324 (a US-built sub-chaser) into a motor torpedo
boat at Sebastopol in 1917, but no Soviet sources con-
firm this. On 12 July 1917 there was no action in the
Bosphorus. However, on the night of 26 July (13 July
in the old calendar) a Russian motor boat attempted to
penetrate into the Bosphorus, and was shelled by the
German/Turkish batteries. The following morning

A hitherto unpublished view of a captured British CMB under the Red Flag under test at Sevastopol in the 1920s.

Author's collection

many bottles were found there, containing an anti-German proclamation from the Revolutionary Russian Fleet to the Turks. (In *Warship* No 8 these boats were mistakenly described as being built in Russia with imported 'Nicholson' engines). Both these facts argue against the idea that the sub-chaser was converted into a motor torpedo boat.

However, it has been established that the Baltic Fleet was due to receive a flotilla of British CMBs in August 1917. After the bitter experience with the first German planing boats in the Gulf of Riga, when a Russian transport was torpedoed and sunk by these ships, a small number of CMBs were ordered in England. They had not been delivered by the British by the time of the October Revolution in 1917. Yet fate decreed that boats of just this type were to sail under the flag of the new socialist Russia. This did not happen until 1920, and therefore this episode belongs to another chapter.

by Raymond Laurence Rimell

Tondern

The First Carrier Strike

Had their full potential as reconnaissance platforms been realised, the Zeppelins' overall effect on naval operations could have been considerable. Here, Zeppelin *L 31* flies over heavy units of the Germany Navy – in the foreground, an *Ostfriesland* class battleship.

Luftschiffbau Zeppelin

Mention the word 'Zeppelin' these days and most people will immediately conjure up mental images of the ill-fated *Hindenburg* burning in mid-air over Lakehurst or squadrons of airships bombing London during World War I. The use of Zeppelins as 'spotters' for fleet operations in 'The Great War' is less well-known and the large, hydrogen-filled dirigibles formed a major arm of the German Imperial Navy.

The author's book *Zeppelin!* chronicles all the airship attacks made upon the British mainland during the 1914–18 war, the defence network that grew as a result, and the eventual checking of the raiders by airmen of the Royal Flying Corps, Royal Naval Air Service and, later, Royal Air Force. The part played by the naval services on both sides was considerable and the book lays particular emphasis on operations such as flying aircraft off towed platforms and the first strategic use of aircraft carriers to launch attacks on targets well beyond the range of land-based fighters, a subject tackled in more detail in this article.

ON THE OFFENSIVE

In the middle of 1918 the Royal Navy laid down plans to mount an air attack against the Zeppelin hangars at Tondern, this base being chosen due to its close proximity to the German Bight, the airships there being particularly well-placed to observe the British Grand Fleet. In due course, two specially-trained flights of RAF Sopwith Camels were deployed to the carrier HMS *Furious* on 29 June this ship, together with the First Light Cruiser Squadron and a number of destroyers, was steaming off the coast of Denmark. Bad weather precluded any

The seven Sopwith Camels on the deck of HMS *Furious* prior to the Tondern raid. Note that national markings on wing upper surfaces have been partially over-painted to render them less visible. Also of note are the deck screens painted in dazzle camouflage.

IWM/SP1156

The 'Toska' shed still burning some hours after the attack on Tondern.

Luftschiffbau Zeppelin

chance of the Camels being flown off and the ships were compelled to return home. On 16 July, Admiral Sir David Beatty reissued orders for 'Operation F7' from the flagship HMS *Queen Elizabeth*, which spelled out the objectives and providing special orders that if the weather was bad the force could stand to for 24 hours before returning to Rosyth.

In the event the weather was not ideal but the task force did not return to port and on the morning of 19 July, as *Furious* lay off the Schleswig coast, seven Sopwith Camels embarked on their historic flight.

First into the air was the leader of the first flight, Captain W D Jackson, whose Camel cleared *Furious*'s deck at 0314, quickly followed by Captain W F (now Sir William) Dickson and Lieutenant N E Williams. Barely an hour later the three biplanes were over the target at 100ft altitude, Jackson diving on the northernmost shed and releasing a brace of bombs, one of which scored a

Captain Bernard Arthur Smart, DSO, who led the second flight of Camels against the Tondern Zeppelin sheds.

B A Smart

The burnt-out wreck of *L 54* in the 'Toska' hangar following
the air strike from HMS *Furious*; beyond lie the crumpled
remains of *L 60*.

Marine Luftschiffer-Kameradschaft

direct hit, the other being a near miss. Dickson and
Williams attacked the large 'Toska' shed which housed
the Zeppelins *L 54* and *L 60*, three of the bombs reaching their target. The hangar burst into flames and an
enormous conflagration followed as the Zeppelins'
hydrogen-filled gas cells caught fire – within minutes the
giant building was completely engulfed.

Close behind Williams as he took off from *Furious* was
Captain Bernard Arthur Smart, DSO, who had shot
down Zeppelin *L 23* some months previously, having
successfully flown a Sopwith Pup from a platform
mounted on the front gun turret of the cruiser (see
Warship 29, p51) HMS *Yarmouth*.

Now Smart was leading a second wave which comprised Captain T K Thyne and Lieutenants S Dawson
and W A Yeulett. The two flights left *Furious* in succes-

sion with no interval between them, the first forming up
to starboard and the second to port, Yeulett, last man
away, taking off at 0320. Although the flights departed
together, Smart's section arrived over Tondern some ten
minutes behind Jackson's, due mainly to Dawson and
Yeulett failing to open up their motors, Thyne having
already returned with engine trouble. Smart's own personal account of the raid was set down in a letter to his
mother a few days later, much of which is quoted in
Zeppelin!. Smart admitted frustration over his comrades' failure to keep up with him, and as the three
Camels arrived over Tondern they met a barrage of
ground fire. Smart wrote later:

> A number of batteries opened out on us and the flashes of
> three close together attracted my attention – close to these I
> saw the three Zepp sheds, two large double ones and one

HMS *Furious* at the time of the Tondern raid in her dazzle scheme. The Camels took off from the forward deck and could not land aboard but ditched into the sea ahead of the ship, or her escorts, and were retrieved.

CPL

small. One of the large ones had a large hole in the roof and was literally belching out thick black smoke from every crack and crevice in the building. I gave the signal and dived on the other big shed at full speed, the 150 knots registered on the indicator giving me a sense of security against the wretched archies [WWI slang for anti-aircraft fire] which, although not particularly well ranged, were properly 'putting the wind up me'! Down and down I came until only 800 feet at which height I dropped the bombs in succession and swerved away. I had a glimpse of one falling short and the other landing in the middle of the shed after which my whole attention was taken up in saving my skin! The aerodrome I now saw to be absolutely thick with men running wildly in all directions and over the roar of the engines I heard the crackle of numerous rifles and several machine guns – it sounded just like a little infantry attack . . .

Smart managed to emerge unscathed and flew toward Brede for a pre-arranged rendezvous with his colleagues. Circling over the town Smart saw no sign of the other Camels and a glance at his watch revealed he had only an hour's fuel left; his chances of returning to *Furious* were fast becoming slim. Torn between waiting for his flight, for whom he was of course responsible, and returning to *Furious*, he choose the latter thinking that 'to return ignominiously without my flight was better than not returning at all'. After a nail-biting return trip, Smart located the task force and ditched his aircraft ahead of a destroyer. Drenched, cold and exhausted he

Above, Col Charles Samson's unsuccessful 30 May 1918 attempt to launch a Camel from lighter *H 3* off Harwich, and below left, Flt Sub-Lt Culley's successful attempt on 31 July. Both were towed by the destroyer HMS *Truculent*.

Peter Cadbury/IWM/Q27511

was hoisted aboard and taken to the Captain's cabin, where he slept for the rest of the day.

When Smart awoke he learnt that four of the pilots had failed to return, their loss attributed to low cloud and poor visibility causing them to loose their way and run our of fuel, the safety margin for which was small. The tale of Smart's comrades became clear later: Jackson had made a forced landing near Esbjerg in Denmark, owing to his petrol running out, and destroyed his machine before being interned; Williams encountered similar problems and landed in Scallinger while Dawson got down safely near Ringkøbing. Neither pilot was able to destroy his machine. (Fliers were under orders to burn their machines if making a crash landing on enemy or neutral territory, to prevent the aircraft falling into enemy hands).

The subsequent summary of operations offered conflicting reports of Yeulett's fate: 'Failed to return. One report stated he was seen to land near Tondern, but a later report says the machine was salved from the sea near Hoyer. No definite news of the pilot.'

Tondern's defences were meagre, being restricted to small arms shouldered by ground troops and on 6 March five Albatross fighter biplanes had been temporarily withdrawn while the levelling of a landing ground was taking place – an event doubtless known to British intelligence. Four men were injured as a result of the Camels' attack and whilst *L 54* and *L 60* were both destroyed, the big 'Toska' shed was soon repaired. The attack was a success and revealed how exposed Tondern really was and the base was thereafter maintained as an emergency landing-ground.

The Tondern raid was of historical importance as being the first time that aircraft were flown from a carrier to attack targets deep in enemy territory. It was a portent of what was to come for a later conflict would see the aircraft carrier play a leading role in the war at sea and in the air.

Zeppelin! A battle for air supremacy in World War I by Ray Rimell is published by Conway Maritime Press at £25.00.

BRITISH NAVAL GUNS 1880~1945 No 15

by N J M Campbell

The turret ship *Trafalgar* showing her amidships embrasures
for her 4.7in QF Mk I guns.

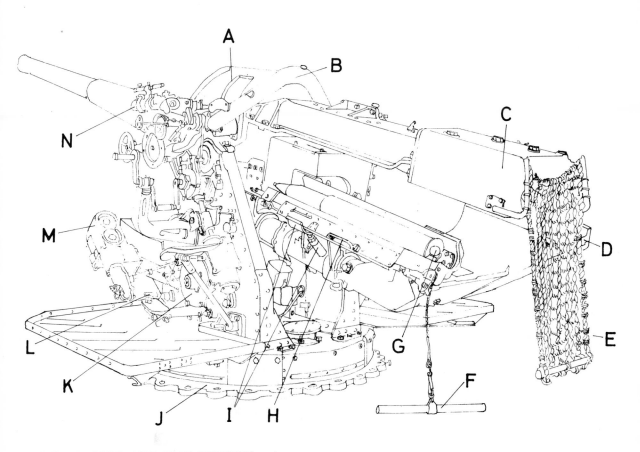

4.7IN MK XVIII MOUNTING (QF MK IX gun)

A Mantlet plate
B Gunsight counterbalance weight beam
C Balance weight
D Balance weight support frame
E Cartridge catch net
F Hand rammer cable hand grip
G Rammer head returning knob
H Loading tray hand grip
I Loading tray locking bolt and bolt release palm lever
J Mounting training base
K Elevating drive main wormwheel gearbox
L Percussion firing footpush
M Elevation receiver
N Layer's monocular gunsight telescope

4.7 inch guns These were all of 4.724in (120mm) actual bore and unless otherwise noted fired separated QF ammunition. The first gun acquired by Britain was a 32 calibre Elswick Pattern M in 1886. This fired a 36lb projectile at 1900fs, and did not enter service, though used in limited numbers by Italy, and the first guns adopted were the 40-calibre marks noted below. There was much argument over the shell weight for these which was originally designed as 40lb, reduced to 30lb at the Admiralty's request and then increased to 36, 40 and finally 45lb.

4.7in QF Marks I to IV These guns differed in construction only, Mk I, Elswick Pattern P, having an A tube, jacket, 5 B hoops to the muzzle, screwed securing ring and breech ring. The interrupted screw breech block with conical fore part, was taken by the jacket. Mk II, pattern Q, differed principally in having 3 B hoops and a short C hoop screwed to the jacket, while Mk III, Pattern T, had a B hoop, 2 B tubes and a shorter C hoop. Mk IV was partly wire wound with B tube, jacket, very short C hoop and breech ring. The breech block was taken by a breech bush screwed into the A tube. The letter A following the mark indicated modifications to the 3-motion BM and the letter B single motion. A single star was added if the breech ring was altered to suit Army field mountings, and two stars are believed to refer to the addition of a cartridge retaining catch for HA fire.

The guns were used by the Army for coast defence and field armament, though mainly by the Navy, and transfers in both directions were numerous. In all 1167 were made – 154 Mk I, 91 Mk II, 338 Mk III, 584 Mk IV – and of these 776 were originally naval with another 110 transferred from the Army. In World War I a total of 13 Mk IVJ and 24 stock guns were obtained from Japan for DAMS, and there were 13 Australian guns not numbered in the British series.

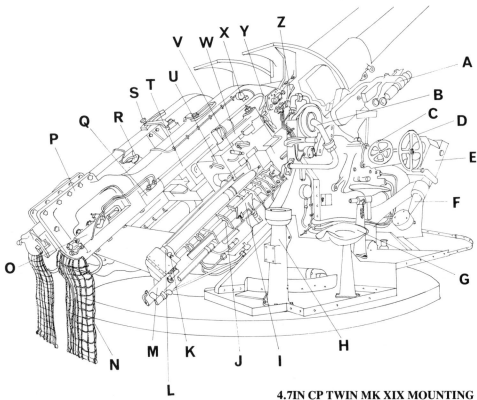

4.7IN CP TWIN MK XIX MOUNTING
(QF Mk XII gun)

A Trainer's monocular sight
B Hydraulic exhaust take-off from elevating structure
C Trainer's power handwheel
D Trainer's hand drive
E Training receiver
F Drive to training receiver 'mechanical' pointer
G Fuze-setter's seat
H Fuze-setting pedestal
I Loading tray unlocking palm lever
J Loading tray
K Hand rammer head
L Power rammer head
M Rammer cylinder
N Spent cartridge catch net
O Intensifier connected to recuperator cylinder gland
P Balance weights
Q Recuperator cylinder
R Loading light
S Semi-automatic/quickfire changeover lever
T Recuperator ram
U Breech mechanism lever locking lever
V Safe-fire lever
W Breech mechanism lever
X 'Rounds fired' counter
Y Breech worker's percussion firing hand-grip
Z Firing circuit 'interceptor' (circuit breaker)

Apart from some coast defence guns, none survived until 1939, but all 4.7in in British warships up to 1914 were Mk I–IV. They were also at that time standard armament for AMCs, though latterly superseded by 6in. Many World War I sloops were armed with these 4.7in, and among others may be noted the *Campania, Princess Margaret* and the rearmed destroyer *Afridi,* while September 1918 figures allot 500 to DAMS.

The earlier mountings, BDI, BDII, UDI and GII were of CP type and these were supplemented by PIII, PIV and PIV*. Some use was made of coast defence mountings, similar to GII and PIV and there were Japanese stock mountings. All allowed 20° elevation except BDI and BDII with 15° which were limited respectively to the *Nile* and *Barfleur* battleship classes as originally completed.

In the earlier part of the First World War 10 PIV mountings from the *Latona* class minelayers were to be adapted for HA fire and assigned to the AA defence of London, but they appear to have been of little use.

4.7in QF Marks V, V* Mark V comprised 7 Pattern Y guns acquired from Elswick for coast defence in 1900, and also in service in the Argentine, Norwegian and Chinese navies among others, while MK V* covered 620 guns made in Japan for DAMS. Both were built up with

A tube, breech piece and 2 B tubes, jacket and short breech ring. In MK V the breech block was taken by the breech piece, but in V* there was a breech bush screwing into the jacket. The breech block was similar to those in

4.7IN MK XX MOUNTING (QF Mk XI gun)

1   Mantlet plate
2   Balance weight
3   Balance weight support frame
4   Loading tray in line with chamber
5   Right gun elevation gear box
6   Hydraulic swivel connection to loading tray
7   Elevation pinion
8   Gun well
9   Drive shaft to elevation receiver 'mechanical' pointer
10 Support tube for loading tray
11 Loading tray unlocking palm lever
12 Power rammer control lever
13 Fuze setting hand crank
14 Loaded tilting tray aligned to fuze setting machine
15 Non rotating ammunition trunking
16 Loading tray in 'out' position
17 Loading tray buffer box
18 Air blast stop valve
19 Loading tray stop pad
20 Recuperator cylinder
21 Breech block in closed position
22 Electric firing lock
23 Loading lamp
24 Tilting tray in line with loading tray
25 Gunhouse roof support plates
26 Mounting hydraulic exhaust main
27 Cartridge at top of hoists
28 Cartridge hoist starting levers
29 Co-axial hydraulic pressure and exhaust pipe at centre of rotation
30 Main hydraulic pressure and exhaust swivel connection
31 Mounting hydraulic pressure main
32 Gunhouse pressure gauge

Mks I–IV but the single motion BM was not interchangeable with that of the previous B guns.

Of the 620 Mk V* guns, 24 were lost in delivery and the remainder were for DAMS apart from 4 in the TGBs *Halcyon* and *Hamadryad* and 2 at Trinidad. In 1939 there were 525 guns left being mostly in DEMS with some in large liners including *Aquitania*, in a few auxiliary warships and in emergency coast defence batteries. In certain conditions it was possible for the gun to fire before the breech was fully closed due to a protruding striker.

The mountings were PV and PX, the latter having two sets of run-out springs instead of one, and cross connected sights. Both allowed 20° elevation.

One 48.9-calibre Elswick QF supplied to the USA found its way to DAMS and then the armed yacht *Eileen* in the First World War.

4.7in QF Mark VI This was a World War I conversion of Army QF Mk I–IV guns to a BL charge and a 3in long obturating case, steel in some. It was hoped to overcome shortage of QF cases and to improve accuracy, but the gun does not seem to have been very successful. The Navy acquired 83 for minor DAMS and mountings were PVII, PVIII and CPIX. The first two of these comprised army cradles on 4in PII/II* and PX pedestals respectively. All allowed 20° elevation. The gun had the chamber increased to 23.328 inches in length with volume 469/490 cu in and with a 6.25lb MD11 charge and 45lb shell, MV was 2203fs.

4.7in BL Mark I, II Mark I was a World War I gun with tapered inner A tube, taper wound wire and full length

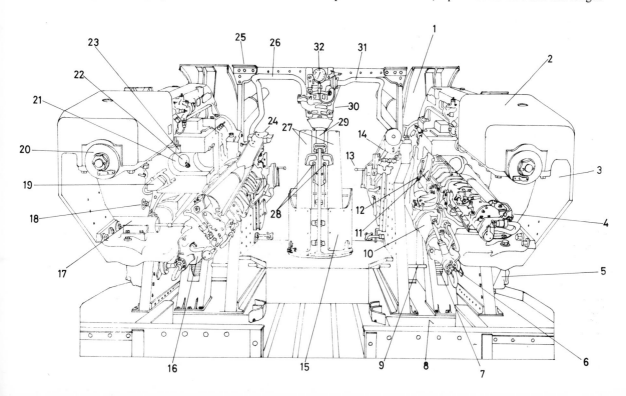

jacket. There was a breech ring and the Welin block was taken by a breech bush located in the A tube. Mk I* differed in having no inner A tube, though originally when large numbers were envisaged for DAMS it would also have had a shortened jacket and B tube. Mk II was of much later date, being ordered in August 1940 and is included for convenience. It had a monobloc barrel with breech ring and breech bush, and was interchangeable with the others. It was originally intended to make 776 Mk I and I*, 400 being for DAMS, but in the event 76 Mk I and III Mk I* were completed with later 32 Mk II. The guns were mounted in the rearmed *Botha* class, the *Scott* and *Wallace* class flotilla leaders, Modified W class destroyers and *Amazon* and *Ambuscade*. In World War II they were in 16 LCG (L) 3 and 4 and in a few other ships.

The CPVI, VI* and VI** mountings all allowed 30° elevation, and can be recognised by the abbreviated shield.

4.7in QF Mark VII A late World War I AA gun design firing fixed ammunition. It was never in service, only 4 being made, and was superseded by Mk VIII from which Mk VII differed in having full length wire and jacket, and in Mk VII* no inner A tube. It was 43 cals in bore length, weighed with BM 3.375 tons and had a chamber 25in long and 475 cu in effective volume. Performance was similar to that of Mk VIII. The mounting was HA X1.

4.7in QF Mark VIII This was the largest calibre fixed ammunition gun ever in service in the RN though the round was considerably lighter and shorter at 76lb and 44.26in than that in fixed ammunition 4.5in QF Mks I and III.

The gun was built with tapered inner A tube, A tube, part length wire, jacket and breech ring. The horizontal sliding block was hand operated with SA opening. The prefixed E and F referring to direct electric or electro-mechanical firing, are occasionally to be found. In all 84 guns were made and it was mounted in the *Nelson* and *Courageous* capital ship classes, the seaplane carrier *Albatross* and the cruiser minelayer *Adventure* only.

The HA X11 mounting was of CP type with 90° elevation and had a 9hp electric motor and hydraulic pump on the mounting to give elevation and training speeds of 10°/sec, twice those by hand. There was also a power rammer but this was unreliable at over 12 rpm, though 15 is recorded.

4.7in QF Marks IX, XII These were essentially separate ammunition QF versions of the BL gun, Mk IX being for single and Mk XII for twin mountings. None of the service mountings had sufficient AA capacity and another fortunate feature was that the shells had a mediocre ballistic form as in previous 4.7in. Totals of 742 Mk IX and 372 Mk XII were made, incorporating many variants. All had horizontal sliding BM, hand operated with SA opening.

Mk IX   – A tube, jacket to 80in from muzzle, breech ring
IXA   – loose barrel conversion, removable breech ring
IX*   – differed from IX in breech ring and SA gear (originally used for 2-part wire wound experimental guns)
IX**   – differences in breech ring to suit CPXVIII mounting
IX**A– loose barrel conversion, removable breech ring
IX**B– new loose barrel guns, differing from IX**A in removable breech ring/jacket connection. 183 made

Prefixes used were: C–percussion firing only; D–EMF and percussion; F–EMF; G–DEF and percussion.

Mk XII   – general construction as Mk IX but removable breech ring
XIIx   – no register on rear of A tube, and breech rings machined to suit A plain A tubes
XIIIB – loose barrel conversion

Mk IX was first tried in a clumsy 60° CPXIII mounting in the destroyer leader *Mackay*, the mounting having later unsatisfactory trials in the destroyer *Bulldog*, while Mk XII was tried in the destroyer *Hereward*. Single service mountings were:

CPXIV   – 30° elevation, A,B,C,D and *Saguenay* class destroyers. A later lightened version in 4.7in sloops only
CPXVI   – 30° elevation, tried in submarines *Thames, Porpoise, Regent, Regulus, Rover*. 4 mountings were converted for destroyers and one was in *Acasta*
CPXVII   – 40° elevation if gun-well covers lowered, E,F,G class destroyers
CPXVIII   – 40° elevation. H,I,Q,R class destroyers including ex-Brazilian and ex-Turkish. Also 4.7in O class
CPXXII   – 55° elevation, S(less *Savage*), T, U, V, W class destroyers.

All were hand-worked except that CPXXII had a spring-operated rammer cocked by the recoil. Mk IX series guns were also in LCG (L) 3 Nos 1–20, the depot ship *Barracuda* and DEMS *Rochester Castle* but the mountings are uncertain.

Mk XII guns were in twin CPXIX mountings which had hydraulic elevation, training and ramming with hoists independent of the mounting. Elevation was 40°. In the 'Tribal' class the mountings were in 2 groups, each powered by a 140hp steam turbine and oil hydraulic pump but in the J,K,N class destroyers each mounting had a 70hp electric motor and pump on the fixed structure.

4.7in QF Mk X Only one of this 40-calibre gun was made, and it was actually a Mk X* without inner A tube.

Full details have not been found but the gun was virtually a separate ammunition Mk VIII. It was mounted for a few years in the submarine *Perseus* in a 50° CPXV mounting. With a 50lb shell and 9.28lb SC103 charge MV was 2465fs.

4.7in QF Mark XI A much improved gun firing a 5/10 crh 62lb shell but a casualty of wartime austerities and only 87 were made. It was built with loose barrel, jacket to 85in from muzzle and the usual removable breech ring and sealing collar. The horizontal sliding breech block was hand operated with SA opening. The twin Mk XX mounting allowed 50° elevation and unlike in CPXIX the guns could be elevated separately. Training, ramming and hoists which were in a fixed trunk about which the turntable rotated, were hydraulically powered but elevation was manual. The oil hydraulic pump and 45 (peak 102) hp electric motor were on the fixed structure.

The gun was in the M class destroyers and *Laforey, Lightning, Lookout, Loyal* of the L class. The fixed hoist trunk caused some ammunition supply difficulties at certain angles of training.

PARTICULARS OF 4.7in GUNS

	4.7in QF Mk I–IV	4.7in QF Mk V*	4.7in BL Mk I, II
Weight inc BM (tons)	2.07/2.1	2.65	3.125/3.138
Length oa (in)	194.1	212.6	219.78
Length bore (cals)	40.01	43.02	45.0
Chamber (cu in)	284	490	665
Chamber length (in)	14.825	26.05	25.80
Projectile (lb)	45	50	50
Charge (lb/type)	12.0 SP	8.67 MD 16	11.45 SC103
	5.44 Cord 20	8.89 SC103	13.78 NF/S164–048
	6.45 MD 16		
Muzzle velocity (fs)	1786	2330	2669
	2125 Cord		
	2215 MD		
Range (yds)	9900/20°/2215fs	11,960/20°	15,800/30°

	4.7in QF Mk VIII	4.7in QF Mk IX, XII	4.7in QF Mk XI
Weight inc BM (tons)	3.087	2.963/2.984: XII 3.238/3.245	3.351
Length oa (in)	197.0	220.62:XII 224.08	247.7
Length bore (cals)	40.0	45.0	50.0
Chamber (cu in)	454	628	670
Chamber length (in)	23.42	30.55	28.0
Projectile (lb)	50	50	62
Charge (lb/type)	9.34 MC19	11.58 SC109	12.81 SC122
	9.19 SC103	13.13 NF/S 164–048	15.38 NF/S 198–054
	10.94 NF/S 164–048		
Muzzle Velocity (fs)	2457	2650	2538
Range (yds)	16,160/45°	16,970/40°	21,240/45°
Ceiling (ft)	32,000/90°		

HM SUBMARINE E 31

Log of her War Service

by Brian Head

The new submarine *E 31* at Scott's shipbuilding yard,
Greenock in 1915.

MoD

Ordered under the November 1914 War Emergency
Programme, *E 31* was laid down in December 1914
and launched on 23 August 1915 at Scott's Yard,
Greenock on the Clyde. The 'E' class formed the major
part of the Royal Navy's submarine force during World
War I and were generally regarded as a well-proven
and sound design. They were the first British submarines to have the hull sub-divided with watertight
bulkheads, thus isolating the boat into 3 main compartments: the fore-ends; control room and the beam
torpedo space; and the engine room, motor room and
stern space. Various improvements were incorporated
as building went on, with lessons learnt from the

experience gained in the first two years of the war *eg*
sounding machines, slopshoots, WCs which could be
blown at depth, hydroplane guards etc. *E 1*, the first
boat of the class, was completed in April 1913. *E 1–8*
had only 2 main watertight bulkheads, as did *E 31*, but
some of the later-built boats had 3 such bulkheads.
Fifty-seven 'E' boats were built over a 4-year period,
including two for the Australian Navy; 24 were lost by
accident or enemy action and 4 were scuttled in the
Baltic at the end of the submarine campaign there.

Scott's only built two 'E' boats (*E 31* and *E 51*). *E 31*
was completed in December 1915. The *E 27–E 56*
group were broadly similar in size and fittings, with an
overall length of 181ft, surface displacement of 667
tons and 807 tons submerged. Six 'E' boats were built as
minelayers. Maximum surface speed when driven by two
Vickers 8-cylinder diesels was 14 knots and maximum

E 31 bow on, taken soon after completion.
The Submarine Museum

The stern view taken at the same time.
The Submarine Museum

The Royal Navy's first purpose-built submarine depot ship,
the *Maidstone*, built at Scott's in 1912.

IWM

speed submerged on electric motors was approximately 9 knots, although 10 knots could be achieved in
short bursts. Endurance was approximately 3200 miles
at 10 knots on the surface and 70 miles at 5 knots
submerged. The maximum safe diving depth was
approximately 200ft (150ft officially), but *E 40* bottomed at 318ft on one occasion with only minor leaks
as a result. All the oil fuel was carried in internal tanks
inside the pressure hull. Two Exide batteries provided
the power source for the 2 electric motors. These
motors developed 840bhp and the diesels 1600bhp.
The batteries generated 220 volts/600 amps from a
total of 224 cells. Each cell weighed 865lb and could
be connected into 4 groups of 56 cells each. They could
then be worked in parallel at 110 volts (group down)
and 220 volts in series (group up).

E 31 had two battery tanks placed amidships with
portable wooden covers. Two fans exhausted the
hydrogen-charged air from the forward tank with a
single fan for the after end. A ventilator for each fan led
outboard at the after end of the bridge. The forward
battery tank with 168 cells was sub-divided to form four
sub-compartments which explains the references in
E 31's log to battery tanks 1–4. 'E' boats also had a
10-ton drop keel which could be released from inside
the control room.

E 31's main armament consisted of a 12pdr gun and
five 18in torpedo tubes – two in the bows. two amidships and one in the stern. The Mark 8 torpedoes had a
range of 3000 yards at a running speed of 41 knots, and
a maximum range of about 6000 yards, by which time
their speed was down to 29 knots. There were two
torpedo loading hatches, fore and aft of the conning
tower. Both hatches were mechanically opened through
gearing from handwheels operated inside the engine
room (after hatch) and the fore ends. The hull hatches
were connected to the hatches in the superstructure
(casing) so they could be opened together for escape
purposes.

The crew of an 'E' boat numbered 31, including 3
officers. On 27 December 1915, when *E 31* was commissioned, Lieutenant-Commander Ferdinand E B
Feilman was in command, with Lieutenant John F
Tryon as First Lieutenant and Sub-Lieutenant Alexan-
der A Love RNR as the Navigator.

Many submarines carried a Royal Naval Reserve
officer as Navigator. They were all recruited from the
Merchant Service and were experienced seamen.
Before the war ended, four RNR officers were given
command of their own boats. Sub-Lieutenant Love was
promoted acting Lieutenant early in 1916 and confirmed in his rank in January 1917.

Lieutenant-Commander Feilman was a very experienced submariner. He was CO of *E 7* in August 1914

Officers inspecting the damage caused to *E 31* by the
Rostock's unexploded 5.9in shell on 4 May 1916, the most
exciting day of the submarine's career.

Author's collection

when she made one of the first patrols into Heligoland
Bight. In February 1915 he took command of *C 32*,
with the 4th Flotilla at Dover. He was appointed to
E 31 in August 1915.

On 8 January 1916, Lieutenant-Commander Feilman took his new boat down the Clyde to Ardrossan
where she joined *E 26* (Lieutenant-Commander
Claude C Dobson DSO – later to win the VC in the
Baltic in 1919 leading an attack by Coastal Motor
Boats on Bolshevik warships at Kronstadt). *E 26* had
also just been commissioned, at Beardmore's yard.

At 0810 the next day, both *E 31* and *E 26* cast off to
begin the voyage south to Fort Blockhouse, at Gosport.
They were escorted by the 4-funnel torpedo boat destroyer *Bonetta* which was acting as a tender for submarines in the Clyde.

E 31 reached Fort Blockhouse on 11 January and
E 26 went on to Dover, and then on to Harwich to join
the 8th Flotilla.. The next day *E 31* started her 'working up' in Stokes Bay, which was followed by six days in
Dockyard hands remedying defects.

Seven of the following nine days were taken up with
more sea trials and exercises, plus a further day for an
experiment with anti-submarine nets at sea. This had to
be cancelled due to dense fog.

On the last day of January 1916, *E 31* entered the
Floating Dock for an overhaul before returning to
Blockhouse jetty on 3 February.

Two more days were spent out in Stokes Bay again,
before she was found ready to join the 8th Flotilla at
Harwich. At 1618 on 7 February, *E 31* slipped from
Haslar Creek in company with *V 1* (Lieutenant Lock-
hart), which was to be based at Yarmouth. The destroyer *Firedrake* had been sent round from Harwich to
provide the escort.

HARWICH – THE 8th FLOTILLA'S BASE

HMS *Maidstone*, together with *Pandora* and, later, HMS *Forth*, lay alongside Parkeston Quay at Harwich. They were the depot ships for the 8th Flotilla.

Maidstone (3500 tons) was the Navy's first purpose-built depot ship for submarines. *Pandora* was a converted merchantman and *Forth* had been a cruiser in former days. *Maidstone* had been launched at Scott's in April 1912 and was distinguished by her sailing ship type bowsprit. She remained at Harwich throughout the war and continued in service until 1929 when she was sold for breaking up.

The other part of the 8th Flotilla was based at Yarmouth with the depot ship *Alecto*. In July 1916 the *Alecto* group was designated as the 8th Flotilla and the *Maidstone* Flotilla became the 9th. The Harwich Flotilla with *Maidstone, Forth* and *Pandora* was the largest Royal Navy submarine flotilla operational in World War I. In June 1917, for example, there were 16 'E' boats and 9 'C' boats attached to the Flotilla. Numbers varied from time to time as boats were detached or transferred but there were only two Captains of the Flotilla throughout the war – Captain Waistell and, from October 1917, Captain Addison.

E 31's log records she made fast alongside *Maidstone* and outboard of *E 29* (Lieutenant Herbert Shove) at 1540 on 8 February 1916. However, all was not well with *E 31*'s machinery and the next 3 days were spent in the Floating Dock. Finally, it was decided that a further spell in the dockyard was required, so on 13 February at 0805 *E 31* slipped from *Maidstone* and proceeded in company with *E 4* (Lieutenant-Commander J T Tenison) and escorted by the destroyer *Brazen*, to Sheerness where at 1445 that afternoon she secured alongside the depot ship *Thames* moored at Queenborough.

E 31 was off at first light, slipping from *Thames* and proceeding upriver at 0655 to Chatham Dockyard where she remained until the middle of March. She undocked on 16 March but thick fog prevented her moving downriver to Queenborough again, until 19 March when she again secured for the night alongside *Thames*. Next day, the destroyer *Cynthia* escorted her back to Harwich.

E 31 GOES TO WAR

Two days later, on March 22, the serious business of preparing for war began, with daily torpedo firing exercises and attacking a destroyer acting as a target. On 7 April, Captain A K Waistell (in command of the 8th Flotilla) having been satisfied that she was now ready to became operational, *E 31* cast off from the depot ship *Pandora* at 1100 to begin her first war patrol.

On 8 April she was in her billet at 54°1'N 5°6'E but saw little activity apart from the occasional trawler, until 11 April when a submarine was observed on the surface off the starboard bow. This was presumed to be a U-boat since no British submarine should have been in that position, and an attack was commenced. Unfortunately, a heavy swell was running and *E 31* broke surface – and then dived to 40ft. The German sub-

marine dived before *E 31* could reach a satisfactory firing position. This incident occurred between 1330 and 1345 in the afternoon. *E 31* had been dived since 0835 that morning and remained so until 1910 in the evening – it was very easy to become the hunted in the comparatively shallow waters off the German coast and the hours of daylight were normally spent submerged.

E 31 returned to the *Maidstone* on the evening of 14 April and the Port Watch was given 4 days leave. On their return, *E 31* went into the Floating Dock for an overhaul and remained there for 4 days. At 0300 she left the Dock on 25 April and slipped from the *Maidstone* at 0730 to proceed to the Lough Light Vessel where she remained on the surface with *E 4* and *D 1* awaiting further orders from *Maidstone*. At 1025 a signal was received to return to Harwich. German battlecruisers had raided the East Coast and brushed with the Harwich cruisers and destroyers, but they escaped before the submarines became involved.

On 1 May the morning was spent making dummy attacks on a destroyer. The next day at 1530, *E 31* left Harwich in company with *E 55* and *E 57* to take part in Operation XX. They were escorted out into the North Sea by the destroyer *Lurcher*. The three submarines parted company with *Lurcher* at 0200 next morning and proceeded to their respective billets.

OPERATION XX

On 4 May, near the Horns Reef, *E 31* was keeping a periscope watch in the forenoon, when at 0930 a Zeppelin was observed to the South heading North West. Half an hour later, the Zeppelin altered course towards *E 31* and she immediately dived to 60ft to avoid any unwanted attention. *E 31* came back to periscope depth thirty minutes later and to the considerable surprise of all concerned, saw the Zeppelin lying on the surface of the water, apparently disabled, about 3 miles away. Lieutenant-Commander Feilman immediately gave the order to surface for a gun action. However, before bringing the 12pdr gun into action, the lookouts reported smoke from 2 vessels bearing West South West. He therefore dived the boat, prepared all torpedo tubes and headed towards the Zeppelin in the hope that she might be attracting some units of the German High Seas Fleet intent on rescue. At 1055 he noted that the smoke had disappeared, so decided to surface and resume the gun action. Firing commenced at a range of 4000 yards with *E 31* closing the Zeppelin. At 3000 yards, three hits were registered and the Zeppelin burst into flames. *E 31* picked up 7 survivors from the Zeppelin (later identified as the *L 7*) before she sank in position 55°25'N 7°17'E.

Lieutenant-Commander Feilman dived on sighting a large vessel approaching and proceeded to prepare for a torpedo attack. However, she turned out to be a Swedish merchantman. At 1215 a large trawler flying the German merchant flag was observed cruising about the spot where the *L 7* was destroyed. She eventually made off to eastward.

It later transpired that the Zeppelin had been fired on by the cruisers *Phaeton* and *Galatea*, one of whom had succeeded in hitting her with a 6in shell, thus disabling her and causing her to make a forced landing.

E 31 was part of a submarine screen positioned off the Danish coast and the Frisian Islands. *E 31*, *E 53* (Lieutenant-Commander J B Glencross), and *E 37* were placed off the Horns Reef, near the Vyl Light and *E 55*, *D 6* (Lieutenant G S White) and *D 4* (Lieutenant P E Phillips) off Terschelling.

Two minefields were to be laid as part of Operation XX, one in the Borkum area by the *Princess Margaret* and the other off the Vyl Light by the *Abdiel*. A few hours later, at dawn, the seaplane carriers *Vindex* and *Engadine* were to launch 9 aircraft for a raid on the airship sheds at Tondern. The submarines were to ambush any German warships sent to intercept the raiding force. The minefields were laid successfully but the seaplane raid was a failure, only one plane succeeding in reaching Tondern and failing to hit any target. Only *L 7* and *L 9* (from Hage) came out to look for the British ships. The escort comprised 16 destroyers of the 1st Flotilla and behind them was the Battle Cruiser Squadron. The main part of the Grand Fleet was to northwards so the scene was set for a major clash with German High Seas Fleet – but *L 7* failed to transmit an enemy contact report before she was shot down.

The clash was therefore deferred to the end of May when the two Fleets met off the coast of Jutland.

The Grand Fleet cruised in the vicinity of the Horn Reef during 4 May but with no enemy vessels sighted, it then returned to its bases.

A NARROW ESCAPE

That night (4 May) *E 31* surfaced at dark, as usual, to begin recharging her batteries. Suddenly, a cruiser appeared out of the darkness, no more than 200 yards away on the starboard bow. The officer of the watch was Lieutenant Love RNR, who showed great presence of mind by immediately putting the helm over to hard-a-starboard and giving orders to dive. The cruiser's turning circle was greater than that of *E 31* and the latter had put her helm over first. The cruiser was obviously intent on ramming but passed about 50 yards off. When abreast of the conning tower, she put on a searchlight as the CO of *E 31* was closing the conning tower lid. She opened fire and the first shot just missed the forward casing. The second shot went through the superstructure forward – 2ft above the hull casing – but did not explode. In all, the cruiser fired about 20 rounds and passed over *E 31* when she reached 60ft on her way to the bottom at 120ft. In retrospect, it was thought that *E 31* had created something of a smoke screen with the exhaust from her diesel engines. The wind was slightly on the port quarter, blowing the smoke ahead to starboard, thus obscuring the lookouts' vision. It was also a very dark night. It was a remarkably narrow escape. The cruiser was thought to be of the *Breslau* or *Yorck* class and later confirmed as the *Rostock* – sunk at the Battle of Jutland at the end of May. On return to base, fragments of the unexploded 6in shell were found embedded in *E 31*'s casing.

E 31 returned to Harwich on 6 May and this time it was the turn of the Starboard Watch to take 4 days leave. Able Seaman Phillips was commended in Lieutenant-Commander Feilman's report for his accurate gunlaying in the sinking of the Zeppelin, as was Lieutenant Tyron, *E 31*'s First Lieutenant, for his handling of the boat, and, of course, Lieutenant Love for his prompt action which undoubtedly saved *E 31*.

BACK TO ROUTINE

E 31 remained at Harwich until the end of May, with her crew undertaking a programme of self-maintenance repairs and servicing. The boat was cleaned up and repainted, leaky battery cells repaired, a new W/T mast installed, torpedoes overhauled, engines tested and torpedo tubes tested by firing dummy shots. On the evening of 30 May, she cast off from *Pandora* at 1900 and headed out for the North Sea again, in company with *E 53* and *D 6*. *Lurcher* provided the escort. *E 31* arrived in her billet on 31 May in position 52°20'N 03°00'E while the Battle of Jutland was being fought. Most of the day was spent submerged and while on the surface at 2105 she was forced to dive hurriedly by a German destroyer. She surfaced at 2200 to recommence battery charging but was put down again at 2330. At 0045 she tried again and finally completed her charge at 0315 on 1 June. Later in the morning watch, a signal was received recalling *E 31* to base and she was alongside *Pandora* by 2010 that evening.

The boat was kept in good order over the next few days by regular attack exercises with local destroyers. Then on 10 June *E 31* proceeded to sea again for a patrol off Terschelling Bank. This particular patrol was mainly notable for a severe gale with accompanying high seas. The North Sea was only 15–16 fathoms in the vicinity of *E 31*'s patrol area and two days were spent primarily sitting on the seabed because there was no real opportunity to carry out a periscope patrol in such weather. Nature relented somewhat on 16 June and *E 31* returned to Harwich on 18 June, arriving at 1905. Half the crew immediately proceeded on 4 days leave.

Lieutenant Tryon left *E 31* during June to take command of *C 12* in the Tyne and was relieved by Lieutenant Douglas Gavin who had been Lieutenant of *C 5* in the *Thames* Flotilla at Sheerness.

E 31's next war patrol commenced on 14 July and the intervening period was spent changing a periscope and with daily attack exercises, including a gun action. This fifth patrol was uneventful with only a few sailing craft and the occasional trawler to be seen. *E 31* returned to the *Pandora* at 0905 on 20 July and the other half of the crew were given 4 days leave. A period of relative inactivity followed, due to the need for various repairs including the replacement of a battery.

TRAGEDY

On 15 August *E 31* went to sea for an attack exercise with *E 41* (Lieutenant A M Winder) and *E 4* (Lieutenant-Commander J T Tenison). To give the flotilla practice in attacking another submarine, *E 41* was carrying out a run with *E 4* and *E 31* attacking her.

Another view of the crumpled casing of the submarine.
Author's collection

E 31 completed a dummy attack on *E 41* but tragedy followed shortly after. *E 41* was off the Cork Sand steering 100° at 12kts when the periscope of *E 4* appeared suddenly on the starboard bow, about 50 yards away, steering approximately 320° and moving fast through the water. *E 41*'s helm was put hard-a-starboard and her engines stopped, but collision was inevitable. *E 4* struck the bows of *E 41* and sank with all hands. In *E 41* an attempt was made to shut the watertight door to the fore-ends but the water was flooding in too rapidly. All hands were ordered on deck but while the men were still climbing up through the conning tower, *E 41* sank by the bows and went down in about a minute and a half in 45ft of water. The rising air pressure in the boat blew open the upper conning tower hatch and carried 2 officers to the surface where they were picked up by the destroyer *Firedrake* which had also rescued Lieutenant Winser and 11 men. There was, however, an amazing escape an hour and a half later from the engine room compartment of *E 41* by Stoker Petty Officer Brown which was a tribute to the man's indomitable courage and professional ability. Both submarines were later salvaged and recommissioned about a year later. The day after the accident *E 31* went into dock at Ipswich and remained there until 1 September.

To be continued

Excellent aerial view of *Poryvistyy* taken on 27 October 1983
in the Eastern Mediterranean. Note rotated position of two aft
76mm mounts.

USN

PORYVISTYY

The last KRIVAK I

by G Jacobs

Poryvistyy is the last of 21 'Krivak I' guided missile frigates to have been completed, and is one of the least known units of the class. Still not listed in *Jane's Fighting Ships* (1983–84 ed), the ship entered the Pacific (in company with the *Kiev* class CVHG *Novorossiysk*) in mid-February 1984.

The *Poryvistyy* was built at the Kamysh-Burun (Kerch) Shipyard. The vessel was laid down in late 1979 (possibly November) and launched during 1981. The vessel apparently was not completed until early 1982, certainly the last 'Krivak I' built at the Kerch facility. If these dates are relatively accurate, it is also after the last 'Krivak II' FFG was completed (*Pitlivyy* in October 1981; Kaliningrad-820 Shipyard). *Poryvistyy* did not enter the Mediterranean until sometime in the late summer of 1983. In January-February 1984 the ship accompanied the *Novorossiysk* task group in rounding the Cape and entering the Indian Ocean. The ship, in company with other units was seen off the eastern Malagasy coast during the task groups northward transit; in late February the task group was operating in the Socotra Islands and off the South Yemen (PDRY) coast. During this time, the Soviet task group conducted ASW and air defence exercises. *Poryvistyy* made a port call at Madras, India; afterwards the ship entered the northern entry to the Malacca Straits on 14 February 1984. The accompanying photo from a RAAF P-3C/Orion aircraft probably was taken about this time. The ship continued in company with the carrier task group. transiting across the South China Sea, en route direct to Vladivostock (main base of the Soviet Pacific Fleet).

Poryvistyy differs in no significant ways from most of the other 'Krivak I' class units; though minor differences do exist in all ships regarding the outfitting of ECM/ESM and communications rigging (see accompanying chart). The class is currently rated as SKR (*Storozhevoi Korabl*/'guard' or patrol ship), a change from their original ratings as large anti-submarine ships. Since completion of the first unit (*Bditelnyy*), only minor updating of ECM/ESM fittings has occurred on any of the units of the class. Three shipyards participated in the construction of the 'Krivak I' series: Kaliningrad Shipyard-820; Kamysh Burun (Kerch); and Zhdanov Shipyard-190. Given the classes dimensions (about 125 × 14.3 metres, but sources differ), the class represents a heavily armed vessel with adequate electronics to perform its intended primary mission of anti-submarine warfare.

Poryvistyy: photo taken in the eastern Indian Ocean in mid-February 1984. 'Owl Screech' fire control director aft is rotated to port facing forward.

Australian Department of Defence

WEAPON SYSTEMS

As the ship's primary role is ASW, the dominant weight allocated for weapons to fulfill this mission is amply evident. The quad SS-N-14 ASW launcher forward provides the ship with a 45km range low-altitutde cruise missile to carry an internal torpedo. While the class lacks an onboard helicopter, ASW attacks can be accomplished by data derived from the VDS inputs and the bow mounted sonar, and from monitoring of aircraft- or helicopter-dropped sonar buoys. For close-in ASW attacks, the ship is provided with RBU-6000 multiple rocket launchers, 12 cylinders to each launcher with an automatic reloading provision. The rockets fire in elliptical patterns and have a maximum range of about 6000m.

The ships are not strong in air defence; however, given their classification as a 'patrol ship' they were not expected to have to provide for their own defence, except for occasional aircraft that get through land-based air defences or any accompanying carrier. The twin-arm SA-N-4 launchers (fore and aft) are controlled by two 'Pop Group' missile fire control radars, and are intended to give the ships 'local' air defence out to 10 to 12km (at an altitude up to 10,000m). The two twin aft-mounted 76.2mm/59cal guns are dual purpose and capable of 85° gun elevation. Maximum gun range is probably 15,000m; about 70 per cent for maximum effective fire.

The ship's two quad launchers for 533mm (21in) torpedoes can accommodate either anti-ship or anti-submarine types (it is more likely the latter are most often carried). Use of the 'long' ASW torpedo has largely gone out of Western navies, but remains a prominent feature of Soviet warships. Used in this role, it probably provides the Soviets with an ASW torpedo capable of a 'stand-off' range of 9000m. The limitations imposed by multiple ASW engagements and potentially long periods at sea will place effectiveness limitations on only having four SS-N-14 missiles onboard; as such, the ASW torpedoes provide a most necessary medium-range back-up system.

PROPULSION SYSTEM

There still remains some doubts as to specifics regarding the gas turbine propulsion system used by the 'Krival' class. A two-shaft COGAG system is used with two gas turbiners, with a single exhaust stack containing two annular uptakes (for cruise turbines?) and two groups of three, fluted exhausts (boost turbines?). One estimate is that two 25,000shp turbines are available; however, the 'Krivak' FFGs have been observed at time making better than 32 knots, indicating a requirement

Close-in forward view shows armament layout of SS-N-14 quad launcher, SA-N-4 SAM twin-arm launcher housing, port and starboard RBU-6000 MRLs port and starboard quad 533mm (21in) torpedo tubes. Two 45mm saluting guns are visible outboard of RBU launchers on main deck. Two Soviet MBK 455M periscopes can be seen above bridge on outer extremity.

USN

far above a combined shp of 50,000. Heating ducts have been noted installed in the last couple years, indicating icing problems in the past when operating in Arctic Circle climates.

FINAL THOUGHTS

While not an exotic design even by Soviet standards, the 'Krivak' class has served a vital function of filling Soviet *numerical* requirements for increased ASW vessels at a time when large numbers of minimally-effective ASW *Kotlin* and *Skoryy* class destroyers were reaching block obsolescence. The bulk of the class, numbering 21 units (plus 11 'II' versions) entered service in the 1970s, and can be expected to remain in service well past the year 2000.

PORYVISTYY ELECTRONIC FITTINGS

Surveillance radars:
Early warning	– Head Net C
Surface search	– Don-2, Don Kay
Navigation	– 2 Shot Rock, Cross Loop A (HF/DF)

Fire control radars: 2 Pop Group (SA-N-4), 2 Eye Bowl (SS-N-14), Owl Screech (76mm guns)
ECM/ESM: 2 Bell Shroud, 2 Bell Squat, 2 Bat-1 counter-torpedo devices
IFF: High Pole B
Communications: Box Yoke (UHF), Pop Art (VHF)
Sonar: One bow mounted, one variable depth sonar (*Moskva* type)

book review

COMBAT FLEETS OF THE WORLD 1984/85.
Their Ships, Aircraft, and Armament
Edited by Jean Labayle Couhat.
English Edition by A D Baker III.
Published by Arms and Armour Press Ltd June 1984
255 × 240mm (10″ × 8″) 1000 pages, approx 2000
illustrations, index. ISBN 0-85368-650-5. £40.00.
Once again the great naval annuals have come around.
Nowadays the warship enthusiast must spend nearly as
much time comparing the two big books as he does
examining their contents. Had *Jane's* been as good as it
has always tried to suggest, the very idea of an English
edition of *Flottes de Combat* would have been a non-
starter. Clearly it was not, and we are left in a very
healthy position, able to sit back and compare.

From its vivid yellow jacket with the inevitable photograph of the *New Jersey's* forward turrets in action off
California to the large section on the 600 ship navy plans
of the Reagan Administration, *Combat Fleets* strives for
the appearance of being the last word. It succeeds
admirably; although it must be remembered that, as G
Jacobs points out in this issue, neither annual is infall-
able, and they seem to share their errors with uncommon
generosity. However, the coverage *is* up to date, the
publishers claim that more than two-thirds of the photographs are new for this edition, and even the most cursory examination would tend to support this contention.
It is this quality in the approach of *Combat Fleets* that
goes a long way to justifying the annual format, despite
the fact that less than one-twentieth of the content will,
on average, change in any one year. The grim days of
twenty-year-old photos in annual publications have
hopefully gone forever. This level of regular replacement makes *Combat Fleets* the better informed, and
thereby the more informative. The large section on the
Royal Navy after John Nott and General Galtieri had
done their worst was particularly valuable.

Supporting material on weapons, sensors and aircraft
also makes this volume more comprehensive. Jane's
other publications tend to reduce this aspect of their
coverage below the essential minimum. Keyed diagrams
clearly indicating the positions of the various shipboard
systems make the whole much more straightforward for
those of us unable to distinguish the many Soviet anten-
nae one from another.

Having covered the positive attributes of *Combat
Fleets*, and they are numerous, it would be well to turn to
the one major criticism that I have to make. The layout
of the text is poor, and gives the impression of being
crammed onto too few (sic) pages for comfort. Here the
larger pages and less crowded layout of *Jane's* make it a
more comfortable book of reference.

Combat Fleets is the cheaper of the two annuals, and
on balance it is better value. Would it be too much to
suggest that the cost-cutting layout is spoiling the ship
for a hap'porth of tar? **Andrew Lambert**

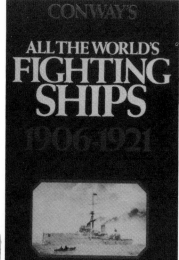
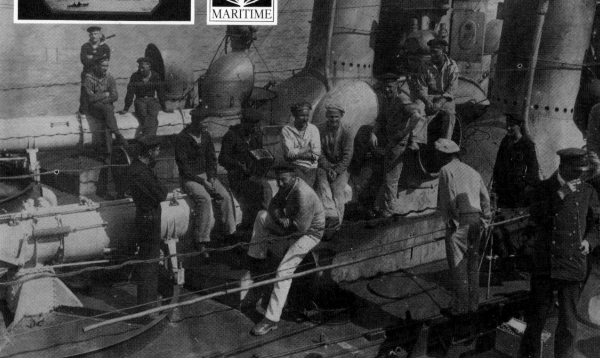

Naval Books

Conway Maritime offer an unrivalled range of authoritative and well-illustrated titles on naval subjects. A free catalogue is available, but some of the leading titles are listed below:

US NAVAL WEAPONS
by Norman Friedman
This exhaustive study by an acknowledged expert on the subject discusses the development and function of every weapon system employed by the US Navy from the birth of the 'New Navy' in 1883 to the present day.
12¼″ x 8½″, 288 pages, 200 photos, 150 line drawings. ISBN 0 85177 240 4. £18.00 (plus £1.80 p + p)

NAVAL RADAR*
by Norman Friedman
A layman's guide to the theory, functions and performance of seaborne radar systems, from their introduction just before the Second World War to the present day, including a catalogue of every major piece of radar equipment to have seen service with the world's navies.
11″ x 8½″, 240 pages, 200 photos, 100 line drawings. ISBN 0 85177 238 2. £18.00 (plus £1.80 p + p)

CARRIER AIR POWER
by Norman Friedman
A penetrating analysis of how carrier warfare operates, with extensive data on the ships and their aircraft.
12″ x 9″, 192 pages, 187 photos, 32 line drawings. ISBN 0 85177 216 1. £12.50 net (plus £2.00 p + p)

ANATOMY OF THE SHIP: THE BATTLECRUISER HOOD*
by John Roberts
The first volume of this new series. Every aspect of the *Hood* is covered in a degree of detail never previously attempted for a recent capital ship, and the standard of line drawings has been highly praised.
9½″ x 10″ landscape, 128 pages, 24 photos, 320 line drawings. ISBN 0 85177 250 1. £8.50 (plus £1.50 p + p)

ANATOMY OF THE SHIP: THE AIRCRAFT CARRIER INTREPID
by John Roberts
The second in this new series, this volume covers the *Essex* class aircraft carrier which is now being refurbished in New York as a floating Air-Sea-Space museum.
9½″ x 10″ landscape, 96 pages, 20 photos, 300 line drawings. ISBN 0 85177 251 X. £8.50 (plus £1.50 p + p)

CAMERA AT SEA 1939-1945*
edited by the staff of *Warship*
"A unique collection of some of the best photographs of World War II at sea" – *Sea Power*
12¼″ x 8½″, 192 pages, 250 photos, 24 colour plates. ISBN 0 85177 124 6. £12.00 (plus £1.50 p + p)

SUBMARINE BOATS
The Beginnings of Underwater Warfare
by Richard Compton-Hall
"Cdr. Compton-Hall has produced a book whose research and many rare photographs and drawings will delight both the technically-minded and the general reader." — *Daily Telegraph*
9½″ x 7¼″, 192 pages, 173 photos and drawings. ISBN 85177 288 9. £10.50 (plus £1.55 p + p)

CONWAY'S ALL THE WORLD'S FIGHTING SHIPS 1922-1946
The second in this highly acclaimed series, the 1922-1946 volume covers all significant warships built between the Washington Treaty and the end of the wartime construction programmes. With over 1000 illustrations, it is the ultimate reference book on the navies of World War II.
12¼″ x 8½″, 464 pages, 506 photos, 530 line drawings. ISBN 0 85177 146 7. £30.00 (plus £2.00 p + p)

CONWAY'S ALL THE WORLD'S FIGHTING SHIPS 1860-1905
The first complete listing of all warships between the first ironclad and the *Dreadnought*. "... must rank with the all-time great naval reference works ..." – *The Navy*. "... all the thoroughness and attention to detail we have come to expect from Conway Maritime ... excellent value". – *Ships Monthly*
12¼″ x 8½″, 448 pages, 471 photos, 506 line drawings. ISBN 0 85177 133 5. £24.00 (plus £2.00 p + p)

A CENTURY OF NAVAL CONSTRUCTION: The History of the Royal Corps of Naval Constructors
by D K Brown R C N C
This behind-the-scenes history of the Royal Navy's designers offers a new insight into the factors governing British warship design from the nineteenth century to the Falklands conflict.
9½″ x 6″, 384 pages, 92 photos, 20 line drawings. ISBN 0 85177 282 X. £20.00 (plus £1.00 p + p)

DESTROYER WEAPONS OF WORLD WAR 2*
by Peter Hodges and Norman Friedman
A detailed comparison between British and US destroyer weapons, including mountings, directors and electronics. "... one of the greatest possible additions to the ... range of naval books ..." – *The Navy*
9½″ x 7¼″, 192 pages, 150 photos, 73 line drawings. ISBN 0 85177 137 8. £7.50 (plus £1.25 p + p)

BATTLESHIP DESIGN AND DEVELOPMENT 1905-1945
by Norman Friedman
The first layman's guide to the design process and the factors governing the development of capital ships. "... an eye-opening study of an extremely complex business ..." – *Nautical Magazine*
10″ x 8″, 176 pages, 200 photos, plans and line drawings. ISBN 0 85177 135 1. £8.50 (plus £1.25 p + p)

MODERN WARSHIP DESIGN AND DEVELOPMENT
by Norman Friedman
"... never before have the problems and parameters of modern warship design been set out so comprehensively, informatively and clearly ... the book should be read by everyone with a concern for the modern naval scene, professional or amateur, uniformed or civilian." – *Journal of the Royal United Services Institute*
10″ x 8″, 192 pages, 167 photos, 65 line drawings. ISBN 0 85177 147 5. £9.50 (plus £1.25 p + p)

AIRCRAFT CARRIERS OF THE US NAVY
by Stefan Terzibaschitsch
"... a definitive history of the US carrier fleet from 1920 until the present day ..." – *Journal of the Institute of Marine Engineers*
11¾″ x 8¼″, 320 pages, 322 photos, 94 plans and line drawings. ISBN 0 85177 159 9. £15.00 (plus £1.50 p + p)

*These titles are available in North America from the Naval Institute Press, Annapolis, Md 21402.

from your Local Bookseller or by post from

Conway Maritime Press Limited
24 Bride Lane, Fleet Street, London EC4Y 8DR

(when ordering direct please add the posting and packing charge noted after the price)

editorial

HMS *Hood* manoeuvring to port at speed in 1937, while serving on the non-intervention patrol off the coast of Spain. Note the tricolour markings on 'B' turret, indicating her nationality to both surface ships and aircraft.
CPL

This issue examines two very different styles of naval development. On the one hand R A Burt takes a new look at the superdreadnoughts of the *Royal Sovereign* class; this dovetails in with the second part of D K Brown's examination of the pre-1914 gunnery trials, the results of which had a considerable influence upon the design of the *Royal Sovereign*, among other classes. These steady, peacetime, design processes were based upon an anticipation of the nature of any future conflict. The majority of the designs arising out of this process were refinements of existing types, largely influenced by the performance of ships already in service. The major errors were more likely to arise out of inaccurate staff forecasts or badly set out design parameters.

On the other hand the unforseen, and often novel demands of war result in a much more direct and rapid design process. This can produce a variety of results, largely dependent upon the available design experience of the nation concerned, and the difficulty of the task that is taken on.

Elio Ando makes a welcome return with a detailed examination of the Italian Navy's Second World War-built *Gabbiano* class ASW corvettes. Inspired by the success of British submarines operating from Malta, these vessels were the first significant anti-submarine ships built for the Italian Navy. However they were relatively conservative in design, and took advantage of the abilities built up by Italy's strong pre-war design base. In consequence they turned out to be both highly successful and extremely durable, although of course far too late.

By contrast Hans Lengerer's study of the Imperial Japanese Navy's attempt to mass produce a more powerful AA weapons system reveals the origins of failure. The Royal Navy had tried 4.5in (12cm) unguided rockets in 1940, and they had been a resounding failure, being removed nearly as quickly as they were fitted. *Hood*'s rocket magazine appears to have been set on fire by an 8in shell from *Prinz Eugen* shortly before she was destroyed by *Bismarck*. The Japanese equipment was hurriedly developed when the US Navy had gained complete air supremacy over the Pacific combat zones. It was installed in most of the surviving aircraft carriers in time to take part in the Battle of Leyte Gulf during October 1944. Neither system ever destroyed a single aircraft.

On the operational side this issue continues Brian Head's detailed log of the war service of H M Submarine *E 31*, a study that emphasises just how much of any vessel's war career was taken up by the tedious, the mundane and the routine. The *Warship* pictorial features that most beautiful and famous of British warships, the battlecruiser *Hood*, during her lengthy peacetime service.

Andrew Lambert

warship pictorial

HMS Hood

April – May 1936

During the interwar years the *Hood* was the largest and most potent symbol of Britain's Imperial power. Her movements during the troubled peace of the mid-1930s provided an accurate pointer to the international crises of the era. The Italian invasion of Ethiopia in 1935 and the resultant difficulties between Britain and Italy drew her to the Mediterranean; the opening moves of the Spanish Civil War brought her to Gibraltar. Later she would wear the tricolour turret markings of the Non-Intervention patrol off the coast of Spain.

These photographs from the album of a sailor lost with the ship when she was destroyed by *Bismarck*, provided a glimpse of the activity of a capital ship that was costing the nation £400,000 a year to run.

by Andrew Lambert

The destroyer *Greyhound* ready to open fire on a radio-controlled Queen Bee target drone. This is indicated by the black flag over her forward funnel (April 1936).

75

The bridge of *Hood* during the AA target shoot.

Greyhound turning at speed to pick up the Queen Bee.

The Queen Bee hits the water after being brought down by *Hood*.

Alongside at Las Palmas, Majorca May 1936, wearing the flag of Vice-Admiral Sidney R Bailey CB, CBE, DSO, commanding the Battlecruiser Squadron.

The Spanish squadron's cruiser flagship *Miguel de Cervantes* clearing Las Palmas. On 23 November 1936 she was to be torpedoed and damaged off Cartagena by an unidentified Italian submarine.

Moored ahead of *Hood* a Spanish Republican squadron comprising three 6in gun cruisers (all *Alfonso* class, the name ship being called *Libertad,* the other two were *Cervera* and *Cervantes*) and six destroyers.

78

The destroyer *Westminster* coming alongside to refuel while at sea. The first view is from *Hood*'s boatdeck.

1 *Hood* during full power trials between Las Palmas and Gibraltar. The forward turrets are trained aft to afford some protection against the spray coming over the bow. Viewed from the starboard machine gun platform.

2 The starboard side with 'A' and 'B' turrets, taken from the pompom embrasure.

3 The stern and wake during the full power trial, from the after searchlight platform.

The boom defences (with attendant vessel) at Gibraltar, May 1936. The carrier *Furious,* the battleships *Nelson* and *Rodney* are also in harbour.

The Emperor of Ethiopia, Haile Sellassie, flanked by admirals (Sir Dudley Pound, the new C-in-C Mediterranean on *his* left), visits *Hood* at Gibraltar while going into exile after the Italian invasion of his country. The Emperor's entourage passes between the ship's 30ft gig and the port 8-barrel MarkV 2pdr pompom mounting on the shelter deck. The Emperor had left Addis Ababa for Djibouti (French Somaliland) whence the cruiser HMS *Enterprise* took him to Haifa in May 1936. The cruiser HMS *Capetown* took the party from Haifa to England.

The Gabbiano Class Corvettes

Part One   **by Elio Ando**

Egeria fitting out in mid-1943 at Monfalcone on the Gulf of Trieste.

Author's collection

The Royal Italian Navy entered the Second World War in June 1940 with very few vessels exclusively designed for the defence of merchant shipping: only the four destroyer escorts of the *Orsa* class, 1168 tons standard displacement and one ship, *Albatros*, which was clearly an anti-submarine type. In consequence the protection of supplies for the Axis armies in North Africa was entrusted to modern destroyers and torpedo boats, along with the old First World War destroyers, now modernised and classed as torpedo boats. In the ten years before the war priority had been given to the construction of submarines, largely neglecting the techniques and tactics of anti-submarine warfare. Therefore by 1941 the Italian Navy had only two sets of echo detection equipment; one aboard *Albatros* and the other in an old minelayer serving at the hydrophone operators school at La Spezia. This type of equipment, activated by supersonic waves, named *periterio,* Italian for asdic derived from the acoustic sounding-line Langerin, had been under development since 1935, but the inadequate

performance and range of those available led to the type being abandoned. The Italian Navy preferred to continue training personnel to use the old 'C' type hydrophone of First World War vintage. This equipment, often used onboard trawlers, relied on highly trained and sensitive ears for its effectiveness.

Because of the growing danger in the first year of the war, from the numerous and highly effective British submarines, it was found necessary, in addition to installing ASW equipment aboard destroyers and torpedo boats, to project a class of destroyer escorts derived from the *Orsa* class, concentrating on AA and ASW armament. The first of 16 vessels of the *Ciclone* class was laid down in April 1941. Furthermore it was essential to establish a school for anti-submarine training. On 1 August 1941 *Antisom,* under the command of Rear Admiral Da Zara, very belatedly began its activities, nearly 14 months after hostilities had begun.

After waiting a month to examine the situation it was decided to institute a four-prong major programme of ASW measures:

1 Building 60 VAS (Vedette Anti-Submarine – submarine chasers) and 60 corvettes.

2 Installing onboard destroyers and torpedo boats

played many of the best qualities of the Italian shipbuilding industry. There were 60 of these vessels, classified as *corvette cacciasommergibili*; bearing the names of the old edged weapons, firearms, insects, birds, sporting animals and minor divinities. Construction began at the end of 1941, 28 were completed before the Italian Armistice with the Allies on 9 September 1943. Others were seized while completing or still on the slipways by the Germans, and then fought against the Allies, including Italy, until 1945. At the end of the war 18 of the *Gabbianos* survived in the Italian Navy, a further four units were added in the following half decade.

HULL AND SUPERSTRUCTURE

The hull of these corvettes was built with a mixture of transverse and longitudinal framing in the centre, completed with internal plating extended up the maindeck. At the ends of the transverse frames prevailed. The main deck was uninterrupted from bow to stern, while the upper deck was broken by the machinery. The plating was either welded or rivetted, a fact entirely dependent upon the technology available to the respective builders.

Twelve transverse bulkheads were carried up to the main deck, three to the upper, dividing the ship into 16 watertight compartments. The forecastle extended from the bow for over half the ship's length. The bridge was built of light alloy, with the captain's charthouse and the

Gabbiano on 8 February 1943 (after escorting troop convoys to and from Tunisia), showing the 100mm/47 gun and the bridge structure.
Author's collection

asdics handed over by the Germans.
3 A large increase in the numbers of operators being trained for hydrophone and asdic equipment.
4 The compilation of tactical rules for anti-submarine operations.

At the same time there were visits to the German Anti-Submarine School at Gotenhafen (Gdynia, Poland), both to study German practice and to gain time. In October 1941 some 60 operators were sent there for six weeks' training, the majority of them chosen from among submarine crews. The first of the German asdic sets was installed onboard the torpedo-boat *Circe* with good results. The VAS were begun immediately. They were vessels of 63 tons standard displacement intended for the defence of coastal routes and could be built rapidly, but their only armament were depth charges carried on side rails.

The same requirement for speed ensured that the corvette design was chosen from among existing plans. The larger of General of the Engineers Corps Fea's projected ships was selected and ordered without modifications or improvements. The 670-ton corvettes dis-

Another view aboard *Chimera* showing the 20mm/65 mountings on the deckhouse. Both this and the preceding photograph were taken on 1 April 1944.

Author's collection

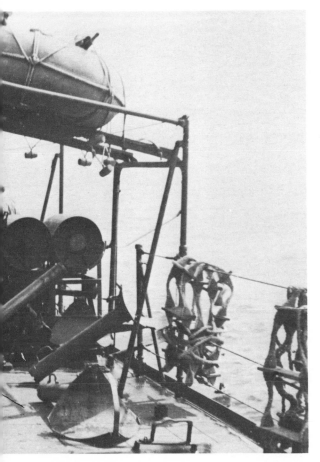

radio room on the first level, and on the second level the forebridge and pilot house supporting the open forebridge. This was the first time that an Italian vessel had carried the open forebridge, very much an English fitting, from which the ship was commanded during combat and largely protected by aerodynamic shelters. Ahead of the bridge the circular radio direction-finding goniometer rotated on a bracket. There was no fire control room, the armament was controlled from the open forebridge by a small 2m rangefinder.

Behind the bridge the mainmast carried the yard for the signal flags, the navigation and identification lights, the searchlight platform and a maintop lookout position. The funnel had an elliptical and tapered form, and was also slightly inclined. It carried the spreader for the radio aerials.

The internal arrangements for the crew placed some of the men under the forecastle, with two more living quarters under the bridge. The petty officers' accommodation and wardroom were in the centre of the forecastle. Under the main bridge, near the stern, in addition to the commander's state room and the officers' wardroom, there were two single cabins and one three-man cabin.

The rudder was of the semi-balanced type, with a surface area of 5.12 square metres and a maximum angle of helm of 35 degrees. The normal steering position was in the forebridge, with a secondary helm in the steering gear room. Three anchors were fitted; the two bower anchors were of the 0.90 ton Hall type and could be used only singly, the other Killich Admiralty type was located amidships on the port side of the bridge.

All the vessels of this class were practically identical; they differed only in minor particulars, such as the cranes for the motor boats, the shape of the forebridge

Details of the depth-charge throwers in *Chimera*.

Author's collection

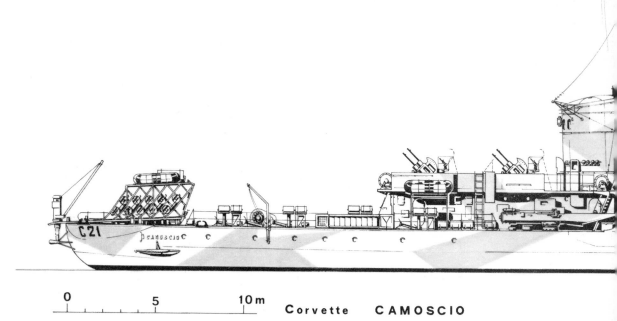

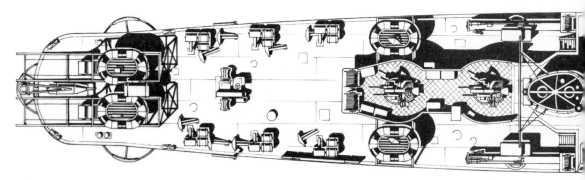

Corvette CAMOSCIO

The corvette *Camoscio* as completed in 1943.
Author's drawing

rail and similarly insignificant matters. Differences between individual ships arose principally out of the major modernisation undertaken after 1951.

MACHINERY

The machinery installation was designed to enable the ships to search for submerged submarines without noise or vibration. Two diesel engines were used for normal cruising, and two electric motors for silent running. The main engines were Fiat M 407 type 7-cylinder two-stroke diesels and were located in a watertight com-

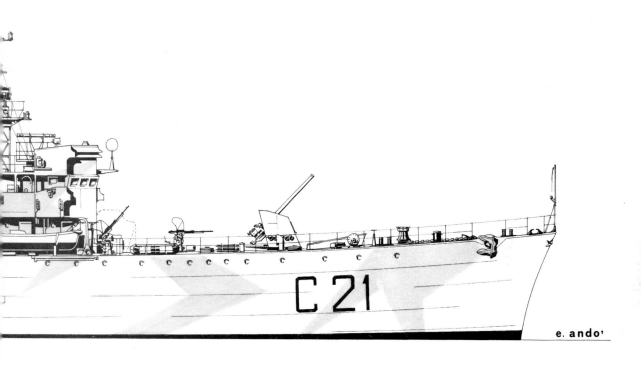

e. ando'

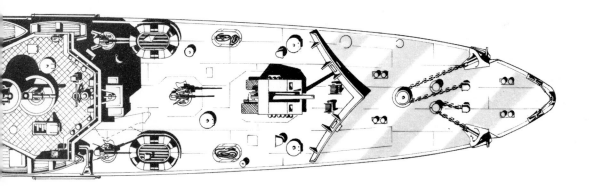

partment amidships. Each gave 1750 Italian horsepower (1725shp) at 430rpm. The exhausts were passed through a silencer before reaching the funnel uptakes. Compressed air was used to start the engines, which being diesels had a maximum time for getting underway of only 15 minutes. Fuel oil, up to 70 tons, was stowed in 14 tanks in the double bottom.

The electric motors were located in the generating station abaft the main engine room. They could be coupled up to the main drive shafts after the diesels had been uncoupled. With 60 batteries in series the electric

motors provided an endurance of 6 hours at speeds up to 7 knots; each motor providing 75hp at 140rpm. The two three-bladed propellers were of 1.8m (5ft 11in) diameter.

An average of the 16 vessels that ran full power trials provides a displacement of 700 tons, with an incomplete armament, power of 3912hp for a speed of 19.86kts.

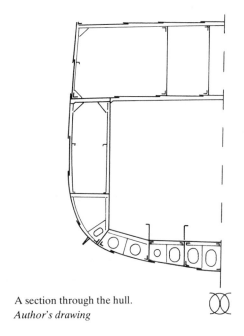

A section through the hull.
Author's drawing

DAMAGE CONTROL
For damage control purposes the hull was divided into three areas, and the crew into two teams. There was no damage control station, and in an emergency orders were given from the engineering office. The water main had 11 hydrants fed by three motor driven pumps. The engine rooms and magazines were protected by automatic sprinklers.

ANTI-SUBMARINE EQUIPMENT
The echo sounder, SCAM 1936 or 1939 type, with transmitter and receiver plates under the keel, had its control panel located under the upper deck just ahead of the main engine room. The repeater was in the pilot-house. For anti-submarine search operations all ships had an asdic, either German or Italian models, located under the upper deck with a spherical housing projecting 95cm (3ft 1¼in) under the keel.

ARMAMENT
Being specifically designed as convoy escorts the ships' armament concentrated on AA and ASW defence.

One 100mm/47 calibre (3.9in) OTO Type 1937 DP gun in a single shielded mounting on the forecastle. The 100/47 was an efficient gun with solid one-piece ammunition; it was the latest development of the guns of the same calibre found aboard cruisers, torpedo boats and submarines.

Three 20mm/70 Scotti IF 1939 or Scotti OM Type 1941 single mountings on the forecastle. One immediately behind the 100mm, the other two beside the bridge. The Scotti was a gas operated, air cooled gun without director control. It had been developed from the 20mm/65 Breda Type 1935, which were mounted in *Urania*.

Four 20mm/65 Breda Type 1935 in twin mountings with fixed, staggered barrels were mounted in emplacements on the central bridgehouse, behind the funnel.

Eight depth-charge throwers, four on each side toward the stern on the main deck. Equipped with 150kg (330lb) depth charges of the German 'G' type, or the similar Italian 'M' type.

Two 'Gatteschi' type depth charge racks, a typical launching platform with 6 trolleys with 2 or 4 depth charges each, able to launch patterns for preselected depths. This armament made it possible to launch a considerable salvo of depth charges onto the submarine under attack.

Two towing torpedoes of the 'Ginocchio' type, these implements were of little military value, and were difficult to use.

Cicogna working up at the anti-submarine training school in early 1943 with the old submarine *H2*, which was used for this purpose.
Author's collection

Flora as completed in 1943.
Author's collection

Two 450mm torpedo tubes, these single mountings were only fitted to the early vessels of the series. They were located on the main deck amidships facing outboard. The torpedoes, Whitehead type 200/450 × 5.75m (18ft 10in) or SI type, weighed 930kg (2050lb). They were omitted from later ships, in accordance with their defensive role.

The ammunition supply was 200 rounds and 60 star-

shell for the 100mm, delivered at 7rpm by an electric hoist from the magazine. The 20mm had 18,2000 cartridges, and relied on a chain of seamen to carry them from the ammunition lockers under the mountings. A total of 86 depth charges were carried, of which 64 were in the magazine behind the officers' quarters.

The ships that fell into German hands, after the Italian Armistice, had their armament modified or integrated with some 20mm/65 1938 type *Flakvierling* quadruple mountings.

CAMOUFLAGE
All these corvettes began their lives, often on the slipway, with the traditional camouflage used by the Italian

Pellicano at speed.
Author's collection

Pellicano turning to port at speed. The ship is shown in her World War II configuration.
Author's drawing

Details of the depth-charge
throwers and racks
in *Danaide*.

Author's collection

Navy from the end of 1941. This involved areas of light
and dark grey, both matt and with a slight blue tinge, and
separated by curves or straight lines. As in all Italian
warships during World War II, the extreme forecastle
was marked with red and white stripes, for aerial recognition. At the end of the war all ships were refinished in a
uniform light grey. Hull letters were in red, the Carley
rafts red and yellow.

MODERNISATION

In the years immediately after the end of the war the
major problem for the Italian Navy was to free the
national waters from mines. Consequently the entire
anti-submarine armament of all the surviving corvettes
was replaced by minesweeping gear.

The large scale modernisation between 1951 and
1956 entailed significant modifications to the superstructure of the ships. The bridge was replaced by a COC
(*centrale operativa di combattimento*). This involved
closing up the windows and opening two or three porth-
oles; the new structure was also one storey higher and
the fore bridge, hitherto open, was partly closed. A small
charthouse was place abaft the bridge; although on some
vessels, destined to be flotilla or divisional commanders'
ships, a new structure extending abaft and before the
bridgehouse was built to increase accommodation. The
depth charge magazine was changed into a petty officers'
wardroom.

The electric motors were removed from the propeller
shafts and used as reserve generators. The batteries were
landed, creating a reserve of both space and weight.
Before 1950 radars began to be fitted, *Gabbiano* and
Ibis being the first ships, mounting an English LWS type
and an American SO 13 type respectively, both on new
tripod mainmasts. After 1956 all 22 vessels had radar;
13 the SO 13, and 3 the ASP/SN6 type: after 1962
another three of the American model were fitted and six
of the Italian NSM 8 type. The other electronic warfare
equipment was restricted to an IFF (Identification,
Friend, Foe) installation.

The other significant alterations took place in the
armament after the end of the period of acting as minesweepers, in 1951-2. Along with the 100mm/47 and the
two 20mm/70 single mountings alongside the bridge

they were also fitted with a twin 40mm/56 on the central
bridgehouse. After the major rebuilds differences in
armament divided the corvettes into two groups. Basically the first group were equipped as AA ships. These
were the *Ape, Chimera, Cormorano, Danaide, Fenice,
Flora, Pellicano, Pomone, Sibilla* and *Sfinge*. Their new
armament was:

Four 40mm/56 in twin mountings on the forecastle and
deckhouse *Folga* retained her 100mm/47 until 1959.
Two 450mm torpedo tubes.
One fixed Mark 10 Hedgehog on the forecastle.
Two Gatteschi type depth charge racks, replaced in
1959-60 with one IMN type rack, which had two layers
and carried 12 Mark 6 depth charges. This was mounted
right at the stern. *Pomona* and *Sibilla* did not have depth
charge racks.

The second group were configured for ASW and
comprised: *Baionetta, Bombarda, Crisalide, Driade,
Farfalla, Gabbiano, Gru, Ibis, Minerva, Scimitarra* and
Urania. Their armament was:
Three 40mm/56, a single mounting on the forecastle and
a twin on the deckhouse. *Bombarda* and *Gabbiano* had
new superstructure ahead of the bridge, and therefore
retained their two 20mm/70.
Two 450mm torpedo tubes
One training Mark 15 Hedgehog, mounted ahead of the
40mm/56 on the forecastle.
Two Gatteschi type depth charge racks, replaced in
1959-60 with two IMN racks at the stern, each with six
Mark 6 depth charges. *Scimitarra* had no rack fitted.

In all ships the 40mm/56 were directed by a Mark 51
fire control system.

In the following years other, minor, modifications
took place, such as *Cormorano, Farfalla* and *Sibilla* having their depth charge racks replaced by a radio-
controlled Meteor P1 target, also located at the extreme
stern. In 1965 *Ape* underwent a further transformation
and returned to service as a mother ship for the *Appog-
gio Arditi Incursori*, the specialist attack squadron who
were heirs to the tradition of the 10th Light Flotilla who
attacked, most notably, the battleships *Queen Elizabeth*
and *Valiant* at Alexandria in 1941. *Ape* was equipped
with a hangar, special cranes and other fittings for this
task, and carried only two 20mm/70.

To be continued

The Royal Sovereign Class Battleships 1913~1948

by R A Burt

Part One

Revenge on her preliminary speed trials in March 1916.
Vickers

When Sir Phillip Watts resigned as Director of Naval Construction shortly after producing the excellent *Queen Elizabeth* class battleships in 1912, his successor Eustace Tennyson d'Eyncourt was faced with the problem of drafting a design for a 15in-gunned version of the *Iron Duke*, a ship which had been part of the 1911 estimates. Furthermore, the Board of Admiralty had it in mind that the new ship should carry 10-15in guns, rather than reciprocate the layout of the *Queen*

Elizabeth which carried eight, mounted in four twin turrets.

Moreover, Their Lordships stated that they would like the vessel to reach a speed of at least 21 knots, which was viewed as adequate for normal North Sea duties with the Grand Fleet. It was proposed that the new class should revert back to using coal and oil mix for fuel – the standard arrangement of the day, rather than emulate *Queen Elizabeth* which had been fitted to burn only oil, and had been designed as a 'special fast battleship' capable of operating with the battlecruiser force if required.

D'Eyncourt and his staff were asked to develop a vessel along these guidelines for the 1913 estimates, and

Ramillies as completed, September 1917, her bulge is already noticeable.
IWM

furthermore, run some experiments toward producing a triple turret – with a view to fitting them into the new ships. Within a month or so, the department of naval construction was able to forward to the Board for approval, some of the designs which they had conceived. Unfortunately, however, the vessel that might carry 10-15in guns had not materialised, because the construction department had felt it impossible to produce a satisfactory layout on the limited displacement given by the Board during the initial specification. Moreover, on examination, five twin mountings as laid out in the *Iron Duke* was seen as unnecessary by D'Eyncourt, as the amidships turret would involve a greater length to the vessel, and a considerable weight increase, not to men-

Ramillies in 1918.
Author's collection

tion the cost and time involved to procure the extra armament and equipment needed.

Also, D'Eyncourt was quick to point out that two extra guns was not generally viewed as a great improvement over the four twin mountings of *Queen Elizabeth* as regards firepower, and furthermore, any consideration of a triple turret would have to be abandoned for the time being, owing to lack of experience, and experimental work involved in such a radical change in British battleship construction. The opinion also prevailed, that, in the event of a knockout blow to a turret, there would be less firepower lost in a vessel fitted with twin mountings.

The Board took all these recommendation into account before finally settling for a layout that showed only eight guns. They were able to approve the initial schematic layout by 31 March 1913, whereupon the new class became designated as the T1 design for a 1st class battleship of the 1913 Estimates. The design, as laid

Resolution c1923 wearing a rear-admiral's flag.
Author's collection

Ramillies in 1919, showing the aircraft platform on the top of 'X' turret.
Author's collection

down, differed from the *Queen Elizabeth* class as follows:

1 The nominal displacement was reduced by approximately 1750 tons, with a reduction of 20ft in length, 2ft in beam, and 3ft on the designed draught.

2 The main armament remained unchanged, but the 6in secondary battery was reduced from 16 to 14 guns. The battery was arranged so that a greater all round

arc of fire could be secured, and by placing the guns further toward the midship section, they were less likely to be washed out in a seaway. The main deck 6in, as first fitted in *Queen Elizabeth*, would now be discarded.

3 The protection to the middle and lower sides amidships would be increased with a uniform 13in of armour, and not taper like that of the *QE*. Behind this, the protective deck was placed a deck higher than before (main deck level) and would be ¾in thicker.

4 The nominal speed was to be 4 knots less, with a mixed fuel arrangement, but the fuel capacity would remain the same.

The freeboard of the new ships was to be the same as in *Iron Duke,* viewed by many of the construction staff as one of the ships' poorer qualities, and they were regarded as wet ships even before they were laid down.

The forecastle level extended aft to 'X' 15in turret, as in *Queen Elizabeth*, although the sides before the secondary battery were less strongly recessed, with the flare being unbroken as far aft as 'A' turret in *Revenge*, and 'B' turret in the others. The rearrangement of the secondary battery, as already mentioned, was placed further back along the main deck level, with a light shelter deck placed above this.

One of the main features of the class, named *Royal Sovereign* class in the summer of 1913, was that the metacentric height had been lowered in order to gain a greater proportion towards steadiness, which in turn would secure a good gun platform. By doing this, however, it meant that the ships would be stiffer, and their stability would suffer; and as a result of this the metacentric height was 2ft less than in *Iron Duke*.

It was understood that if any considerable flooding took place in the ships as a result of action damage, they would not be able to maintain stability as well as previous designs.

To counteract this somewhat, a different means of protection was adopted as follows:

1 By raising the height of the protective deck to main deck level, it meant that the vessels had a better protected freeboard well above the deep load waterline. Furthermore, the maximum thickness of armour was to be carried right up to the deck.

2 The provision of armoured longitudinal bulkheads fitted between the main and middle deck levels, on each side amidships.

It was realised at the time, that any change in policy with the protection would result in a ship which would be prone to heavy rolling, even though a slow roll.

This, however, was an accepted fact, because the benefits of a greatly increased level of protection, even when the ships rolled and exposed the sides, which would be a uniform 13in, outweighed any of the disadvantages of stability.

ARMOUR

The maximum armour distribution was almost identical to that of *Queen Elizabeth*, but as already mentioned, it was 13in throughout and did not reduce to 8in below the waterline as in the latter. The armour was rearranged to provide increased protection to the middle lower side

TABLE 1: LEGEND for T1 design (final)

Length	580ft pp	
Beam	88ft 6in	
Draught	28ft 6in	
Displacement	25,750t	
Sinkage	91 tons per sq in	
Freeboard	26ft foward	
	16ft amidships	
	18ft aft	
Height of turrets	'A'	30ft 6in
from load waterline	'B'	40ft 6in
	'X'	33ft
	'Y'	23ft
Shaft horse-power	31,000 for 21kts	
Fuel	900t coal, in normal conditions	
	3000t in maximum conditions, plus	
	1500t oil	
Armament	8 × 15in, 16 × 6in, 4 × 3in AA, 4 ×	
	21in torpedo tubes	
Armour	(Main belt was to be 15ft 9in above	
	waterline, 5ft below)	
Main belt	13in	
Extensions	4in-6in	
Bulkheads	4in-6in	
Barbettes	10in-4in	
Turrets	11in	
CT	11in	
Signal tower	6in	
Wood backing	for main armour 4in of teak	
Decks	1in on forecastle, 1¼in-1½in upper,	
	1in-1½in-2in on main, and 3in-4in	
	lowerdeck aft.	
General equipment	750ft	
Armament	4750t	
Machinery	2550t	
Armour	8250t (including backing)	
Coal	900t minimum	
Hull	8630t	
Board margin	100t	
Designed condition	25,750t	

amidships, with a greater height of armoured freeboard below the principle protective deck.

The leading modifications over that of *Queen Elizabeth* were as follows:

1 The main armoured belt was uniform and not tapered.

2 The height of the belt was 15ft 1½in above water in the *Queen Elizabeth*, compared with 13ft 9in in *Royal Sovereign*. However, in *Queen Elizabeth* the belt ran 5ft 4½in below water (some of which was 8in) and the *RS* had 7ft at a thickness of 13in.

3 The main belt was carried up to the main deck level at 13in whereas it was reduced to 6in in *Queen Elizabeth*, and 8in and 6in in *Iron Duke*.

4 The extension belt forward, which was 6in thick, was made to run slightly higher up than before, and the belt ran right through to the bows, where it reduced to an inch in thickness. The after extremities of the belt, terminated in a bulkhead just before, instead of after, the rudder head.

5 The main belt and sloping deck armour between middle and main deck levels was reinforced by a longitudinal bulkhead of ¾in, and set well inboard on both port and starboard of the ship. This bulkhead extended from 'A' to 'Y' barbette, and was originally

Royal Oak in 1917. *IWM*

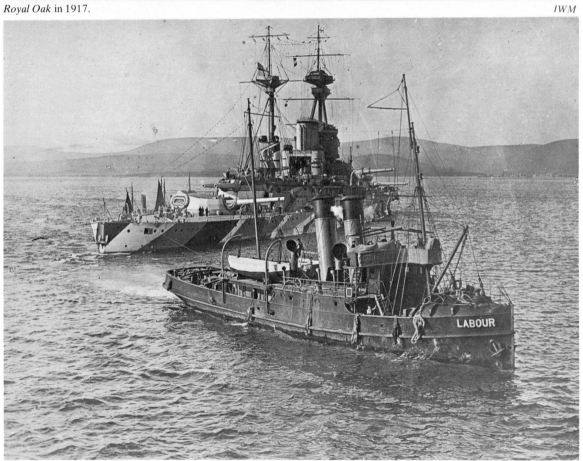

Revenge during the winter of 1917. She is wearing the normal
type of camouflage, consisting of five colours.
IWM

to have been backed with coal protection before an all oil policy was adopted. (See machinery.)

6 An increase to 2in on the deck inclines, and more 2in thickness on the flat before thinning to 1in.

7 1in armour added around the stemhead between the forecastle and upper deck.

8 Anti-torpedo bulkheads were reduced from the uniform 2in thickness in *Queen Elizabeth*, to 1½in and 1in.

This class were the first British battleships to revert back to any armoured protection carried through to the extremities of the ship since the *Neptune* of 1911. Having stated this, however, the 1in thickness placed at the bows, was really little more than a placebo.

The weight of armour devoted to each ship was approximately 8240 tons. All main strakes were of the Krupp's process, with the exception of the decks, centreline bulkheads, battery traverses, funnel uptakes and anti-torpedo bulkheads, all of which were of high tensile steel.

The 13in belt amidships extended to abeam the centres of 'A' and 'Y' barbett, with the upper edge reaching main deck level, about 7ft 9in above the load waterline. Forward of the belt, there was a 6in strake that extended for approximately 42ft, and then reduced to 4in terminating some 34ft before the stem. The upper edge of the 6in run was carried slightly above the main deck level, with the bottom at the same height as the 13in run. Aft of the ship, the 13in run was met by a 6in strake, which extended to about 50ft from the stern, and at the same height as the midships section. Outside this, it reduced to 4in.

Above the 13in belt, there was a 6in thickness that extended from 'A' barbette to 'X', and between main and middle deck levels. The 1in forward strake was a short patch at the stem between the upper and forecastle levels.

The main bulkheads were 6in on the forward fitting which ran obliquely inwards from the extremities of the 13in belt and 6in side armour, to the outer face of the side armour of 'A' barbette between lower and upper decks. The after bulkhead was also given a 6in thickness, and ran inwards much the same as that forward, meeting 'Y' barbette before it terminated. There was a stem bulkhead of 1½in that closed the extremities of the short patch of side armour at the stemhead between the forecastle and upper deck levels. A 4in bulkhead closed the ends of the 4in belt aft between lower and main deck level. There were special bulkheads of ¾in which ran logitudinally port and starboard from just outside 'A' to abreast 'Y' barbette: these were set well inboard of the ship's hull.

The deck protection varied in thickness according to location: the forecastle deck was 1in amidships over the 6in gun battery, while that of the upper deck ranged from 1¼in to 1½in, and ran from 'A' to 'Y' barbettes. The main deck was 2in on the inclines which reached just onto the flat; after this it was reduced to 1in throughout the ship. The middle deck was from the outer base of 'Y' barbette and was fitted with plates of 2in-3in- and 4in that terminated at the stern of the ships. The after

extremities once outside the after bulkhead, sloped strongly down to meet the lower deck at the stern. There was a 2in inside bulkhead with 4in and 3in outside this to cover the steering gear. The lower deck which was forward ran underwater, and extended from the base of 'A' barbette through to the stem of the ship where it was met by a bulkhead; the deck was 1in inside this bulkhead, and 2½in once outside.

The protection given to the barbettes varied a great deal: the 'A' fitting sported thicknesses from 10in to 6in. The outer face was 10in above the main deck level, with 6in below this Inner Faces were 9in and 7in above the upper deck reducing to 6in through the upper level to the main deck. Sides were 10in above the upper deck, and then reduced from 10in to 6in from upper to main deck level. 'Y' barbette was 9in on the face from above main deck, and reduced to 6in below this, the rear being 9in and 7in and 4in below main deck. The sides were 10in above, and 6in below main deck. Turrets were given 13in on the face plates, while the sides were 11in. Rears were also 11in, and the roof consisted of 4¾in to 5in plates.

The battery armour was 6in, and ran amidships between upper and forecastle deck levels, with a 4in bulkhead closing each end. The 2in centreline bulkhead, which was complete through the whole length of the 6in battery except in the wake of the funnel uptakes, extended from the 4in bulkhead to 'B' barbette. The 1½ traverses extending some 15ft inboard of ship were between the 6in guns, and were carried up to the full height of the battery. The gunshields (6in) were 3in, and the sighting hoods which were also 3in, were located near the 4th and 5th guns, on the forecastle deck level.

The main conning tower was 11in on the sides, and had a 3in roof, 4in floor, 6in base, and a 6in tube. The torpedo CT was 6in on the sides, 4in tube and a 2in floor. Funnel uptakes were 1½in.

The anti-torpedo bulkheads which ran longitudinally both port and starboard between forward and after magazines were 1½in to 1in thick. They reached down from the middle deck to keel level and were met by traverse bulkheads.

ARMAMENT

The main armament of *Queen Elizabeth* was perpetuated in the *Royal Sovereigns* with four twin turrets mounted on the centreline. There was parallel procedure in both classes except that the nominal height of the forward and after turrets was reduced by approximately 1ft forward, and 6in aft. And the director tower was placed on a tower just beneath the top, instead of on the roof of the top. On paper, the *Royal Sovereigns* were given wider arcs of fire for the 15in guns, but later, in practice, the arcs were practically identical.

Consideration was given to securing a better position for the 6in secondary battery, as that of the *Iron Duke* and *Queen Elizabeth* classes had been sited too far forward and were prone to being washed out in a seaway. The start of the battery in the *Royal Sovereigns* was positioned farther back, nearer the midships section, and approximately 238ft from the bows. This was

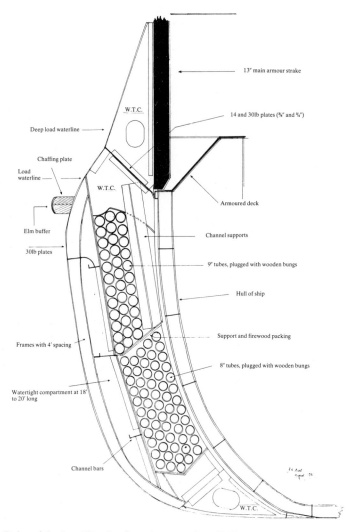

13" main armour strake

14 and 30lb plates (⅝" and ¾")

W.T.C.

Deep load waterline

Chaffing plate

Load waterline

W.T.C.

Armoured deck

Elm buffer

Channel supports

30lb plates

9" tubes, plugged with wooden bungs

Hull of ship

Frames with 4' spacing

Support and firewood packing

8" tubes, plugged with wooden bungs

Watertight compartment at 18' to 20' long

Channel bars

W.T.C.

Bulge of the *Ramillies* showing tube protection, 1917.

Royal Oak at sea in late 1917.
IWM

Royal Oak in 1917.
IWM

accepted as a worthy improvement over the former classes.

In the original design, the shell stowage was given as 80 rounds per gun, but later, it was able to accommodate 100 rounds per gun. The magazines and shell rooms were situated at the foot of the central trunk, with the shell rooms one deck below the magazines. After World War I, consideration was given to placing the magazines above the shell rooms (1922) but after a short enquiry, this move was seen as a bad move, mainly because it would cause numerous problems. These, in the main, were (1) Reduced rate of loading. (2) Reduced capacity for shell stowage. (3) Great expense. (4) Such alterations would exceed the terms of the London// Washington Treaty.

UNDERWATER PROTECTION

Throughout the years which led up to World War I, the subject of providing vessels with adequate underwater protection had been the subject of much debate. Experiments had been conducted in the early months of the war in some of the old pre-dreadnoughts. Charges of explosive were placed against strategic bulkheads and certain parts of the hull, to ascertain the effect and record the damage. These experiments were, in the main, carried out at Chatham Float, where midship sections were made to different scales, and then tested upon. They would then, if possible, do this to one of the old disposable ships, to gather important data toward the construction of a suitable method of underwater protection.

By 1915 the investigations had proceeded to a point where a 400lb charge of TNT had been tested against shaped steel plates, and showed considerable degrees of success. The results obtained indicated that there was, with a tube form of protection, a certainty of reducing the effect of a torpedo carrying that weight of explosive, and furthermore, would ensure that the inner bulkheads of the vessel struck by the torpedo would remain intact.

D'Eyncourt, the DNC sent a letter to the Board on 7 September 1915 stating that 'It could be safely anticipated that any ship would be greatly improved regarding underwater defences if fitted with this latest and relatively easy method of protection'. This method of construction, had been designed to fit to one of the new *Royal Sovereign* class, then under construction. *Ramillies* was the vessel chosen because of her advanced state of construction and the clear space available for launch-

Another view taken at the same time.
IWM

ing. The scheme adopted was understood to be a little inferior to that of the test piece at Chatham but, the only suitable method that could be formulated for a ship on the stocks.

It must be remembered that in a ship where bulge protection is an original portion of the vessel, a better product in design could be manufactured, but adding to a ship's outer hull certainly had no shortage of problems, although this had been adequately overcome. Moreover, a big part in the fitting of such protection was that the building programme should not be disturbed, and assurance was   the vessel would take the water on the date provisionally put forward by the builders.

The form of the protection in the shape of additional bulges was placed on each side of the vessel, and made up of watertight compartments that were partially filled with small steel tubes on 9in in diameter. This was in the top section only, and that of the lower section would have 8in tubes. There was an extra divisional bulkhead placed on the inner compartment which would be backed by wood (fir) supporting. The watertight compartments were 18-20ft long, and although the length of the tubes fitted are not specified, each had to be plugged

with wooden bungs driven well into the tubes, once in place. The tubes were ¾in thick, and fixed into position by more wooden packing. The bulges (or blisters) were shaped to fit the hull, and were approximately 220ft long, by 7ft 3in wide. Their plating was ½in thick.

After it had been approved for *Ramillies* to receive her bulge type protection, it was thought, that the extra bulbous shape might reduce the ship's speed. To combat this the DNC asked the experimental department at Chatham and Haslar, to conduct some experiments, and give a reliable estimate of the bulge's effect. A model was made, and tests were conducted. To everyone's surprise however, a report to the DNC stated that the effect had considerably exceeded expectations, and although a loss of 1-2 knots was expected, the ship would still be capable of over 21 knots in all weathers. Moreover, it was found that the bulges would have a bonus not expected, in the sense of a damping effect to any abnormal rolling that might occur. The original cost of the bulges was £150,000, apart from the extras that might be included.

When *Ramillies* put to sea and went through her lengthy series of trials, it was considered that the ship was little impaired by the bulges, and the rest of the class should be approved for being fitted with a similar form of protection. *Revenge* and *Resolution* were fitted with

Royal Oak at anchor in 1917, one of her sisters is over her bow.
IWM

Resolution at Rosyth in 1918.
Author's collection

bulges during 1917-18 (see appearance changes) but as further experiments had been conducted on different bulges since *Ramillies'*, these ships were fitted with an improved type without the tubes inside. The bulge was in two parts as before, with the bottom section being empty, and watertight: the top part consisted of a wood offal and cement filling. It was considered that this method was much better than the *Ramillies* fitting, because of the substantial saving in weight by leaving out the tubes. *Royal Sovereign* was fitted with her set during her long refit of 1920, but *Royal Oak* did not receive her set until as late as her 1922-1924 refit, when another improved type was fitted. This time, the bulges rose above the waterline, and up onto the sides of the ship, almost reaching the 6in gun battery. Another of the alterations had been to include water sections throughout the bulge, but it was stressed that if the bulges let in water, they would be less effective; they were to have at least 15-20 per cent of air inside those compartments filled with freshwater, in the initial fitting. In 1927 *Ramillies* had her early shallow bulges removed, and was given a set almost identical to those of *Royal Oak*.

During 1924 tests were made pertaining to the bulges, and it was found that 14 revolutions per minute had been needed to steam at 14-15 knots, before the bulges had been fitted: now, however, it required only a 5 per cent increase to reach speeds of 12-20 knots.

After *Royal Oak* had been fitted with her full bellied bulges, she was inclined on 2 June 1924, with the following results:

'A' condition: Ship fully equipped with 900 tons oil on board, plus water protection in the bulges.
Displacement: 29,160t
Draught: 28ft 3½in
GM: 6.3ft

'B' condition: Ship as above but with 3300 tons oil on board (not water protection).
Displacement: 32,200t
Draught: 30ft 11½in
GM: 6.3ft

'C' condition: Ship as above, plus reserve food tanks full and water protection.
Displacement: 32,800t
Draught: 31ft 4½in
GM: 6.3ft

Light condition was at 27,920 tons and a GM of 6.2ft.

When *Resolution* was docked some years later, on 26 August 1930, an inspection of her bulge showed considerable corrosion had taken place. The top part of the bulge, where the wood offal was placed, had let in water, and the offal had rotted with the concrete being badly pitted. Not only had corrosion set in, but the wood packing had been thrown in loosely, and not placed in the correct order when initially fitted. Forward of frame 22, and abaft 228, the packing was so loose, that it was of no practical use whatsoever, and, moreover, the sea-water which filled the compartments had rendered the

1 *Royal Sovereign* at sea in 1917, with *Resolution* and *Revenge* abeam.
IWM

2 *Revenge* in 1927 or later, with a *Nelson* class battleship ahead.
Author's collection

3 *Resolution* in the first years of peace.
Author's collection

4 *Royal Sovereign* at anchor in Scapa Flow, 29 June 1917.
Author's collection

3

4

whole length of the bulge ineffective, and hardly in a position to intercept a torpedo attack. Later, as other units of this and the *Queen Elizabeth* classes were found to be the same, there was a much closer inspection, on the fitting and watertight joints of the bulges.

MACHINERY

The main propulsion machinery consisted of two sets of turbines arranged in three watertight compartments divided by two longitudinal bulkheads. The two main and two auxiliary condensors were located near the main midship compartment, but the auxiliary condensor and auxiliary machinery was in a separate compartment on the wings of the ship. Each ship had four shafts. The high pressure ahead and astern, plus the cruising turbine, were arranged on the outer shafts in each wing compartment, whilst the low pressure ahead and astern turbines (in one casing) were located on the inner shafts in the middle compartment. Parsons reaction turbines were fitted in all ships of the class, with a designed revolutionary speed of 300 per minute.

As first designed, the ships were given a mixed firing system of coal and oil, but on Lord Fisher's recall to the Admiralty on 30 October 1914, one of the first moves he made, was to convert the *Royal Sovereign*s to all oil burners. As a result, the shaft horsepower was increased to 40,000 from 31,000, and speed increased from 21 to 23 knots. This conversion was approved in December 1914, by which time, the vessels were nearing the launching stage (*Royal Oak* already launched in November) but this change, however, did not seem to pose a problem. The oil stowage was to be the same as an all coal stowage, which was almost identical to the *Queen Elizabeth* class at 3400 tons maximum. The fuel arrangements were improved over the preceding class, by using fittings which made for easier re-fuelling with a connection on the upper deck from where the oil would be filtered before reaching the tanks.

Owing to the amount of reduction in boilers, it had now become practicable to fit one uptake only, and in doing so, they became the only British dreadnoughts with one stack.

To be continued

BRITISH NAVAL GUNS 1880~1945 No 16

by N J M Campbell

4.5in guns All naval guns were actually of 4.45in bore while the Army field howitzer of 1914-18 and the BL medium field gun of 1939-45 were 4.5in. The Army QF Mk II AA gun was however virtually identical to the naval Mks I and III and was 4.45in. This calibre was better suited to shells of about 50lb than 4.7in and the ballistic form was much improved.

4.5in QF Mks I, III These only differed in details of the firing mechanism, Mk I having electric and percussion with the latter eliminated while Mk III had electric only.

The construction comprised a loose barrel, jacket, removable breech ring and sealing collar. There was a horizontal sliding breech block with hand operated mechanism and SA opening. Guns had to be dismounted to change barrels. Fixed ammunition was fired by guns in the earlier mountings as noted below, but the round which was up to 49in and 91.75lb was inconvenient, and shells also tended to separate from the cases, so that in later mountings separate ammunition was fired.

In all 5 experimental guns, 46 Mk I and 524 Mk III were made. From 1937 Mk I were in the aircraft carrier *Ark Royal*, the depot ships *Forth* and *Maidstone*, with 3 guns in the battleship *Queen Elizabeth,* in *Valiant* and 4 in the battlecruiser *Renown*. Of the twin mountings Mk II had a distinctive low shield, Mk III an open backed one, while Mk IV was a turret mounting with revolving trunk, the others having hoists independent of the mounting. Elevation in all was 80° and they were powered by an electric motor and oil hydraulic pump. Mountings and ships were as follows:

Mk I – single UD, fixed ammunition, not in service.
Mk II BD, fixed ammunition – *Queen Elizabeth, Valiant, Renown, Illustrious, Victorious, Formidable, Indomitable*
RP 10 Mk II* BD, fixed ammunition – originally intended for *Albion* class aircraft carriers, never mounted
RP 10 Mk II** BD, fixed ammunition – *Implacable, Indefatigable*

4.5IN MK II BD MOUNTING

A Mantlet plate
B Training receiver
C Trainer's manual handwheel
D Trainer's power drive handwheel
E Right gun loading tray
F Right gun fuze-setting machine
G Gunhouse deck level
H Fuze-setting tray
I Loading access steps
J Ventilation fan and trunking
K Revolving 3-round scuttle
L Balance weight
M Securing flange for upper portion of gunhouse (at gundeck level)
N Breech-worker's platform
O Layer's manual handwheel
P Layer's power driven handwheel
Q Left gun QF/SA lever in 'Quick-fire' position
R Left gun QF/SA lever in 'Quick-fire' position
S Right gun QF/SA lever in 'Semi-automatic' position

4.5IN RP10 MK IV MOUNTING

A   Captain of turret's lookout hood
B   Exhaust fan trunking
C   Trainer's sighting port door
D   HP air bottle for air blast
E   Right gun shell hoist trunking
F   Shell 'legend' at foot of shell hoist, to ensure correct projectile position, nose to the rear
G   Waiting shell
H   Automatic shell release, synchronised with hoist movement
I   Right gun shell and cordite hoist operators' platform
J   Waiting cartridge
K   Single-stroke cartridge hoist
L   Fixed mounting training base
M   Left gun shell and cordite hoist structures
N   Right hand gunhouse access door
1   Original gundeck level in Mk II mountings
2   Revised gundeck level for Mk IV mountings

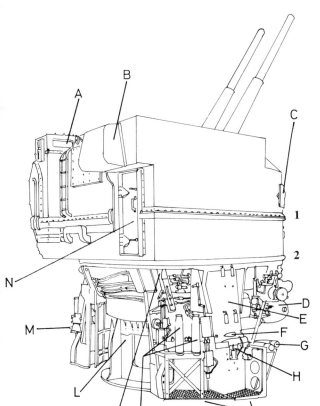

RP 10 Mk II*** BD, separate ammunition – the post-war completed *Eagle, Ark Royal*
Mk III UD, fixed ammunition – *Ark Royal,* cruisers *Seyella, Charybdis,* and depot ships *Forth, Maidstone, Tyne, Hecla, Adamant*
RP 10 Mk IV separate ammunition – *Savage*, first 16 'Battle' class destroyers
RP 10 Mk IV* separate ammunition – Last 8 'Battle' class

4.5in QF Mk IV This was ballistically identical to the above and of similar construction, but was modified to suit converted 4.7in CP XXII mountings known as 4.5in Mk V and mounted from 1943 in *Savage* and 'Z' and 'Ca' class destroyers. Elevation remained at 55° and separate ammunition was fired. RP 50 Mk V mountings with electric training and elevation were in the 'Ch', 'Co' and 'Cr' class destroyers, and RP 50 Mk V* in the last 8 'Battles'. Improvement to RPC and alterations in nomenclature resulted in Mk 5* Mod 1 mountings in the modernised 'Ca' class and Mk 5* Mod 2 in the 'Tribal' frigates. Modifications to the Mk IV gun included removal of alternative percussion firing in Mk V* mountings, more generous radii on some breech components and alterations in nomenclature as in mountings. In all 199 guns were made.

4.5in QF Mk V Of similar performance but differing in construction and faster working BM, this gun was developed during the Second World War but was first tried in the destroyer *Saintes* in 1947. Separate ammunition was fired and the breech block which moved vertically, opened hydraulically and closed by spring operated racks. The breech ring which incorporated the recoil and run-out cylinders, was screwed and shrunk on the jacket, and the loose barrel which was withdrawn to the rear, was held in place by retaining and locking plates attached to the breech ring. The twin RP 41 Mk VI mounting was of true turret type with 3 upper and 3 lower hoists per gun for AA shells, other shells and cartridges. Elevation was 80°. RP 41 Mk VII which was never in service, was intended for the *Malta* class aircraft carriers and probably for the final *Lion* battleship design. It differed principally in the roller path diameter being increased from 11ft to 14ft. The Mk V gun and Mk VI mounting with their later variants, were in many postwar ships comprising the *Daring* and 'County' classes, *Whitby, Leopard, Salisbury, Rothesay, Leander* and broad beam *Leander* class frigates, as well as the Australian 'Battle' and *Daring* class destroyers and *Yarra* and *Swan* class frigates. In all about 300 guns were made.

4.5in/8cwt QF Mk I This was originally developed *c* 1943 for Armoured Vehicle Royal Engineers Churchill tanks under the auspices of Major-General Jefferis. It was inadequate in this role and in spite of its extremely low performance was adopted for some coastal forces craft in the absence of anything better. The naval order was apparently for 3 prototypes and 106 guns, and it was agreed in September 1945 to accept 98 that were assembled though the requirement was only 60. Construction comprised – barrel and removable breech ring with vertical sliding SA breech block, and fixed ammunition was fired. Mk I mountings were power worked and allowed 12° elevation; 36 were made with a very few hand worked 30° Mk II.

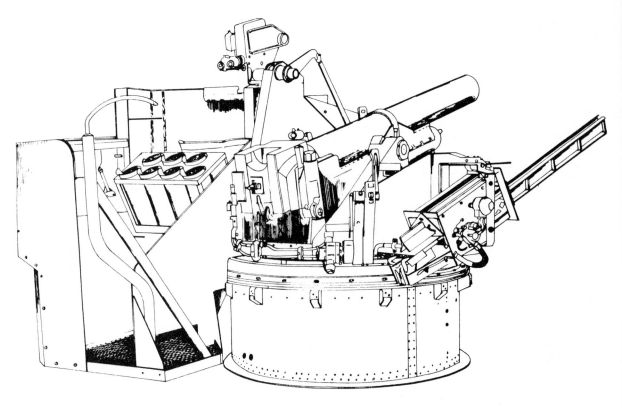

The 4.5 inch 8cwt gun on Mark 1 mounting, a drawing from the forthcoming 'Anatomy of the Ship' volume on the Fairmile 'D' MTB.

4.5in Mk 8 This 55-calibre gun currently mounted in the missile destroyer *Bristol* (since 1973) the *Sheffield* and *Manchester* destroyer and *Amazon* frigate classes is listed under the mounting Mk number as is now the usual practice. The gun and single mounting, which has a glass reinforced plastic shield and allows 55° elevation, were designed for use against fast surface targets and reliability and accuracy together with the minimum crew were given greater importance than a very high rate of fire, the latter being about 25 per minute. A muzzle brake and fume extractor are fitted to the barrel. Training and elevation are electric with Thyristor RPC and hydraulic loading gear. Ships fitted with this gun were supplied to Argentina, Brazil, Iran, Libya and Thailand, some of which countries look very odd customers in 1985. Performance figures for the British gun do not appear to have been published, but the following are thought to be correct for the export version. Weight of gun plus BM 2.38 tons, shell 46lb, charge 16.2lb multitube, weight of fixed round 82.2lb, MV 2850fs, range 24,000yds or 11.8nm.

PARTICULARS OF 4.5in GUNS

	4.5in QF MkI, III-V	4.5in/8cwt QF MkI
Weight including BM (tons)		
MkI, III	2.814	0.400
IV	2.759	
V	3.315	
Length oa (in)	211.75	89.06
MkV	241.25	
Length bore (cals)	45.0	18.88
Chamber (cu in)	600	137.5
Chamber length (in)	25.06/25.15	8.82
Projectile (lb)	55	14.69
Charge (lb/type)	11.035 SC122	1.148 NQ/R 014 × 048
	13.63 NF/S 198-054	
Muzzle Velocity (fs)	2449	1500
Range (yds)	20,750/45°	3300/9° 58′ (sight limits)
Ceiling (ft)	41,000/80°	

The Japanese aircraft carriers Junyo and Hiyo Part Two

by Hans Lengerer and Tomoko Rehm-Takahara

Junyo at Sasebo on 28 May 1946.
Author's collection

In reply to the US Naval Expansion Bill of 17 May 1938, known in Japanese naval circles as the Second Vinson-Trammell Act, the IJN decided on 8 September 1939 to convert the submarine depot ships *Takasaki* and *Tsurugizaki* into carriers. Also in 1939 the Fourth Fleet Completion Programme came into force. The American answer was the so-called 11 per cent Naval Expansion Bill, known in Japanese naval circles after its sponsoring senators as the Third Vinson-Trammell Act, signed on 14 June 1940. Only one month later, on 19 July 1940, the so-called Stark plan, a 'Two Ocean Navy' plan with a

70 per cent increase in the total tonnage of naval vessels and an increase in naval planes to 15,000, was signed by President Roosevelt. Japan considered it necessary to continue in the naval armament race and answered with the Fifth and Sixth Naval Replenishment Programmes neither of which was ultimately realised. The two nations were locked in an unlimited and seemingly endless armaments race.

As described in the earlier part, the IJN wanted to achieve parity with the USN in the number of carriers. It was considered that the two *Shokaku* class carriers, included in the Third Fleet Replenishment Programme of 1937, would have balanced American carrier strengths as envisaged by the First Vinson-Trammell

Another view of *Junyo* at the end of the war.
Author's collection

Junyo from overhead.
Author's collection

Bill, but it was also reported that 8-10 carriers, most probably 9 carriers would be built according to the Second and Third Vinson-Trammell Bills. The IJN had included only 3 carriers in the Third and Fourth Programmes (*Shokaku, Zuikaku* and *Taiho*). In order to reduce the difference the IJN decided to requisition the liners *Kashiwara Maru, Izumo Maru,* and *Kasuga Maru* and speedily convert them into carriers. The three liners requisitioned belonged to the first requisition, conversion and equipment of vessels that was ordered along with the first work of the War Preparation Programme

Michael Wunschmann's superb 1:1200 scale model of *Junyo* in 1945.
Jürgen Peters

(*Shusshi Junbi Keikaku Dai ichi chaku sagyo*) on 15 November 1940 due to worsening international relations and especially because the IJN was unable to take any measures to counteract the Third Vinson-Trammell Plan.

Unofficially the building yards received the order for conversion in October 1940, officially the Ministry of Transportation gave it on 10 February 1941. At the same day the Navy Ministry purchased *Kashiwara Maru* and *Izumo Maru* as auxiliary carriers. The price for the purchase of the equipment of both ships amounted to Yen 48,346,000 (£4,834,600). For the aircraft and weapons the IJN had to spend Yen 27,800,000 (£2,780,000). The money was granted with the Special War Budget for different categories of ships for fiscal

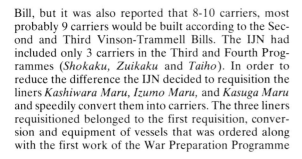

year 1941 (*Showa 16 rinji gunji hi, Zatsuekisen*). To convert the three liners the Diet allowed during the 76th session Yen 38,073,000 (*Kasuga Maru*) and during the extraordinary 77th session Yen 76,146,000 (*Kashiwara Maru* and *Izumo Maru*), grand total of Yen 114,219,000.

In order to keep the conversion secret the ships received temporary designations. *Kashiwara Maru* was called no 1001 ship (*Dai 1001 bankan*), *Izumo Maru* no 1002 ship. The conversion drawings were immediately accepted as building plans and the conversion begun. The construction as passenger liners was well advanced and the ships completed up to the main deck. Despite the fact that a part had to be broken up in order to install the lower hangar on the middle deck, and some alterations had to be carried out on the hulls and the interior of the ships, *Izumo Maru* was launched as early as 24 June 1941. Two days later, on 26 June 1941, *Kashiwara Maru* followed. At their launching day the ships were named *Hiyo* and *Junyo* respectively. Because *Hiyo* was launched two days earlier than *Junyo*, the ships were classified as *Hiyo* class.

The Nagasaki yard of Mitsubishi needed barely 11 months to complete *Junyo* (now building number 901). She was commissioned on 3 May 1942 as auxiliary aircraft carrier (*Tokusetsu kokubokan*) and was classified after 14 July 1942, after participating in the diversionary operation to the Aleutian Islands, as a regular aircraft carrier (*Kokubokan*) *Junyo* in the IJN register of its warships (*Gunkan*). *Hiyo* was completed and commissioned on 31 July 1942 and classed at once as an aircraft carrier.

TECHNICAL DESCRIPTION

Hiyo and *Junyo* were the only carriers converted from merchant ships that saw action as fleet carriers. The IJN operated their other carriers, converted from passenger liners (*Taiyo* ex-*Kasuga Maru*, *Unyo* ex-*Yawata Maru*, *Chuyo* ex-*Nitta Maru*, *Kaiyo* ex-*Argentina Maru*, and *Shinyo* ex-*Scharnhorst*) primarily for transporting aircraft and material and to a far lesser extent for the training of pilots. By contrast Allied escort carriers were used almost entirely for their intended roles of ASW, screening, AA operations etc. For these tasks the Allies preferred to convert middle or small merchant ships while the Japanese produced the largest ships ever converted from liners. Only the Italian *Aquila* would have surpassed them in size if her conversion had been completed. Next to them came the escort carrier conversion of the British liner *Pretoria Castle* with a displacement of 17,392 tons and capable of operating 50 aircraft. Because this ship only carried out her trials in January 1945 and was used exclusively for training she was reconverted into a liner after the war. However the *Hiyo* conversion was so complete that their reconversion would not have been possible. They could fulfill their task as fleet carriers, ie attack carriers, with some restrictions, for the machinery plant was not subject to conversion and only a few alterations were allowed to the hull. More detailed conversions would have needed a lot of workers, material and time: none of which Japan could spare at the time of their conversion.

After completion the ships displaced 24,150 tons standard with trial displacement of 27,500 tons. The hull had an overall length of 219.32m (719ft) (*Hiyo* 220m/721ft), the length at the waterline was 215.3m (706ft) and between the perpendiculars 206m (675ft) (*Hiyo* 206.3m). The beam measured at the waterline was 26.7m (87ft). The depth from keel to the flight deck was 21.79m (71ft) and from the waterline to the flight-deck about 13.64m/44ft (this measure varied according to the displacement and the draught) with a mean draught of 8.15m (26ft). With the combined funnel/island bridge, their large almost rectangular flight deck

and their continuous gun galleries for AA guns and MGs, fire directors etc they looked like regular fleet carriers and resembled British *Illustrious* class fleet carriers in some respects. Only from the shape of the hull, especially with regard to stem and stern and the small length/beam ratio, typical of merchant vessels, could the observer recognise their humble origin.

In comparison with the purpose-built carrier *Hiryu*, whose measurements differed only in minor respects but displaced about 7000 tons less, it becomes clear how much their operational qualities, ie speed, armour, number of aircraft suffered from the limitations forced on the constructors by their origins

If the *Hiyo* class is compared with the *Shokaku* class, carriers that displaced only about 1500 tons more but were nearly 40m (141ft) longer, the contrast becomes still more clear. Despite the fact that they could never completely fulfill their missions as attack carriers and taking into consideration the limitations to which the constructors had had to pay attention it can be seen that the Japanese constructors constructed carriers nearly the value of *Hiryu*.

A comparison between the nomenclature of the decks as liner and carrier shows the following differences:

Main deck	=	Uppermost deck
Upper deck	=	Upper deck
Second deck	=	Middle deck
Third deck	=	Lower deck
Fourth deck	=	First hold
Hold	=	Second hold

Above the main deck there were:

| Bridge deck | = | Flak deck |
| Promenade deck | = | Flight deck |

The interior of the carrier is adequately illustrated in the figures and needs no further mention here.

FLIGHT DECK

The promenade deck was lengthened to the bow and stern and became the flight deck. In contrast to the fleet carriers' flight deck it had no expansion joints because it was the strength deck. Although the installation of catapults would therefore have been possible the ships had none, like the other Japanese carriers, because the IJN failed to develop a catapult. The flight deck was nearly rectangular, unarmoured and had longitudinal wooden planking except for about 17m (55ft) on either end which was bare steel. At the bow its breadth was 16m (52ft), after that it expanded symetrically to 27.3m/89ft (shortly before the island bridge) and began to reduce again symetrically about 6m (19ft) before its after end to a width of 25m (82ft). Originally the con-

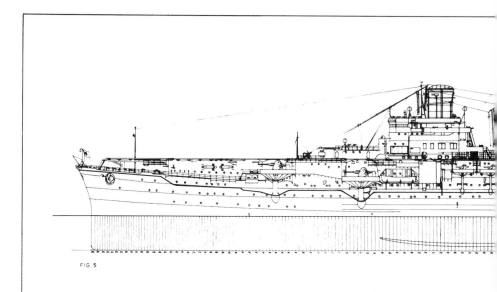

FIG 5

Full elevation of *Junyo* as completed.
Michael Wunschmann

structors had planned a length of 208.6m (682ft) but they were completed with a flight deck 210.3m long (690ft). Compared with the medium class of standard carrier, *Hiryu,* the breadth was equal, the length 6.6m (21ft) shorter. With the length and the breadth of 27.3m (89ft) on about 70 per cent of the length the flight deck would have been large enough to enable simultaneous operations of some aircraft but the lack of catapults delayed flight operations. The deck began shortly after the bow (a common feature of nearly all Japanese carriers) and ended with a long curve (1.2m/4ft on a length of about 15m/49ft immediately before the stern in order to make the approach flight more easy and to slow down approach speeds. If planes were carried on the flight deck, they were lashed to securing points, consisting of flush bars set in hemispherical recesses in the flight deck. Sufficient lashing points were provided to enable planes to be secured in almost any position on the flight deck. From 1944 on securing points were also used for lashing a number of the newly developed (1943) portable 25mm machine cannon in single mounts.

ARRESTING GEAR AND CRASH BARRIERS
For slowing down the approach speed of the aircraft 9 arresting wires were stretched across the flight deck. One arresting wire was before the forward elevator, 8 between the fore and aft elevators. In case of flight operations they were held, at a minimum height of 160mm, by lifting bars at the extreme edges of the flight deck. Each wire was led down over guide pulleys to an

arresting gear compartment below the lower hangar deck. *Junyo* and *Hiyo* had the Kure type model 4 arresting gear (*Kure shiki yon gata chakkan seido sochi*). In this type (and also other Kure types) the two ends of a wire were led to the two sides of a winding drum inside and affixed to which was a squirrel cage made of high resistance bronze. The drum and squirrel cage rotated around a six pole stator energised with 120 amperes at 220 volts at the maximum setting. The setting was chosen according to the weight of the plane.

In order to stop aircraft whose arresting hook had not engaged a wire the carriers were equipped with two fixed crash barriers of the Naval Air Technical Department type model 3 (*Kusho shiki san gata kasso seichi sochi*) in the vicinity of the bridge. Some Japanese sources say that both carriers had also two transportable barriers (at the fore and middle part of the flight deck) of the same model and type but the Americans found only three (two fixed and one portable) when they inspected *Junyo* in Sasebo harbour on 6 October 1945 (*vide* Air Technical Intelligence Group, Advanced Echelon, FEAF, APO 925, FF12-5(25)A8-2(CV) Series No 89 – Report No 34, dated 28 October 1945 – Inspection of Japanese Aircraft Carriers). Each fixed barrier had three wires that were led from the ends of each barrier to a separate air-hydraulic arresting unit installed at the port side on the upper hangar deck. If an aircraft engaged the wires a system of pulleys caused a ram to be pushed into a hydraulic cylinder, thus forcing oil through a series of restrictions into an air loaded accumulator. The shape of

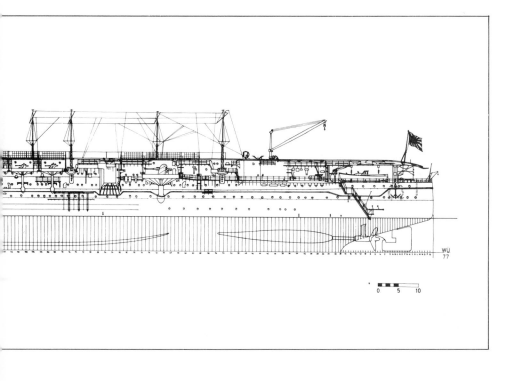

Flight deck view of *Junyo*.
Jürgen Peters

Junyo from the side.
Jürgen Peters

the restrictions and the increasing pressure of the air in the accumulator resulted in a rather high retardation and much less movement in comparison to the arresting wires. The barriers were raised and lowered by compressed air within 2.5 seconds.

Barriers were used only if there were a deck park forward. In operations the after one was used, the forward one was kept for training and as a spare.

WIND CATCHER
Before the forward elevator there was a wind catcher. It was raised if aircraft were on the flight deck and lowered in case of flight operations. About 30 per cent of its area were holes. It was operable up to a wind speed of 50m/s (180km/hr or 97kts) and could be raised within 30 seconds by wind speed of 35m/s (126km/hr or 68kts). When lowered it housed in a recess flush with the deck.

4-TON-AIRCRAFT CRANE
A collapsible 4-ton-crane was located on the port side and directly behind the aft elevator. Like the wind catcher, arresting wires and crash barriers it housed in a recess flush with the deck when lowered. It was used predominately for lifting aircraft on board when the ship had entered a harbour.

EQUIPMENT FOR NIGHT LANDINGS
Athwartships outriggers were installed at the after end of the flight deck to assist pilots in their landing approach. Flight deck night lighting consisted of fluorescent tubes about 20cm (8in) long. There were a number of other markings and equipment but there is not enough space to deal with them all and therefore this part will close with mention of the searchlights that were also installed for night landings, but, for well founded reasons, seldom used. *Junyo* and *Hiyo* had four 110cm (44in) searchlights that were located as follows: no 4 was directly in front of the airplane crane, no 2 also to port on a level with the funnel, while no 3 was installed to starboard and more forward than no 3. While these searchlights could disappear into recesses below the flight deck no 4 one was installed in a sponson on the outer side of the bridge.

AVIATION GASOLINE FILLING POSITIONS
There were a lot of filling positions for aviation gasoline on the flight deck. They were supplied by two main gasoline lines, one for A type (high octane fuel for starting up and high bursts of speed) and the other for B type (lower octane fuel for cruising). Sufficient fixed A type filling stations (positions) were provided to ensure

that any position could be reached with a 25m (82ft) flexible hose. Twice as many filling positions were provided for B type fuel. Hoses were filled with pistol type filling valves.

HANGARS

The depth of the ships allowed the arrangement of double hangars of closed type. The upper hangar was below flight deck and uppermost deck, the lower between uppermost and middle deck. The hangars were about 153m (502ft) long, about 5m (16ft) high and about 15m (49ft) wide. Because few Japanese carrierborne planes had wings that folded completely considerable ingenuity was required to achieve close stowage. In the first planning an aircraft complement consisting of 12 (+4) fighters Type 96 (Claude), 18 (+2) dive bombers Aichi D3A (Val), and 18 (+0) torpedo bombers Nakajima B5N (Kate), grand total 48 (+6) was intended but later this was altered to 12 (+3) fighters type zero (Zeke, later Zero) making a grand total of 48 (+5). Based on war lessons the complement was altered again to 21 (+3) Zeros, 18 (+2) Vals, and 9 (+0) Kates. Of these 8 to 9 were usually carried on the flight deck although it was possible to stow them in the hangars.

Funnel uptakes, boiler downtakes, and exhaust trunks cut deeply into the effective width, but two partial lines of folding wing aircraft could be squeezed in. Engines could not be started up in the hangar decks, the sides, as already mentioned, were completely enclosed and ventilation inadequate.

Hangar ventilation was based on a complete renewal in 10 minutes. As a measure against flash the mouths of the exhaust trunks were covered with fine mesh copper gauze, the latter being protected by expanded metal coverings. When planes were fueling in the hangars – they had the same aviation gasoline system as described in the flight deck section – the elevators were kept in their lowest position to ensure a good current through the hangars.

The first measure against fire was to divide the hangars into spearate sections by means of roller, blind type fire curtains. These were of vertical type, the roller having its axis vertical at one side of the hangar, and the top and bottom of the curtain being guided in slots supported from the deck above and the hangar deck. Both hangars were divided by five curtains into 4 sections. Arrangements were provided to spray the fire curtains in an emergency from the fire-main.

Fires within the subdivisions formed by the fire curtains were fought with foam. No overhead sprinkler was provided, but a fire main extended the length of the hangars on either side and was fitted with goose necked nozzles which projected a horizontal stream across the deck. Foamite hoppers were provided at intervals along the bulkhead but did not appear very effective due the their awkward location for servicing. The foam system was controlled from fire observation stations built out from the hangar bulkheads. The foam solution supplied to the sprayers from the system consisted of a 2 per cent solution of a special salt water soap in sea water, which was pumped into the foam mains by large capacity pumps at first hold deck level. The ends of the main foam line were connected to the firemain so that water spray could be used if foam supply failed.

ELEVATORS

As described previously (see hangar) the wings of most Japanese carrier aircraft were only partially folding, if at all. Although this feature permitted the most rapid handling, it reduced the number of planes stowed in the hangars and also necessitated very large elevators. Therefore *Junyo* and *Hiyo* had two square elevators with rounded edges, a side length of 14.07m (46ft) and displaced 0.53m (21in) to port. They were located in the fore and aft part of the flight deck.

Elevators were unarmoured and were capable of lifting a maximum load of 5 tons. The time to raise or lower elevators from lower to flight deck was 15 seconds.

TABLE 2: ALTERATIONS TO AIRCRAFT COMPLEMENT	Fighters		Bombers		Torpedo bombers		
	Type 96 (Claude)	Type 0 (Zero)	Type 99 (Val)	Suisei	Type 97 (Kate)	Tenzan	Total
1st Plan (at time of planning conversion	12 (4)		18 (2)		18 (0)		48 (6)
1st alteration (because the Type 0 fighter became operational)		12 (3)	18 (2)		18 (0)		48 (5)
June 1942 (*Junyo* only) Aleutian operation		6 (2)¹	15 (4)				21 (6)
July 1942 (after reorganisation of the Combined Fleet)		21²	18		9³		48 (?)
December 1942 (after South Pacific Naval Battle)		27⁴	12⁵		9	48 (?)	
June 1944 *Junyo*		27	9	9		6	51
Hiyo		27	18			6	51

Notes 1 12 type 0 fighters of the 6th Kokutai (flight group) were carried as additional complement. They were to be stationed at Midway Island after its capture by the Japanese invasion troops.
  2 Reinforcement of fighters because of war lessons
  3 The first time torpedo bombers were on board.
  4 See 2
  5 Because of heavy losses and insufficient replacement fewer planes were carried.
  6 During 1943 the complement varied.

Elevators were operated by wire cables wound on motor operated drums and were guided by heavy vertical stiffeners being occupied by balance weights. The cable drums were fitted with friction brakes that came into operation immediately after the current was shut off. The brakes held the elevator in position at the upper hangar and served as a precaution against failure of power. Positive detents, hinged about vertical axes at the four corners of the aperture in the flight deck, were swung into position when the elevator was brought to rest at flight deck level and thus cushioned the cables from shock when the elevator stopped.

The elevator machinery was installed in a pit between the lower hangar deck and the deck below. The elevator pits were bridged by portable gangways at lower deck level.

Junyo's island and forward lift.
Jürgen Peters

AVIATION GASOLINE TANKS AND SYSTEM

The aviation gasoline was carried in two groups of tanks, one forward and the other abaft the machinery spaces. Each group of tanks was divided into two sections, one section containing A type fuel the other one B type fuel.

Each tank was fitted with a fixed suction pipe reaching to within 100mm (4in) of the bottom, having a float-operated hinged toe piece 600mm (2ft) long, which ensured that the suction was never from the bottom of the tank unless the latter was empty. The tanks were also fitted with sumps 100mm deep, to which all water and sullage drained. The aviation gasoline pumping space contained three separate pumps, one for A type fuel, one for B type fuel, and the third for dirty water and sullage. Each of the two clean fuel pumps was connected through a strainer to the suction pipes of the appropriate tanks and delivered through a rising main to the main gasoline line. The sullage pump was to the sullage suctions of all tanks and to a small sullage tank, located in the pump compartment, into which all water or condensate from the air escape pipes drained. The sullage pump discharged overboard. The gasoline supply and sullage

pumps were all of 'gear wheel' type, driven by electric motors in the compartment above.

Suitable cross connections were provided to use the A type fuel pump to pump B fuel and vice versa should the other pump break down. The hangar and flight deck filling positions were supplied by two main gasoline lines, one for A type fuel and the other for B type fuel. These mains were situated in the middle section of the lower hangar and in the end sections of the upper hangar, with rises to the middle section of the upper hangar and the flight deck. The gasoline tanks formed a part of the ship's structure and their installation was easy because position and measures were already decided when they were planned as luxury liners. They were surrounded by an airspace full of inert gas (CO2). Arrangements were also provided for filling in an emergency the space above the aviation gasoline in the tanks, and spaces around pump, valve, and working compartments, with the same gas.

Outside the air spaces they were protected by 25mm Ducol steelplates. These precautions were found to be inadequate in the early stages of the war and, after the Battle for the Marianas (Philippine Sea) in June 1944, the top and side air spaces were filled with concrete as a further protection against bomb and, to a far lesser degree, torpedo damage.

Starboard quarter view of *Junyo*.
Jürgen Peters

AIRCREW ACCOMMODATION

Along the outer side of the hangar walls the living quarters for aircrews were established. In their configuration as liners these areas were to be part of the passenger cabins. In *Junyo* this part had already been completed with wooden walls and was not altered because it would have taken too much time. At this time fire prevention measures were not given much consideration. In *Hiyo* cabins had not yet been established and this ship was completed with thin steel walls within this area. In *Junyo* all wooden walls were replaced by uninflammable material (steel) after the Battle for the Marianas.

Japanese naval pilots and navigators were generally in the ratio of three petty officers and warrant officers to one commissioned officer. Pilots and navigators of petty officer rank were quartered in a separate mess and had sleeping places like the tier type bunks of the USN. Commissioned officers were given normal type cabins. Hatches from these living quarters were generally double and had double ladders for quick access to the bridge and flight deck.

BRIDGE

The bridge was a characteristic feature. It was positioned on a prominent platform before the middle frame to starboard in order not to narrow the flight deck and to disturb flight operations. Its measurement exceeded all bridges built before on Japanese carriers. For the first time funnel and bridge were combined into a funnel/island bridge. Japanese carriers built before *Junyo* and *Hiyo* always had funnels that came athwart out of the side plating of the hull usually directly below the flight

114

Stern view of *Junyo* with Kate and Val aircraft being armed
with torpedoes and bombs.

Jürgen Peters

deck, and angled towards the waterline. This was
because the Naval Air Technical Department feared the
disturbance of flight operations by the hot exhaust from
vertical built funnels. On the other side a number of
people had the opinion that if the ship heeled over to a
large degree funnel openings would dip into the water
and the machinery be disabled. They also urged that a
vertical standing high funnel would not disturb flight
operations. Because this form of funnel was planned for
the carrier *Taiho* it could be tested in *Junyo* and *Hiyo*.
Therefore the ships were built with the combined fun-
nel/island bridge, the funnel being 17m (55ft) high and
sloped outward at 26° in order to keep away exhaust
from the flight deck. The shape had been decided after
experiments in the wind tunnel.

From a quarter view, the ships looked somewhat
strange. Except *Junyo, Hiyo,* and *Taiho* only *Shinano*
was built with this superstructure. On all other carriers
the IJN continued the athwart funnels already
described.

To be continued

ATTACK AND DEFENCE
by D K Brown RCNC

No 5

Prior to World War I – Part Two

Edinburgh after the trials of 1909–10.
Author's Collection

HMS BELLEISLE

These trials were carried out on 4 September 1900 with the target ship moored head and stern. She was cleared for action and in as representative state as possible with steam up and with all items of equipment in place. Hammocks, sailors' kit, cabin woodwork, canvas and boats were all in their usual place for action. On the other hand, the decks were flooded beforehand, as a precaution against fire and the pumps were kept running to pour water over the decks as firing began.

The objects of the trials were, quoting the 1915 Gunnery Manual, threefold:

(a) To ascertain the risks of fire in action on account of wood fittings, where such precautions have been taken as may reasonably be expected in a well-disciplined ship.

(b) To give officers a more accurate idea of the extent of damage likely to be caused by various descriptions of projectiles when fired under conditions as nearly resembling an actual engagement as possible.

(c) To give means of considering the best means of rapidly making good such damage as might occur.

It will be noted that the trial was not envisaged as giving information on protection by armour since *Belleisle* had wrought iron plate, with a maximum thickness of 12in.

The firing ship was the battleship HMS *Majestic* which opened fire from astern of *Belleisle* at a range of 1700 yards. She then passed, at 10 knots, up the port side of the target at about 1300 yards, ceasing fire at 1700 yards on the port bow. *Majestic* was in action for about 7 minutes during which time she fired 8 rounds of 12in common shell, 7 rounds 12in AP shot and about 100 6in lyddite at the bow and battery and a further 100 6in common at the stern. In addition some 400 12pdr common and 750 3pdr AP shells were fired. Full charges were used for all rounds.

Observers believe that about 30-40 per cent of the rounds fired were effective (*Brassey's Naval Annual 1901*). There is no evidence that any of the 12in AP shot hit the armour though some may have passed completely through the light structure.

Four 12in common shell seems to have hit. One hit the upper port after corner of the battery (6in wrought iron) and exploded doing immense damage to the fittings in the battery and 'killing' all the dummy crew members. Another struck the belt amidships (either 12in or 8in thick) and made a large hole which contributed to the rapid sinking of *Belleisle*. Two others hit the unarmoured hull forward destroying the funnel and making a large hole in the deck.

One 6in shell (probably common) penetrated 6in wrought iron. The lyddite shells caused very severe damage aft, bending decks upwards and rupturing them as well as destroying the sides. The 6in common caused lesser but still severe damage and repair of damage to unarmoured structure was seen as very difficult.

Six small fires were started but all were easily and quickly extinguished. It was fortunate that there was no major fire since all hand pumps and all fire mains above the armoured deck were destroyed.

All boats were destroyed as were all flag halyards. During the firing *Belleisle* was covered in thick black smoke from bursting shell and her crew would have had difficulty in seeing the enemy. The official notes commented that 'High capacity shell will do great damage and demoralise the crew. Fittings on the sides of armour protection should be removed as the gear stowed there would be flung about violently under impact'. *Belleisle* sank after the firing but was salvaged soon after and scrapped in 1904.

The torpedo gunvessel *Landrail* was used for trials on the control of gunfire while several ships were firing simultaneously (*Exmouth, Albermarle, Triumph* and *Prince George*). Only practise (inert) projectiles were used and she was sunk on 4 October 1906 in Lyme Bay.

The trials against HMS *Hero* in 1907 and 1908 were also primarily for tests of fire control, with two ships firing, but live ammunition was used and some material lessons were obtained. Three separate attacks were carried out, each lasting about 6 minutes, with the firing ships steaming at 15 knots at a range of 8000 yards. Common shell was fired from the 12in guns and both common and lyddite from 9.2in and 6in guns. After the last attack (18 February 1908) *Hero* sank to the bottom in shallow water and hence no examination was possible below the lower deck.

The unarmoured structure was almost totally destroyed and the effect of 9.2in lyddite was particularly impressive. Only one serious fire was started, in coal bags stowed on the upper deck. In a few places there were minor fires in hammocks but, though woodwork was shattered, it did not burn. Splinter damage to voice pipes and communication wiring was noted.

THE EDINBURGH TRIALS 1909-10

This series of trials was more elaborate and more carefully planned to gather information than had been any of the previous ones. Replicas of different structural components were built into *Edinburgh* and tested in turn under what were then seen as realistic conditions. The striking velocity of each projectile was adjusted to that corresponding to 6000 yards for a 4crh round. At that range the angle of descent of a 12in shell is $2° 58°$ ($6in-4\frac{1}{2}°$) and to simulate a little list or roll the ship was heeled to $10°$ during firing against the deck targets. In most of the trials *Edinburgh* was actualling rolling several degrees so the results in terms of angle of attack are only approximate.

In the first series of tests, the value of the thin armour in keeping out heavy lyddite shell was demonstrated. Two 4in KC plates were erected on the side of the forward superstructure and these were fired at by 13.5in, 9.2in and 6in lyddite while the two larger calibres were also fired against the unprotected superstructure. Also fired were 12pdr and 3pdr shell, but these were relatively ineffective. The 6in and 9.2in lyddite fired against the armour had little effect though the bigger shell did produce some damage behind the plate. The deck in front was considerably damaged. A 9.2in shell exploding, perhaps only partially, in the unarmoured

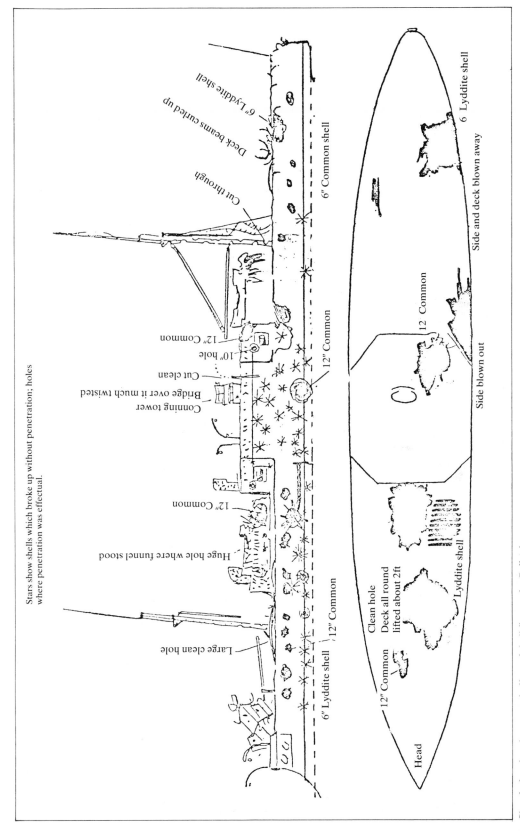

Stars show shells which broke up without penetration; holes where penetration was effectual.

6" Lyddite shell

Large clean hole

12" Common

Huge hole where funnel stood

12" Common

Coning tower
Bridge over it much twisted
Cut clean
10" hole
12" Common

Deck beams curled up
6" Lyddite shell

6" Lyddite shell

Cut through

6" Common shell

12" Common

6" Common shell

6 Lyddite shell

Side and deck blown away

12 Common

Side blown out

12 Common

Side blown out

Clean hole
Deck all round
lifted about 2ft

Lyddite shell

12" Common

Head

Sketch showing the general effect of shell fire on the *Belleisle* as viewed from outboard.

From the Engineer

superstructure, caused severe damage, blowing large holes in the deck above and below and wrecking all fittings in the vicinity of the blast.

The effect of the 13.5in lyddite was even more dramatic. The first round hit the 4in plate and burst outside, wrecking the bow and lower deck in the vicinity and making a hole 3ft × 2½ft in the armour. The plate was forced back bodily some 2ft 3in at the after end. Great damage was caused in the rear by broken pieces of the plate but there was no blast effect inside the compartment.

The next round hit the unarmoured superstructure and completely wrecked the large compartment in which it burst. Side plating was blown out over an area 25ft × 8ft and the decks above and below were destroyed. A large hole was made in the side opposite the entry point of the shell and a small fire was started.

Another 13.5in lyddite shell fired at the uninjured forward 4in plate confirmed that this thickness would keep out most of the effects of such a shell. This series of tests showed once again the devastation which could be caused by large HE shell and that such projectiles could be kept out by thin armour.

In the next text a 13.5in lyddite shell was fired at the funnel casing hitting it about 20ft above the level of the boilers. Steam had been raised in the two boilers under the funnel and was at 25lb psi pressure and small fires (coal) were lit at the back of the furnaces. The armoured gratings kept out most of the fragments but not the blast which severely damaged the furnace and smoke box doors and would probably have blown a proper furnace fire into the stokehold. Blast damaged the steam pipes and valves and even bent the floor plates. A few splinters got into the stokehold and hit one dummy stoker.

Damage above deck was severe but very localised since the explosion was free to vent. Once again, and in a different way, the power of large HE shells was clearly shown.

Three small sections of protected deck were tested next: K with 2in KNC chilled armour over 1in mild steel; L with 1½in KNC over ¾in mild steel; M with 1½in mild steel over ¾in mild steel. A ¾in side plate was used to explode the shell above the deck. APC and CPC 12in shell all produced holes in the deck about 7ft × 2ft and fragments produced considerable damage below. A 12in lyddite shell forced the decks down about a foot, fragments penetrating decks L and M but not K.

Some further tests were carried out with a 2in side burster plate and thin (¾in × ⅝in) decks. Some considerable protection was given even against 12in lyddite. In the next series of trials sections of side and deck were built which were representative of typical small cruiser protection. These included:

A (which was in two parts)
  3in side and ⅜in deck
  2½in side and ¾in deck
D 1¼in KNC over ½in mild steel deck ¾in screen
E 1in nickel steel over ¾in nickel steel deck ¾in screen
F 1in nickel steel over ¾in mild steel deck ¾in screen

Heavy shell of all kinds bursting above the deck made sizeable holes in it and fragments caused damage below. The nickel steel reduced the extent of damage somewhat. Target A showed that the advantage of ¾in deck over ⅜in was negligible and that the weight was better put into side armour increasing the probability of the explosion of HE shells taking place outside the ship.

The 1915 edition of the Gunnery Manual describes these trials in great detail with numerous fascinating sketches. There is also a very lengthy section of General Observation, on the *Edinburgh* trial, summarised below:

1 'It is of great importance from every point of view to keep out large, high capacity, high explosive shell as these are an extremely formidable projectile.' The report said that such shells have a tremendous smashing effect locally, and break up decks and bulkheads near the burst, opening up the ship. The splinters from lyddite shell are small (average ½oz) and projected over considerable distance though they have little penetrating power due to their irregular shape. They will cut into wood and destroy fittings, especially electric cables. One shell hit under the bridge where there were a number of cables and voice pipes all of which were cut, many several times. Firing circuits to the lighter guns mounted in the superstructure were cut.

These splinters glanced off steel structure and had a remarkable ability to get round corners. Exposed personnel such as signalmen and gun crews were at great risk. Against heavy structure the blast effect was quite localised and blast proof structure, such as funnel casings, could be constructed if desired. It should be realised that a 13.5in lyddite shell had about the weight, striking velocity and bursting charge of an Exocet missile.

2 'The comparatively large fragments of common shell will penetrate decks and bulkheads to a much greater extent than lyddite.' Few lyddite splinters passed through more than one bulkhead and many not that. Common shell causes comparatively little local damage but will open the ship up in a more far reaching manner. The big splinters of common shell do not visually travel far from the line of the shell, unless they glance off heavy structure and, indeed, usually went out through the far side of the target vessel.

Structure, other than the thickest armour, should be attacked by a mixture of common and lyddite shell.

3 The value of side armour was clearly demonstrated (note that this was at the equivalent of 6000 yards firing range) and its use wherever possible was seen to be desirable. Armour decks were effective in deflecting shells which hit them at the shallow angle of the trails but in so doing fragments of deck would be broken off and cause serious damage in the compartment below. The space under an armoured deck was thought to be unsuitable for important stores or equipment.

4 The effect of a hit from a large HE shell on the funnel or casing might be very serious.

The experiments demonstrated the value of even thin side armour in resisting the explosion of large HE shell but 'they also demonstrated what, perhaps, was not thoroughly realised before, viz, that armoured deck plates, of existing thickness, at any rate, do not afford

Belleisle as salvaged after sinking as a result of the 1900 trials.
Author's Collection

real protection to the vitals of the ship when attacked by
heavy high expolsive shells unless used in conjunction
with thin side armour'.

The lessons for ship design were seen to be:
(a) side armour should be carried to as near the ends of
the ship as possible and cover as large an area as
possible
(b) weight is better used in side armour than in deck
protection
(c) in small ships the weight given to protection is better used in side armour than on decks
(d) the extra cost of KNC steel over nickel steel is
unjustified for decks.

A retrospective view of lessons learnt will be found at
the end of this article.

EMPRESS OF INDIA 1913

The firing against HMS *Empress of India* on 4
November 1913 was to give officers and men experience
in firing live shell against a real target and few material
lessons were sought. The target was held by a single
anchor and was attacked in turn by a number of ships.
The cruiser *Liverpool* started firing lyddite shell; 16 6in
in 1 minute 58 seconds and 66 4in in 3 minutes 7 seconds. At a range of 4750 yards it is believed that she
scored 7 hits with 6in and 22 with 4in shell. Against a
large and stationary target that does not seem a very
impressive performance but contemporary writers were
impressed. They believed that a light cruiser could inflict
important damage on a battleship caught unprepared in
poor visibility.

The battleships *Thunderer, Orion* and *King Edward
VII* then fired in turn. The first two fired 40 13.5in
common shell in 4 minutes 17 seconds and 4 minutes 7
seconds at a range of 9800 yards. They scored 7 hits plus
1 ricochet and 9 or 10 hits respectively (*Orion* scored 5
hits from 17 rounds in her second minute). *King Edward
VII* then engaged at 8500 yards with 12in (16 rounds for
5 hits), 9 2in (18 rounds for 7 hits) and 6in (27 rounds for
5 hits).

There was then a concentrated firing from *Neptune,
King George V, Thunderer* and *Vanguard* at ranges of
8000-10,000 yards. All guns used reduced charges.

Ship	Rounds fired	Type
Neptune	24	20 common 4 practice
King George V	23	common (old type ex-*Royal Sovereign*)
Thunderer	25	common (old type ex-*Royal Sovereign*)
Vanguard	23	practice

Some 22 hits were obtained in just over 2 minutes. By
1645 *Empress of India* was badly on fire with one foot
trim by the stern. The whole ship's side was red hot. She
settled slowly by the stern and listed slowly to starboard
finally turning over and sinking at 1830. No holes were
observed in the armour belt.

During the firings the wind was Force 2 to 4 and it was
noted that there was considerable advantage in firing up
wind when cordite smoke would be blown clear of the
firing ship. Smoke on the target occasionally interrupted
fire and made the fall of the smaller shells difficult to
spot. The fore top of *Empress of India* was clear of
smoke and control could have been maintained. It was
suggested that a much thicker floor to the top was desir-

HMS *Royal Sovereign* at Portsmouth, the sister of the 1913
target battleship *Empress of India. Royal Sovereign* was
scrapped in the same year.
CPL

HMS *Conqueror*, class name sister to the 1907–08 target ship
Hero. They were shallow draught turret rams built in
1879–88.
CPL

able to keep out both splinters and fire. The bow of *Empress of India* was always clear of smoke and it was suggested that ships should be given an emergency fire control position right forward.

In this case, for the first time, serious fires broke out, initiated by *Liverpool*'s lyddite shells and spread by later hits. The wooden decks, unbacked by steel, were thought to be a prime cause. Many hatches were blown open giving a good draught to the flame.

The 1915 Gunnery Manual sums up as follows: 'That the infliction of the first hit is of the utmost importance was fully borne out by this firing. In addition to the feeling of elation on obtaining the first hit and the opposite effect on the enemy, the subsequent immediate development of a large volume of accurate and rapid fire would render it difficult, perhaps even impossible, for the opponent to reply.' The need for guns to be continuously ready, particularly in poor visibility and for steering from the conning tower was emphasised.

MINOR TRIALS

There were a number of other trials in which replicas of specific parts of the structure of modern ships were built and tested, either at Shoeburyness or on target ships. In 1902 some test sections were built onto the *Belleisle* representing the protection of the *Drake* and *Monmouth* armoured cruiser classes.

The *Drake* target consisted of 4 6in KC plates with representative supports, half being backed by a coal bunker and half not. Two 6in cast steel, AP rounds (2crh) were fired at a velocity corresponding to 2300 yards and caused no damage. Two 9.2in shells were then fired at an equivalent range of 5800 yards and both penetrated and burst just behind the plate. The plate backed by a coal bunker was more severely damaged but the bulkhead behind and the decks remained intact, the coal having absorbed the heavy splinters and the blast. Damage overall was much more serious when unbacked.

The *Monmouth* target was of four 4in KC plate. Three out of four 6in (equivalent range 4100 yards) penetrated and burst behind as did both 9.2in shells. Once again, the effectiveness of the 9.2in shell was noted; it would pierce at least 6in of cemented armour and burst behind causing severe damage. It was also noted that it was important to have upper side coal bunkers full in action. The interior of all armoured positions, manned in action, should be as free as possible from fittings which might themselves become lethal projectiles, under the shock of an explosion. Gun positions should be divided by traverses.

In 1906-7 a casemate representing that of the *Devonshire* armoured cruiser class was tested at Shoeburyness. The armour was 6in KC with a $\frac{1}{4}$in mild steel screen behind to which the fire control instruments were secured. The armour kept out 7.5in common shell (2crh) at equivalent ranges of 6000-8000 yards but was easily penetrated by capped shell.

The hazard caused by flying fittings was again noted and recommendation made as to the best way of mounting and securing electric lights and cables. Cement used to give a smooth finish to the inside of armour caused no problem. The casemate was given six coats of paint inside and out and the floor covered with corticene. There was no fire even when a 7.5in lyddite shell was fired in through the gun port.

In 1907 a series of tests was carried out against two targets representing turret roofs. In both targets the plating was 3in KNC but 'A' was made up of small plate while 'B' was in two large plates. They were fired at with impact angles of 10° and 15° with 12in common and 7.5in and 6in common and lyddite. The velocities of the shells corresponded to the range giving an angle of descent of 10°.

Calibre	Equivalent Range (2crh)
12in	11,400 yards
7.5in	8400 yards
6in	7400 yards

The 15° impacts represented the additional effect of a 5° roll.

The 6in shells caused no direct damage but sheared many rivets and bolts, an effect much more marked with the 7.5in shells. The 12in shells caused very severe damage due to shock and blast, damage being more severe with the smaller plates, thought it was noted that it was the supporting girders rather than the plates which failed.

The lessons learnt were:

(a) to prevent flying bolts and rivets causing injury. A 3in rope mantlet close under the roof girders was found to be very effective

(b) avoid openings in the roof which would admit blast

(c) provide strong support to the roof

(d) avoid obstructions on the turret roof which would cause a shell to detonate rather than glance off. Light guns should not be mounted on turret roofs

(e) lyddite shell gave a shower of splinters which would cause damage and injury all round the turrets – eg bridge, etc.

These were only some of the numerous tests carried out against armoured structure.

STOPPING TORPEDO CRAFT

Many ways were tried to stop torpedo craft before they could launch their weapon. In 1902 the effect of ricochet fire from 6in and 4.7in guns was tried against an old torpedo boat at a range of 1200 yards without much success.

There were many experiments using shrapnel from big guns, mainly carried out on shore but also using the destroyers *Skate* (1902) and *Ferret* (1911). Different numbers and sizes of balls were tried but none were particularly effective. Two special rounds of 12.5in case shot, each containing 100 balls, were made and fired from an old rifled muzzle loader against *Skate* at 800 yards. Considerable damage was caused but it was thought that such shot would be useless over 1200 yards and would cause unacceptable damage to the rifling of guns.

Typical of the shrapnel firing was one against *Ferret* at a range of 1900 yards with the ship moored bow toward the gun, with heel at 30° to the line of fire. Four 12in

HMS *Hero* with shell holes during the 1907–08 trials.
NMM

rounds were fired, each containing 353 12oz oil hardened steel balls. The swept zone was about 800 yards × 130 yards, the four rounds achieving 32, 13, 24 and 2 hits respectively.

Conventional shell was tested in 1899 against a target at Shoeburyness representing a torpedo boat, fitted with a boiler and coal bunkers. One pounder shell was ineffective while 3pdr common shell was usually stopped by the first bulkhead in end on fire. Broadside on 3pdr shell burst well inside the boat and could damage the boiler after passing through a full coal bunker.

In 1894-5 similar trials were carried out with 6pdr and 12pdr guns. It was concluded that, end on, the 12pdr was the smallest gun that could stop a torpedo boat with a single shot though 3pdr and 6pdr would cause serious damage.

In 1906 the destroyer *Skate* was used for trials with 3pdr, 12pdr and a 4in BL (25lb shell). The 3pdr rounds did little damage and were unlikely to have stopped the boat. Twelve pound shells, both end on and at 13° inclination (bow nearest) caused serious damage. The 4in shell and, in particular, the lyddite-filled rounds caused serious damage. Further tests against *Ferret* in 1909-10 confirmed the value of lyddite shell. A 4in projectile would make a hole about 29ft × 20ft (common shell 8ft × 5ft) in the side plating (5 or 8psi). The common shell showed to advantage when hitting a full coal bunker.

The blast, splinter and probably morale effect on personnel would be much greater with lyddite.

SAFETY OF AMMUNITION

Many tests were carried out on the safety of shells and cordite charges when hit by shells. Concern was felt after some of the incidents in the 1904-5 Russo-Japanese War. In one the armoured cruiser *Iwate*'s starboard, forward 6in casemate was blown up after a Russian shell hit and exploded a shell in the racks, this explosion then detonating all the Shimose filled projectiles in the casemate.

In the Battle of Tsushima a 12in shell burst in the after turret of the battleship *Fuji* and 8¼in charges caught fire and burnt fiercely for some time. There were 6 HE shells in the turret at the time but none exploded. Fires also occurred in nitro cellulose - less charges in the Russian armoured cruisers *Rossiya* and *Gromoboi* on 14 August 1904.

British tests showed that powder filled shell could explode if hit directly by a shell but that only the one shell actually hit would explode. Lyddite shell would not explode if hit by common shell of 6in calibre or below. Larger common shell or lyddite shell would cause sympathetic detonation which could spread to adjoining

POWDER BURST

LYDDITE BURST

○ ○ PIECES OF PLATE OR STRUCTURE.

End on view. Note all plating is ordinary thin skin plating unless otherwise stated.

– ← – – – TRACK OF SHELL AND BURST

13·5" LYDDITE AT SUPERSTRUCTURE. *N⁰ 6.*

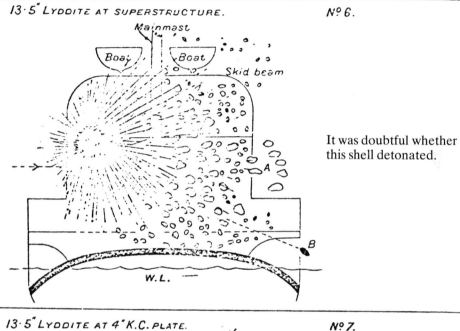

It was doubtful whether this shell detonated.

13·5" LYDDITE AT 4" K.C. PLATE. *N⁰ 7.*

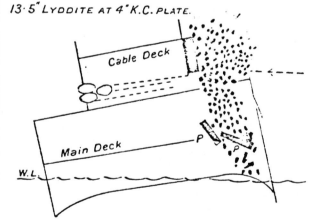

P.P. Pieces of old 6″ plate which had been placed on deck to strengthen it.

N⁰ 8.

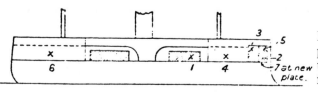

Diagram showing the position of the hits and the two 4″ K.C. plates erected forward.

SHELL PENETRATION OF EDINBURGH

shells if close. A 13.5in lyddite shell (191lb burster) detonated a similar shell 10ft away but not one at 15ft. The danger zone was 2ft 9in for a 9.2in and 1ft for a 6in shell.

The battleship *Revenge* had a cordite explosion in her 6in magazine in 1899 and the cruiser *Fox* in 1906 due to spontaneous combustion. In *Revenge* all three cartridges in one case burnt while in *Fox* one of four cartridges in the affected case was not ignited. In an experiment in 1897 a stack of cordite was ignited in the open and detonated leaving a crater 26ft wide and 9ft deep.

The effect of flash in an ammunition trunk was studied at HMS *Excellent* in 1891-2. Various combinations of 4.7in and 6in shell and cartridges of powder and cordite were tested. In no case were shells sympathetically detonated but cartridges, particularly powder filled, would burn or explode. It was recognised that ammunition trunks should not communicate directly with a magazine and that there should be at least 12in between the trunk and a magazine hatch.

Other tests showed that shells exploding in oil tanks could cause a fire if they burst above the oil but were unlikely to ignite a full tank.

Attempts were made to develop an anti-submarine shell that would dive and after a short delay detonate a high explosive filling. These experiments do not seem to have been very successful though submarines *A 1* and *A 3* were sunk in 1911-12, while at periscope depth, by conventional lyddite shell. These tests were not thought to be significant as the submarines were of obsolete construction.

This article has only described the more important of the many full scale tests in the years before World War I.

RETROSPECT

It is clear that the Royal Navy, in the opening years of the twentieth century, made determined attempts to discover what would happen in war. The tests were carried out in realistic conditions, for the fighting ranges then envisaged, and the lessons learnt were carefully digested. Use was also made of the very detailed reports from observers in the Japanese Fleet during the war with Russia.

The great destructive effect of large HE shells was appreciated and the value of even thin armour in keeping blast and splinters out of the ship was realised. The danger of communications, both electrical and voice pipes, being cut by splinters was realised.

It was appreciated that fittings would fly and act as secondary projectiles when the structure to which they were attached was hit. Damage below armoured decks was likely from fragments of deck (spalling) and from flying bolts and rivets. Such damage was even more likely in the case of hits on turret roofs and rope mantles were found to give protection.

Serious fires were uncommon in these tests even when attempts were made to provoke them by excess paint, hits in oil tanks, etc. It was noted that damage to fire mains and hand pumps would make fire fighting difficult.

All these tests were carried out at comparatively short (simulated) range – 6000-8000 yards being usual. Such ranges seemed realistic by the thinking of the day as the results of firing against *Empress of India* did not produce a very high proportion of hits. Even so the captain of *Neptune* thought that hitting at 6000-8000 yards was too easy and that battle practice range should be increased to 12,000 yards. Only in the spring of 1914 did Beatty get permission to carry out a firing at 16,000 yards. Had longer ranges been tried, the deficiencies in deck protection which were observed might have seemed more serious. It should be noted that the German Navy did not envisage fighting at much more than 10,000 yards and that their decks were usually a little thinner than those of British ships.

While the danger of flash travelling down ammunition trunks was realised it does not seem that the effects of a very large mass of cordite being ignited in a confined space was studied. The defects in armour piercing shells were clearly known by 1910 but nothing was done to remedy them until after Jutland. Again, the idea of a close action with normal impact was a contributory factor to lack of appreciation of the problem.

All in all, the trials were comprehensive and the Royal Navy had a far better idea of what war meant than almost any other navy, the Japanese being the only rival.

The 12cm Multiple Rocket Launcher of the Imperial Japanese Navy

by Hans Lengerer & Tomoko Rehm-Takahara

The growing danger of the annihilation of their fleet by Allied aircraft led the Japanese to develop rocket launchers as a shipboard weapon. After the Battle for the Marianas, with its shocking result for the Japanese, the Naval Technical Department ordered the Kure Naval Arsenal to design a multiple rocket launcher for shipboard use in June 1944.

Prior to this only the crudest troughlike rocket launchers were used by the IJN. Late in 1943 naval officers observed the test firing of Army 20cm (8in) rockets [The Imperial Japanese Army had begun theoretical studies of solid fuel rockets as early as 1931 but more than 10 years elapsed before production for operational use was realised.] and the decision to manufacture such rockets for naval land forces was made. The Navy began production of 20cm rockets, which were not an exact duplicate of the Army 20cm rocket in March 1944, and by May 1944 trial production of the heavy 45cm (17.7in) rocket began. After ground test firing this rocket on Kamegakubi Island near Kure, this weapon, the largest solid-propelled rocket used operationally by any nation in World War II saw action in the Philippines.

By July 1944 the 12cm (4.7in) incendiary shrapnel AA rocket and its launcher, the subject of this article, were developed and earmarked for 5 carriers and 2 battleships. Next, armour piercing anti-tank rockets with shaped charges in 8cm (3.1in), 10cm (3.9in), and 20cm (8in) calibre were put into production during April 1945 but they were never used in action.

The solid propellant for the naval rockets was developed and manufactured at the Second Naval Powder Factory, Hiratsuka, and the designing and manufacturing of metal parts was carried out at the Kure Naval Arsenal, which also developed the launcher for shipboard use. Test firing of rockets took place on the already mentioned island of Kamegakubi. Because of their 'cut and try' process, rather than by new theories on optimum design rules, and less efficient and precise manufacturing methods than the Americans, the performance was, in general, below the American standard.

DEVELOPMENT
When the Kure Naval Arsenal received the order in June 1944 only one month was allowed for designing

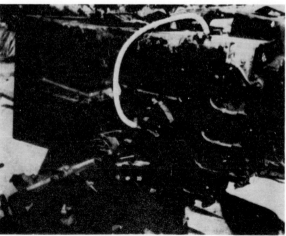

The left hand side of the rocket launcher showing the elevating and training mechanism.
Author's collection

The right hand side of the launcher.
Author's collection

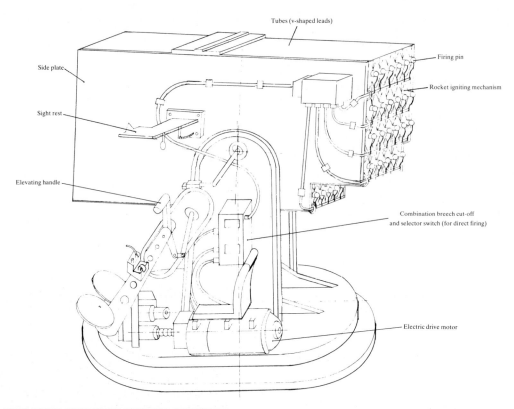

Tubes (v-shaped leads)

Side plate

Firing pin

Sight rest

Rocket igniting mechanism

Elevating handle

Combination breech cut-off
and selector switch (for direct firing)

Electric drive motor

FIGURE 1: THE 12CM 28-TUBE ROCKET LAUNCHER

and producing the first model. In view of the short time, the 25mm triple machine-gun mount already in use by the IJN since 1941 was modified for this purpose. In order to install as many tubes as possible it was decided to fire 12cm rockets. Twenty-eight barrels were fitted to this launcher. Only a few alterations to the machine-gun mount were necessary: a completely new cradle for the 28 'barrels' was fitted; thin steel cabinets were fitted on

A right-front view with an indication of the size of the whole system.

Author's collection

either side of the mount to protect the crew from flames; the firing switch was changed to a rotary switch, to allow the rockets to be fire in a ripple.

The gun department of the Kure Naval Arsenal carried out the design very speedily and within the time allowed the first model was tested and proved so satisfactory that in the course of the following month (August 1944) the first ships received their rocket launchers. Figure 1 shows the 12cm 28-tube rocket launcher. In this launcher the first three rows (from top to bottom) were fitted with six barrels each, the next two with five each. This space was needed to install a part of the steering gear but about one month later a 30-tube rocket launcher appeared with two more 'barrels', ie five rows with 6 tubes each.

THE FIRE DIRECTOR SYSTEM

To control the multiple rocket guns the Type 95 short range HA fire director system (*Kosha sochi*) was used extensively although its derivative, the simplified short range HA director system Type 4 modification 3, could also be used.

The Type 95 director (*Shageki sochi*) was the standard one in use by the IJN and controlled the rocket gun mounts remotely by a Ward-Leonard system, ie the training and elevation motors were interconnected by synchronisers to prevent the motors getting out of step. The Ward-Leonard system was used on the mount and received signals from the Type 95 director.

The system was based on the 'course and speed' principle and was originally copied from the French Le Prieur mechanical lead computing sight (commonly called LPR by the IJN) although in a few cases an open ring sight or an optical ring sight (etched glasses) were used. The general arrangement and the training and elevation electric circuits are adequately illustrated but a few remarks may be helpful.

TABLE 1: 12CM 28-TUBE ROCKET LAUNCHER

Length of the launcher rails (barrels, tubes)	150cm/4ft 11in
Length of the cradle (rocket firing container)	150cm/4ft 11in
Height of the cradle (rocket firing container)	75cm/30in
Height of the rocket launcher mount	135cm/4ft 5in
Width of the cradle (rocket firing container)	85cm/2ft 9½in
Firing mechanism	Electrically released firing pin
Rate of fire	28 rockets in 6-10 seconds (theoretically) 16-20 rockets per minute (practically)
Elevation	+5° − +80° (no depression)
Traverse	Complete revolution
Elevating speed (loaded)	About 12°/sec
(empty)	About 10°/sec (electric) About 9°/sec (manual)
Traverse speed (loaded)	About 12°/sec
(empty)	About 18°/sec (electric) About 12°/sec (manual)
Maximum range at 30° elevation	About 4200m/4593yds
Maximum height at 80° elevation	About 2300m/2515yds
Weight of the elevating ports	599kg/1320lb
Weight of the loading ports	780kg/1720lb
Weight of the box plate etc	191kg/421lb
Weight of the tubes (rocket firing container)	395kg/870lb
Complete weight with 28 rounds loaded	2494kg/5498lb
Loading time	About 3-5 minutes
Fixtures	1 Uses the 25mm triple MG mount. 2 Anti-flash shells are attached. 3 A 28-round salvo was difficult and may have had catastrophic results. 4 Training radius 1.37m 5 Operation radius about 2m 6 The rocket launcher had the appearance of a large rectangular segmented box, mounted in an ordinary 25mm MG triple mount. 7 The rockets are arranged in five layers. Each of the top three layers held six rockets, and the lower two ones held five each.

The control officer had a scooter control which had two pairs of vibrating contacts; one for elevating and one for training. These contacts were vibrated by means of an eccentric cam. If the scooter control was moved, one side of the pairs of contacts will complete the circuit for a longer time than the other and the generator will therefore be triggered so that the motors will be driven at high or low speed accordingly and in the appropriate direction.

The maximum target speed that could be set in this system was 600 kilometres/hour (431kts). When the demand for higher speed targets was made, the only satisfactory solution which would be supplied was the addition of the above-mentioned etched ring sight in the control officer's telescope which provided for 700, 800 and 900km/hr target speeds.

The most serious deficiencies of the system were that the multiple mounts could not be trained and elevated rapidly enough while the sight was inadequate for high speed targets.

The rear of the launcher. Note that there are six rockets in each of the top two rows, and only five in the other two. *Author's collection*

THE ROCKET LAUNCHER

As already mentioned the 12cm (4.7in) AA 28-tube and 30-tube rocket launchers were installed on ships for use. They fired a large number of 12cm incendiary shrapnel shells to knock down torpedo or dive bombers that attacked the ship. The rocket launcher is adequately illustrated in the accompanying figures and photographs and needs no further explanation here. Table 1 contains the essential characteristics and capabilities.

THE INCENDIARY SHRAPNEL ROCKET SHELL

The principle of the 12cm rocket shell is like that of ships and planes which push the water or air backwards with their propellers and move forward from the reaction. In rocket guns the projectile is propelled in flight by reaction to the backward expulsion of high pressure gases.

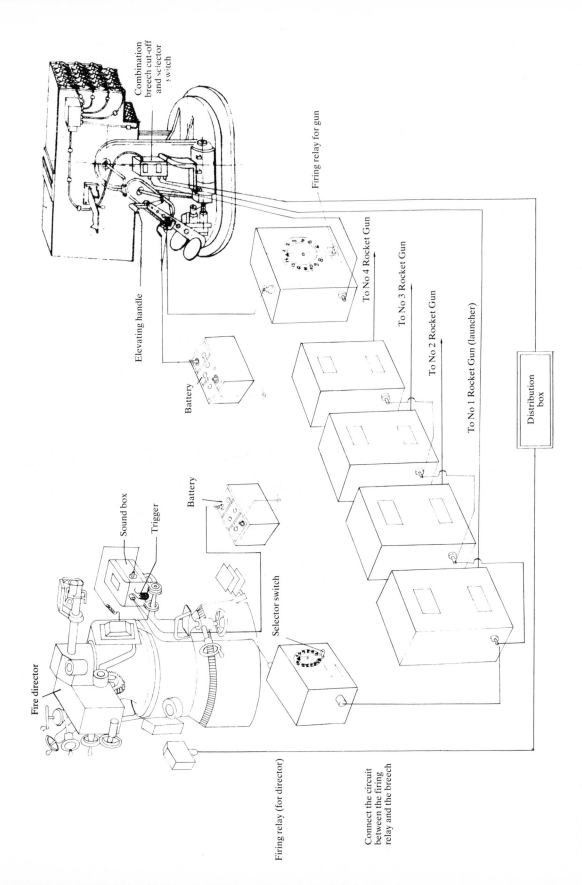

Combination breech cut-off and selector switch

Firing relay for gun

Elevating handle

Battery

To No 4 Rocket Gun

To No 3 Rocket Gun

To No 2 Rocket Gun

To No 1 Rocket Gun (launcher)

Distribution box

Sound box

Trigger

Battery

Selector switch

Fire director

Firing relay (for director)

Connect the circuit between the firing relay and the breech

FIGURE 2: FIRE CONTROL ARRANGEMENTS FOR THE ROCKET SYSTEM

TABLE 2: 12CM ROCKET INCENDIARY SHRAPNEL SHELL

Projectile's outside diameter	12cm/4.7in
Length of projectile	73.05cm/2ft 5in
Complete weight	22.45kg/49lb 8oz
Weight of bursting charge	200 grams/7oz
Propellant	Powder
Weight of propellant	3.56kg/7lb 13oz
Number of grains	7
Outer diameter of grain	35mm/1⅜in
Inner diameter of grain	5mm/¼in
Length of grain	360mm/14¼in
Combustion time of propellant	1.6 seconds
Weight of booster charge (ignitor)	35 grams/1¼oz (block powder)
Pellets	60 special phosphorous incendiary pellets
Weight of the incendiary charge	440 grams/15½oz
Average internal pressure	85kg/mm²
Number of nozzles	6
Maximum nozzle diameter	11.5mm/⅜in
Stabilisation	Spin 3600rpm (0-25°)
Fuze (time)	5.5-8.5 seconds delay
Fuze (model)	Type 5 combination model 2
Maximum initial velocity	About 290m/sec or 787fps (increased elevation led to a delay of the initial velocity)
Maximum range, horizontal (with 8.5 seconds delay)	About 1650m
Maximum range, vertical (with 5.5 seconds delay)	1050m
Lateral depression	100m
Longitudinal depression	100m

Table 2 contains the essential characteristics and capabilities.

ESSENTIAL PRECAUTIONS IN HANDLING

As described before, the rocket launcher was controlled by the same fire director system that controlled the 25mm MG in double or triple mounts. Manual control and firing was to be avoided. When the sight of the 25mm gun had to be used a greater superelevation of the rocket was necessary.

Upon firing, there was violent flame and blast, especially near the breech, hence it was important not to permit personnel to be there, especially after the breech switch was on, ie ready. Between the rocket launchers of a group (in general 3 or 4) and directly behind them thin steel plates were installed as a screen against flames. Furthermore, since at the time of firing the anti-flash shield (on the mounts) and a deck area about 3m deep and 1in wide became hot because of the flames, water had to be sprinkled to cool them. For this reason water filled cartridge pouches were set up near the mounts (inner side, after part). However, as the electric circuit was not waterproof, water could not be allowed to get into it.

When firing exceptionally by direct aiming, the 'firer' and 'azimuth trainer' had to stay behind the anti-flash shield and, in addition, had to wear adequate protective

clothing, ie flying suits or fire-proof garments and flying shoes, flying gloves, and gas mask. Further it was not permitted to fire all rockets at the same time, but 14 or 15 salvos could be fired before the launcher had to be loaded again. When the relay was turned too quickly fire became practically instantaneous, causing breakdowns in the weapon and unforeseen fire damage.

Loading the launcher, the personnel had to take the following precautions:

The switchgear for the system, installed onboard the aircraft carrier *Katsuragi*.
Author's collection

1 The loading positions of the red and blue shells must not be mistaken.
2 The rocket must not be loaded in reverse.
3 The launching rails ('barrels', tubes) must not be loaded doubly.
4 Excessive jarring must be avoided.
5 The firing plugs had to be tight.

The loading time was about 3 to 5 minutes and depended upon the experience of the personnel.

With regard to the launcher, the following precautions had to be observed:

1 The launcher rails had to be handled properly and

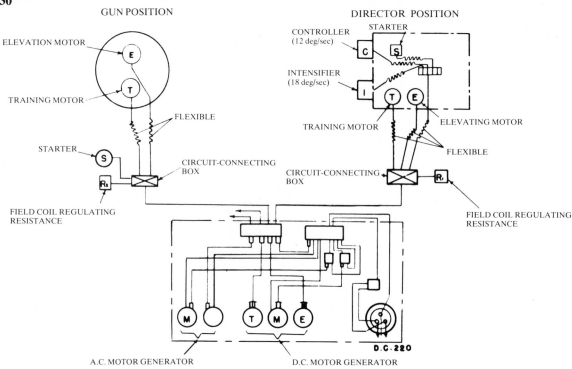

FIGURE 3: THE ELECTRICAL CIRCUIT DIAGRAM

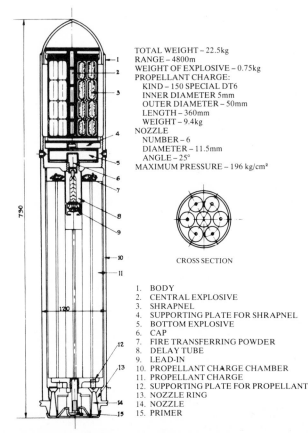

TOTAL WEIGHT – 22.5kg
RANGE – 4800m
WEIGHT OF EXPLOSIVE – 0.75kg
PROPELLANT CHARGE:
    KIND – 150 SPECIAL DT6
    INNER DIAMETER 5mm
    OUTER DIAMETER – 50mm
    LENGTH – 360mm
    WEIGHT – 9.4kg
NOZZLE
    NUMBER – 6
    DIAMETER – 11.5mm
    ANGLE – 25°
MAXIMUM PRESSURE – 196 kg/cm²

CROSS SECTION

1. BODY
2. CENTRAL EXPLOSIVE
3. SHRAPNEL
4. SUPPORTING PLATE FOR SHRAPNEL
5. BOTTOM EXPLOSIVE
6. CAP
7. FIRE TRANSFERRING POWDER
8. DELAY TUBE
9. LEAD-IN
10. PROPELLANT CHARGE CHAMBER
11. PROPELLANT CHARGE
12. SUPPORTING PLATE FOR PROPELLANT
13. NOZZLE RING
14. NOZZLE
15. PRIMER

kept smooth, but oil and inflammable coating must be avoided.

2 It was important to inspect the firing plugs, before and after firing (see also above), in order to determine whether they were secured (about 6mm in firing) and clean.

3 Since electric firing circuit was the only method of firing for the gun, it was necessary to make advance preparations.

As to the projectile it might be helpful to read the following sentences with regard to figure 5.

1 The motor body contained the propellant (that was identical with smokeless powder). Therefore, high temperature and great humidity had to be avoided, and the body had to be kept in a cool and dry place. In practice, the temperature should be kept below 40°C and misfire was feared if the booster charge absorbed moisture. Fire was, of course, forbidden.

2 In the shell body there was a cannister containing the special phosporus incendiary. Heat in excess of 100°C or rough handling might cause the special phosphorus to leak. Hence, it was necessary to handle the shell gently.

3 A temporary cover was attached to the bottom of the motor base plate. It was for protection and water-proofing and should not be removed without cause. However, before firing took place, it had to be removed without fail. Below the temporary cover there was still a water-proofing paper (cellophane).

FIGURE 4: SECTION OF THE 12CM SHRAPNEL ROCKET

The primer could be inserted and firing done without removing all cellophane. The powder with primer attached was fired as it was.

4 In order to avoid disturbance during flight, the various connections, which were screwed together, had to be sufficiently tight.

5 In case the shell was exposed to rain or had fallen into water, the inside of the propellant tube had to be inspected and if there was moisture, it was necessary to wipe and dry the propellant and the inside of the motor body. However, at this time it was necessary to be careful that the delay element cylinder was screwed tight and did not receive a jolt.

In order to prevent penetration of fire to the bursting charge through the delay element cyclinder threads a copper washer was attached.

METHODS OF INSTRUCTION AND TRAINING
In 1944 the Yokosuka Naval Gunnery School, Anti-aircraft Department, Special Gunnery Section, did publish a pamphlet about the weapon that was captured on Okinawa by the American troops and translated into English. This translation will be cited without alterations.

A Instruction and training are based on a minutely detailed plan and on the commanding officer's perserverance and spirit. The gun crew,

under the officer in charge, and the piece are a unit. The aim should be to achieve the weapon's best combat performance. It is also necessary to cultivate a very vigorous war-like spirit and a steadfast and immovable belief in ultimate victory.

B Concerning plans for instruction, the rocket gun's special characteristics should be made known, and the basic instruction should progress, by degrees, from instruction on each part to that covering the whole plan.

C Training should be based on combat-like conditions. First of all, it is necessary that training be repetitious. Training with actual targets (planes, etc) should be regarded with great importance, and, furthermore, night training should be carried out. In order to get the most out of training, observation of demonstrations and investigation of results should be carried out.

D Training concerning emergency measures to be taken for damage or defects occurring in ordnance should be related to battle experience, so that should such conditions develop in reality, they could be dealt with thoroughly. Further, those measures must become so familiar that they can be carried out quickly and effectively.

FIGURE 5: BALLISTIC PERFORMANCE OF THE ROCKET

The numerals on the trajectory indicate the time of flight and 0 indicates point of shell burst on 55 seconds and 8 seconds delay.

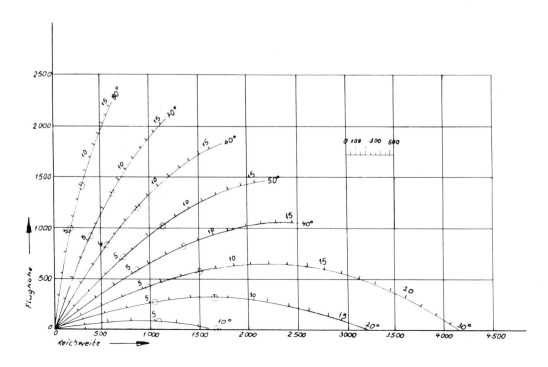

SUITABLE STANDARD FOR METHOD OF FIRING

For the defence against aircraft the following methods were developed. They were considered to be sufficiently accurate for this purpose.

Appropriate Time	Firing Officer's Command		Essentials of Control	Name of Firing Method
Dive Bombing (Small number of planes)	Diving 'A' Method	(a)	Adjust sight at fixed sitting.	Diving 'A' Method
		(b)	Correct sighting.	
		(c)	When it is ascertained that the enemy planes have begun their dive, track the 2nd or 3rd plane from the leading plane; usually 3 or 4 salvos are fired against each plane.	
		(d)	Carry on salvo fire.	
Dive Bombing (Many planes at once)	Diving 'B' Methods	(a)	Follow the Diving 'A' Method.	Diving 'B' Method
		(b)	Continue firing to the neighborhood of the enemy planes' diving point.	
Torpedo Bombing (Small number of planes)	Torpedo 'A' Method	(a)	Adjust sight at fixed setting.	Torpedo 'A' Method
		(b)	Sight on enemy planes.	
		(c)	Carry on salvo fire.	
Torpedo Bombing (Many planes)	Torpedo 'B' Method	(a)	Follow the Torpedo 'A' Method.	Torpedo 'B' Method
		(b)	Turn to the vicinity of point of enemy torpedo firing; and sight on a horizontal line, firing at about 15° elevation	

SHIPS EQUIPPED WITH ROCKET LAUNCHERS

During July/August 1944 12cm 8-tube rocket launchers were installed aboard the carriers *Zuikaku, Junyo, Unryu,* and *Amagi.*

During September/October 1944 12cm 30-tube rocket launchers were installed aboard the carrier *Katsuragi,* and the battleship/carriers *Ise* and *Hyuga.*

As a general rule carriers had four mounts, and battleships three. They were installed at each side of the ship. *Junyo* differed insofar as this ship was equipped with six mounts only instead of eight.

LANDBASED ROCKET LAUNCHERS

Naval land forces were also equipped with it for use ashore. For this purpose the rocket launcher was mounted on a rotary pedestal manufactured at the Sasebo and other Naval Arsenals in 1944 and 1945. The pedestal is shown on the accompanying photographs and differs in many respects from the 25mm MG triple mount used aboard of ships. These mounts were devised for the defence of the Japanese home islands.

The control panel aboard *Katsuragi.*
Author's collection

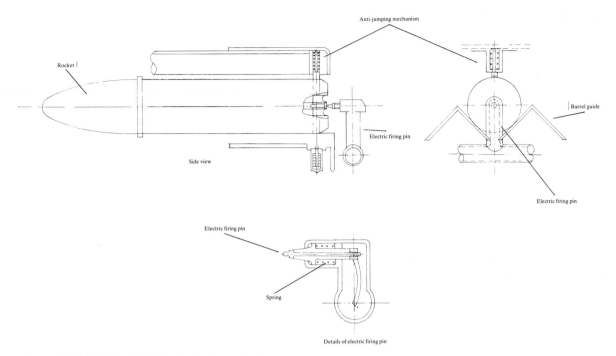

FIGURE 6: ROCKET IN FIRING POSITION

FIGURE 7: GENERAL ARRANGEMENT

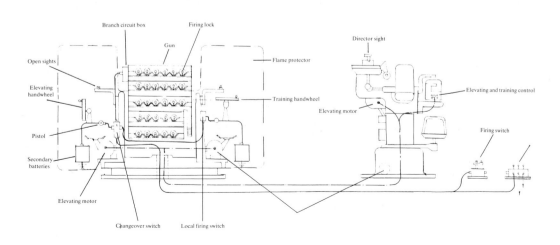

HM SUBMARINE E31

Log of her War Service

by Brian Head

Part Two

E 31 at Harwich in 1918.
Author's collection

On 5 September 1916 Lt-Cdr Feilman took *E 31* to sea for her sixth war patrol. She arrived in her billet at 0400 on 6 September. The first five days were uneventful with mostly neutral shipping and trawlers observed. At 1300 on 11 September the smoke of a number of ships was sighted to eastward. By 1400 *E 31* was closing what looked like three cruisers. All tubes were brought to the ready. The vessels were apparently pursuing a zigzag course at irregular intervals and there were three groups totalling ten ships in all, plus two destroyers and a Zeppelin in company. *E 31* maintained contact whilst endeavouring to reach an attack position. The Zeppelin was not making the approach very easy and at 1530 it was right

overhead when *E 31* was at periscope depth. The enemy vessels now appeared to be minesweepers or minelayers accompanied by two destroyers and the chase continued until 1745 when Lt-Cdr Feilman decided to abandon the attack as the enemy was then about 3 miles away and steaming rapidly to the eastward. (Position 54°24′N 5°37′E.)

AUTUMN 1916

The last day of the patrol was spent in a full gale so no doubt all concerned were glad to return to Harwich on 14 September were *E 31* secured alongside *Forth*. Half the crew were given leave and on their return *E 31* entered the floating dock for three days maintenance work. The day after she undocked, *E 31* was ordered to sea at 2215. The destroyer *Melampus* escorted her out and she was in her billet at 0800 next morning, 26 September. Again, this turned out to be a very uneventful patrol and she returned to *Maidstone* three days later.

After two days in, which included a day's exercise attack to ensure no 'rustiness' *E 31* cast off from *Maidstone* at 0930 for her eighth patrol. She was in her billet at 0520 on 4 October and once more suffered at the hands of the autumn gales. This was a particularly bad spell with five continuous days and nights of severe gales from the southwest. On 5 October, the log records *E 31* as lying on the bottom in 23 fathoms and the boat still rolling. Visibility was very poor, with heavy rain, and charging the batteries was a very hazardous operation, with the boat plunging and rolling on the surface head to sea and shipping water down the conning tower. On 7 and 8 October it was noted that battery charging had to be commenced with the conning tower hatch closed and the diesel engines being started by a charge. Finally, on 10 October, the gale moderated to 'fresh wind and rough sea'. *E 31* proceeded to Harwich on the surface and reached *Forth* on the 11th. Half the crew went on leave the next day. It needs little imagination to guess how they needed that break. Living conditions at sea in an 'E' boat were never comfortable.

On 18 October orders were given at 2100 for the boat to be on standby, with two days fresh provisions, the boat fully manned and the crew sleeping in the boat. Obviously some emergency was being anticipated. Just after midnight, *E 31* cast off from *Maidstone* and made her way down the estuary with *E 43* (Lt-Cdr V M Cooper) and *E 53* (Lt-Cdr J B Glencross) accompanied by the faithful *Lurcher*. Several divisions of destroyers and light cruisers passed in an easterly direction, but there was no excitement for *E 31*. Having arrived at her appointed station by 0800 she spent most of the forenoon at periscope patrol and surfaced at 1100 on hearing an explosive charge dropped by *Lurcher* as a signal. She remained on the surface in company with *Lurcher* and *E 43* until 1700 when both submarines began the return trip to Harwich where *Forth* was reached by 0140 next morning.

Trafalgar Day 1916 was marked by *E 31* entering the floating dock to have her No 1 fuel tank examined for a suspected leakage and two days later she rejoined *Maidstone*.

At 2325 on 24 October *E 31* went to sea again with *E 55* (Lt-Cdr G H Kellett) and *E 53*, escorted by *Melampus*. This was again a short-lived patrol. She reached her billet at 0650, dived at 0715 on periscope watch, surfaced every hour for W/T watch and at 1015 all three submarines were ordered to return to base.

The depot ship *Maidstone* at Harwich, with *E 31* and *H 21* alongside.
HMS *Dolphin*.

E 31 alongside one of the German floating docks surrendered in 1918, showing her 12pdr gun.
HMS *Dolphin*

A few days at Harwich, interspersed with exercise attacks, ended with *E 31* casting off from *Maidstone* at 1440 on 6 November for her next patrol. Lt-Cdr Feilman's orders were to patrol to the North and East within 10 miles of the Schouwen Bank Light Vessel. He was also to patrol the Steen Deep if the weather was favourable. There was a warning that submarine nets were thought to have been laid in positions 51°42′N 3°3′W, each being marked by a buoy. A sunken German minelayer was known to be in position 51°50′ N3°15′E. These three positions were, therefore, to be avoided. *E 31* reached her billet by 2320 that night and the next day ran into more foul weather. In position 51°49′N 3°22′E the log records high seas running with a strong southwesterly wind.

U-BOATS ATTACKED

At 0725 on 9 November destroyers were sighted to the southward and Lt-Cdr Feilman decided to proceed to attack. Twenty minutes later they were identified as a force of British light cruisers and 4 destroyers. Coming to the surface at 0920, a U-boat was sighted on the surface to the west. *E 31* dived immediately and started an attack. An hour later, when the range was 1½ miles,

the quarry dived. Feilman however, took the view that the enemy boat was in the vicinity for a purpose and estimated she might reappear again, given time. He surfaced and proceeded NW for a couple of hours to lie in wait. However, after keeping a periscope watch for about four hours and sighting nothing, he decided to return to his billet.

At 0945 next morning, a submarine was again sighted on the surface. *E 31* got to within 2 miles when the U-boat dived and the attack had to be abandoned. Feilman decided this activity was worth reporting and at 1155 he came to the surface and made a signal to *Maidstone* – 'Submarine Minelayer Schouwen Bank 0930 proceeding west'. He was then in position 51°50′N 3°23′E.

On 12 November, a floating mine was sunk by rifle fire – they were a hazard to friend and foe alike. Later, in the afternoon, another U-boat was sighted. This time *E 31* was able to get into a firing position and fired her first torpedoes of the war 'in anger'. The U-boat was sighted at 1510 and both bow tubes were fired 6 minutes later. Both missed. One torpedo passed astern and the other broke surface and appeared to pass underneath the enemy boat, aft.

At 0725 next morning came another encounter with a U-boat. She was observed coming to the surface astern of *E 31* which was herself on the surface. Lt-Cdr Feilman immediately dived the boat to make an attack but his adversary had obviously only been taking a quick 'breather' or else he was suspicious, because he dived while *E 31* was manoeuvring for a torpedo shot.

At 1140 that morning two torpedo boats were sighted proceeding northwards. An attack started but was broken off when they were identified as Dutch (*Ophir* class). *E 31* returned to tie up alongside *Forth* at 0915 on 14 November and half the crew were given leave in the usual way.

A couple of days were spent in the floating dock and no further operational patrols carried out until early December. In the meantime there were exercise attacks. On 1 December a party of MPs were taken on board for a demonstration dive off *Forth*. Nothing too risky!

On 6 December *E 31* began her 12th war patrol, casting off from *Forth* at 1115 and arriving on station at 0500 next morning. At 1645 another submarine was sighted which, on being challenged, proved to be *E 56* (Lt-Cdr C L Dering). The next five days were devoid of incident until at 1130 on 12 December, an explosion was heard while *E 31* was submerged. Ten minutes later a submarine was sighted on the surface to the northward, but proceeding away from *E 31*. After failing to get into a suitable position for a submerged attack, *E 31* was brought to the surface for a gun action, but the enemy was having none of it and quickly submerged. (Position 54°24′N 3°30′E.) This was the last incident of 1916, although the return to Harwich on 14 December was made in dense fog, going slow ahead and sounding the foghorn continually.

The starboard watch enjoyed 4 days leave prior to Christmas and the boat had a brief visit to the floating dock again before spending the rest of the Christmas period alongside *Maidstone*.

1917 – A CHANGE IN COMMAND

The morning of New Year's Day 1917 found *E 31* doing attack exercises and Lt-Cdr Feilman promoted to Commander, but it was not until 10 January that she next went to sea for an operational patrol. Casting off from *Pandora* at 0740 she followed some minesweepers out from Harwich. Her billet was in position 54°50′N 40°25′E, reached on 11 January. The patrol was noted only for the very stormy weather including snow squalls. A noon sight was possible on only one day out of 8 at sea. She returned to *Pandora* on 18 January. Half the crew were given four days leave the next day and Commander Feilman left the boat early in February being relieved by Lt R W Blacklock on 5 February.

Commander Feilman was appointed as CO of *K 14*, one of the large steam-driven Fleet submarines. He replaced Commander Goodhart who had been lost in the accident involving *K 13* on 29 January when she had been carrying out trials in the Gareloch. Goodhart had been aboard *K 13* for experience before taking over *K 14* which was completing at Fairfields.

After a day in the floating dock for a checkover there followed a week spent exercising the crew in attack drill or doing various maintenance jobs.

On 7 February *E 31* moved across to the Shotley Pier – a place of earlier memories for many of the crew, no doubt, with the masthead of HMS *Ganges* shore establishment for boys training clearly visible across at the Parkeston Quay where the depot ships lay. The old ironclad cruiser *Minotaur* was moored off Shotley jetty having been renamed *Ganges* when the original old 'wooden wall' was towed away. *E 31*'s log described her being alongside Shotley Pier for experimental purposes. This did not take too long as she returned alongside *Maidstone* at 1330.

On 13 February *E 31* slipped from *Pandora* at 0740 for her 14th war patrol and her first under Lt Blacklock's command. Minesweepers preceded her, and she reached her appointed station at 1405 that afternoon, in position 52°16′N 2°13′E. Later that night she shifted to another pre-arranged billet and came to the surface at 0545 to keep a lookout by moonlight. However, the weather was overcast so *E 31* dived again 25 minutes later.

The following two mornings saw her keeping a look out surfaced in the moonlight around 0500. Dense fog prevented the same procedure on 18 February but she was there again the next morning. At 0545 she surfaced but was quickly submerged again 5 minutes later when an unidentified vessel was seen approaching. *E 31* went to the bottom and kept a listening watch on the hydrophones as the surface ship was heard passing backwards and forwards overhead. Next day two Dutch destroyers were seen exercising off Texel Island; 21 February was a day of dense fog and on the 22nd *E 31* returned to base. Half the crew were given the customary 4 days leave. On their return, the crew kept in trim with the usual exercise attacks.

On 4 March *E 31* cast off from *Maidstone* for her 15th patrol at 0730. This was a short 5-day patrol, the only incident being the sighting of another submarine the first afternoon. Apart from that the weather was stormy with gales, heavy seas and snow. Parkeston Quay was no doubt a welcome sight at 1500 on the afternoon of 9 March.

REFIT

A lengthy period for maintenance and refitting now followed. On 11 March *E 31* sailed for Chatham, escorting *C 22* (Lt O North) also going for a refit. During this period, all the crew were given 10 days leave. A Poulsen Arc wireless transmitter was fitted to replace the Spark transmitter as the main set, and the 12pdr gun was removed from fore to aft. The wireless office, or silent cabinet as it was also known, was very small in 'E' boats, being about 4 feet square, on the port side. In *E 31* it was situated just aft of the beam torpedo tubes. Some of the 'E' class had one of their amidships torpedo tubes removed in order to facilitate the fitting of Poulsen Arc equipment which gave a much longer range than the Type 10 Spark transmitter. There was just room for one operator to sit at the operating position. The aerial was led away up to the deck tube (on the starboard side of the casing) extending to the height of the guardrail stanchions. Apart from the main wireless aerial which was carried between 2 masts laid horizontally alongside the port side when not in use, 'E' boats also had a portable mast at the after end of the bridge. It was made up of 2 or 3 sections, and the top of the mast when housed was just below the level of the periscope brackets. The aerial itself was led from the top of the mast to eyeplates or tripods, forward and aft, on the casing. Kite aerials were also used – usually in the form of box kites, flown from the bridge to enable longer range of transmission and reception to be achieved. Operational orders for Harwich submarines sometimes contained instructions for the use of kites in order to communicate with the Admiralty station at Grimsby. *E 53* made a particular mention of the successful use of her kite aerial when on patrol in March 1918.

RETURN TO THE NORTH SEA

Working-up attack exercises followed on 11 and 15 May and on the 16th *E 31* returned to the war. She cast off from *Pandora* at 0410, to go back to the North Sea.

At 0730 on 17 May, while on the surface, a U-boat was sighted. Lt Blacklock immediately took *E 31* down to periscope depth, altered course 195° and brought the bow tubes to standby. However, 5 minutes later it was clear the U-boat was fast moving out of range and was already an estimated 4 miles distant. *E 31* therefore continued on her way to her billet in position 53°55′N 4°00′E, which she reached at 1600. The only incident noted over the next four days was unidentified sound signalling picked up on the hydrophones while submerged. On 22 May the sea was too rough to remain at periscope depth (22ft). On 23 May two Zeppelins were sighted at 1815 while *E 31* was on the surface. Lt Blacklock decided to dive the boat but remained just below periscope depth. He surfaced at 1900 – only to find a Zeppelin right overhead. This time *E 31* went to the bottom of the North Sea and stayed there for the next two hours.

The fore ends of *E 31*. From the amount of loose equipment and rag lying about in this and subsequent internal photographs it must be presumed that they were taken while *E 31* was undergoing a refit.

HMS *Dolphin*

She returned to Harwich the next day. On 25 May half the crew were given four days leave. Gun trials took place on 30 May, with a day on exercise attacks on 1 June and 7 June when she joined *E 4*, (Lt-Cdr J D Gaimes) now salvaged and refitted after the tragedy of the previous August. On 12 June whilst exercising with the destroyer *Firedrake*, *E 31* was recalled from sea and given orders to proceed on patrol at 1330. She tied up alongside *Pandora* at noon and rapidly took on torpedoes and other stores from *Maidstone*.

E 31 was under way at 1355 and on billet at 0215 on 13 June in position 53°15'N 4°05'E. The patrol was relatively devoid of incident. Apart from some fog the weather was fine and calm except for the evening of the 18th when heavy rain was encountered.

Numerous Dutch fishing vessels were sighted and at 2115 on 14 June, a suspicious vessel caused the torpedo tubes to be brought to standby. By 2207 the vessel had been proved to be friendly. On 20 June *E 31* returned to *Maidstone* at midday and half the crew were given four days leave from the 21st.

Due to a leak from Z tank into the battery tank, *E 31* spent three weeks in the hands of Dockyard and *Maidstone* staff. The batteries were taken out and placed on the quayside and the battery tank rerivetted, cleaned and caulked with rosbonite. All the battery cells were then replaced.

On 15 July *E 31* had a trial run to the exercising grounds to trim the boat. The next day was occupied with an exercise attacking *Firedrake*. Sailing was cancelled on 19 July due to bad weather but on 20 July *E 31* commenced her 18th war patrol casting off from *Maidstone* at 0900 and proceeding in company with *E 47* (Lt E C Carre). It was an uneventful patrol and *E 31* was back alongside *Maidstone* on 28 July at 0600. Half the crew were given four days leave. On 2 August a diver reported that one of the propellers was chipped on all

blades. *E 31* went into the floating dock for a replacement propeller to be fitted, which was done the same day.

GERMAN SWEPT-CHANNEL ENTRANCE DISCOVERED

E 31's next operational patrol took place from 7-15 August. Lt Blacklock's operational orders instructed him to cruise until darkness fell, close to the Texel shoals. *E 42* (Lt C H Allen), *E 41* (Lt-Cdr N Holbrook, VC) and *E 45* (Lt-Cdr G S Watkins, DSO), together with a submarine from Yarmouth, would also be on patrol in the area. Warning was given that a minefield was to be laid on the night of 12 August to the southeast of *E 45*'s area. *E 31* was to endeavour to attack a patrol vessel before that date, which was thought to be operating in the vicinity of 54°5'N 5°1'E.

Leaving *Maidstone* at noon on 7 August, *E 31* was on billet at 0100 next morning. Her log records she commenced a submerged patrol close to the Texel buoys at 0323. At 0920, a suspicious vessel was sighted and the torpedo tubes brought to standby. At 1020 he proved to be a neutral. The same thing occurred at 1620 and again it was a neutral.

E 31 transferred to a new billet on 9 August but ran into a SW gale. The sea was too heavy for a periscope depth patrol, so Lt Blacklock decided to remain at 60ft and surface every hour for a brief look round the horizon.

On 10 August at 0500 a spar buoy was sighted and this was thought to indicate the Borkum swept-channel. At 1130 German minesweepers were sighted to the southward and 4 explosions were heard. This was to be a long day submerged as *E 31* made her way carefully round the edge of the German minefields to ascertain the correct position of the entrance to the swept channel. Diving at 0315 she surfaced at 2000 – nearly 17 hours later.

The next day, at 0930, 14 German M-class minesweepers were observed sweeping in the vicinity of 53°56'N 5°00'E. Lt Blacklock decided they should not be allowed to proceed about their business undisturbed and prepared to attack. However, an explosion shook the boat considerably and the sound of several more mines exploding persuaded him that manoeuvering too close to the edge of a British minefield (W3 on Admiralty charts) did not recommend itself and he therefore abandoned the idea and, as he put it, 'hauled out'. Mine explosions were heard throughout the day, 30 being counted.

E 31 moved to a new billet on 12 August, arriving on station at 0200. The new minefield (W9) was to be laid that night but the operation was cancelled. *E 31* failed to receive the relevant signal that the operation was to be postponed for three days, so she spent a quiet day waiting while no British minelaying force arrived.

On the evening of 13 August another 8 explosions were heard some distance away, so obviously sweeping operations were still going on. The signal which *E 31* had missed, was sent by the 'I' method – whereby one shore station transmitted a signal ostensibly addressed to another shore station but the text being intended for a

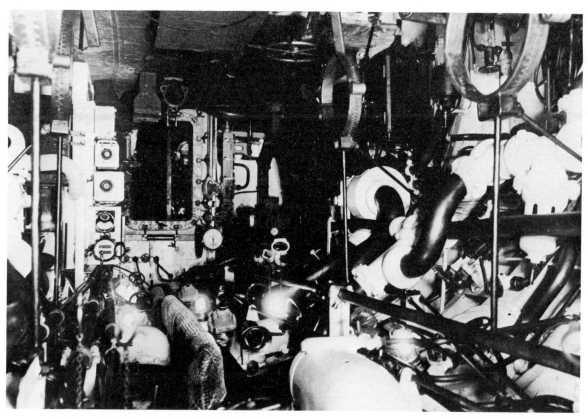

The beam torpedo space, looking aft. The wireless office is to starboard.

HMS *Dolphin*

third party listening but not transmitting. Thus the presence of the third party is not revealed to the enemy. *E 31* had to maintain strict W/T silence lest German direction finding equipment should be able to pinpoint her position.

The next day, the starboard engine suffered a broken No 6 cylinder. This was scheduled as her last day on patrol so she therefore returned to Harwich, albeit limping. A German UC boat was sighted on the surface at 1754 on 15 August but she dived immediately and no attack was possible. By 2200 that night *E 31* was secured alongside *Pandora*.

Blacklock immediately made his report and it was clear that *E 31* had found the correct location where the German swept-channels through their minefields came to an end. There were buoys at 54°05′N 5°30′E as well as in positions about five miles to the south and east.

That same night, the British minelaying force went out to put down 1000 mines about ten miles to the west of the end of the swept channel reported by Lt Blacklock. The new field was designated Field 56.

There was an interesting consequence of this patrol by *E 31*. At least two U-boats were sunk in the new minefield laid the night *E 31* returned. One was *U 50* on 31 August and the other was *U 88* on 5 September. *U 88* was commanded by Walther Schweiger, the man who sank the *Lusitania* when in command of *U 20* in May 1915.

The reconnaissance by *E 31* had obviously been a skilful and dangerous operation by her commanding officer. The mine was a major hazard to submarines in 1914-18 and 13 British submarines are believed to have been sunk by mines in the Heligoland Bight alone.

In World War II submarines were equipped with a sonar system that detected moored mines when the boat was submerged. World War I submariners had no such aid. They just had the sound of the mine mooring cable rubbing down the outside of the hull. The tension inside *E 31* when manoeuvring within, and on the edge of, the British minefields being swept by the Germans and then the German minefields whilst ascertaining the precise position of the swept channel, must have been acute. There is no indication of the drama in the brief notes in the log – but when Ordinary Telegraphist Head went home on leave at the end of that trip, his father heard him talking in his sleep, and found him counting – counting the mine explosions.

To be continued

book review

SEEK & STRIKE
Sonar and the Royal Navy 1914-1954
by Willem Hackmann
Published by HMSO Books 29 November 1984
487pp (25cm × 15cm), 77 illustrations, 27 tables,
appendices, index.
ISBN 0 11 2904238 (£15.95)

Willem Hackmann has earned himself the gratitude of
all naval historians. This book is a magnificent
achievement, combining a wealth of primary research
in the archives of Britain and the United States with a
lucid analysis that can be followed by those not expert
in acoustics and electronics. No subsequent study of
submarine, destroyer or escort design will now be complete without making the fullest use of this pioneering
study.

Starting with attempts to transmit signals to the early
submarines, and then to locate icebergs in the wake of
the *Titanic* disaster Dr Hackmann takes a firm grip on
the astonishingly diverse history of both passive hydrophone and active sonar equipment. The cut off date
of this work relates to the introduction of the nuclear
submarine and the still secret nature of the basic
research undertaken thereafter. He demonstrates how
the Royal Navy maintained itself in the position of the
leading anti-submarine force by designing a complete
weapons package, rather than merely improving sonar

equipment. For example the ahead-thrown weapons
Hedgehog and Squid were introduced to allow the
escort vessel to maintain sonar contact with a submarine while attacking, something that had been
impossible while the astern-launched depth charge
remained the only effective weapon. Dr Hackmann has
little to say about the influence of sonar on ship design;
but he has a great deal to say about the effect of warship characteristics on sonar design. This accurately
reflects the priorities of the interwar period, when the
constructor severely limited the size of any hole in the
keel for sonar fittings.

On the theme of passive hydrophones this book illustrates the astonishing performance of those developed
by the Germans before World War II for use in U-boats
and surface ships. The set in the cruiser *Prinz Eugen*
apparently provided an accurate range and bearing for
HMS *Hood* before any other form of contact was established on 24 May 1941.

The wider theme of the increasing importance of sci-
entific research is ably carried through the book, and
lifts it above the dry and overly factual account that
could have been produced. Occasionally it becomes
obvious that this book is the work of a technological
historian and not a naval writer. However, it would be
churlish in the extreme to complain of this, instead we
should be grateful for this enlightening book.

Andrew Lambert

As&As

GRAF ZEPPELIN PART 1 (*Warship* 31, p154) from Günter Ulbrich, Kiefernweg 4, W Germany.

In the above cited article, the author states, that only the USA had 8in (203mm) guns in aircraft carriers. However, this is not quite true. For 8in mountings were not only shipped by *Lexington* and *Saratoga* but also by the Japanese carriers *Akagi* and *Kaga*. From completion in 1927 and 1928 respectively, both ships were equipped with ten 8in guns *vice* eight in the US carriers. Four guns were mounted in twin turrets at the fore end of the No 2 flight deck and six were mounted aft in hull casements. During the modernisation of *Kaga* from 1934 to 1936 the turrets were removed and four guns in casemates added. *Akagi* lost her turrets in the modernisation from 1936 to 1938 and retained only the casemate guns. With this main armament both ships served for the rest of their careers until their loss in the Battle of Midway.

ARETHUSA CLASS CRUISERS PART 2 (*Warship* 32. Photograph of HMS *Galatea*, p263) from Lt-Cdr John M Maber, RN (Retd) Corsham, Wilts

I fear that the flags flown in the photograph of HMS *Galatea* have little to do with White Russians. British warships used to fly a Red Ensign over International Code flag M (a white St Andrew's cross on a blue field) when entering and leaving naval ports where the channel was restricted. This is confirmed in *Flags for Ship Modellers and Marine Artists* by Alec A Purves (new impression by Conway Maritime Press, 1983), page 34. In any case the Imperial Russian ensign was the reverse of code flag M, ie a blue saltire on a white field.[*This was a piece of risky captioning prompted by the fact that* Galatea *had served in the Black Sea since November 1918 with the White Russians. She then sailed for the Baltic with General Gough joining Admiral Sir Walter Cowan's squadron in May 1919 but after his 17 May (not 30 March as stated in the text on p264) action (covering Estonian landings) off Seskar Island to the Kronstadt approaches with the Bolshevik destroyer* Gavriil *and 4 minesweepers.*
Randal Gray]

D M Milligan of Penrith, Cornwall made the same correction adding that this particular signal was changed *c*1938 to code flag M over the Pilot Jack.

AUSTRALIA TO MAKE IMPORTANT NAVAL HISTORICAL FILM

The Ministry of Defence (UK) has given approval to an Australian Company to dive and film the wrecks of HMS *Repulse* and HMS *Prince of Wales* as part of a documentary to be made on the history of these ships. The expedition to the South China Sea will be made in May 1985 and the Australian release of the film should coincide with the RAN 75th Anniversary in 1986.

To those who served in these two ships at any time and in the escorts of Force Z-HMAS *Vampire*, HMS *Electra*, HMS *Express* and HMS *Tenedos*. *CAN YOU HELP?*

Personal recollections and photographs of the ships and of their final action on 10 December 1941 are needed. Also accounts from those serving in Singapore at the time.

Please write to Commander Gordon Dalrymple, PO Box 139, Collaroy Beach, NSW 2097.

Naval Books

Conway Maritime offer an unrivalled range of authoritative and well-illustrated titles on naval subjects. A free catalogue is available, but some of the leading titles are listed below:

US NAVAL WEAPONS
by Norman Friedman
This exhaustive study by an acknowledged expert on the subject discusses the development and function of every weapon system employed by the US Navy from the birth of the 'New Navy' in 1883 to the present day.
12¼" x 8½", 288 pages, 200 photos, 150 line drawings. ISBN 0 85177 240 4. £18.00 (plus £1.80 p + p)

NAVAL RADAR*
by Norman Friedman
A layman's guide to the theory, functions and performance of seaborne radar systems, from their introduction just before the Second World War to the present day, including a catalogue of every major piece of radar equipment to have seen service with the world's navies.
11" x 8½", 240 pages, 200 photos, 100 line drawings. ISBN 0 85177 238 2. £18.00 (plus £1.80 p + p)

CARRIER AIR POWER
by Norman Friedman
A penetrating analysis of how carrier warfare operates, with extensive data on the ships and their aircraft.
12" x 9", 192 pages, 187 photos, 32 line drawings. ISBN 0 85177 216 1. £12.50 net (plus £2.00 p + p)

ANATOMY OF THE SHIP: THE BATTLECRUISER HOOD*
by John Roberts
The first volume of this new series. Every aspect of the *Hood* is covered in a degree of detail never previously attempted for a recent capital ship, and the standard of line drawings has been highly praised.
9½" x 10" landscape, 128 pages, 24 photos, 320 line drawings. ISBN 0 85177 250 1. £8.50 (plus £1.50 p + p)

ANATOMY OF THE SHIP: THE AIRCRAFT CARRIER INTREPID
by John Roberts
The second in this new series, this volume covers the *Essex* class aircraft carrier which is now being refurbished in New York as a floating Air-Sea-Space museum.
9½" x 10" landscape, 96 pages, 20 photos, 300-line drawings. ISBN 0 85177 251 X. £8.50 (plus £1.50 p + p)

CAMERA AT SEA 1939-1945*
edited by the staff of *Warship*
"A unique collection of some of the best photographs of World War II at sea" – *Sea Power*
12¼" x 8½", 192 pages, 250 photos, 24 colour plates. ISBN 0 85177 124 6. £12.00 (plus £1.50 p + p)

SUBMARINE BOATS
The Beginnings of Underwater Warfare
by Richard Compton-Hall
"Cdr. Compton-Hall has produced a book whose research and many rare photographs and drawings will delight both the technically-minded and the general reader." — *Daily Telegraph*
9½" x 7¼", 192 pages, 173 photos and drawings. ISBN 85177 288 9. £10.50 (plus £1.55 p + p)

CONWAY'S ALL THE WORLD'S FIGHTING SHIPS 1922-1946
The second in this highly acclaimed series, the 1922-1946 volume covers all significant warships built between the Washington Treaty and the end of the wartime construction programmes. With over 1000 illustrations, it is the ultimate reference book on the navies of World War II.
12¼" x 8½", 464 pages, 506 photos, 530 line drawings. ISBN 0 85177 146 7. £30.00 (plus £2.00 p + p)

CONWAY'S ALL THE WORLD'S FIGHTING SHIPS 1860-1905
The first complete listing of all warships between the first ironclad and the *Dreadnought*. "... must rank with the all-time great naval reference works..." – *The Navy*. "... all the thoroughness and attention to detail we have come to expect from Conway Maritime ... excellent value". – *Ships Monthly*
12¼" x 8½", 448 pages, 471 photos, 506 line drawings. ISBN 0 85177 133 5. £24.00 (plus £2.00 p + p)

A CENTURY OF NAVAL CONSTRUCTION: The History of the Royal Corps of Naval Constructors
by D K Brown R C N C
This behind-the-scenes history of the Royal Navy's designers offers a new insight into the factors governing British warship design from the nineteenth century to the Falklands conflict.
9½" x 6", 384 pages, 92 photos, 20 line drawings. ISBN 0 85177 282 X. £20.00 (plus £1.00 p + p)

DESTROYER WEAPONS OF WORLD WAR 2*
by Peter Hodges and Norman Friedman
A detailed comparison between British and US destroyer weapons, including mountings, directors and electronics. "... one of the greatest possible additions to the ... range of naval books..." – *The Navy*
9½" x 7¼", 192 pages, 150 photos, 73 line drawings. ISBN 0 85177 137 8. £7.50 (plus £1.25 p + p)

BATTLESHIP DESIGN AND DEVELOPMENT 1905-1945
by Norman Friedman
The first layman's guide to the design process and the factors governing the development of capital ships. "... an eye-opening study of an extremely complex business..." – *Nautical Magazine*.
10" x 8", 176 pages, 200 photos, plans and line drawings. ISBN 0 85177 135 1. £8.50 (plus £1.25 p + p)

MODERN WARSHIP DESIGN AND DEVELOPMENT
by Norman Friedman
"... never before have the problems and parameters of modern warship design been set out so comprehensively, informatively and clearly ... the book should be read by everyone with a concern for the modern naval scene, professional or amateur, uniformed or civilian." – *Journal of the Royal United Services Institute*
10" x 8", 192 pages, 167 photos, 65 line drawings. ISBN 0 85177 147 5. £9.50 (plus £1.25 p + p)

AIRCRAFT CARRIERS OF THE US NAVY
by Stefan Terzibaschitsch
"... a definitive history of the US carrier fleet from 1920 until the present day..." – *Journal of the Institute of Marine Engineers*
11¾" x 8¼", 320 pages, 322 photos, 94 plans and line drawings. ISBN 0 85177 159 9. £15.00 (plus £1.50 p + p)

*These titles are available in North America from the Naval Institute Press, Annapolis, Md 21402.

from your Local Bookseller or by post from
Conway Maritime Press Limited
24 Bride Lane, Fleet Street, London EC4Y 8DR
(when ordering direct please add the posting and packing charge noted after the price)

CONWAY MARITIME PRESS

editorial

Overhead view of the new 'Duke' class Type 23 frigate HMS *Norfolk*.

MoD

This issue features two major articles on the hitherto little studied area of the first postwar generation of surface combat ships. These have now almost all ended their effective lives, at least in the hands of their original constructors. This opens up two new areas of enquiry: firstly, as John Jordan demonstrates in his article on the French *Surcouf* class destroyers, comes the question of the role these ships were designed to fulfill, the degree to which the lessons of World War II had been assimilated and how these new designs stood up to the test of time.

The rising cost of naval armaments ensured that many of these ships remained in service, after having their weapons and sensors updated, to the end of their economic lives. This will be the case with the last few ships of the *Surcouf* class. The Canadian *Mackenzie* type firgates appear, in Thomas G Lynch's article on the problems of finding a successor, to have been expected to soldier on well beyond this limit. This article highlights the second area of interest, the whole issue of continuity in design and construction policy and the alternative policies of rebuild or replace. The French and Canadian policies stand in direct contrast to that of Holland. Faced with the block obsolescence of their entire navy the Dutch sold two cruisers and seven destroyers to Peru in the early 1970s. Only one of these ships, the cruiser *De Zeven Provincien,* had been subjected to a major rebuild. This fleet was then replaced by one based around the two *Tromp* class guided missile destroyers and thirteen *Standard* frigates.

In recent years the Royal Navy has tended to follow the Dutch practice. Perhaps the lessons learnt trying to keep the old *Ark Royal* at sea, the highly uneconomic careers of the *Tiger* class cruisers and the reconstruction of the *Victorious* provided some inspiration here. Consequently a number of relatively modern units have been sold abroad to make way for more capable types, or just to make some money out of them with no hope for replacement, long before their economic careers were over. The 'County' class guided missile destroyers are the best example. These large ships were blessed with a missile system that was never effective. To retain any combat value they required a major rebuild.

The Canadian Patrol Frigate controversy emphasises the problem of preparing new generations of warships. Cost is now the major factor, ships are designed to meet financial limits, and often cut down to the detriment of their military capability. The Type 42 destroyers were a good example of this. On the other hand once the function of any new ship is determined the increased availability of surface to surface missiles and advanced point defence systems has tended to increase the size and cost of every new design. Even such projects as the Type 23, intended to be an 'austere' cost limited design, has now become so capable that it approaches the specification of the 'luxury' Type 22. The only significant differences that now remain are the alternative sonar and extra helicopter of the Type 22.

Andrew Lambert

Surcouf

The French Postwar Destroyers

Part I by John Jordan

THE POSTWAR ESCORTEURS d'ESCADRE

Designed in the immediate postwar period and completed during the 1950s, the 18 ships of the T47, T53 and T56 types have served throughout the past three decades, during which time they have constituted the nucleus of the French surface fleet. As with the *Leander* class frigates of the Royal Navy, a number of ships of the class have undergone major reconstruction to enable them to keep pace with the rapid developments in naval technology which have taken place during the period. A study of the class from its origins through the various modifications therefore gives a valuable insight not only into the development of French weapon and sensor technology since the war, but also into the important changes in French tactical thinking which have prompted these modifications.

THE FRENCH NAVY POSTWAR

Although France was technically among the victors in 1945, the state of her navy was more akin to that of one of the defeated Axis powers. Her territory had been occupied for five years, during which time ship design and construction had all but ceased, and the pride of the Marine Nationale, the *Force de Raid,* had been scuttled at Toulon (November 1942). It was therefore to be expected that the designs for new ships in the immediate postwar period would be based largely on the types under construction or projected when France capitulated in June 1940. The suggestion, however, which has appeared in a number of sources that the T47 design was derived from that of the 'super-destroyers' *Volta* and *Mogador* is almost certainly wide of the mark. For in spite of superficial similarities between the two classes, the adoption of the T47 design as the standard French postwar destroyer in effect marks the abandonment of the *contre-torpilleur* as a type.

THE DEMISE OF THE CONTRE-TORPILLEUR

The *contre-torpilleur* of the interwar period was designed for surface warfare in the Mediterranean. It was envisaged that the *contre-torpilleurs,* operating in homogeneous divisions of three ships, would act independently or semi-independently of the major surface units, employing their heavy guns and torpedo armament in lightning strikes on enemy shipping and shore installations, and relying on their exceptionally high speed for protection. Since Italy was the projected 'enemy', range was a relatively minor consideration.

Even at cruising speed, endurance was generally calculated on the principle that it should be adequate only for transit to the ports of French North Africa.

These calculations, and consequently the very *raison d'être* of the *contre-torpilleur* as a type, were seriously undermined by Italy's late entry into the Second World War. The Marine Nationale was, in the event, presented with a few opportunities to use these ships in the manner intended. They were employed instead on long-range patrol and escort work in the Atlantic, tasks for which they were fundamentally unsuited. Their fuel consumption was heavy, their bunkerage too small, and there were frequent breakdowns in their high-performance guns and machinery.

The Marine Nationale of 1945 was quick to accept that its prewar operational concepts had been invalidated by wartime developments, and immediately set about rebuilding its once-great fleet around the aircraft-carrier. Two such vessels, *Dixmude* (ex-HMS *Biter)* and *Arromanches* (ex-HMS *Colossus)* were transferred from Britain in 1945 and 1946 respectively, and in August 1947 parliamentary approval was given to an 18,500-ton carrier of French design, the PA28. This ship attracted considerable opposition from the Air Force and, in a climate of financial stringency, was duly cancelled in 1950. The requirements, however, of operations in French Indo-China led to the acquisition on loan of two US Navy carriers of the *Cowpens* class in 1951 and 1953 respectively, while at the same time work proceeded on a more advanced home-grown design, culminating in orders for the two carriers of the PA54 (*Clemenceau*) type in 1954–55.

THE T47 DESIGN

The new tactical organisation established a requirement for a destroyer-sized escort capable of operating at fleet speed, with the task of protecting a carrier task force against hostile aircraft and submarines. This requirement was, in fact, closer to that which spawned the *torpilleurs* of the *Le Hardi* class of the late 1930s than it was to the tactical concepts which inspired the *contre-torpilleurs. The Le Hardi* class had been designed as escorts for the fast battleships of the *Dunkerque* and *Richelieu* classes, and as the maritime tactics of the period took little account of the potential of naval aviation, their main armament was naturally designed for anti-surface warfare, with low-angle guns and "long" anti-ship torpedoes. Nevertheless, there are a number of important similarities between the ill-fated *Le Hardi* class and the T47 which suggest that it was this type, rather than the late *contre-torpilleurs*, which formed the basis of the postwar design.

The *Le Hardi* class differed radically from their predecessors that standard '1500 tonnes' destroyers of the 1920s, in that they were given an adequate margin of speed to enable them to accompany the new battleships even in adverse weather conditions. They were therefore designated *torpilleurs d'escadre* (ie *fleet* torpedo boats). The postwar requirement was also for a *torpilleur* (hence the 'T' in T47), and although the type designation of these vessels underwent a succession of changes

Chevalier Paul 7 June 1957, emphasising the size of the 5in and 57mm gunhouses.
L & L van Ginderen

Guépratte 20 October 1961, showing the deck layout aft.
L & L van Ginderen

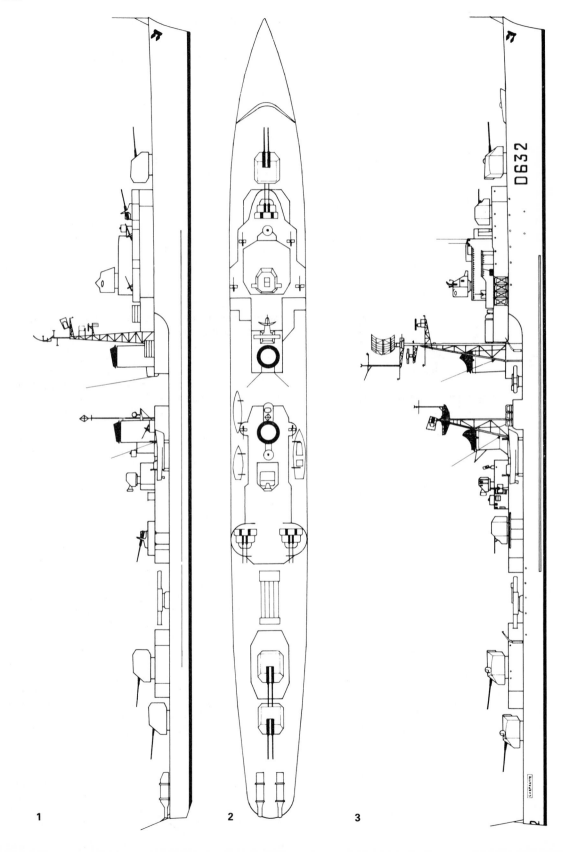

1   2   3

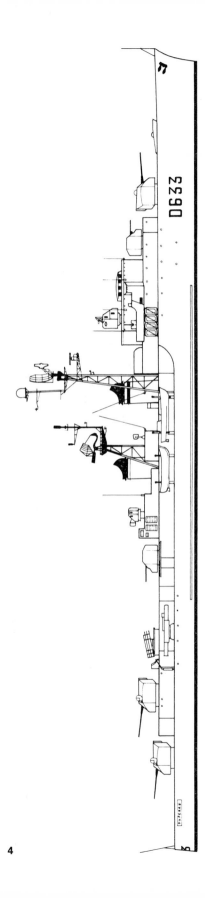

1 Profile of the T47, based on the official drawing of 1951.
Drawn by the author

2 Overhead view of the T47, also from the official drawing of 1951.
Drawn by the author

3 *Guépratte* in 1959. Comparison with the original outline given in the drawings illustrates the significant increase in top hamper.
Drawn by the author

4 *Duperre* in 1964, a member of the modified T53 subgroup.
Drawn by the author

during the early 1950s, when the first ships of the *Surcouf* class were under construction, the designation finally adopted in 1955, *escorteur d'escadre* (fleet escort), is strongly reminiscent of that applied to the prewar type.

Also reminiscent of the *Le Hardi* class was the layout of the main armament. Both types had their major calibre guns in three twin enclosed mountings, one mounting being located forward and two aft. The guns of the *Le Hardi* were 130mm (5.1in) calibre weapons, whereas the *contre-torpilleurs* mounted 138.6mm (5.5in) guns. The 127mm (5in) calibre selected for the T47 is therefore closer to that of the prewar *torpilleurs*. Moreover, a modified *Le Hardi* design under consideration by the French Naval Staff in 1938 would have had the low-angle 130mm Model 1930 replaced by a new dual-purpose gun of the same calibre to provide more effective anti-aircraft protection for the battleships. In the event it proved impossible to proceed with this design owing the the outbreak of war and the subsequent military crisis, but as this was one of the major designs on the drawing board when France capitulated there can be no doubt that it influenced the design of the T47 (see table).

The hull selected for the T47 was substantially larger than that of the *torpilleurs d'escadre,* but smaller than that of the later *contre-torpilleurs.* The increase in size was largely related to the lessons learned by the French Navy in the course of wartime operations. The major weaknesses of the *torpilleurs* and *contre-torpilleurs* designed in the 1930s were found to be:
   – poor endurance in ocean operations
   – the weakness of their close-range AA batteries
   – the fragility of their machinery and artillery (the result of over-emphasis on high performance).

In the T47 the emphasis was shifted away from high performance and onto staying power. Bunkerage was increased considerably over that of the prewar designs, endurance at the cruise speed of 18kt rising to 5,000nm, as comparted with only 4,000nm for *Volta* and *Mogador,* and about 3,500nm for the *Le Hardi* class. A powerful secondary battery of three twin 57mm AA mountings was adopted – a factor which was largely responsible for the increase in length over the prewar *torpilleurs*. However, in spite of the increase in hull dimensions and displacement, installed horsepower was

TABLE 1: A COMPARISON BETWEEN THE POSTWAR T47 AND THE PREWAR MOGADOR AND LE HARDI

The figures in brackets for the *Le Hardi* type relate to the proposed AAW modification, which undoubtedly influenced the design of the T47.

Class	MOGADOR	LE HARDI	T47
Displacement (tons)	2,884 (st)	1,772 (2,215)	2,750
	4,018 (fl)	2,557 (2,929)	3,740
Length (metres)	137.5 (oa)	117.2 (118.8)	128.6
	131 (pp)	111.6	124.5
Beam (metres)	12.67 (max.)	11.1 (12.7)	12.7
Draught (metres)	4.57	4.2	5.4
Freeboard (metres)	3.7	3.11	3.75
Turbines	2 sets Rateau	2 sets Rateau/Parsons	2 sets Rateau
Boilers	4 Indret 35kg/cm²	4 Sural Penhöet 35kg/cm²	4 ACB-Indret 35kg/cm²
	385° superheat	358° superheat	385° superheat
Horsepower (shp)	92,000 (normal)	58,000 (62,000)	63,000
	105,000 (max.)	66,000	
Speed (knots)	39 (designed)	38	34
Oil Fuel (tons)	709	470	800
Endurance	4,000 at 18kt		5,000nm at 18kt
	3,000nm at 20kt	2,760nm at 20kt	
Complement	14 officers	10 officers	19 officers
	228 men	177 men	328 men
Armament	4 × 2 138.6mm Mod 34	3 × 2 130mm Mod 30	3 × 2 127mm Mod 48
		(3 × 2 130mm CA)	
	2 × 2 37mm Mod 33	2 × 1 37mm Mod 33	3 × 2 57mm Mod 51
	2 × 2 13.2mm Mod 29	2 × 2 13.2mm Mod 29	4 × 1 20mm
	2 × 3m 2 × 2 550mm	1 × 3, 2 × 2 550mm	2 × 3 long 550mm
			2 × 3 short 550mm
	2 × 8 200kg DC	1 × 8 200kg DC	

little higher than that of the *Le Hardi* class, and was only two thirds that of *Mogador*. The designed speed of 34 knots was still high by the standards of other navies, but was regarded by the French as only just adequate if the ships were to accompany major surface units – the later *contre-torpilleurs*, which were intended to operate independently, were designed to go into action at speeds of 36–39 knots, and achieved even higher figures on trials.

MAIN ARMAMENT

The 127mm mounting developed for the T47 was of a completely new design. The only French dual-purpose mounting of the prewar period had been the 130mm Model 1935 which made up the secondary battery of the battleships *Dunkerque* and *Strasbourg*. This weapon, which was mounted in twin and quadruple turrets, was not a great success, and the twin D-P mountings of the same calibre envisaged for the improved *Le Hardi* type were to have been of a new model. In the postwar period the Marine Nationale had few surviving destroyers armed with the 130mm gun, and these were elderly vessels which would soon be discarded. There was therefore no compelling reason to perpetuate this calibre, and for the T47 design the French adopted the equivalent US Navy calibre (5in/127mm) to enable the ships to use American munitions. As well as presenting an early example of the sort of standardisation among the western allies which would be reinforced by the creation of NATO in 1949, the decisions was undoubtedly influenced by the instant availability of well-tried 5in munitions for use against both surface and air targets, at

a time when French military research and development was hamstrung by the fragility of the country's postwar economy. The 127mm Model 1948 would become the standard major-calibre AA weapon of the Marine Nationale during the 1950s, and would be installed not only in the new fleet escorts but also in two 9,000-ton anti-aircraft cruisers, *De Grasse* and *Colbert*.

THE AA BATTERY

The medium-calibre AA battery of the T47 comprised three twin 57mm mountings, of which one was sited immediately beneath the bridge, while the other two were placed side by side abaft the second funnel. The after mountings were located well clear of the superimposed 127mm mounting and therefore enjoyed clear arcs on stern bearings.

The 57mm calibre was intermediate between the Royal Navy's 40mm and the US Navy's new 3in (76mm) gun, and was adopted by a number of other European navies during this period. The gun itself was designed and manufactured by Bofors, and entered service with the Royal Netherlands Navy in 1953 aboard the cruisers of the *De Ruyter* class, and subsequently with the Swedish Navy on the destroyers of the *Halland* class.

The enclosed mounting adopted for the Swedish and Dutch vessels was fully-automatic and radar controlled, and weighed 24 tonnes. Possibly the weight of the mounting was considered excessive by the French, as it represented 50 per cent of the weight of each of the 127mm mountings which comprised the main armament (the Swedish destroyers had only two twin 120mm mountings, with one twin 57mm superimposed above 'A' mounting). An early official drawing of the T47 class dated 1951 shows the 57mm guns in open mountings similar to those of the US Navy's 3in gun. However, a full-enclosed mounting of French design weighing 16 tonnes was finally adopted to provide better protection for the gun-crews. The French thereby avoided some of the maintenance problems experienced by other navies with their open-mounted AA guns, and the 57mm mountings were retained on the four vessels which underwent AAW conversions during the early 1960s.

The official drawing which dates from 1951 also shows six single 20mm Oerlikon guns, of which four were to be located in the bridge wings and the other two immediately abaft the second funnel. In the event the bridge structure layout was revised and only the pair of Oerlikons at the after end of the bridge wings was fitted, together with the after pair abreast the high-angle fire control director.

TORPEDOES

The 1951 drawing had the torpedo tubes in a quadruple bank located on the centre-line between the midships 57mm mountings and the after 127mm deckhouse. The tubes were of the conventional long, anti-ship type, and were of the traditional 550mm (21.7in) diameter. No attempt at standardisation with other allied navies was made in this direction, perhaps because the French retained large stocks of unused torpedoes from the pre-war era.

The primacy of the anti-aircraft role of the T47s (they were laid down as *escorteurs rapides anti-aériennes*) was apparent not only in the care and attention lavished on the gun and sensor outfit of the vessels, but also in the distinctly secondary consideration given to anti-submarine weapons in the early stages of the design. The 1951 drawing shows only twin depth-charge racks simi-lar to those of the prewar ships above the stern, while details of the class published at this time mention only that consideration was being given to other A/S weapons similar to the US Navy's Hedgehog and the Royal Navy's Squid.

In the event a completely novel solution was adopted. The centreline quadruple bank of long torpedo tubes aft was replaced by two triple mountings on either side of the upper deck (an arrangement favoured by the French in their prewar construction because of the greater possibilities for rapid engagement on fore and aft bearings). Between the two funnels two further triple mountings for 'short' anti-submarine torpedoes were installed on the deck edge, with box-shaped magazine lockers immediately abaft them each containing three reloads.

The L3 anti-submarine torpedo developed for the T47 class and for the *escorteurs* of the E50 and E52 classes was only 4.3m long, as compared with 6.7–7m for a standard anti-ship torpedo. The maximum range of the L3 was 5,500m, and its acoustic active guidance system was effective out to a distance of 600m and down to a depth of 300m, given favourable acoustic conditions. If the target was not detected within the predicted time, a pre-programmed circular or helical search pattern was followed. The L3's maximum speed of 25 knots was adequate in the immediate postwar period, when few submarines were capable of exceeding 15 knots under-water, but this 10-knot margin over diesel boats was quickly eroded with the advent of submarines with nuclear propulsion in the mid/late 1950s, and speed was increased to 35 knots in the L5 torpedo which succeeded the L3 in the 1960s.

The 550 diameter of the L3 meant that it was also compatible with the longer tubes. These, however, normally carried the heavier K2 anti-ship torpedo. Few details have been published about the K2, except that it weighed 1,100kg and was designed for employment against fast surface vessels. A maximum speed of 50 knots is reported.

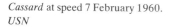

Cassard at speed 7 February 1960.
USN

TABLE 2: WEAPONS DETAILS

	127mm Mod 1948	57mm Mod 1951
Length (cals)	54	60
Elevation	+80°	−8°/+90°
Muzzle velocity (m/s)	810	865
Max range (metres)	22,000 (12nm)	13,000 (7nm)
Practical range (metres)	9,000 (air targets)	5,000 (air targets)
Projectile (kg)	32	2.96
Mounting (tons)	48	16
Rpm per barrel	15–18	60

	L3 torpedo	L4 torpedo
Length (metres)	4.3	3.13
Diameter (mm)	550	533
Weight (kg)	910	540
Warhead (kg)	200	–
Speed (knots)	25	30
Range (metres)	5,500	–
Depth (metres)	300	–
Guidance	Active acoustic (600m)	Active acoustic

RADARS AND SONARS

At the outbreak of war in 1939 no French surface ship was equipped with radar whether for surveillance or for fire control, nor were destroyers fitted with sound-ranging equipment for the detection of submarines. The installation of such devices on those vessels which served with the Allies during World War II and the acquisition of ex-British and American escort vessels in the immediate postwar period gave the French much useful experience in operating allied radar and sonar/ASDIC equipment, and encouraged an awareness of the significance of these developments. Although they benefited considerably from the transfer of American and British technology in the postwar period, the French were not content to leave the design and manufacture of such important items of equipment to their allies. The major sensors planned for the T47 class would therefore be of French design and manufacture.

The long-range air search radar developed for the T47 was the DRBV 20A, which was characterised by its distinctive antenna – a large parabolic cylinder of lattice construction with a horizontal array of dipole elements. Operating in the metric P-band, this radar does not appear to have been particularly successful, as it was quickly succeeded in French naval service by the DRBV 22, which resembled much more closely the contemporary US Navy sets.

The long-range DRBV 20A was backed up by a shorter-range dual-beam set for air and surface surveillance. The DRBV 11 was an S-band radar, with better low-level performance than the DRBV 20, and was intended to provide precision tracking and designation of air and surface targets prior to their engagement by the 127mm and 57mm guns.

The 1951 drawing shows both the DRBV 20A and the DRBV 11 mounted on a tall British-style lattice foremast. The second funnel was to have had only a short HF/DF pole mast forward of it. When completed, however, the ships were given twin tripod masts, stepped around the funnels, giving a more pleasing appearance.

The foremast carried the DRBV 20A air search antenna, and the mainmast the DRBV 11 target designation radar. There was a small DRBV 30 navigation radar on the forward side of the foremast, and a Mk 10 IFF antenna on the after side, while HF/DF aerials were shared between both masts.

Fire control arrangements also had to take wartime developments into account. The large main armament director, with its integral 5-metre stereoscopic range-finder, was essentially conservative in conception, but by the time the first ships of the class had been completed it carried a DRBC 11 fire control radar. The antenna, comprising a lattice dish reflector with a small feed horn slung beneath, was fitted on the port side of the director in most of the early vessels, but *Bouvet* had her antenna to starboard, and in the last four units *(Maillé Brézé, Du Chayla, Cassabianca* and *Guépratte)* it was mounted atop the director. The DRBC 11 operated in the S-band, and was primarily for surface engagement.

On a small deckhouse abaft the second funnel was a smaller director associated with the DRBC 31 radar. The DRBC 31 was an X-band radar for high-angle fire control, and was designed especifically to control the twin 57mm mounting. It has been retained on all vessels of the class which have kept their 57mm mountings since conversion.

For anti-submarine operations two sonars were developed. The first, the DUBV 24, was a long-range panoramic sonar for underwater surveillance. No technical details have been published, but the type number suggests operation in the medium/low-frequency band. The 5,500 maximum range of the L3 torpedo is indicative of the detection parameters of the sonar. In addition to the DUBV 24 the T47 was fitted with a DUBA 1 short-range 'searchlight' attack sonar. Operating in the high-frequency band to provide more precisely-defined target data, this sonar was housed in a retractable dome and was to be used in conjunction with close-range anti-submarine weapons.

PROPULSION

The vertical small-tube boilers adopted for the T47 series were derived from those employed in the *contre-torpilleurs* of the *Mogador* type. These had proved particularly successful in service. The rapid build-up of pressure atainable with this type of boiler enabled the *contre-torpilleurs* to increase speed from 15 knots to 35 knots in a matter of minutes, whereas a full 20 minutes would have been necessary had a boiler of classical design been employed. Natural circulation made the boilers inherently more reliable than those of the forced circulation type adopted for the *Le Hardi* class.

THE SURCOUF CLASS

Twelve ships were built to the basic T47 design. The first was ordered under the 1949 naval programme, a second the following year, then a batch of four in 1951 and six in 1952. Four shipyards participated in the construction programme, although no less than eight of the 12 ships were built by the naval dockyards of Brest and Lorient. All were completed between 1955 and 1957. There

TABLE 3: SURCOUF (T47) CLASS

Type	Programme	No	Builder	Laid down	Launched	Completed
T47A	1949	D 621 *Surcouf*	Lorient	Jul 51	3.10.53	1.11.55
	1950	D 622 *Kersaint*	Lorient	Nov 51	3.10.53	20.3.56
	1951	D 623 *Cassard*	A C Bretagne	Nov 51	12.5.53	14.4.56
	1951	D 624 *Bouvet*	Lorient	Jun 52	3.10.53	13.5.56
	1951	D 625 *Dupetit-Thouars*	Brest	Mar 52	4.2.54	15.9.56
	1951	D 626 *Chevalier Paul*	F C de la Gironde	Feb 52	28.7.53	22.12.56
T47B	1952	D 627 *Maillé Brézé*	Lorient	Oct 53	26.9.54	4.5.57
	1952	D 628 *Vauquelin*	Lorient	Mar 53	26.9.54	3.11.56
	1952	D 629 *D'Estrées*	Brest	May 53	27.11.54	19.3.57
	1952	D 630 *Du Chayla*	Brest	Jul 53	27.11.54	4.6.57
	1952	D 631 *Casabianca*	A C Bretagne	Oct 53	13.11.54	4.5.57
	1952	D 632 *Guépratte*	F C de la Gironde	Aug 53	9.11.54	6.6.57

were minor differences between the first six units ordered (Type T47A) and the final six (Type 47B). In the second sub-group the spacing of the second and third 127mm mountings was changed, and there was some revision of the ventilation trunking arrangements.

THE T53 DESIGN

Long before the first ship of the *Surcouf* class was completed, a new revised design was drawn up. The T53 incorporated a number of improvements over the T47, most of which related to the air defence mission.

Both major radars of the T47 were replaced by new models. Atop the foremast, in place of the DRBV 20A air surveillance rade, was the large distinctive aerial of the DRBI 10 three-dimensional radar. The DRBI 10 employs a Robinson feed with a broad, square lattice antenna, which produces a narrow beam. The feed moves up and down as the antenna rotates, producing a wavy scanned area and providing height-finding data as well as target range and direction.

The DRBC 11 dual-function S-band radar on the mainmast was replaced by the DRBV 22, an L-band air surveillance radar with an antenna similar in configuration to that of the US Navy's SPS 6.

The functions and frequency operation of the new radars suggest a shift away from Royal Navy wartime practice (ie long-range metric air warning radars plus short-range dual-purpose sets) in favour of US Navy practice, which favoured medium-range air search sets combined with large three-dimensional sets for ships with radar picket or air defence duties. The T53s would later be fitted with US Navy-type TACAN (Tactical Air Navigation) aerials atop the foremast for aircraft control.

The shift away from preoccupations with surface warfare in favour of a totally AAW-orientated approach was reinforced by the replacement of the S-band DRBC 11 fire control radar by a smaller X-band anti-aircraft radar designated DRBC 30. As in later ships of the T47 type the DRBC 30 was mounted centrally atop the main armament director.

ANTI-SUBMARINE WARFARE

The T53 had an identical sonar outfit to that of the T47, but the anti-submarine torpedo tubes, together with their reloaded lockers, were discarded in favour of a sextuple 375mm A/S rocket launcher, which was located on the centre-line atop a new deckhouse which connected the 127mm mounting in 'X' position with the midships 57mm mountings. The rocket launcher was developed specifically for the French Navy by Creusot-Loire, and could use the complete range of Bofors 375mm anti-submarine rockets. Engagement ranges of between 260m and 3,600m are reported.

TABLE 4

375mm A/S rocket launcher	
Elevation	0–92.5°
Range	655–3,625m
Rate of fire	1 round/sec
Weight of launcher	16t

THE DUPERRE CLASS

Five ships of the T53 type were ordered under the 1953 naval programme, and these were to have been followed by a sixth unit (the T47s and T53s, following traditional French practice, were intended to operate in divisions of three ships). However, authorisation of the sixth unit was to be delayed until 1956, and when the ship was finally ordered it was to a drastically revised design.

Acknowledgement: The author wishes to thank Robert Dumas for his assistance in the preparation of this article. The assistance was in the form of answers to specific questions posed by the author, who therefore accepts full responsibility for any errors of fact or omission which remain.

to be continued

TABLE 5: DUPERRE (T53) CLASS

Type	Programme	No	Builder	Laid down	Launched	Completed
T53	1953	D 633 *Duperré*	Lorient	Nov 54	2.7.55	8.10.57
	1953	D 634 *La Bourdonnais*	Brest	Aug 54	15.10.55	Mar 58
	1953	D 635 *Forbin*	Brest	Aug 54	15.10.55	1.2.58
	1953	D 636 *Tartu*	A C Bretagne	Nov 54	2.12.55	5.2.58
	1953	D 637 *Jauréguiberry*	F C de la Gironde	Sep 54	5.11.55	Jul 58

The French Dreadnoughts

The 23,500 ton Courbet Class Part I

by Robert Dumas

THE ORIGINS OF THE COURBET DESIGN

The Naval Programme of 1906 provided for the construction of 16 battleships by 1919. The Conseil Superieur de la Marine (CSM) established at a meeting in October 1907 the specification of the battleships to be built in 1909 and 1910. The table below gives the specification originally decided on. These ships would have been no more than modified semi-Dreadnoughts of the *Danton* class, already rendered obsolescent by the *Dreadnought*.

Displacement	21,000 tons (not to be exceeded)
Armament	4 305mm guns in twin turrets
	100 rounds per gun
	12 240mm guns in broadside twin turrets
	150 rounds per gun
	18 100mm guns in armoured casemates
	400 rounds per gun
	4 torpedo tubes
Protection	Identical to the *Danton* except that the internal torpedo protection was suppressed
Speed	20 knots
Coal	900 tons with emergency stowage for 1800 tons
Machinery	Entirely turbine
Anti-torpedo nets	

NOTE: the CSM expressed the view that the adoption of oil fuel should await the results of trials in another battleship.

On 15 November 1907 the Minister of Marine, Gaston Tomson, ordered the design department to prepare a project for a battleship along the lines given above. He added, 'At the same time, they should study a variety of designs with single calibre armaments of 305, 274 and 240mm guns, apart from that all the other aspects of the ship should be the same (secondary armament, speed, protection, cruising range tonnage etc,) the only difference should be in the main armament'. It was a decision of great importance: it was the first time that those responsible for the French Navy had envisaged the construction of a *Dreadnought* type battleship.

A detailed programme for Project A was prepared along the lines indicated by the CSM, established by the design department and adopted by the Chiefs of the service on 25 January 1908. The results of these studies

Paris in 1912, while still under construction.
Author's Collection

were sent to the dockyards for the engineers, who were requested to confer on the design of the new battleship. The Minister postponed this communication on 1 February 1908, and the design department was invited to examine the construction of the different designs outlined in time for a meeting on 15 February.

In a note of 10 July 1908, Engineer General Lhomme presented two designed in response to the opinions stated by the CSM and the Minister of the Marine.

Courbet as completed in 1913.
Author's Collection

Paris making 21.5 knots on trials 11 July 1914.
Author's Collection

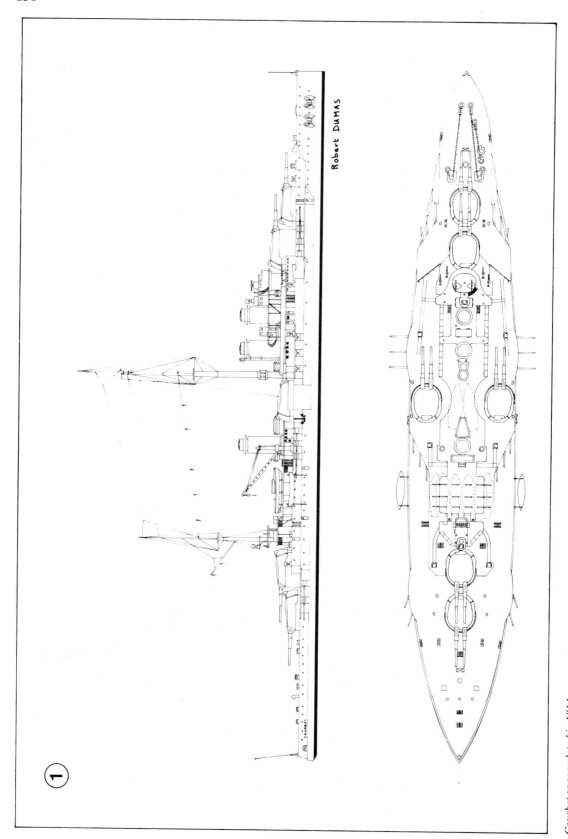

Robert Dumas

① COURBET

Courbet as completed in 1914.
Drawn by the author

	PROJECT A	PROJECT B
Length	160m	161m
Breadth	26.34m	26.60m
Draught	8.60m	8.77m
Displacement	21,600 tons	23,200 tons
Armament	4 305mm guns in twin turrets	12 305mm guns in twin turrets
	12 240mm guns in twin turrets	18 100mm guns in casemates
	18 100mm guns in casemates	12 47mm guns
	12 47mm guns	
	4 submerged torpedo tubes	4 submerged torpedo tubes

Rounds per gun for both designs
305mm 100
240mm 150
100mm 350 + 50 overload
47mm 450

Protection
250mm belt reduced by 20mm toward the extremities

Height of the belt above the waterline	2.45m	2.35m
Thickness at the waterline	220mm	220mm
Depth below the waterline	1.65mm	1.65mm
Armoured decks	48mm	70mm

Turrets and casemates

305mm turrets		270mm–290mm
240mm turrets		180mm–240mm
100mm casemates		100mm
Torpedo Nets		

Machinery	all Turbines
Speed	20 knots
Fuel	900 tons of coal (normal load), 2700 tons supercharge. Eventually 300 tons of coal would be replaced by 300 tons of oil.

In these two projected designs there exists a fundamental difference in the conception and mounting of the main armament. This point led to the design department making a number of remarks. In the Projected ship A the presence of two forward 305mm turrets in the same place as the 18 100mm guns in casemates would reduce the arcs of fire of six guns, and these should be mounted in a separate battery round the forward 305mm turret.

In Projected ship B the engineers proposed the abandonment of the classic hexagonal disposition of the turrets. This would be replaced by a pair of superimposed turrets fore and aft, leaving only one turret on each broadside. This solution required extra displacement in the bow to support the extra weight. The stability of the ship was considered vitally important, and with regard to the effects of pitching and rolling the new design had to be equal to that of the hexagonal arrangement. The design department wanted to replace the 18 100mm guns with 12 138.6mm, and increase the thickness of the batter to 150mm.

Following these observations the CSM ordered the modified project B(1) to conform to these suggestions.

This design will henceforth be referred to as B1.

In August 1908 the projected designs A and B1 were sent, on the orders of the Minister of the Marine, to the Admirals commanding the seagoing fleets. They all approved of the general disposition of B1, anticipating the inconvenience that would arise from the great height above the waterline of the forward superimposed turret. The guns of this turret were in effect 13 metres above the waterline, and the floor of the conning tower was 15 metres above the same point. The two Admirals did display a marked preference for the 138.6mm guns but insisted that more should be fitted. Their opinions were passed on to the design department.

However, in a note prepared for the October 1907 meeting of the CSM, the General Staff had recommended the study of three and four gun turrets. These offered a novel solution to the problem of the distribution of heavy artillery. In particular they had favoured a design with combined triple turrets in the axial positions with twin turrets on the broadside. Inspired by these projections, and bearing in mind the opinions of the Admirals the design department studied, without special orders a third project, C, carrying 12 305mm and 18 138.6mm. This armament provided, as did B1, a broadside of ten guns. It also offered the possibility of moving the forward turret back from the bow and lowering the conning tower, allowing a reduction in the immersion of the bow and a 1000 ton reduction in displacement.

PROJECT C	
Length	159m
Breadth	26.60m
Draught	8.77m
Displacement	22,200 tons
Armament	12 305mm in two triple turrets and three twin
	18 138.6mm guns in casemates (275 round per gun)
	12 47mm
	4 submerged torpedo tubes
Protection	As in A, B and B1
Machinery	Turbines
Speed	20 knots
Fuel	As per A and B

These three projects (A, B and B1) were officially examined by the CSM on 24 December 1908. They decided that A was inferior to the other two projects. The Admirals declared that 'from now on the importance of a single calibre was settled by the improved accuracy obtained that no longer required discussion'. As a result of this A was definitively abandoned and the choice was now between B1 and C. The CSM declared that there was enough evidence in favour of the latter project 'which brings together the conditions which are indispensable to a modern battleship: a powerful and homogenous armament, defensive armament effective at long range and adequate protection'.

The adoption of the two triple turrets permitted the suppression of one turret. This reduced the silhouette and improved the seagoing qualities. On the other hand the arrangement of the secondary armament and the

1

2

3

1 *Jean Bart* entering the dockyard basin at Bizerta on 17 August 1916 after being hit by a torpedo fired by the Austrian submarine *U 12* which struck her in the bow, flooding three compartments. She reached port under her own steam from the French patrol line in the southern Adriatic.
Author's Collection

2 *Jean Bart* in the Bizerta basin.
Author's Collection

3 *France* in 1922, the year in which she was lost, after striking an uncharted rock in Quiberon Bay. She was the only dreadnought battleship to be lost as a result of an error of navigation.
Author's Collection

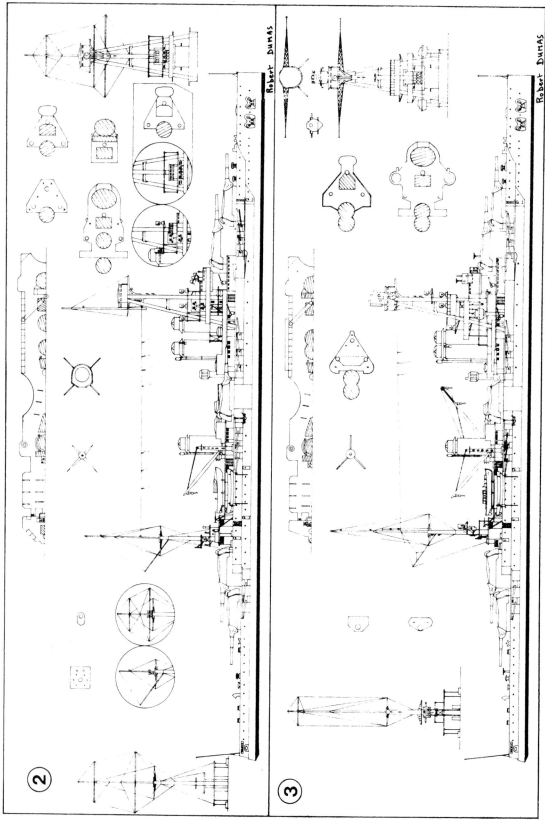

1 *Paris* in 1923.
Drawn by author

2 *Paris* in 1929.
Drawn by author

Robert Dumas

Robert Dumas

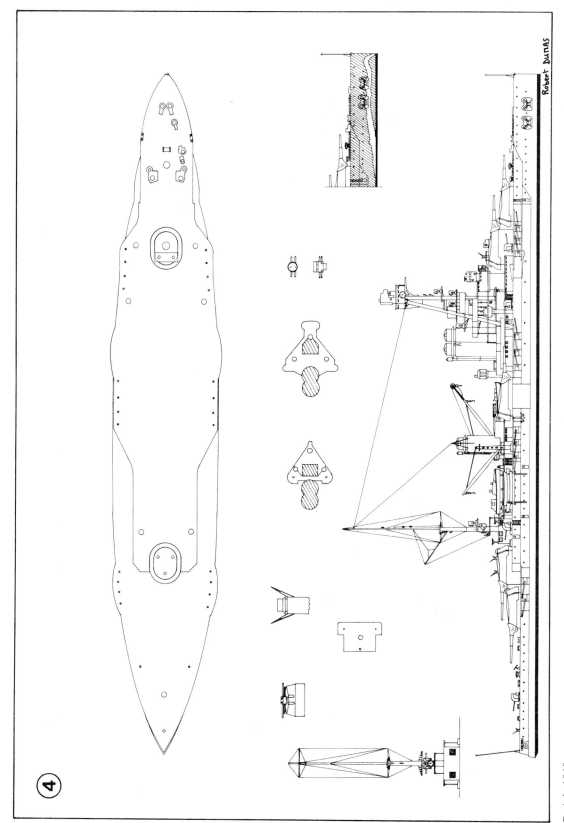

Robert Dumas

Paris in 1940.
Drawn by author

protection of the central battery were better arranged in B1. Meanwhile the Admirals had many reservations about triple turrets. They did not think it would be possible to fire all three guns simultaneously. Despite this risk they decided to continue the study of the triple turret, alongside work on twin turrets of the British pattern, which they considered more spacious and better organised than French models.

The nomination of Vice Admiral Boue de Lapeyrere as Minster of Marine on 24 July 1909, gave a precise direction of these studies. He demanded the establishment of a definitive project based on the main armament of B1 and the secondary battery and protection of C. Only 4 of the 12 47mm guns were retained. The energetic minister did not stop there; making a series of major decisions. The English pattern turrets were adopted, torpedo nets were abandoned (decision of the Minister 25 November 1909), the number of 138.6mm guns was increased from 18 to 22 (decision of the Minister 17 December 1909).

The result of these decisions, given to the design department, was the production of the definitive project outlined in the table below.

CHARACTERISTICS OF THE DEFINITIVE PROJECT

Full load displacement	23,467 tons
Overall length	166m, 165m between perpendiculars
Breadth at the waterline	27m, 28m overall
Draught	8.852m
Armament	12 305mm (1910 model) in 6 twin turrets 22 138.6mm guns (1910 model) in casemate batteries 4 47mm (1902 model) 4 450mm torpedo tubes
Protection	Belt 270mm reducing to 180mm at the extremities Casemates Four armoured decks 30mm, 30mm, 12mm & 40mm
Turrets	320mm Barbettes, 280mm Conning tower 300mm
Machinery	4 Parsons Turbines of 28,000shp
Speed	21 knots

After the adoption of the definitive project by the CSM and the inclusion of two battleships in the 1910 Budget, the Minister of the Marine placed the orders for the *Courbet* and *Jean Bart* on 11 August 1910. In the following year two more ships, *Paris* and *France* were budgeted for and ordered on 1 August 1911.

To accelerate the construction of the *Courbets,* new methods of building were adopted. Engineer Constructor Lyasse, chief of the design department examined the plans and modified them in accordance with his suggested alterations.

1 To order at the same time as the ship, the engines, boilers, turrets and guns etc.

2 To provide the constructors with outline plans of the ship, and detailed plans of the decks, as soon as the orders were signed.

3 Within six weeks send on detailed plans.

These measures led to a considerable reduction in the time taken to build the *Courbet* class (*Courbet*–38 months, *Jean Bart*–36 months, *Paris*–33 months and *France*–35 months). Such times compared favourably with those taken to construct the *Patrie* class (60 months on average).

The construction of the four *Courbets* marked the beginning of an important modernisation of the battlefleet. By the size of this effort France proved that she was determined to make up for the backwardness of the preceeding years. Unfortunately this rapid, if overdue, naval rearmament led to a certain number of errors in design.

The range of the main armament (12,500ms) was insufficient.

The rangefinder was a small item with a 2.74m base.

The ship was coal fired.

The protection was badly designed.

These were the principal weaknesses revealed during the First World War. At the end of the war these problems had to be attended to in order to improve the efficiency of the class.

To be continued

Paris in 1939, immediately before the outbreak of the Second World War.

Author's Collection

Paris leaving Brest in 1923 after her first rebuild.
Author's Collection

The Canadian Patrol Frigate

by Thomas G Lynch

HMCS *St. Laurent* in the mid-1950s. These were among the
finest post-war designed ships in the world, but by the
mid-1970s were obsolescent.

DND Photo

With the announcement on 18 August 1983 of a $3.85
(1983) billion contract to St. John Shipbuilding and
Drydock Company Limited the 15 year search for a *St.
Laurent* replacement seemed to be over. NATO countries, especially the US, had been sceptical of ever seeing
it come off the drawing boards and indeed criticism of
the costs had been made both in Canada and abroad.
Setting all arguments aside, the first batch of six are now
on order, with the first steel to be cut in October and the
first section arriving on the ways in July 1985, the 75th
anniversary of the founding of the Canadian Navy.

Just how did the Canadian Navy get itself into a situation where elderly frigates were expected to soldier on
into the 30th year of service? A brief history of postwar
construction helps to understand the current situation.

HISTORY

During the 1950s and early 1960s, Canada embarked
upon the construction of an evolving anti-submarine
warfare destroyer type, starting with the *St. Laurent*
class. These were revolutionary in hull design and construction, being one of the first postwar warship class to
be built in a precision pre-fabricated manner, without an
actual keel-laying. They were also the first warships
designed in Canada to ever enter service with the-then
Royal Canadian Navy.

As improvements were identified in submarine performance, the armaments and sensors were changed to
match the challenge, first with the *Restigouche* and
Annapolis Class. Mid-way through construction of the
latter, a large helicopter hangar, flight deck and helicopter assist landing equipment were required and installed.
Likewise, the *St. Laurents* were retrofitted with a helo
deck and hangar to reflect the current ASW requirement
for a large helicopter, but it was realised as early as 1962
that the *Annapolis* class was the end of the road for this
hull design. Missile systems of the day were just too large
and bulky. The *Restigouche* class began to be modernised extensively with ASROC and a huge lattice mast
to reflect their role as a pure ASW frigate, but only four
were done before budget cutbacks forbade refits of this
expense. Variable depth sonar updated the ships'
underwater abilities to meet the threat of the early
1970s.

Continual, progressive naval construction was considered vital. Accordingly, Naval Services Headquarters
began to examine a more versatile ship, generically
known as the General Purpose Frigate. This was a bigger
and better *St. Laurent* hull design with a near-cousin of

the *MacKenzie* class Y.100 steam development adopted. By 1964, however, the project with its sophisticated DATAR command and display system was judged to be too expensive. It was the first setback to the carefully planned gradual obsolescence programme outlined in the 1964 White Paper on Defence. This would not be addressed and only partially rectified with the construction of the DDH–280 'Tribal' class destroyers nearly six years later.

The 280s were the last gasp of the Naval Constructor Design Office in Ottawa. Too many talented people had been lost in the period 1964–67. From then on, the ships and equipment would have to be designed or tailored to naval specifications by the prime contractor.

In 1973, naval construction entered a barren wasteland. The careful, phased construction of the 1964 White Paper was thrown out in the 1971 White Paper which shifted first priority of the Canadian Navy from ASW to 'sovereignty protection'. That this had been part of the Navy's mandate since 1910 was ignored by the government in the Paper. Nothing new in construction was announced, since this same Paper made official the virtual freeze on defence spending that had started in

1969. By 1975 Maritime Command planners had determined that a minimum of 20 warships would be necessary to fulfill the tasks set by the government of the day. The real need for a replacement for the Argus CL–28 long range patrol aircraft, however, the Centurion main battle tank and the fleet of mixed CF–104, 101 and CF–5 fighters brought the replacement programme to a virtual standstill. By 1980, the situation of the *St. Laurents* was becoming acute and embarassing. Cracks in the superheater header in some of the 'steamer' frigates had the entire fleet immobilized in November 1981 while examination of all these ships were carried out. Some ships were out of operation for months while the situation was diagnosed and corrected.

In the spring of 1984, HMCS *Assiniboine* returned from southern exercises with fractures of upper deck stringers and plating. This was later traced to buckling of stiffeners and ship plate in the fuel tanks directly below the damage, but it still served as a warning that these ships were past their prime. They had been engineered to give 20 years of faithful service, but were being pushed for another ten years with only token or 'band-aid' DELEX refits.

In 1978 a revised replacement programme was announced that would see a first batch of six ships produced during the latter half of the 1980s to replace the ailing *St. Laurents*. It was then projected that a repeat class of the same sort would take up the slack as the last

A modernised *St. Laurent* class, HMCS *Skeena*. The versatility of the hull design was obvious with the major modifications of the late 1960s and 1970s, such as VDS and the capability of carrying a heavy ASW helicopter.
CAF Photo

The later 1960s modifications of the *Restigouche* class
reflected the uncertainty being felt within the Navy by 1969.
Only the decision to build the DDH-280 class *Tribals* stopped
this expensive modernisation programme at four of class.
Gatineau.
CAF Photo

of the *Restigouche* class retired in the early 1990s.
Finally in 1983, after two changes in government, three
revisions of time scale and four Ministers of National
Defence, the contract was signed. It seems that a thaw in
defence spending had been accomplished, but was it too
little, too late bearing in mind that in 1975 naval planners had expressed a need for 20 ships? This had now
dwindled to six new ships, plus the 16 steam frigates and
four DDH-280s. From the frigate number must be
deducted the *MacKenzie* class of four, these being
training ships only. The follow-on batch of six CPFs has
not materialised. According to informed sources within
MARCOM, the political climate of a late summer elec-
tion will delay the decision on Batch Two until at least
November of this year or even later, setting this portion
of the replacement programme back at least another six
to eight months.

Although the above figures show 24 effectives, the
figures are deceptive. By 1996 all of the steam frigates
will have been retired, leaving only the CPFs and the
Tribals, a total of 16. Just to maintain the minimum
figure, a second batch will be necessary . . . and the
Tribals will be 22 years old plus.

The 1983 signing for the construction of the first six
CPFs came under servere criticism too. Although St.
John Shipbuilding had won the final contract for the
ships over SCAN Marine of Quebec (rumours of unfair
assistance were voiced by St. John representatives

throughout the competition stage), they were forced to
watch 60 per cent of the direct benefits of the contract
awarded to Versatile Vickers for design work and
Marine Industries Limited of Quebec who will build
three of the six as sub-contractors. Additionally, these
same companies are potential competitors when the
second batch contracts are awarded. Finally, the Minister announced that a $650 million (1983) contract for
the TRUMPH refits for the four 280s was awarded to
Davie Shipyard in Quebec without disclosure of any
other bidder.

THE SHIPS

The ship revealed in the contract signing in 1983 shows a
state-of-the-art conventional hulled warship. Roughly
comparable with the NATO Standard Frigate layout,
the ship is nearly 1000 tonnes heavier and suffers from
an apparent inferiority in throw-weight in conventional
gunnery. (1 × 57mm versus 2 × 76mm on the NSF.)
However, with the Candian switch to a surface-to-
surface offensive weapon such as Harpoon, the gunnery
role was revised to emphasize a more dual role, pre-
dominantly air defence.

The weapon/sensor fits are fairly well balanced. The
greatest deficiency in the Navy's ships had been the near
non-existence of anti-missile defence, other than the
largely passive Corvus/P4 chaff counter-measures. Even
in the later system the CPF will have a decisive influence,
bringing into the forefront the new Plessey SHIELD
Rapid Bloom system using the new P5 and infra-red
decoy rockets. Added to this are the 57mm pre-
segmented round, the Mk 15 Phalanx 20mm close-in
defence mount and the new vertical-launch Sea Sparrow
missile system, utilizing the RIM–7M with their depen-

The building of the four 280 Class *Tribals* spelt the end of new
warship construction for over ten years before the CPF was
announced. Here, *Athabaskan* readies for her launch, 27
November 1970.
CAF Photo

TABLE II: MARITIME COMMAND OPERATIONAL SHIP TIME FRAME
Copyright: T.G. Lynch

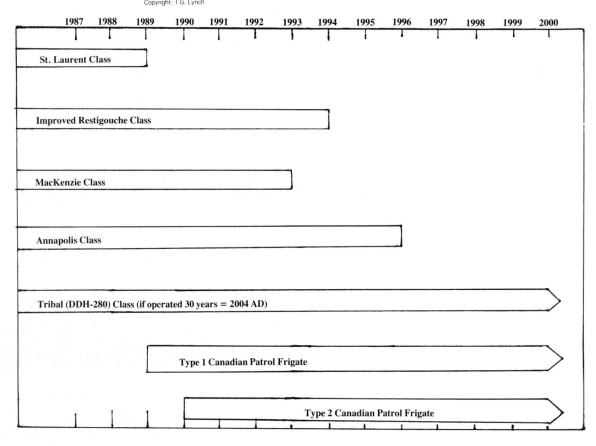

dable jet vane control (JVC). These, with sophisticated electronic jamming, will go a long way to redressing the deficiencies in the Canadian fleet.

The CPF will mark a large departure from Canadian evolution in warships, showing the large gap that has existed between the technology of the steam frigates and the threat of the 1980s.

1 The CPFs will mark a retrenchment from the fully COGOG DDH–280s to CODOG, the cruise power being provided by a medium speed, French-built Pielstick 20-cylinder PA6 V 280 diesel. For greater speeds, General Electric LM 2500–30 gas turbines with a Deschelde cross-connect gearbox will be fitted. Final transmission of power will be by twin shafts to two Escher-Wyss controlled-pitch propellers, the latter having a cavitation inception speed of 22 knots. The engines and gearbox are raft-mounted and fully hooded for exceptional quietness. Control of the engineering spaces will be via the Hawker Siddeley Dynalec 6000 machinery control system.

2 The CPFs will be the first Canadian-built warship to be without at least one NC MK 10 Limbo ASW mortar. ASW duties have been fully transferred to the first enclosed Mk 32 mod 5 triple torpedo tubes on a Canadian ship, angled at about 30° from the fore and aft line. These appear from behind a sliding panel in the leading edges of the helicopter hangar structure.

3 Anti-ship firepower will be switched from the conventional gun mount in previous Canadian warships to the RGM–84A–2 Harpoon missile. With a range of 80 miles plus, it is a definite step in the threat environment of the 1980s and 90s.

4 The Canadian-developed, variable-depth sonar (AN/SQS–504/505) will be dropped in favour of the Canadian hybrid version of the Gould Inc., AN/SQR–19 tactical towed array sonar. Called CANTASS, it is the towed array (or 'wet-end') of the SQR–19 married to state of the art Canadian data processors. This in turn will probably be refitted to the DDH–280 during the TRUMPH refits.

5 The venerable Canadian anti-acoustic torpedo device (CAT II) will finally be replaced by the AN/SLQ–25 NIXIE system. Canadian manufacturers are in place and the contract amounts to $19.7 million (1984). Of course this will be retrofitted to the 280s and possibly the *Annapolis* class frigates.

6 The substitution of the Dutch Signaal VM–25 STIR fire control/tracking radar over the M–22 series as seen on *'Tribals'* is a natural progression, especially when it is remembered that Sperry of the US is using it in conjunction with the Mk 92 mod 2 Fire Control System on the FFG–7 frigates. In the case of the CPF two will be fitted and preliminary computer studies showed that there would be 'gathering' problems with the rear unit. Although not confirmed, it was noted that this second STIR antenna was shifted to a higher position early in the defination stages.

7 CPF will be the first Canadian ship to employ Shipboard Integrated Communications System (SHINPADS) and Shipboard Integrated Communications System (SHINCOM). The former links computers within the ship and in turn others in the fleet, while the latter is a very shophisticated internal communications system. Both are highly resistant to failure or damage, doing away with bundled independent systems and eliminating miles of copper wiring on the 'Tribal' class. These will also be seen in the TRUMPH and DELEX refits to the 'Tribals' and *Annapolis* classes respectively.

Two programmes of logistical support are a necessary part of the programme. The first is Integrated Logistics Support (ILS) and the second, software development.

The first entails developing the training facilities necessary for initial combat system integration and training of user/maintainer personnel. This centre is being built by PARAMAX, the wholly Canadian company founded by Sperry to handle the combat systems integration. Called the Combat System Test and Support Facility, (CSTSF), it will begin operation training sometime in April, 1987.

Secondly, but still part of the first package, is the Personnel Training Centre (PTC) or CPF operator and maintainer training for main propulsion control and the Combat System Training Centre (CSTC) for the training of combat systems officers and personnel. The latter facilities will be with Canadian Forces Base Halifax, Nova Scotia and training should begin in October, 1987. Additionally, spares and supplies for the operation support of the ship will begin to arrive in Halifax in 1987 and appropriate stores within CFB Halifax are being planned as part of the programme. The second part of logistical support will be the necessary software. Here the system is truly awesome. Ship software for Machinery Control Systems (MCS) and Combat Control Systems (CCS) amounts to 1,120,000 cells (remembering that one cell equals 16 bits). Facility software amounts to 900,000 cells – diagnostics needing 240,000, training 160,000 and 200,000 pages of documentation.

A weary HMCS *Saguenay,* here nearing her 25th year in service in 1981, is expected to soldier on until at least 1990. The ships are without basic anti-missile defence.
Maritime Command Museum

HMCS *Annapolis,* one of two of class, will be the last steam
frigate to retire in 1994.
CAF Photo

An artist's impression of the new CPF at sea in the mid-1990s.
CPF Office

CANADIAN PATROL FRIGATE SPECIFICATIONS

Dimensions	
Displacement	light 3866 tonnes
	deep 4254 tonnes
Length	(oa) 133.5m
Beam	maximum 16.4m
	waterline 14.8m
Draft	4.6m
Propulsion	1 Pielstick 20 cylinder PA6–280 med.
Cruise	speed diesel; 8000shp
Main	2 G.E. LM 2500–30 gas turbines, 30,000shp each. Deschelde cross-connect gear box, twin shaft, Escher-Wyss CPP
Speed	30kt+
Range	diesel – (15kt) 4500nm+
Sensors	AN/SQR–19 TACTASS towed array,
Inderwater	passive
	AN/SQS–505 in C5 fixed hull mount dome
Surface	AN/SPS–49(V) long range air search
	Sea Giraffe 150 HC medium range air search (G/H band)
	Sperry Mk 127E navigation radar (X-band)
	VM 25 STIR fire control/illuminator radar X 2 (I/J band)
ESM	CANEWS (0.5–18Ghz)(500Khz–500MHz)
ECM	Ramses
	SHIELD Rapid Bloom, P5 round, infra-red decoy
Electronics	RF Harris 13 rec/7 trans HF transceiver
Radio	9 RT–1244(v) UHF transceivers
	2 RT–246 land support VHF systems
	2 MRT 66 Maritime mobile transceivers
	Message processing SHINPADS
	Interior communication SHINCOM
	Underwater telephone AN/WQC–2A (AN/WQC–510(v))
Command &	Processors – AN/UYK–502 and
Control	AN/UYK–505
	Display – AN/UYQ–501
	Data Bus – AN/UYC–501
	Sensor switchboard: combined, radar and sonar
Misc	AN/SLQ–25 NIXIE torpedo decoy
	AN/UYS–502 sonobuoy processor
Electrics	3 × 1000Kw MWM/Telefunken diesel generators
	1 × 500Kw MWM/Telefunken diesel generators
Weapons	Bofors 57mm Mk 2 auto gun mount
Anti-air	16 RIM–7M Sea Sparrow vertical launch SAM modules (12 reloads)
	Phalanx Mk 15 20mm close-in defence mount
Anti-ship	8 (4×2) Harpoon RGMA–2 S/S missile canisters
ASW	2 × Mk 32 mod 5 triple TT
	24 × Mk 46 mod 5 (MAST) ASW torpedoes
Helicopter	1 CH124A Sea King or equivalent
	1 DAF Indal Recovery Assist, Secure and Traverse (RAST)
SATCOM	1 AN/WSC–3(v)2 UHF transceiver (2 × OE–82C antannae)
	1AN/SRR–1 fleet broadcast receiving system.
Manning	225 all ranks

As can be seen, the demand for the prime and sub-contractors to supply a complete logistics package as well as design and built a suitable warship has been largely met, but at the expense of time, which is in short supply. The only justification and hence saving for this odeal would be:

1 St. John Shipyard gets a second contract for Batch Two of CPF.

2 That one or more repeat batch orders are placed.

What might be seen in Batch Two? Maritime Command would like to see the vertically launched lightweight Sea Wolf point defence system installed. Secondly, if science and the armaments industry can come through, at least a basic area defence system, although this is unlikely in the time set aside to build Batch Two. The only sysytems available are suitable only for warships of over 8,000 tonnes, precluding their use. In any case, Batch Two should be announced within months and a decision to build further ships of this class by mid-1985. But where will Maritime Command go from there?

In the last number of years, numerous naval authorities have said that the day of the conventional-hulled warship were numbered. Friction between the ship and water has been sited as the greatest barrier to higher, quieter speeds, along with the limitations placed upon weapon/sensor suites by a slim displacement hull. Defence Research Establishment, Atlantic, Halifax is a good indicator.

Since World War Two DRA(A) (or Naval Research Establishment as it was known until recent times) has played an important part in defining Canadian naval needs. They were largely instrumental in documenting the results of several experimental hydrofoil craft through the 1950s and 1960s that resulted in the developmental hydrofoil warship, HMCS *Bras d'Or*. Looking again into the future, DRA(A) provide two alternatives in their current testing programmes.

1 Hydrofoil ships Experiments with the ill-fated 400 ton developmental hydrofoil *Bras d'Or* showed that indeed a warship smaller than 3500 tonnes would operate in almost any weather condition the North Atlantic could dish out. In tests with two conventional steam frigates in April, 1971 in Sea States 7–8, *Bras d'Or,* while hull-borne, had better sea-keeping capabilities than a frigate, having to steam in figure-eights about the two ships to maintain contact in less than two cable lengths of visibility.

A proposed conceptual design of a 400–450-ton hydrofoil warship that would meet both the needs of the Canadian Navy and the US Navy was put forward by the Canadian Naval Liaison Officer to the David Taylor Model Basin in 1979 that would use fully-submerged hydrofoil elements rather than the unique surface-piercing ones of *Bras d'Or*. Built for about $100 million complete (1983), they would be capable of speeds of up to 50 knots and carrying out many of the tasks assigned to more expensive, general purpose frigates, such as search and rescue, anti-submarine patrols, fisheries protection patrols and sovereignty interdiction. Although these hydrofoil craft would be far inferior in range and adaptability, their relative cheapness and frugality in manpower (50–60 versus 230 for the CPF) would allow far more specialised payloads to be carried on a common design (Canada's 'small, but many' concept of the FHE–400 era revived) hull in far greater numbers (approximately 2.8 for the cost of one CPF).

However, as pointed out by numerous naval experts, the hydrofoil ship would still not solve the problem of Artic patrols nor could they operate wholly on their own. AORs for their support would not be able to be defended successfuly by hydrofoil warships, needing larger weapons platforms to do so effectively. The hydrofoil warship would only be a partial solution to the conventional hulled warship, albeit a cost effective one.

2 SWATH Ships Currently these are being intensely studied by DRE(A), with unmanned scale models being tested in the waters of Bedford Basin. SWATH stands for Small Waterplane Area, Twin Hull and the advantages lie in their many-fold increase in stability over a conventional hull in moderate to very rough seas and the wide variety of tonnages possible, from 400 tons up.

SWATH is basically two torpedo-shaped underwater hulls with four supportive, streamlined upright columns that in turn support a broad, flat payload deck. Looking somewhat like a catamaran with stilts, the ship offers little wave impact surface to on-coming waves; pitch, heave and roll can be largely dampled out by movable 'fins' or stabilizers. These traits will allow SWATH to sustain greater speeds in rough weather and with the propulsive machinery housed in the under-water 'torpedoes' in larger versions, far less movement would be apparent, with a very high metacentric centre. The largest problem to date experienced by DRE(A) has been the down-scaling of a working model, since the machinery must be housed on the payload deck and complex 'Z' drives employed.

However, with the current level of funding to this project, it will be near the end of this century before a viable warship design is available.

To sum up the future for Maritime Command: until at least after the turn of the century, conventional warship hulls will remain paramount. However, as the benefits of SWATH become more and more apparent, and the cost of warships per unit continues to soar, these two types of warship will come to the forefront. This is especially true when one considers that the cost of the final ship in Batch One will be in excess of $300 million $1994 and no firm figures are even projected for Batch Two.

What will the fleet look like by the turn of the century? Taking in the many variables, at least 12 patrol frigates will be built, with the possibility of a Batch Three being ordered by 1990. A minimum of six new submarines are planned and the first of these should begin to appear by mid-decade (1995). The DDH–280 *Tribals* will have completed their-mid life TRUMPH refits by the late 1980s and still be viable weapons platforms. Lastly, concrete decisions will have been made on a class of SWATH ships, with hydrofoil craft a strong second contender.

With a new resolve within the Canadian government to repair the damage done by 16 years of deliberate neglect by a past government, Canada's navy should once more be a viable fighting force and worthy of the trust of her NATO partners.

The Canadian/US (CUSH) 4500 tonne conceptual drawing put forward by the Canadian Liaison Officer in 1979.
Credit: DRE(A)

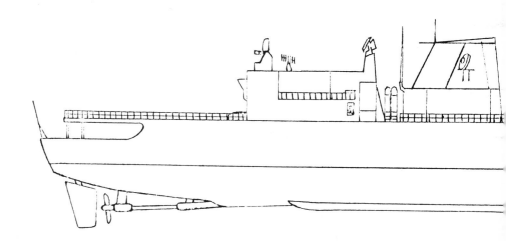

An artist's impression of a 4500 tonne SWATH ship in Canada's service after the turn of the century.
Credit: L B Jenson by permission

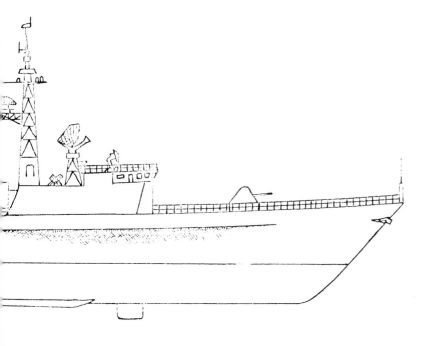

Roanoke

A Civil War Battleship

by Francis J Allen

The American Civil War (1861–1865) caused the United States Navy to design or build several unusual warships. The most surprising of these, in size if nothing else, were the sea going vessels on the monitor principle. The majority of these types, notably *Dictator* and *Puritan*, the two largest, were never completed to the original design. USS *Roanoke*, (1854–1883) however, was converted into such a vessel.

Roanoke was originally built as a huge steam frigate of the *Merrimack* class. As large as contemporary 90-gun steam battleships in the British and French Navies, the class were ruined by their weak and unreliable machinery. At best they reached 9.5 knots, but such a performance was infrequent and could not be depended upon. *Merrimack* ended her days as the famous CSS *Virginia* (known universally as the *Merrimac*, of *Monitor* and *Merrimac* renown).

In her original form the *Roanoke*, along with her sister, the *Colorado*, came close to meeting a violent end at the hands of her ex-sister, the *Virginia* at the Battle of Hampton Roads. After destroying the wooden sailing ships *Cumberland* and *Congress*, *Virginia* went home leaving *Roanoke* hard aground and *Colorado* unable to move because her machinery was disabled.

After this demonstration of her uselessness for combat with the purely coastal forces of the Confederate Navy, *Roanoke* was taken out of service and laid up at Brooklyn Navy Yard on 25 March, 1862. On the orders of the Navy Department she was then cut down to the gun deck and covered with iron armour tapering from $4\frac{1}{2}$ inches amidships to $3\frac{1}{2}$ inches at the stem and stern; and $1\frac{1}{2}$ thick on the deck. Three twin turrets of the Ericsson type were then installed at the Novelty Ironworks. The Ericsson turret was supported on a central spindle that rested on the keel. In action the considerable weight of the turret was carried on the spindle, rather than on a race mounted in the upper deck, as was the case in the British system of Captain Cowper Coles. When at rest the Ericsson turret rested on a special plate laid into the deck.

Roanoke was recommissioned on 29 July, 1863. She then served in the North Atlantic Blockade Squadron until 25 June, 1865, when she was laid up at Brooklyn Navy Yard until sold for scrap on 27 September, 1883.

As a warship the ironclad *Roanoke* was not a success. Her draught, which had already caused problems at Hampton Roads, still precluded her from taking part in coastal operations. Yet her low freeboard, forced by the use of turrets, caused problems with seakeeping on the broad oceans. Similar difficulties were encountered by the Royal Navy with its cut down wooden warship, *Royal Sovereign* (described in *Issue 32*). Both ships were only suitable for harbour defence: they were neither true monitors, nor battleships.

USS *Roanoke* (1855–1883) shown here before her conversion to an ironclad in 1862.

US Navy NH45364

USS *Roanoke* (1861–1883) under conversion to a monitor, at the Novelty Iron Works, New York, in 1863.

US Navy NH50462

USS *Roanoke* seen here at the Brooklyn Navy Yard probably following her decommissioning in June 1865. The ship-of-the-line to the left in the background is the USS *Vermont*. The *Vermont* was in use as a receiving ship there until September 1865.

NH48105

The *Roanoke*, as converted.

Displacement	3435 tons.
Dimensions	273ft oa, 38½ft beam, 22¾ft draught.
Machinery	Two direct-acting trunk engines – speed 9 knots.
Protection	The armoured belt extended from 4ft below to 6ft above the waterline. It tapered from 4½ inches down to 3½ inches. The deck was 1½ inches thick, being composed of two ¾in plates laid flat across the top of the belt.
Armament	6 11in smooth bore Dahlgren guns.

The Royal Sovereign Class Battleships 1913~1948

Part II **by R A Burt**

Royal Oak at Portsmouth in September 1936. She had just completed a major refit at a cost of £1,000,000. *Royal Oak* remained the best of the class until she was sunk at Scapa Flow.
Author's Collection

APPEARANCE CHANGES AND MODIFICATIONS

The *Royal Sovereign*s were well proportioned and finely balanced vessels. The single uptake made them look both distinctive and impressive. When viewed from bow-on, they were the very image of the layman's idea of a battleship; only the arrangement of the upper bridges, which were different in all ships, produced a somewhat unbalanced effect away from the funnel when viewed from the broadside. The upper bridge was carried slightly abaft the mast, and the navigating bridge projected unusually forward. In the *Ramillies*, the bridge was shortened at the rear, and did not extend behind as much as the others after her completion.

In 1918, whilst operating at sea together, it was most difficult to tell them apart, especially from a distance. There were however, a few identitfying features which separated the class from one another:

Ramillies
1 Tall searchlight tower fitted over the upper bridge on the foremast.
2 Low searchlight towers fitted abreast the mainmast.
3 Low breastwork around the upper pairs of 6in guns.
4 Lower yard on foremast at director platform level.

5 Completed with shallow bulges, although these were hidden from view when at deep load.

Resolution
1 No foretopmast in 1916/17.
2 Very long gaff at the starfish.

Revenge
1 Fo'c'sle sides recessed from abaft outer face of 'A' barbette, whilst it was abaft 'B' in the rest of the class.
2 Very prominent caging to funnel.
3 Two yards on foretopmast, one in others.

Royal Sovereign
Shorter gaff from heel of topmast.

Royal Oak
1 Flange high up between tripod legs (only vessel with this).
2 Very long gaff from heel of maintopmast.

No bulges in any ships except *Ramillies*.

WAR PERIOD: 1916–1918
1916/17
1 extra, later, 2 × 36in lamps added in maintop in *Royal Oak* and 1 in *Royal Sovereign* over the control top. *Revenge* fitted for towing kite balloons.
Extra precautions fitted as a result of Jutland, but uncertain if any armour protection additions fitted.
Rangefinder baffles were temporarily fitted to the main top mast and funnel in *Royal Oak*, and on funnel only in

Revenge. These were removed by mid 1917.

1917/18

Control tops enlarged. Deflection scales painted up on 'A' and 'Y' or 'B' and 'X' turrets.

Range clocks fitted to face of control top, or on a short pole over this, and also, at rear of SL tower abaft mainmast.

High angle rangefinder fitted on roof of control top.

Searchlight equipment in first 4 ships improved (all but *Ramillies*).

Funnel platform replaced by two large 'coffee box' type towers with 2 × 36in lamps in each.

After superstructure searchlights were removed from *Royal Oak* and *Royal Sovereign* and remounted on new platform against other side of mainmast.

Searchlight transferred from lower bridge position, to that of new SL towers around funnel. SL removed from tops in *Royal Sovereign* and *Royal Oak*.

Armoured casemates fitted to upper deck 6in guns in *Resolution* and *Royal Sovereign* (1918).

All vessels fitted with underwater bulges by 1920 increasing beam to 101–102ft except *Royal Sovereign* December 1920 and *Royal Oak* 1924. *Resolution* and *Revenge* during November 1917–February 1918. Middle and lower bridges in *Resolution* and *Revenge* were extended aft and the extremities connected by means of curved screens. Upper bridge in *Revenge* extended back almost to the funnel. Short topmast fitted to *Resolution*, which was completed without this feature. The foretopmast in *Royal Oak* was temporarily removed in 1917. This was also removed in *Royal Sovereign* but replaced later with foretopmast of same length.

Signal struts fitted forward from starfish in *Ramillies* and *Royal Sovereign* below control top.

Revenge in early 1919, illustrating the final extent of her wartime modifications. Searchlight towers, splinter protection for the bridge and the range clock at the masthead are the most obvious detail changes.

IWM

LAUNCH FIGURES: REVENGE

Length	580ft 0½in pp
Beam	88ft 7⅜in (as moulded – 88ft 3⅜in)
Draught	(on launch 13ft 6in forward, 16ft 9¾in aft)
Length of engine	
rooms	69ft 11½in
Length of boilers 1	38ft 0⅝in
rooms 2	38ft 1in
3	38ft 0¾in

Breakage at launch
Longitudinally in a distance of 436ft 9in: 1⅛in hog
Transverse in a distance of 78ft 10in: ¹⁄₁₆in sag

Water density at
time of launch   35.25 cubic sq feet
Displacement   11,954 tons

Gear (on board at
time of launch)   363 tons machinery
1,487 tons armour
370 tons of ballast, men and equipment

Recorded weight
of hull on launch 9.734 tons

Metacentric height, and stability (GM)
Royal Oak as inclined in 1917

'A' condition	Ship fully equipped with 900 tons oil on board, plus feed tanks full to working height
Displacement	27,970 tons
Draught	30ft mean
GM	2.01ft
'B' condition	Ship as above although 3,380 tons oil, plus reserve tanks full to capacity
Displacement	31,130 tons
Draught	33ft 7in
GM	3.40ft

Stability in the above conditions
'A'   34°
'B'   33.5°
Light condition 26,750 tons.
GM   1.14ft
Stability vanishes at 'A' condition 53° 'B' condition 58°

Ramillies differed somewhat from her sisters, owing to the addition of the bulges.

'A' condition GM: 4ft   **Displacement** 30,400 tons
'B' condition GM: 4.5ft   **Displacement** 33,570 tons

Norman Wilkinson-type dazzle camouflage painted up on *Ramillies* and *Revenge*. Experimental painting was for the purpose of confusing rangetaking equipment, especially that of submarines. *Ramillies* sported her scheme of grey shades and 6 colours from November 1917 until March 1918, whereafter she was again painted all grey.

1918

Large base rangefinder fitted at rear of 'B' turret and 'X' turret in *Revenge*, but only on 'B' in *Ramillies* and *Revolution*. Small rangefinder added between SL towers at rear of funnel in *Royal Sovereign*, which was intended primarily for the purpose of checking distances from the next ship astern during 'pair ship' concentration shoots, when the leading ship was controlling fire of both ships. Searchlight tower location was experimental with this class and various locations for lamps can be seen in photographs throughout this period.

A medium based torpedo rangefinder was fitted over the TCT in *Resolution* which replaced the original rangefinder. The searchlight tower over the bridge in *Ramillies* was removed.

Airplane platforms fitted over 'B' and 'X' turrets in all.

1919–1921

Deflection scales were painted out by 1919. Large base

rangefinder added to rear of 'B' turret in *Resolution*, *Royal Oak, Ramillies,* and *Royal Sovereign* had similar fitted to rear of 'X' turret.

2 small rangefinders (1 in *Resolution*) mounted between after pair of searchlights on funnel in *Resolution, Revenge, Royal Oak.* 24in signalling searchlight removed from forward superstructure and mounted on middle bridge in *Revenge*. Sternwalk fitted in *Revenge*. Long struts fitted to forward starfish in *Resolution* and *Revenge*.

Royal Sovereign, as refitted May 1921 until September 1922

1 Large base rangefinder fitted at rear of "B' turret.
2 Rangefinder removed from between searchlight towers at rear of funnel.
3 Range clocks added over 'X' turret with additional one over control top.
4 High angle range finder added on small tower over bridge.
5 SL tower abaft mainmast was removed.

Other vessels of the class had the searchlight removed from towers abaft the mainmast, but the towers were retained in some vessels until 1924/5. Armoured casemates to upper 6in guns, now fitted to the rest.

Royal Sovereign in 1922/3 in peacetime livery after a refit. The rangefinder at the rear of B turret can be seen.
Author's Collection

Ramillies in September 1929 undergoing a refit. The bridge and funnels of a County class cruiser can be seen over the forward turrets.
Author's Collection

Revenge at Devonport, December 1931.
Author's Collection

Royal Oak refit, September 1922 until June 1924

1 Large base rangefinder fitted to rear of 'B' turret.
2 Rangefinder clocks removed from between the searchlight towers.
3 Range clock added over 'X' turret.
4 High angle rangefinder added in small tower over bridge.
5 A very prominent high fitting anti-torpedo bulge fitted, extending almost up to the 6in gun battery.
6 Middle bridgework extended back to reach funnel.

There was much modification in the location of range clocks through the class. Rangefinders were removed from *Resolution* and *Revenge* in 1924. The searchlights were removed from the middle bridge in *Ramillies* and *Resolution*. (July to October 1924 in *Resolution*) Clinker fitted to funnel during the refit of 1924, thus being very distinguishable from the rest of the class.

1924/5

Rangeclocks over control tower removed in Resolution and *Royal Sovereign* (by July 1925 in *Resolution*. Range clocks added over 'X' turret in *Ramillies* and *Revenge*).
36in lamps removed from middle bridge in *Revenge, Royal Oak* and *Royal Sovereign*.
2 × 24in signalling lamps on middle bridge in *Revenge* were remounted in forward superstructure, and an extra pair of 24in were temporarily mounted on 'B' turret, these being removed from the turret by 1926.
A signal and distributing office was added at the rear of the upper bridge in *Revenge*, and this served for identification of that vessel for many years to come.

Revenge 1926/7

1 The signalling searchlight was transferred from the forward superstructure to the lower bridge.
2 The office at the rear of the upper bridge was enlarged considerably.
3 A taller topmast was fitted to the mainmast.

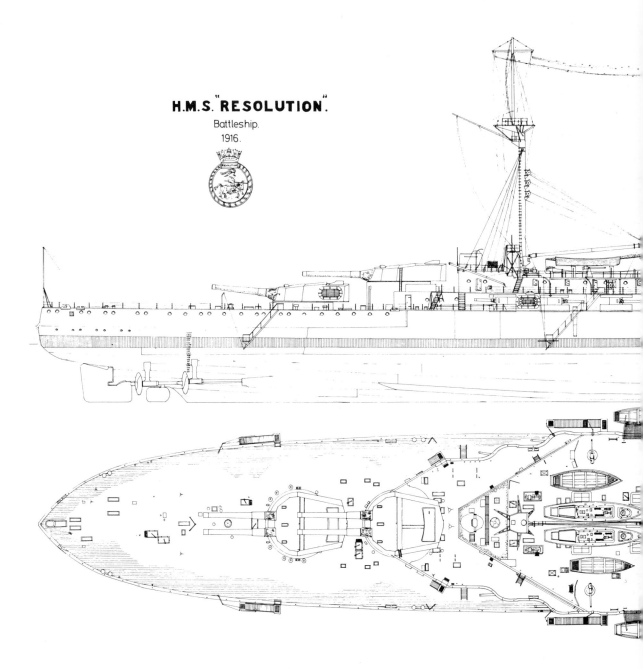

H.M.S. "RESOLUTION".

Battleship.
1916.

Resolution as built, 1916 (R A Burt. Redrawn from official plans now held by the NMM).

Ramillies: September refit from 1926 to April 1927
1 Control top modified and enlarged.
2 Upper pair of 6in guns were removed, although the casemates were retained.
3 Extra pair of 4in AA guns were added on the shelter deck abeam funnel. (3in AA had been replaced by 4in in all vessels during 1924/25).
4 IARF mounted in small tower on bridge.
5 24in lamps remounted from forward superstructure lower bridge.
6 High sloping roof fitted to upper bridge. (Bullet-proof).
7 Foretopmast and lower yard removed.

One feature *Ramillies* retained throughout her long life was the small row of scuttles just beneath her upper

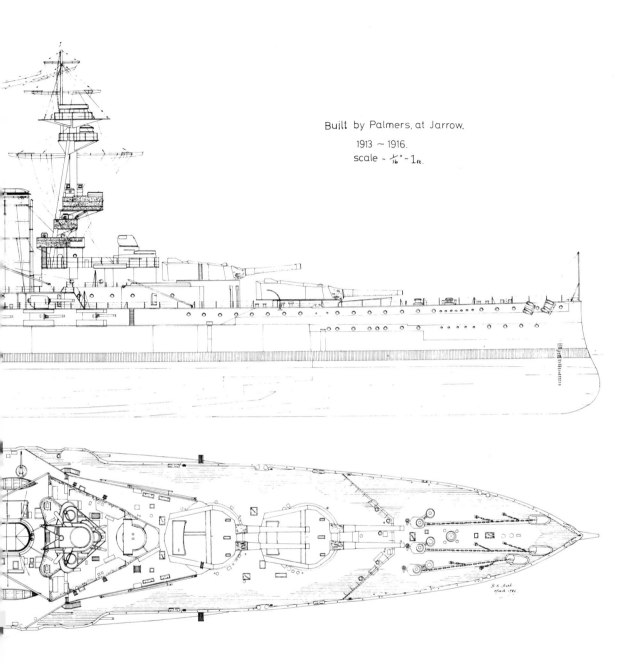

Built by Palmers, at Jarrow.

1913 ~ 1916.

scale - $\frac{1}{16}$" - 1ft.

bridge, an excellent point for identification.

Resolution **as refitted December 1926 to December 1927**
1 Control top enlarged and modified.
2 Range clocks added over 'X' turrets.
3 Upper pair of 6in guns removed, although casemates retained.
4 Extra pair of 4in HA guns as in *Ramillies*.
5 Training catapult (McTaggart type) fitted on quarter-deck, right aft, with crane.
6 Foretopmast, and yard below director removed.

7 Extra signalling struts fitted to starfish below the control top.
8 Topgallant mast fitted to mainmast.

Revenge
24in lamps removed from middle bridges.
1 24in lamp mounted on small platform very low before the bridge.

Resolution in drydock at Devonport, undergoing a refit. She is already fitted with a funnel cap.
Author's Collection

PARTICULARS OF VESSELS AS COMPLETED

Displacement *Royal Oak*
27,970 tons, load condition
31,130 tons deep load
Ramillies
30,400 tons load condition
33,570 tons deep load
Revenge
29,590 tons load condition
32,820 tons deep load

Length 580ft 3in pp
614ft 6in waterline
620ft 6⅞in over all (*Ramillies*)

Beam 88ft 6in
101ft 5½in (*Ramillies* after bulging)

Draught (mean) 30ft in the load condition. 33ft 7in deep load

Royal Sovereign **Built at Portsmouth Royal Dockyard**

Laid down	Launched	Completed	Handed over
15.1.1914	29.4.1915	8.4.1916	May 1916

Royal Oak **Built at Devonport Royal Dockyard**

15.1.1914	17.11.1914	1.5.1916	

Revenge **Built by Vickers of Barrow**

22.12.1913	29.5.1915	24.3.1916	

Resolution **Built by Palmers Shipyard**

29.11.1913	14.1.1915	7.12.1916	

Ramillies **Built by Beardmores Shipyard**

12.11.1913	12.9.1916	5.5.1917	September 1917

Armament as completed
8–15in Mk 1 42 calibre
14–16in Mk XII 45 calibre
2–3in A
4–3 pounder
5 machine guns
10 Lewis guns
Torpedo tubes
4 21in submerged, broadside and fixed at 90° and 2° depression
21 21in torpedoes carried. Mk II, IV and IVHB

Searchlights
First four ships were fitted with 8–36in lamps which were located as follows:
4 on forward bridge (2 port + starboard))
2 on base of funnel
2 on after superstructure
All vessels fitted with 2 24in signalling lamps
Ramillies carried 11 36in lamps as completed

Rangefinders (1918)
30ft fitted in 'B' and 'X' 15in turrets
1 15ft fitted in 'A' and 'Y' turrets
1 15ft fitted in gun control tower
1 12ft fitted in spotting top
2 9ft fitted on forebridge or platforms abreast funnels
1 6ft 6in fitted on forebridge

Battle signal stations
There were two separate and well enclosed stations located on the main deck level. Each were provided with signal lockers, and there were arrangements for working the signals through W/T trunks which ran through the decks above.

Fire control
The gun directors for the main armament were fitted in a tower aloft, and in an armoured tower. "X" 15in turret is also fitted with director gear. Follow the pointer gear is fitted to all sights, and flexible voice pipes are fitted for night control.

Complement
Ramillies	1917:	936
Revenge	1917:	940
Resolution	1916:	910
Royal Oak	1916:	1,909
Royal Sovereign	1921:	1,240
Resolution	1923:	1,012

Anchors
2 145cwt stockless bowers
1 145cwt stockless sheet
1 60cwt stern anchor, Admiralty pattern

Boats
2 50ft steam pinnaces
1 42ft launch
1 36ft pinnace
3 32ft cutters
2 27ft whalers
1 16ft skif dinghy
1 13ft 6in balsa raft

Boat derricks
1 60ft–65ft boat hoisting derrick which is located at the base of mainmast. In addition to this, there were also 2 32ft and 2 35ft wooden derricks for use with light boats and supplies.

Height of 15in gun from LWL
'A' 30ft 6in	'B' 40ft 6in
'X' 33ft	'Y' 23ft

Wireless
Main office:	Type 1–16
2nd office:	Type 2–34
3rd office:	Type 9
Fire control office:	Type 31

Destroyer office fitted in *Royal Oak* and *Revenge*, with modified Type 9 installed

Height of sighting slits in conning tower from lower waterline: 50ft
Height of fore funnel: 74ft
Height of lower masthead: 120ft
Depth of keel from battery: 44ft 6in

For further details of alterations, see appearance changes

Royal Oak **as refitted from March 1927 until June 1927**
1 Control top enlarged and modified.
2 Range clocks over control top removed.
3 Upper pair of 6in guns removed.
4 Extra 4in HA AA guns added.
5 Foretopmast and yard below director platform removed.
6 Extra signal struts fitted on starfish below top.
7 Topgallant mast added to main.

Royal Sovereign **refit from October 1927 to June 1928**
1 Control top enlarged and modified.
2 Upper pair of 6in removed, and this time the casemates also.
3 Extra pair of 4in HA AA guns fitted.
4 Foretopmast and lower yard removed.
5 Extra signal struts, as in *Royal Oak*.

Revenge **as refitted from January 1928 to January 1929**
1 Control top enlarged and modified.
2 Upper pair of 6in guns and casemates were removed.
3 Extra pair of 4in HA AA guns fitted.
4 AA observation post fitted both port and starboard below the director tower.
5 RDF equipment fitted. DF cabinet located at rear of director platform, with aerial at the rear of control top.

A close-up of the bridge of *Resolution* in 1933.
Author's Collection

TABLE FOR MACHINERY

Boilers	18
Make	Babcock and Wilcox in *Revenge, Ramillies* and *Royal Sovereign*. Yarrow in the other two
Designed Shaft Horse Power	40,000
Designed speed	23 knots
Total tube surface	63,846 sq ft in first three as above 69,840 sq ft in other two
Number of boilers in each room	6
Fuel	900 tons minimum; 3,400 tons maximum
Diameter of screws	inner: 10ft outer: 9ft 3in
Pitch	inner 10ft (in first three) outer 9ft 6in inner 8ft 9in (in other two) outer 9ft 3in
Weight of machinery	2,550 tons (dry)
Main feed pump output	(vertical steam reciprocating single cylinder) 71.4 tons per hour
Auxiliary feed pump output	35.7 tons per hour
Designed revolutions of shafts	300 per minute
Radius of action	10 knots at 7000 miles Full speed at 2700 miles
Number of screws	4
Number of blades	3

6 Forward section of each searchlight tower was enlarged to bring forward a pair of lamps in each. The after section was raised along with the lamps.
7 Plane platforms were removed from the turrets.
8 The bridge was enlarged.
9 Flag signalling was transferred from the fore to the mainmast. The after superstructure was enlarged to accommodate the required staff.
10 Taller gallant added to the mainmast.
11 Signal yard at head of maintopgallant, and close above starfish.

Resolution **1930/1**
1 Fo'c'sle deck 6in casemates removed (by March 1931).
2 HA RF on control top was replaced by HA Director.
3 After pair of torpedo tubes were removed (by March 1931).

Royal Sovereign
HA RF on control top replaced by HA Director.

Revenge **May 1931**
1 HA RF replaced by HA director.
2 Range clocks over "X" turret were removed.

Revenge **as refitted from May to December 1931**
1 Multiple 2 pounder (pom-pom) 8 barrel, were fitted on a raised platform on the starboard side of the shelter

1

2

3

4

1 *Ramillies* in July 1935.
Author's Collection

2 *Ramillies* in April 1936.
Author's Collection

3 *Resolution* in October 1936 carrying the experimental 4in between decks mounting above the second 6in casemate. This mounting, with 4.5in guns was later fitted to the fleet aircraft carriers of the *Illustrious* class and the rebuilt battleships *Queen Elizabeth* and *Valiant* and the battlecruiser *Renown*.
(Wright & Logan)

4 *Royal Oak* in March 1937, carrying the tricolour markings of the non-intervention patrol on B turret.
Author's Collection

deck abeam the funnel (none to port).
2 Modified type of DF fitted.
3 Base of searchlight towers on starboard side cut away to accommodate 2pdrs.
4 24in lamps removed from fore, and remounted on small platform low on mainmast.
5 Signal struts raked well aft, and fitted below starfish below control top.

Ramillies 1931/2
1 Range clocks over 'X' turrets were removed.
2 Upper deck casemates were removed by July 1932.

Royal Oak
1 Range clocks were removed from over 'X' turret by April 1932.
2 Upper deck 6in casemates removed from April to July 1932.
3 HA DF replaced by HA director.

Royal Sovereign **as refitted from January to November 1932**
1 Range clocks over 'X' turret removed.
2 Multiple 2pdr pom-pom's added on raised platform around funnel on both port and starboard. Platform cut away to accommodate pom-poms arcs of fire.
3 AA observation posts fitted at each side of 15in director platform.
4 After pair of TT were removed.

5 New rectangular shaped searchlight towers fitted around funnel, with after pairs of lamps raised higher than those aft.
6 Training catapult fitted on the quarterdeck, right aft, with a crane to serve this.
7 Plane platforms were removed from turrets.
8 Bridge was modified and enlarged.
9 Deep supporting flanges added below navigating platform.
10 Lower bridgework was extended back around the funnel base to meet the new SL towers.

Resolution **1933**
1 Range clocks removed from over turrets.
2 The starboard 4in AA guns were replaced by an experimental twin 4in AA mounting, and a gas-tight turret. This was a prototype for those eventually fitted to the *Queen Elizabeth* class shortly before the Second World War.
3 Multiple 0.5in AA four barrelled guns were added abeam the conning tower on the shelterdeck level.

Royal Oak **1933**
After pair of TT removed. Plane platforms removed.

Ramillies **as refitted from January 1933 until August 1934**
1 Multiple pom-pom added around funnel as in others.
2 Multiple 0.5in AA added abeam conning tower.
3 HA DF on control top replaced with HA director, and after director added on a platform on the main tripod legs.
4 Tripod legs fitted to mainmast.
5 After pair of TT removed.
6 Torpedo control tower and rangefinder removed.
7 Training catapult fitted to port side of 'X' turret with crane to serve this fitted on platform on after superstructure.
8 Plane platforms removed from turrets.
9 Bridge enlarged and modified.
10 Roof over upper bridge made more steeper, with prominent flanges for support placed below the navigating platform.

Ramillies **1935**
HA RF fitted to mainmast to support HA directors.

Royal Sovereign
Multiple 0.5in AA guns added as in others HA RF removed from bridge (May to July 1935).

Royal Oak refitted from June 1934 until August 1936
1 6in director towers relocated port and starboard on new platforms on foremast below 15in director.
2 Single 4in AA replaced by larger mounted twin fittings.
3 Multiple 2pdrs added around funnel as in others.
4 Multiple 0.5in guns added around CT.
5 AA RF removed from over bridge and from control top.
6 HA director platform fitted on legs of tripod although director not yet fitted at this date.
7 4 × 21in torpedo tubes added (experimental) port and starboard in recessed ports in fo'c'sle before 'A' turret.
8 The remaining forward pair of TT were removed.
9 RDF equipment fitted.
10 The 36in searchlight lamps were replaced by 44in.
11 Training catapult was fitted as in *Ramillies*, although of a different type to *Ramillies*.
12 The upper part of the bridge was completely renewed with an open structure giving a clear view all round.
13 Tripod legs fitted to mainmast to support the director.
14 Maintopgallant removed and topmast was reduced in height.
15 The lower part of the bridge was extended back around the funnel as in the *Royal Sovereign*.

Resolution as refitted from December 1935 to September 1936
As above in *Royal Oak*, with the exception of a different face for bridgework.

Revenge refit July 1936 to March 1937
1 Torpedo rangefider and tower was removed.
2 36in lamps replaced by 44in.

Royal Sovereign March 1937
1 Multiple 2pdr temporarily removed.
2 36in lamps replaced by 44in.
3 Catapult and crane removed.
4 Catapult and base on quarterdeck was retained.

Royal Oak April 1937
1 HA director fitted on control top and on platform on tripod legs.
2 Flagpole fitted to each mast.

Ramillies May 1937
1 36in lamps replaced by 44in
2 Tower over bridge was replaced by large open platform which extended back around tripod legs.

In 1937 red, white and blue stripes were painted on 'B' turret in those vessels operating around Spanish waters, for recognition. Also large letters were seen on the turret tops such as to the vessels name: ie *Ramillies* – RA. *Royal Oak* – RO. *Revenge* – RE etc. *Royal Sovereign* was under refit from June 1937 until February 1938, and was fitted much the same as the rest of the class (see *Royal Oak*).

Resolution January 1938
2 pounder AA guns were fitted to those mounts that had been purposely fitted in 1936.

Ramillies June 1938
1 Catapult removed but crane was retained.
2 Remaining pair of TT removed.
3 Single 4in AA replaced by twin fittings.
4 Topgallant mast reduced in height.

Revenge refitted from early 1939 to August 1939
1 Single 4in AA replaced by twin mountings.
2 Multiple 2pdr added around funnel.
3 Multiple 0.5in AA added abeam CT.
4 HA director added on control top, raised well clear of top.
5 After HA added in place of torpedo director tower.
6 DF aerial removed from over top. Modified type of aerial fitted at head of main topgallant.
7 Base of searchlights cut away to accommodate pom-poms.
8 Signal and distributing office at rear of bridge removed.
9 Clinker screen fitted to funnel.
10 Signal yards were removed from maintopmast.

WARTIME ALTERATIONS:
No major alterations, but ships became very heavy in appearance owing to the ever increasing additions in AA defence.

STEAM TRIALS ON COMPLETION

Revenge

Date	24.3.1916
Type of trial	4 hours, full power, preliminary
Location	Firth of Clyde, Skelmorlie
Sea	Smooth
Wind	Light breeze, NNE
Ships bottom	Clean
Draught forward	33ft 2in
Draught aft	32ft 7in
Steam pressure in boilers	220lb /sq in
Steam pressure at turbines	204lb/sq in
Speed	20.773 knots
Boilers in use	18
Heating surface	63,800 sq/ft
Fuel consumption	1.19lb/shp/hour
Oil pressure	75lb/sq in
Oil temperature	75°F
Screws inner	10ft
outer	9ft 3in
Pitch of screws	9ft 6in

Revolutions taken on 4 runs whilst on the Measured Mile

	Starboard inner	Starboard outer	Port inner	Port outer	Speed kts
1	300	310	308	312	20.966
2	302	314	300	312	20.655
3	302	312	298	310	20.85
4	308	314	308	316	20.667

Speeds recorded whilst on overload were as follows

1	22.140kts at 43,080 shp
2	21.710 at 42.610 shp
3	22.031 at 42,350 shp
4	21.898 at 42,680 shp

STEAM TRIALS

General for class, as completed.

Nature	Date	Speed	SHP	Revs.
Royal Sovereign				
MM. 2hr, FP	22.5.16	21.75kts	41,112	320.4 mean
Royal Oak				
MM. 1½hr, FP	9.5.16	22kts	40,360	328
Revenge				
MM. 2hr, FP	24.3.16	21.9kts	41,938	326
Resolution				
MM. 2hr, FP	30.12.16	Not known	41,405	317.75
Ramillies				
MM. 2hr, FP	1.10.17	21.5kts	42,414	325

Although full sets of trials were not carried out in the class owing to hostilities, the above shows that the best speed attained was a little over 22 knots. All of the above trials were run at full load.

A further set of figures are available after the bulges were added. *Royal Sovereign* was still under refit when these trials were carried out.

February 1921. Full Power trials

	Speed	SHP	Ships bottom
Revenge	21.1kts	40,940	foul
Resolution	21kts	40,306	foul
Royal Oak			
(no bulge)	21kts	40,395	foul
Ramillies	20.8kts	37,710	Slightly foul

A further set of trials were made in March, when the ships bottoms were even worse, and *Royal Oak* had been at sea for 7 months without cleaning bottom.

Revenge	Speed: 19.4kts for 41,320shp
Royal Oak	20.8kts for 40,498shp
Ramillies	20.9kts for 41,480shp
Resolution	20.5kts for 40,196shp

1940/1

0.5in AA removed and 8 to 10 20mm AA added on 'B' and 'X' turrets, superstructure, shelter deck forward, and quarterdeck at the extreme ends.
Ramillies painted up in a one-off dazzle type of camouflage believed to consist of blues and greys.
Clinker screen to cap for *Ramillies*.
Revenge, and *Royal Sovereign* were both camouflaged with early versions of the dazzle theme: both were unofficial.

1941/2

Radar fitted for control of main armament (Type 284).
Radar fitted for control of 4in (Type 285).
Radar fitted for air warning: Type 79 in *Ramillies* at first.
Type 279 in *Revenge* and *Resolution*.
Radar fitted for surface warning (Type 273).
Original DF aerials on masts removed.
Modifications of bridgework in *Ramillies, Resolution* and *Royal Sovereign*. Maintopgallant removed in *Ramillies, Revenge* and *Resolution*.

1942/3

Two forwardmost 6in guns (port and starboard) removed.
6 twin 20mm AA added in *Royal Sovereign*.
Radar fitted for 2pdrs (Type 282).

Directors for this were port and starboard abeam bridge.

1944 *Ramillies*

1 Twin 20mm AA mounted on 'B' and 'X' turret, and on quarterdeck right aft.
2 VHF equipment added before Normandy beach landings.
3 Special type of missile jamming aerials mounted at base of main tripod (Type 650).

Resolution and *Revenge* were relegated to subsidiary service at the end of 1943. Admiralty disruptive camouflage painted up in *Ramillies* and *Resolution*. *Revenge* retained the same camouflage from 1942. *Royal Sovereign* was camouflaged and refitted for special service with the Russian Fleet, and renamed *Archangelsk* (Archangel). All vessels fitted with funnel caps by 1942.

PARTICULARS FOR SHIPS

Displacement	
Revenge	31,875 tons load condition
	33,230 tons deep load
Resolution	28,013 tons light load
	34,249 tons deep load
Ramillies	30,507 tons light load
	34,032 tons average action load
	35,507 tons deep load
Royal Sovereign	29.948 tons light load
	33,491 tons average action load
	34,836 tons deep load
Length	As completed
Beam	Average: 101ft 4in, except *Ramillies* at 102ft
Draught	29ft 4⅛in average at light load, to 33ft 6½in in the deep
Complement	from 1,037 to 1,240
Armament	8 15in Mk I, 42 calibre, unchanged as built
	8 6in
	8 4in (twins) AA
	24 2pdr and 12–22 20mm AA in *Ramillies*
	Small AA guns removed in *Revenge* and *Resolution* after becoming training ships at Devonport
	Royal Sovereign up to 42 20mm AA and 24 2pdr
	Quadruple pom-poms fitted to turret tops (and quarterdeck in *Resolution*)
	In all ships by 1942
	Resolution 24 2pdrs and 10 20mm AA
	Revenge 10 single 20mm AA
Armour	As completed except in *Resolution, Ramillies* and *Royal Sovereign*
	Extra 2in over magazines on main deck level
Searchlights	4 44in
	4 24in, (signalling) in *Revenge,* 2 in others
Machinery	As completed
Fuel capacity	As completed
	Radius reduced owing to wartime additions
	Speed decrease for same reason
Average speed	19 knots

to be continued

The Japanese aircraft carriers Junyo and Hiyo

Part 3   by Hans Lengerer and Tomoko Rehm-Takahara

PROTECTION

The lack of real protection was a result of the limitations imposed by the conversion. The installation of side armour, torpedo protection measures (bulges, armoured bulkheads etc), and an armoured flight deck would have reduced speed. Becauase it was feared that the ships could not operate within a division of warships with their comparatively low speed of 25.5 knots, only a minimum of protection was allowed.

Along the machinery spaces there were installed 2 × 25mm Ducol steel plates (50mm) on the 20mm thick hull plates. Furthermore turbines and boilers compartments were divided by means of one longitudinal and several transverse bulkheads. This protection might be sufficient against framents of bombs and shells, and MG bullets but not against direct hits.

The aircraft gasoline tanks, ammunition and bomb magazines were before and abaft the machinery spaces, the torpedo stowage being adjacent to the after bomb room. They were protected by 25mm Ducol steel plate. Beside this very light protection, more narrow framing and better watertight subdivision than normal merchantmen was considered as further (also insufficient) protection against torpedo, bomb, and shell damage.

As mentioned Junyo received a 'concrete armour' around her gasoline tanks after the sinking of Hiyo during the battle for the Marianas. After June 1944 concrete was also used as protection for AA bridge, etc.

ARMAMENT

The aircraft complement has already been dealt with in the chapter on hangars.

At the time of completion Hiyo and Junyo were armed with 12 12.7cm AA guns L/40 type 89 (6 double mounts) and 24 25mm MGs type 96 model 2 (8 triple mounts). AA guns and MGs were installed on sponsons along the flak deck, half of them on each side of the ship. On the port side the first AA gun was located level with the wind catcher, the next one level with the forward elevator, and the third level with the aft elevator. On the side the first was installed parallel to that on the port side; the next two were close together behind the bridge.

In order to direct the fire of these guns two type 94 fire directors were provided. One director was installed on the fore part of the bridge, directing the fire on starboard, the other one shortly behind the port aft 12.7cm AA gun, directing the fire of the guns on that side. When Junyo commissioned only the 4.5m stereo range finder of the fire directors were installed, the other parts were fitted subsequently.

The authors regrettably do not know whether or not Hiyo already had the complete fire directors at the time of her commissioning.

Four triple mounts were located in the middle part of the flak deck to port, the others aft on the starboard side. Directing the fire of the MG's two type 95 fire directors were on sponsons near the MG group at both sides of the

Junyo at the end of the war.
Author's Collection

A bow view, showing the angle of the funnel.
Author's Collection

Junyo broadside on.
Author's Collection

Junyo with an *Akitsuki* class anti-aircraft type destroyer.
Jurgen Peters.

ship, a total of four directors. Each director directed 2 triple mounts.

The bombs were stowed in separate compartments before and abaft the machinery spaces, the torpedo-room being adjacent to the after bomb room. The complement consisted of:

Number of pieces	Weight of bomb in kg
54	800
198	250
348	60
240	30

and

27	Torpedoes type 91

Six torpedoes could be readied for operation at the same time. With this arrangement there was a combined bomb and torpedo hoist aft and a smaller bomb hoist forward, serving both hangars. Bombs and torpedoes were lifted from their stowage bins on to light trolley by means of hydraulic hoists, and the trolleys were wheeled out on to a platform raised about one metre above deck level. This arrangment was adopted to allow a coaming of this depth to be worked around the bomb lift, thereby preventing aviation gasoline vapour from pouring into the bomb room hoists, fitted over the raised platform, enabled the bombs and torpedoes to be lifted onto special dollies, which were used for transport inside the hangars or from the upper hangar to the flight deck by means of the after elevator. The dollies were manually operated light ones for bombs of 250kg or less and a heavy type for bombs of over 500kg and torpedoes. Loading bombs and torpedoes onto planes was normally carried out on the flight deck, but there are cases of it being done in the hangars.

MACHINERY

The machinery spaces were divided by a longitudinal and some transverse bulkheads into six compartments. Four were used as boiler rooms, two as turbine rooms. The machinery plant consisted of six boilers and 2 turbine sets, ie they had two propeller shafts. The machinery spaces of *Junyo* were in general arrangements, identical to those of *Hiyo*. On *Junyo* six Mitsubishi watertube boilers with three steam drums (fuel oil consumption only) generated steam with a pressure of 40 kg/cm² (about 39bar) and a temperature of 420°C and supplied it at 35bar and 405°C at the turbine inlet to two Mitsubishi-Curtis action turbine sets with double reduction gears. The *Hiyo* had the same turbine sets but received six of the seldom used Kawasaki-La Mont (Japanese term-Se-go) forced circulation boilers.

One set of turbines consisted of 1 HP, 1st IP, 2nd IP, and LP (double flow) turbines, ie four turbines per shaft. The turbine set had a performance of 28,125shp per shaft at 170rpm. The astern power was 15,500shp per shaft at 144rpm. The HP and the first IP turbines operated at 4145rpm, the second IP at 3325rpm and the LP at 2392rpm.

The arrangement of the machinery of *Hiyo* and of *Junyo* was nearly identical, the difference was that on *Junyo* the HP astern was incorporated into the 2nd IP casing. Because the ships were planned as merchant ships they had no cruising turbines like the warships of the IJN. The shaft had a diameter of 440mm, was 36m long and weighed 55 tons. With 5.5m diameter the propeller was the largest fitted to a Japanese CV.

On their official trials *Hiyo* made 25.63 knots with 56,630shp, *Junyo*'s performance is documented as 26 knots at 51,000shp with a trial displacement of 27,000 tons. (The authors do not completely trust 51,000shp, this might be an error in the Japanese source and might in fact be 57,000shp).

The weight of the machinery was 3823 tons including water in the boilers (*Hiyo*), without water 3568 tons. Divided through the performance the ratio for one HP was, with water in the boilers 68kg, without water 63kg. The ratio of the *Hiryu*, already compared with the *Hiyo* class, was 17kg and 15kg respectively. From this data we can see that the machinery of the *Hiyo* class, built as luxury passenger liners, was four times as heavy as that of a regular CV.

With 4100 tons fuel oil the ships had a (designed) cruising radius of 10,000 sea miles at 18 knots. In fact

Flight deck plan of *Junyo*.

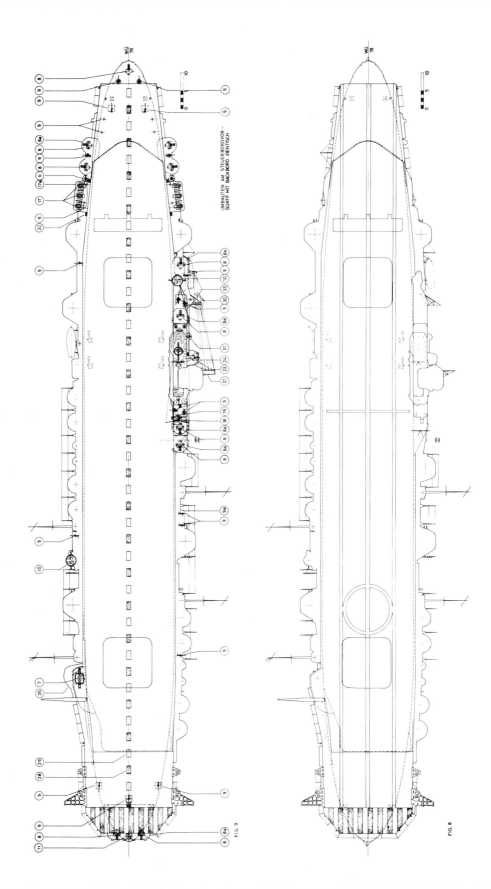

UMBAUTEN AM STEUERBORDVOR –
SCHIFF MIT BACKBORD IDENTISCH

FIG. 9

FIG. 8

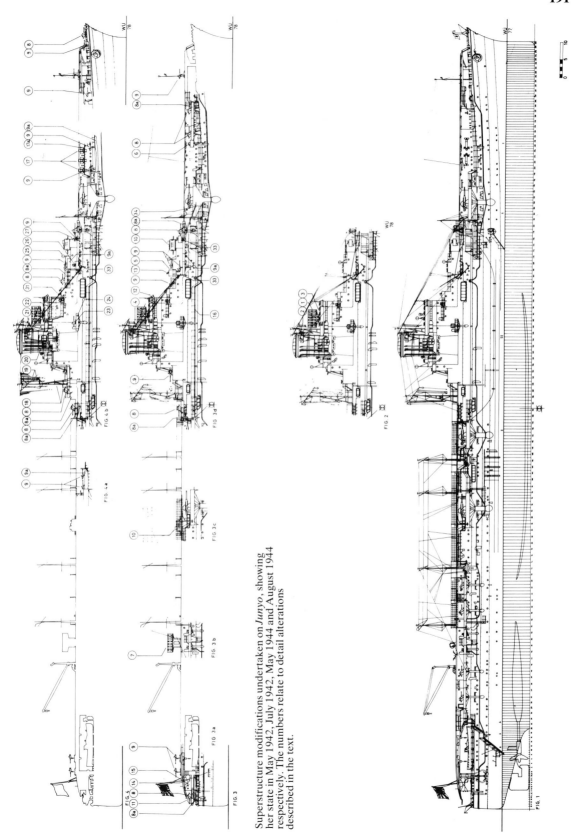

Superstructure modifications undertaken on *Junyo*, showing her state in May 1942, July 1942, May 1944 and August 1944 respectively. The numbers relate to detail alterations described in the text.

Two perspectives of Michael Wunschmann's superb model of *Junyo*.

the *Junyo* obtained 12,251 sea miles, and *Hiyo* 11,700 at the same speed.

There were also two auxiliary boilers in the aft boiler room. They were cylindrical boilers running on fuel at a pressure of 10.5bars. Between the aft boiler rooms and the turbine rooms there was the reserve engine room with 3 2000kVA turbo generators, 1 250kVA, and 1 145kVA diesel generator. On the ships 225 V AC was used.

Because of their low speed of 25.5 knots there were problems in launching the fast aircraft, in service from about the middle of the war, during calm periods. At the time of the A go operation (Battle for the Marianas) no training with the new aircraft model Suisei had been possible at Tawi Tawi and the pilots had to fight with insufficient training. Taking into consideration that the ships were planned as passenger lines a higher speed could not be provided. As mentioned earlier they could have been used more effectively if the development of Japanese catapults had not failed, and they had been equipped with them. There were also a number of problems with the merchant ship machinery plant and the crew could not rely on it, especially as it was difficult to operate. Directly before the South Pacific Battle (Battle off Santa Cruz Islands) *Hiyo* had to return to Truk because of a machinery break down which must have had an influence on the outcome of the battle.

RADIO EQUIPMENT
Two tiltable wireless radio masts were fitted on each side of the ships. They were lowered during flight operations. In the radio rooms there were two long-wave transmitters, four short-wave transmitters, one combined long- and short-wave transmitter and 21 receivers. Three loop antennas for direction finding were fitted on the bridge; the fourth elsewhere.

DEGAUSSING COIL
When commissioned the ships were fitted with a degaussing coil for magnetic mines

SHIP'S BOATS
A feature aft below the flight deck was the stowage of four 12m boats (two motor boats and 2 motor launches). Two were stowed fore and aft in deep wells and two on skids directly over the other two on the upper hangar deck level. All four were handled with trolley hoists supported from the athwartship I-beams extending outboard underneath the flight deck. These boat hoists had a capacity of 5 tons. Also on this level were one 8m motor launch and one 6m traffic boat. Two 13m landing boats (the Japanese called them special landing boats) were stowed on the deck below. Besides these, two 9m lifeboats were carried on both sides of the ships on a level with the bridge.

SYNOPSIS
Except for their low speed and inadequate protection the ships of the *Hiyo* class were comparable with the middle class regular CV *Hiryu* in their capability as fleet CV's. After having lost four CVs in the battle for Midway the IJN brought these ships into operation with the main body of the CV fleet. They were the only ships in the world that became regular CVs through conversion from merchant ships, and they acted as fleet CVs in two of the most fierce sea/air battles during the war in the Pacific.

FATE
As already mentioned the carriers took their place in the main body of the CV force in some engagements of the Pacific War. *Junyo* participated in the Battle in the

South Pacific (Battle off Santa Cruz Islands) and the Battle for the Marianas. *Hiyo* was a member of Vice Admiral Ozawa's CV force in the last mentioned battle only. During this battle *Hiyo* was lost.

Hiyo Sunk during the Battle for the Marianas by one bomb hit and one torpedo hit on 20 June 1944 7.32pm. Position 16° 20′N/132° 32′ E. Stricken from Navy list on 10 August 1944.

Junyo Damaged by two torpedo hits during an attack by the American submarines *Redfish* and *Sea Devil* near Nomosaki on 9 December 1944 at about 1.30am. One torpedo exploded in the starboard engine room, the other one near the bow on the same side. About 5000 tons of water poured into the ship, increasing the draught to about 10 metres and giving the ship a list to starboard. The port engine was still operable and *Junyo* reached Sasebo under her own power on the same day. Repairs went on until March 1945 but were never finished due to lack of materials. She was anchored, camouflaged, in the bay of Ebisu (near Sasebo) from 1 April 1945. Classified as reserve warship (yobikan) after 20 April 1945 she lay immobilised thereafter and saw no operational service until the end of the war even though she was classified as guard ship (keibokan) on 20 June 1945. Captain Maehara, the last commanding office (he took over command on 12 May 1945) received orders to strip her of all armament and other installations on 5 August 1945. This job had been practically completed by October 1945. This was done to use her guns and equipment for other purposes, but the end of the war prevented these weapons from seeing further service.

When the members of the (American) Air Technical Intelligence Group boarded *Junyo* on 8 October 1945 they reported after the inspection that any attempt to repair or complete the ship would be a waste of material and labour. They considered her good only for scrap. *Junyo* was stricken from the Navy list on 30 November 1945 and broken up (scrapped) from 1 June 1946 until 1 August 1947 by the Sasebo Ship Company.

[11]The rocket launchers installed on a number of large Japanese warships for AA defence have already been dealt with at some length in another article published by the author in *Warship 34*.

TABLE 4: INSTALLATION OF RADAR

Time	Name of ship	Number and type of radar	Location
July 1942	*Junyo*	1 × 21 go	On bridge
Autumn 1942	*Hiyo*	1 × 21 go	On bridge
March 1943	*Hiyo*	1 × 21 go	On flight deck instead of searchlight no 4
July/August 1943	*Junyo*	1 × 21 go	as above
Spring 1944	*Junyo* *Hiyo*	1 × E 25	At signal mast on bridge
July/August 1944	*Junyo*	1 × 13 go	At signal mast on bridge

TABLE 5: REINFORCEMENT OF LIGHT AA WEAPONS

Time	Name of ship	Number and type of gun	Location
Spring 1943	*Hiyo*	4 × 25mm triples	Forepart of flak-deck port and starboard
		2 × director type 95	2 each
July/August	*Junyo*	as above	as above
Autumn 1943/Spring 1944	*Hiyo* *Junyo*	4 × 25mm triples	2 on stern; before and behind island bridge one each
		12 × 25mm singles	Before and behind the island bridge, on the flight deck transportable
July/August 1944	*Junyo*	3 × 25mm triples	1 × on bow, before and behind island bridge one each
		2 × 25mm twins	1 × bridge instead of searchlight no 1 1 × location unknown
		18 × 25mm singles	various places on flight and flak decks
August 1944		6 × 12cm rocket with 28 tubes	3 each on both sides of the ship on sponsons before the fore 12.7cm AA gun on flak deck

1. In October 1944 the *Junyo* had the following armament
12 × 12.7cm AA guns in six double mounts
15 × 25mm MG in 19 triple mounts
4 × 25mm MG in 2 double mounts   91 barrels
30 × 25mm MG in 30 single mounts
6 × 12cm rocket launchers with 28 tubes (168 tubes)

2. The data concerning the rocket launchers is quite contrary to that of Mr Fukui Shizuo gives in his book '*Japanese Naval Vessels Illustrated 1869–1945, Vol. 3 Aircraft Carriers, Seaplane Tenders, Torpedo Boat and Submarine Tenders*', p.338 (table 7–3). He writes that CVs received four mounts on each side of the ship (BBs three mounts only), and gives other locations on *Junyo*.

Right side
Opposite to the tiltable (collapsible) aircraft crane, four mounts were installed on the former MGs platform which was, after the removal of two triple mounts, lengthened in order to get the area needed for their installation. To control their fire, the fire director of the former MG group was used.

Left side
Above the aircraft engine test room a large sponson was built (some metres abaft the sponson for the original aft MG group consisting of two triple mounts) and four rocket launchers installed. The sponson for the original aft MG group was enlarged and one of the removed MG triple mounts (see right side) installed together with the fire director for the rocket launchers.

Because of the violent flame and blast which developed upon firing, thin steel plates were installed between the rocket launchers of a group (in general 3 or 4) and behind them as a screen against flames. These screens are clearly visible in the photographs taken as Sasebo and identical to Fukui's photo no 3375. Therefore the authors place little reliance on the accuracy of Mr Fukui's data, and in this case they think that *Junyo* was equipped with three 12cm 28 tube rocket launchers on each side of the ship directly before the forward 12.7cm AA guns.

As&As

BATTLESHIP BISMARCK by Hans Gally

Numerous books have been written about the battleship *Bismarck*. This article, therefore, confines itself to some little-known facts which were but briefly – if at all – mentioned in previous literature but which should, in any case, be of interest to lovers of ships. The writer only deals with technical details and modifications which should be helpful when it is necessary to classify illustrations of the ship in a chronological order and to correct faulty statements.

ALTERATIONS AND MODIFICATIONS OF THE WARSHIP

In the short time between commissioning of the ship (August 1940) and her sinking (May 1941) major alterations and modifications of her superstructure were carried out only once. This occurred in December 1940/January 1941 at the shipyard of Blohm & Voss,

Hamburg. At that time a number of vents located at the barbette of turret 'Berta' were lowered and the suction ports were protected against jets of water. In addition, one large gas turbine bulkhead was mounted at either side of the rear bridge deck in front of the vent ports (for the boilers), after the ventilator grids had suffered considerable damage during gun tests in the Baltic Sea at the end of 1940. Finally, the vent ports close to the large shipboard crane and near the catapult launching gear were altered in order to reduce the entrance of jets of water. Further and-less important-reconstruction work is not dealt with in this paper.

RANGE FINDERS OF THE HEAVY ARMAMENT

When commissioned in August 1940 the ships had no range finders for the heavy and secondary armament (38cm and 15cm quick firing guns). The range finders on the foretop command post and aft command post were installed either late in October 1940 or November 1941.

The range finder on the forward command post was

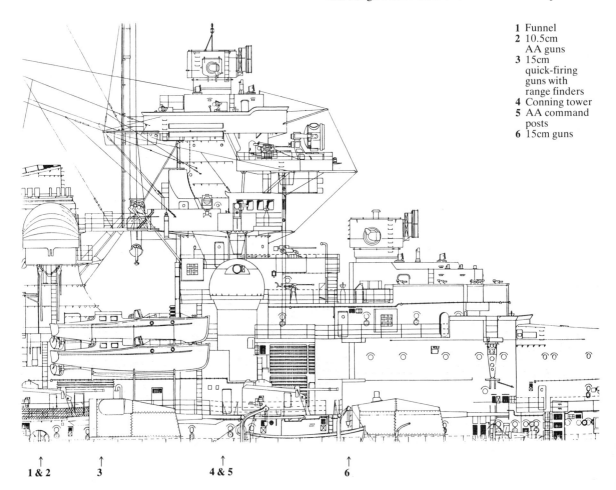

1 Funnel
2 10.5cm AA guns
3 15cm quick-firing guns with range finders
4 Conning tower
5 AA command posts
6 15cm guns

1 & 2   3   4 & 5   6

installed in Kiel (March 1941), its 'mattress' (Radarantenne) presumably in Gotenhafen.

HEAVY AA – ARMAMENT AND FIRE CONTROL

The heavy anti-aircraft armament consisted of 16 10.5cm quick firing guns, calibre L/65 in twin mountings on each side of the superstructure. The forward eight guns were quick firing guns, construction 1933, in tri-axially stabilised twin mountings construction 1937, abbreviated.:

10.5cm SKC/33in 10.5cm Dopp LC/31.

The after eight guns were quick firing guns, construction 1933 Neue Art (new design), abbreviated:

10.5cm SKC/33 na in 10.5cm Dopp LC/37.

The ship had the forward four twin mountings from the very beginning. The aft four twin mountings were installed in Gotenhafen either in the last days of October 1940 or in November 1940. The protective shields of the forward and aft guns differed in appearance.

The heavy AA–armament was controlled by two tri-axially stabilised directors located one on each side of the bridge superstructure and by two emergency control positions (Hilfsleitstände), one immediately after the main mast and one immediately forward of 'C' turret

After superstructure of *Bismarck*, also in April 1941.

('X' turret on British ships).

The emergency control positions were stabilised only in height. They were open ie there was no overhead protection for the crew.

The spherical anti-aircraft command posts were missing (plus the associated computer Reg VI) presumably to keep the terms of delivery to the USSR. They were never installed in the ship.

CHANGE IN THE LIGHT AA – ARMAMENT (2CM – FLAK)

When the ship was commissioned, the light flak armament consisted of 12 2cm machine guns (MG C/38 in LC 30) singly mounted on the superstructure and the funnel. It was improved in 1941 by the addition of 2cm army mountings (Heereslafette) and Flak 38 quadruple army mountings as follows:

1 One additional 2cm army mounting on turret A in Kiel harbour (March 1941,

2 Two additional 2cm army mountings after the aft command post in April/May 1941 (Baltic Sea/Gotenhafen) and

3 Two quadruple mountings on the searchlight platform of the conning tower (after April 1941).

The singly mounted 'Heereslafette' (army mountings) were removed before the ship left Gotenhafen in May 1941.

1 AA emergency control position
2 2cm AA gun
3 Range finder
4 37cm AA guns
5 10.5cm AA guns
6 AA Emergency control post
7 15cm guns
8 Big aircraft hangar
9 10.5cm AA guns

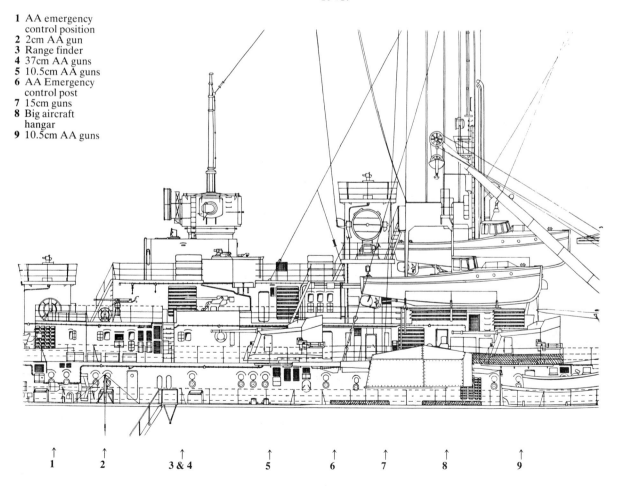

1   2   3 & 4   5   6   7   8   9

3

4

1 Forward superstructure of *Bismarck* in September 1940, on her departure from Hamburg. The range finders have not been installed.
Federal German Archive

2 Aft superstructure of *Bismark,* passing through the Kiel canal in September 1940. The 10.5cm AA guns have not been installed.
Federal German Archive

3 Vents on 'B' turret before alteration.
Federal German Archive

4 The same vents after alteration.
Federal German Archive

THE SHIP'S AIRCRAFT AND HANGARS
There were two small aircraft hangars on each side of the funnel and a big hangar below the main mast. Each small aircraft hangar could accommodate one Arado 196; while the big hangar was capable of holding two aircraft (and not four). Consequently the ship carried only four Arados 196 A and not six (as often quoted).

THE SHIP'S BOATS
Bismarck carried on its starboard side only one captain's gig, although she had skids for two. After April/May 1941 her cutters and dinghies were aboard. *Bismarck* then carried additional life-rafts of different size and form.

SHIP'S COLOURING
From January 1941 until 12 May the *Bismarck* carried three black and white zig-zagged camouflage stripes. The colour of the turret-roofs was either carmine or (presumably before leaving Gotenhafen in May 1941) dark grey. Unfortunately there were no coloured photographs available of this time and statements of survivors differ.

Colour photographs of the warships *Prinz Eugen* (with 'zig-zag camouflage') and *Tirpitz*, taken in spring 1941, give every reason to believe that the turret covers and slopes were painted carmine coloured before the beginning of May 1941.

The colour of the turret roofs was painted over on 22 May 1941 when *Bismarck* left Grimstad-Fjord. It was now grey. On 26 May 1941 the turret roofs of the heavy and secondary armament were painted yellow but the heavy seas washed away the colour of the 15cm guns.

In spite of intensive studies a number of relevant questions still remain unanswered. The author will be grateful for receiving further hints, corrective information and supporting materials.

Hans Gally
Josef-Stöhrer-Weg 13
7505 Ettlingen

The Gabbiano Class Corvettes

Part Two   **by Elio Ando**

CAREERS

The first ship to enter service was *Gabbiano*, on 3 October 1942. Until the Italian armistice on 9 September 1943 all corvettes, once completed and after a brief period of battle training joined the *Squadriglie* (Divisions); two or three *squadriglie* made up a Gruppo (Flotilla). These were primarily employed as anti-submarine escorts; largely on the route between Sicily and Tunisia in support of the Axis armies in North Africa, and in coastal convoys along the Italian peninsula and the islands of Sicily, Sardinia and Corsica.

After the armistice all those vessels that reached allied bases in accordance with the terms of the agreement were employed escorting allied convoys. Those that were still in the hands of the northern building yards, or in northern harbours, fell into German hands and served against the Allies until the end of the war.

At the end of the war the surviving ships served as minesweepers in the postwar clearing up operations. Thereafter they served in the training flotilla right up to the end of their careers. Corvettes of this class also served in the *Gruppo Navale Costiero* (Coastal Flotilla), the *Gruppo Navale di scortia* (Escort Flotilla), the *Gruppo Navale Logistico* (Supply Flotilla), the *Com-*

ando Motosiluranti. (MTB Headquarters), as training ships for engineers and sonar operators and as naval district ships.

In the following tables the career details of each ship are given, with a synopsis of her war service. They are listed in numerical order of the original hull numbers. The eight entries for each ship are:

1   Hull letter up to 1949.
2   Hull letter up to 1952.
3   Pennant number after Italy joined NATO.
4   Pennant number under the German flag.
5   Builders. An Ansaldo, Genoa: Br Breda, Porto Marghera: Ce Cerusa, Vottri: CRDA,M Cantieri Riuniti dell'Adriatico, Monflacone: CRDA,T Trieste: NM Navalmeccanica, Castellemmare di Stabia: OTO,L Odero Terni Orlando, Livorno.

6   Laid down.
6   Launched.
8   Completed.

Procellaria sinking on 31 January 1943, she is being assisted by the German motor raft M7481.
Author's Collection

Gabbiano entering Pireaus Harbour 6 February 1943. At the
left is the destroyer *Pigafetta*.

Author's Collection

Gabbiano   C11   –   GB   F571   Ce   14.1.42
23.6.42   3.10.42
Assigned to the 1st Corvette Squadron, 3rd A/S
Gruppo, based at Trapani. From January 1943 served as
a convoy escort on the route to Tunisia. Before the
armistice carried out 102 war missions, with 18 A/S
sweeps and 22 escort cruisers. She took part in the action
which led to the scuttling of HM submarine *Sahib*, which
was first damaged by depth charges and then engaged on
the surface with gunfire. During her war service she
steamed 14,383 miles, the most of any of this class.

At the armistice she was at Palermo and fought off
four German motor rafts before reaching Malta. She
then took part in convoy escort duties between Bizerta
and Algiers. Removed from the list in 1974.

Procellaria   C12   –   –   –   Ce   14.1.42
24.9.42   29.11.42
Joined the 1st Corvette Sq and a month later, at dawn on
31.1.43, while in formation with Italian and German
vessels between Bizerta and Trapani struck a mine and
sank after three hours.

Cormorano   C13   –   CM   F575   Ce   14.1.42
20.9.42   6.3.43
Served with the 2nd Corvette Sq shooting down a torpedo bomber on 21 August. At the armistice was at
Bastia and reached the rendezvous of Portoferraio (El-
ba) after sinking one German A/S vessel and two motor
rafts. Based at Malta and later Taranto with the allied
convoy patrols. Deleted in 1971.

Pellicano   C14   –   PE   F574   Ce   14.1.42
12.2.43   15.3.43
Operated from Naples with the 1st Corvette Sq in 39 war
missions. From 15 September at Malta for two weeks,
then at Taranto. In service until 1969.

Cicogna   C15   –   –   –   An   15.6.42
12.10.42   11.1.43
With the 1st Corvette Sq out of Trapani. On 14 March
1943 attacked HM submarine *Thunderbolt* with depth
charges and sank her. Hit by bombs while at anchor at
Messina, she was set on fire and grounded. When Sicily
was evacuated the wreck was scuttled.

Folaga   C16   –   FO   F576   An   15.6.42
14.11.42   16.2.43
Alloted to the 2nd Sq in the Tyrrhenian Sea. Took part
in 44 A/S operations and 11 escort missions. On 18
August took part in the sinking of HM submarine *Saracen*. After the armistice escorted allied vessels in the
waters of Southern Italy. Career ended 1 Aug 1965.

Ibis   C17   –   IB   F561   An   18.6.42
12.12.42   3.4.43
Originally with the 1st Sq out of Naples. Had 35 war
missions with a probable damaging of a submarine on 18
June. On 25 August shot down a Mosquito aircraft.
Served with the allied forces after the armistice. Deleted
1971

Gru   C18   –   GU   F566   An   5.7.42
23.12.42   29.4.43
As *Ibis*, active 1943 to 1971.

Antilope   C19   Uj6082   –   –   OTO,L
20.1.42   9.5.42   11.11.42
Joined 1st Sq at Trapani. On 3 March 1943 collided with the destroyer escort *Pegaso* and was heavily damaged. After temporary repairs reached the builders yard, where she was hit by bombs. Siezed by the Germans, and found stranded and half sunk at the end of the war.
Gazella   C20   –   –   –   OTO,L   22.1.42
9.5.42   6.2.43
Operated from Maddelena (Sardinia). On 5 August ran into a mine barrage and sank in one minute.
Camoscio   C21   Uj6081   –   –   OTO,L
25.1.42   9.5.42   6.2.43
Assigned to the 1st Sq at Naples. On 24 July damaged by air attack and returned to Naples and then Livorno, where she was seized by the Germans. Sunk by British and American ships off Toulon on 17 August 1944.
Capriolo   C22   Uj6083   –   –   OTO,L
3.6.42   5.12.42   –
Alce   C23   Uj6084   –   –   OTO,L   27.5.42
5.12.42   –
Renna   C24   Uj6085   –   –   OTO,L   31.5.42
5.12.42   –
All three had similar fates. Siezed by the Germans while fitting out at Livorno, and towed to Genoa for fitting out. Uj6085 sunk in the harbour during an air raid, the other two scuttled on 24 April 1944.
Ape   C25   –   AP   F567   NM   6.5.42
22.11.42   15.5.43
Belonged to the 4th, and later the 2nd Sq in the Tyrrhenian Sea. 31 war missions. After the armistice escort service out of Malta and Algiers. In service until 1980 as supply ship A5328 with the raider men.
Vespa   C26   Uj2221   –   –   NM   4.5.42
22.11.42   2.9.43

The Italian Royal family aboard *Baionetta* en route to Brindisi on 10 September 1943. King Victor Emmanuele III is sitting in the centre of the group.
Author's Collection

No war service before the armistice. Seized by the Germans at Pozzuli and towed to Genoa. Active until 24 April 1944 when she was scuttled.
Lucciola   C27   –   –   –   N   22.6.42   21.3.43
–
Fitting out at Castellamare on 13 September, when siezed by the Germans and scuttled. Later raised and rebuilt as a merchant ship.
Grillo   C28   –   –   –   NM   26.6.42   21.3.43
–

Uj202, ex-*Melpomene*, under the German flag. Note the quadruple 20mm 'Flakvierling' immediately abaft the 100mm/47.
Author's Collection

Uj203, ex-Tersicore, sunk on 20 April 1944 by an air raid at Monfalcone.

Author's Collection

Cicala C29 – – – NM 30.9.42 27.6.43 –

Calabrone C30 – – – NM 1.10.42 27.6.43 –

Cavalletta C31 – – – NM 3.12.42 – –

Libellula C32 – – – NM 3.12.42 – –

All had the same fate as *Lucciola,* scuttled and in part broken up.

Scimitarra C33 – SC F564 Br 24.2.42 16.9.42 15.5.43

Began her war service with the 4th Sq at Argostoli (Greece). 17 A/S missions and 5 escort cruises. Removed from the list in 1971.

Baionetta C34 – BA F578 Br 24.2.42 5.10.42 15.5.43

At the time of the armistice was training at Pola. Carried the Italian Royal family from Pescara to Brindisi on 9 September. On 28 November torpedoed by a German submarine but reached base. In service until 1971.

Colubrina C35 Uj205 – – Br 14.3.42 7.12.42 –

Ready at Venice on 9 September, sabotaged, later fell into German hands. Sunk in harbour during an air raid 27 March 1944.

Spingarda C36 Uj208 – – Br 14.3.42 22.3.43 –

Seized, repaired and commissioned by the Germans at Venice. Sunk by gunfire near Zara by the Hunt class destroyers *Wheatland* and *Avon Vale* on 1 November 1944.

Carabina C37 Uj207 – – Br 28.9.42 31.8.43 –

Similar fate to *Colubrina,* sunk by air attack ?.2.44.

Bombarda C38 Uj206 BD F549 Br 31.8.42 – –

Seized by the Germans at Venice, incomplete. Sabotaged by them when they evacuated the city on 26 April 1945. Refloated and commissioned into the Italian Navy in 1951, and remained in service for 27 years.

Artemide C39 Uj2226 – – CRDA,M 9.3.42 21.9.42 28.11.42

Initially at Trapani with the 1st Sq. Hit a mine on 21 February 1943 and reached Trapani towed by the destroyer escort *Pegaso.* On 15 April reached Livorno for a complete repair. Fell into German hands on 9 September and towed to Genoa. Found scuttled at the end of the war.

Persefone C40 Uj2227 – – CRDA,M 9.3.42 28.8.42 10.10.42

With the 1st Sq out of Palermo, operating between Trapani and Bizerta. Shot down one aeroplane. On 9 September at La Spezia for repairs, was sabotaged and later refloated. On 25 April lay sunk in the harbour of Genoa.

Euterpe C41 Uj2228 – – CRDA,M 2.4.42 22.10.42 20.1.43

Assigned to the 2nd Sq. On 24 April 1943 participated in the sinking of HM submarine *Sahib.* At La Spezia with *Persefone,* had the same fate.

Minerva C42 – MI F562 CRDA,M 2.4.42 5.11.42 24.3.43

War service in the Adriatic and off Sardinia in 51 missions. On 15 August participated in sinking by gunfire HM submarine *Saracen.* At the armistice reached Portoferraio, and served as an escort out of Palermo, Malta and Taranto. In service until 1 July 1969.

Driade C43 – DR F568 CRDA,T

After the end of the war the corvettes were used for minesweeping. Here *Flora* leads three of her sisters.
Author's Collection

9.5.42   7.10.42   14.2.43
Operated with the 3rd Sq in 89 war missions, 17 A/S sweeps and 18 convoy escort cruises. At Taranto on 9 September, joined the allied escorts. Deleted 1 July 1966.
Danaide   C44   –   PO   F573   CRDA,T
16.5.42   18.11.42   4.4.43
20 escort missions and 28 A/S sweeps with the 2nd Sq. On 9 September reached Portoferraio. Later operated out of Malta and Palermo. Removed from the list 1 January 1968

Pomona   C45   –   PO   F573   CRDA,T
16.5.42   18.1.42   4.4.43
After training at Pola, was at Brindisi with the 3rd Sq. Surprised there on 8 September, and continued with the allied escort flotillas. Deleted 1965.
Flora   C46   –   FL   F572   CRDA,T   16.5.42
1.12.42   26.4.43
Similar career to *Pomona*, 11 A/S sweeps and 5 escort missions. At the armistice was at Naples, thereafter operated between Palermo and Bizerta. Decommissioned 1969.
Sfinge   C47   –   SF   F579   CRDA,T   20.6.42
9.1.43   12.5.43
Command ship of the 3rd Sq principally on the Brindisi to Albania route. After the armistice active in the Tyrrhenian Sea. Active until 1977.
Chimera   C48   –   CH   F569   CRDA,T
27.6.42   30.1.43   26.5.43
With the 4th Sq based at Argostoli. Shot down a stuka on

27 September 1943. Then operated between Malta. Removed from the list in 1971.
Sibilla   C49   –   SB   F565   CRDA,T
20.6.42   10.3.43   5.6.43
As *Chimera*. Out of serivce in 1971.
Fenice   C50   –   FE   F577   CRDA,T
27.6.42   1.3.43   15.6.43
Command ship of the 4th Sq. Completed only one war mission. Removed from the list 1965.
Tuffetto   C51   Uj2222   –   –   An   15.3.43
25.8.43   –
Seized while fitting out. Fought under the German flag out of Genoa, where she was found scuttled at the end of the war.
Marangone   C52   Uj2223   –   –   An   15.3.43
–   –
Strolaga   C53   Uj2224   –   –   An   15.3.43
–   –
Ardea   C54   Uj2225   –   –   An   15.3.43   –   –
Both seized on the slips, uncertain if ever completed. Scuttled in Genoa harbour.
Daino   C55   Uj6087   –   –   OTO,L   1.3.43
–   –
Cervo   C56   Uj6086   –   –   OTO,L   25.2.43
–   –
Seized on the slip at Livorno, where the former remained. The latter was towed to Genoa. Both were scuttled in habour still completed.
Stambecco   C57   Uj6088   –   –   OTO,L
4.3.43   –   –

1 *Driade* in 1952, note the modified armament.
Author's Collection

2 *Driade* after the major reconstruction of the 1950s. She had become a specialised anti-submarine corvette.
Author's Collection

Seized on the slip and destroyed by an air raid on an unknown date in 1944.
Crisalide C58 – CR F547 NM 22.4.43 8.12.47 25.9.52
Seized on the slip by the Germans, who began to break her up. At the end of the war was rebuilt and commissioned in 1952. In service until 1971.

1

2

Flora, showing the typical profile of the *Gabbianos* reconstructed into anti-aircraft corvettes.
Drawn by the author

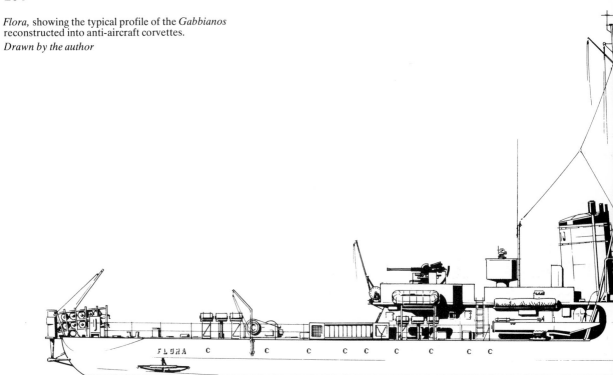

FLORA   as A/A corvette (1959)

Driade, a typical anti-submarine corvette.
Drawn by the author

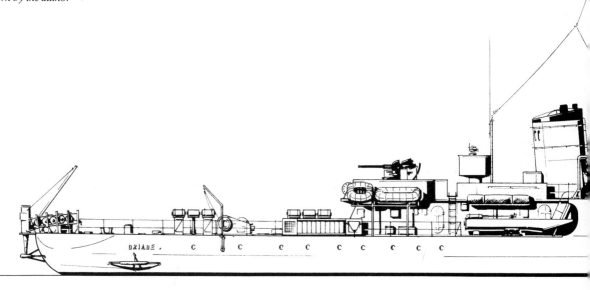

DRIADE   as A/S corvette (1961)

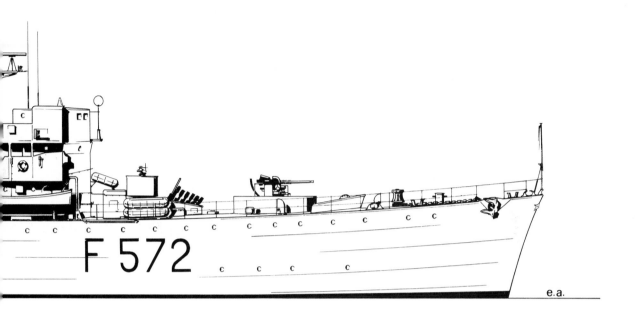

F 572

e.a.

F 568

e.a.

Farfalla C59 – – F548 NM 21.4.43
4.1.48 10.12.53
As with *Crisalide,* in service 1953 to 1971.
Maggiolino C60 – – – NM – – –
Cucciniglia C61 – – – NM – – –
Not complete at the time of the armistice.
Scure C62 Uj209 – – Br 20.10.43 – –
In German hands. Damaged in an air raid on 1 May 1944 and afterward scuttled.
Clava C63 – – – Br 20.10.43 – –
Zagaglia C64 – – – Br ?43 – –
Both seized and broken up by the Germans while still on the slip.
Urania C65 – UR F570 CRDA,M 1.10.43 21.4.43 1.8.43
The armistice came during her working up period. Operated along the coastal routes with the allies. Deleted in 1971.
Berenice C66 – – – CRDA,M 1.10.42 20.5.43 1.9.43
Left Trieste on 9 September, and was sunk just outside the harbour by German field guns.
Egeria C67 Uj201 – – CRDA,M 5.2.43 3.7.43 –
Captured by the Germans while fitting out. Fought under the German flag. Damaged by gunfire, or an air raid on 29 February 1944. Found sunk at the end of the war.
Melpomene C68 Uj202 – – CRDA,M 25.3.43 29.8.43 –
Commissioned by the Germans. Sunk near Zara on 1 November 1944 by HMS *Wheatland* and HMS *Avon Vale.*

Tersicore C69 Uj203 – – CRDA,M 15.4.43 – –
Launched, but still incomplete when sunk by air attack on 20 April 1944.
Euridice C70 Uj204 – – CRDA,M 1.7.43 – –
As *Tersicore,* sank by air attack one month later, on 25 May 1944.

TABLE 1: GABBIANO CLASS CORVETTES

Displacement (tons)	standard 670
	normal 728
	full load 737
Dimensions (metres)	
Overall length	64.40
Between perpendiculars	58.80
Maximum beam	8.71
Mean draught at standard displacement	2.53
Machinery	2 shaft diesel (Ansaldo-Fiat, or CRDA-Fiat)
	2 electric motors
	3,500ihp (designed), 150hp with electric motors
	2 three bladed propellors
Speed	18 knots (designed)
Endurance (knots)	4,400 at 10 knots, search speed
	3,000 at 16 knots, cruising speed
	1,500 at 18 knots
Armament (original)	1 100mm/47 D/P; 3 20mm/70 AA
	3 20mm 65/AA; 2 450mm torpedo tubes
	8 depth charge throwers
	2 depth charge racks
	2 towed depth charges
Complement	5 (+2 war) officers; 12 petty officers; 93 men

Flora and *Daniade* awaiting their final demolition during the 1970s.　　　　　*Author's Collection*

HM Submarine E31

Log of her War Service Part 3

by Brian Head

E 47 in floating dock at Harwich.
IWM

NEW BRIDGE SCREEN

On 17 August, *E 31* was given a major improvement. The ERAs from *Maidstone* spend 5 days fitting a brass screen to the bridge. Until then, the only protection for those standing a watch on the bridge was a canvas screen that had to be rigged on surfacing. The top of the conning tower was no more than about 8 feet above the deck casing – which was often awash. The discomfort and difficulty in rigging and sheltering behind the canvas screen in winter in the North Sea can readily be imagined. The new screen was made of brass to avoid interference with the magnetic compass.

On 29 August, a distinguished expert came aboard for an exercise with the light cruiser *Concord*. He was Norman Wilkinson, the marine artist but now a Lieutenant RNVR. *Concord* had been given a particular type of camouflage painting and Lt Wilkinson took observations form the periscope. The purpose being to ascertain the effectiveness of the camouflage or whether some other design might be preferable. *Concord* was a light cruiser (3750 tons) of the *Centaur* class serving with the Harwich Light Forces.

BACK TO THE BIGHT

31 August was occupied with exercise attacks on a submarine target and on 2 September *E 31* exchanged her forward periscope with *E 4*, as it needed repair and she was standing by for the next patrol. She should, in fact, have sailed on 2 September but bad weather caused a postponement and her 20th War Patrol commenced the next day at 1020. She left Harwich in company with *E 45*. (Lt Commander G S Watkins DSO.)

At 1507 she submerged to periscope depth, sighted an aeroplane and went deep to 70 feet. The first encounter with aircraft other than Zeppelins. An hour later she resumed patrol when all was clear. *E 31* arrived on billet at 0409 next morning – familiar territory, patrolling within sight of the Texel Buoys and the Dutch coast, averaging 15 hours continuously submerged each day. Two Dutch cruisers and a Torpedo Boat Destroyer were seen, evidently relieving each other on patrol. The log also noted that a W/T routine was kept at 0340, daily. Nothing of any note occurred during the patrol, although HMS *Skilful* and 3 TBDs were sighted on September 9th. *E 31* returned to *Maidstone* at 1600 on 11 September.

3

1 *E 31*, looking forward from the control room.
HMS Dolphin

2 The port side of the control room, looking aft.
HMS Dolphin

3 Another view from the port side of the control room, looking aft, clearly showing the ship's bell.
HMS Dolphin

THE DOVER PATROL

A couple of days were spent in the Floating Dock whilst half the crew were on four days leave and then it was back to exercise attacks in a plan with Lt Edmund Phillips of *E 52* for the two boats to have a break from the monotony of North Sea patrols. Instead, the idea was to operate from Dover, lying in wait at night for U-boats trying to slip through the patrols and the Dover Barrage – an anti-submarine barrier of nets and mine fields. The plan was duly approved by Captain Percy Addison newly appointed as the flotilla Senior Officer in succession to Captain Waistell and on 9 October, the two submarines left *Pandora* with the destroyer *Lurcher* as escort. They reached Dover at 1600 and secured alongside the *Arrogant*, another old cruiser which had been converted to a submarine depot ship, there being a small group of elderly B and C class submarines based on Dover for coastal protection duties. *Arrogant* was also depot ship to anti-submarine motor launches based

there as part of the Dover Patrol.

Before commencing operations in the Dover Straits, *E 31* and *E 52* were painted dark green on all exterior surfaces. This would help to render them less visible at night, in the moonlight.

Now began a succession of patrols at night, with the days spent alongside *Arrogant* in Dover Harbour. The two *E* boats were ordered to keep constant W/T watch whilst on the surface but they were not to report by W/T except for an absolute necessity. If they required assistance, Q Wave (500kcs) was to be used. This was (and still is) the Merchant Ship frequency.

E 31's first patrol was on 13 October. She cast off from *Arrogant* at 1700 and was escorted by the destroyer *Myngs* to the Barrage. At 1840 she cleared the Barrage, parted company with her escort and proceeded to her assigned billet to lie in wait for any U-boat hoping to make passage through the Straits. At 2101 *E 31* arrived on billet and divided to trim the boat. It was essential when running awash to keep a perfect trim on the boat as there would be little margin for error if she became unstable. For the next six hours *E 31* patrolled on her electric motors, at slow speed, just awash. At 0300 the main engines were clutched in and course was set for Dover in order to clear the Barrage by daybreak. There was no point in letting the enemy see you or the whole object of the exercise would be wasted. HMS *Myngs* was waiting to escort *E 31* back to Dover and at 0800 she was all fast alongside *Arrogant* again. *E 52*

to take advantage of moonlit nights to lie on the surface with just the conning tower above the water and wait at the points where the U-boats were throught to be passing through the Dover Straits. Navigation was difficult with wind and erratic tides and the danger of sandbanks. *E 31* was three times swept through the Barrage by mistake, once when submerged, so it was not a very effective barrier to the U-boats.

E 31 didn't go out again until 21 October. This time, HMS *Miranda* provided the escort. At 1914 a German submarine was suddenly encountered travelling in the opposite direction. The two submarines passed rapidly on the starboard side, too close to attack each other, and the German was immediately lost in the darkness. *E 31* was in her billet at 2030 but no further enemy contacts were obtained. At 0310, she went ahead on main engines and was alongside *Arrogant* by 0830.

Out again on 23 October in very unpleasant weather with a rough sea, strong north-westerly wind and squally rain showers, she again drew a blank.

The next patrol was on 27 October, with the *Falcon* as escort. The only incident reported was star shells observed to the south east.

On 29 October, the weather was again very unfriendly with rising sea, cloudy sky, squally showers and a freshening wind. It was a 1030 return to *Arrogant* instead of the usual 0830.

E 52's SUCCESS

The night of 31 October/1 November saw *E 52* score with the sinking of *UC 63* torpedoed on the surface. One survivor was picked up. *UC 63* was on her way back through the Straits after a patrol of the Bay of Biscay and laying mines off the Isle of Wight. She was sunk about 16 miles east of the Barrage north of Le Sandettie Shoal at 0112 on 1 November. *UC 63* was part of the Flanders Flotilla, based on Bruges and Zeebrugge.

E 31 was due to go out on the evening of 1 November and she cast off at 1630 only to have to return to harbour by 1730 because the weather was too thick, being very misty and rainy, overcast sky and a moderate south easterly wind blowing. The success of *E 52* the previous night had improved morale very considerably and Lt Blacklock was eager to score for *E 31*. However, it was not to be. *E 31* was again frustrated on 2 November when she had to return to harbour because of fog, less than two hours after leaving.

On 3 November, *E 31* put to sea again, this time her escort was HMS *Morris* in clear, but cloudy weather. Nothing was seen and she returned to Dover by 0800 next morning.

She tried again on 6 November, being escorted out by HMS *Afridi*. Again, *E 31* drew a blank. On 12 November she went into Floating Dock for three days maintenance and half the crew were given four days leave.

E 31's next patrol was on the night of 21/22 November. She left Dover at 1600 in company with the destroyer *Viking* and was in her billet by 1750. Blacklock dived the boat at 2050 and remained on periscope watch until 0515 the next morning, before returning to *Arrogant*.

Out again on the evening of 23 November, *E 31* sailed in company with *C30* (Lt C Buckland RNR) and the destroyer *Melpomene*. This time she remained running on the surface on main motors until 0030 then changed to a new billet east of the Falls Bank. At 0515 *E 31* surfaced having patrolled her second billet submerged. She was all fast alongside *Arrogant* by 0830.

Further patrols were carried out on 27 November and 29 and 5 December. It was then decided that *E 31* and *E 52* should return to Harwich, as no more U-boats had been encountered since Lt Philip's success on 1 November.

RETURN TO HARWICH – AND THE NORTH SEA

Both submarines left Dover at 0900 on 10 December in company with the destroyer *Firedrake*. They reached Harwich at 1700 on the following day, having anchored overnight in the North Edinburgh Channel.

On 13 December, contractors' workmen from Ipswich started clearing the port intermediate shaft for taking out and the crew were preparing to remove part of No 3 battery, a leak having reoccurred in the foreward battery tank. All torpedoes were returned to store for overhaul on 15 December. The battery cells were replaced on 2 December and six torpedoes taken on board on 21 December. On 22 December the contractors' men were still at work on the port intermediate shaft. They had Christmas Day off but resumed next day, finally finishing the job on 27 December. Four more torpedoes were then taken on board, and *E 31* pronounced ready for sea.

Half the crew had been given the customary four days leave on 15 December and on 22 December the crew were employed repainting *E 31* in her normal grey livery and restoring her number to the bridge screen.

A trial run was carried out on 28 December to test the engines and trim the boat and adjust compasses. All was found to be satisfactory.

The next day, *E 31* left Harwich at 0835 for her 33rd war patrol. She arrived in her billet (54°24'N 4°05'E) at 0715 on 30 December. A W/T routine was kept at 0530 on 31 December and throughout the patrol.

New Year's Day 1918 passed uneventfully but on 2 January the weather deteriorated alarmingly with a severe gale blowing and halfway through the forenoon, Blacklock gave up all attempts to maintain a periscope patrol. *E 31* bottomed at 135ft. Just to add to their problems, the gyro compass broke down. The storm continued for the next two days and daylight was spent on the bottom of the North Sea. Constant hydrophone watch was maintained.

Eventually, the gale moderated and on 5 January, repairs were made to the starboard engine on the surface. This took nearly two hours. The only other incident in the day had been the recording of two explosions at 0130 in rapid succession. The origin was unknown. *E 31* returned from patrol at 1630 on 6 January. Half the crew went on four days leave and she was not required for operations again until the end of the month. On 14 January, *E 31* carried out an attack exercise with *Melampus*.

Attack exercises were also conducted on 23 January

Aft spaces viewed from the control room.
HMS Dolphin

with *E 44* and *E 41*. On 25 January, W/T operators went to instruction. Obviously it was thought desirable to ensure the professional standards of the telegraphists were kept up. With the change-over from Spark to Poulsen Arc transmitters, the most newly-joined Boy Tel or Ord Tel might be the most experienced operator on board as he would have completed a special Poulsen Course at the Signal School before joining. Because skilled operators were in short supply, it was difficult for operational boats to release their telegraphists for courses and it was not unknown for the junior operator to teach the senior hand – usually a Leading or Petty Officer Telegraphist – the finer points of handling the Poulsen Arc set.

On 29 January, after a start delayed by fog, *E 31* left Harwich with *E 45* at 1230. Her operation orders were to watch the exit from German minefields – the centre of the exit channel being located at 54° 45'N 06° 15'E. There was also a warning that if a W/T transmission was made, giving details of enemy vessels coming through the exit, then *E 31* was to move from the position where she sent the signal. There was a strong possibility of German DF (Directional Finding) stations getting a bearing on her position.

On 30 January, at 1055 whilst proceeding on the surface, she was forced to dive rapidly by a Zeppelin

The engine room, looking foward.
HMS Dolphin

sighted on the starboard beam. *E 31* remained submerged until 1708 when she surfaced again and continued on towards her billet, where she arrived at 2135 and commenced a moonlight patrol.

The next day, in position 54°59'N6°00E, the hydrophone operators picked up two U-boats, *U 59* and *U 60*, exchanging underwater signals. On 3 February, more such signals were intercepted between *UC 64* and *U 104* during the afternoon and also between the

U-boats and a third station – thought to be Heligoland.

The next dax, *E 31* received a recall signal by W/T and returned to *Maidstone* on 6 February. Half the crew were given leave next day. She remained at Harwich for the remainder of February. 15 February was spent exercising with *Lurcher* and the 19th with *E 41*. On 26 February, a most unusual event took place. At 1000 that morning, full Divisions were held for the Harwich Forces, after which there was a march past and review by His Majesty King George V. One can imagine the practice drills that went on beforehand in order to reacquaint the submariners with the nicities of parade ground marching, but only one march past rehearsal was noted in *E 31*'s log – 22 February after Divisions.

On 27 February, *E 31* went onto the Floating Dock for 2 days. *E 31* departed on her 35th war patrol on 5 March (having been postponed from 4 March when she left Harwich at 0800 in company with *E 33*). On 7 March, her log records the fact that the weather was too severe for surface patrolling. She was then off the North Dogger Bank (55°52'N4°42'E). The weather moderated sufficiently for a surface patrol on 8 March and on 11 March at 2230 a signal was received ordering her to proceed to a new billet. At 0613 next day she was passing submerged at 60ft through minefields and arrived on her billet at noon in position 54°42'N7°25'E. At 1510 that afternoon she sighted a German seaplane and dived to 60ft. This was the first time a German

The stern tubes and motor room.
HMS Dolphin

aeroplane had been encountered since the previous August. It was to become a more familiar event and foreshadowed the increasing use of aircraft in the anti-submarine role. Late that evening at 2044, *E 31*'s log records another passage through a minefield at 60ft. The next morning, whilst on the surface, another submarine was sighted. *E 31* did a rapid dive. At 1115 Lt Blacklock decided to surface again – and so did the other submarine, which, on being challenged, turned out to be *E 53*. The two boats closed and their captains were able to exchange news. This was a very unusual occurrence as it was rare for two submarines to be operating so closely together. The only other incident of the patrol was the sighting of 3 Zeppelins that same afternoon.

On 14 March *E 31* returned to base in company with *E 33*. On 15 March half the crew were given four days leave, and Sub-Lt Blood was promoted to acting Lieutenant. March 26 was a day of exercise attacks and Captain(S)'s inspection took place on 28 March.

On 30 March *E 31* was on patrol again. On this occasion Lt Blacklock was ordered to take station off the Dogger Bank South Light Vessel and be available for direction to a number of pre-determined positions by wireless signal. Any vessels sighted in these areas were to be attacked, but after each attack *E 31* was to return to its patrol area. The secondary aim of the patrol was to observe the movements of the enemy so that minefields could be laid out to best advantage. At night the patrol was to be made on the surface with continuous W/T watch being kept at the pre-arranged times for submarines. During the day there would be a submarine

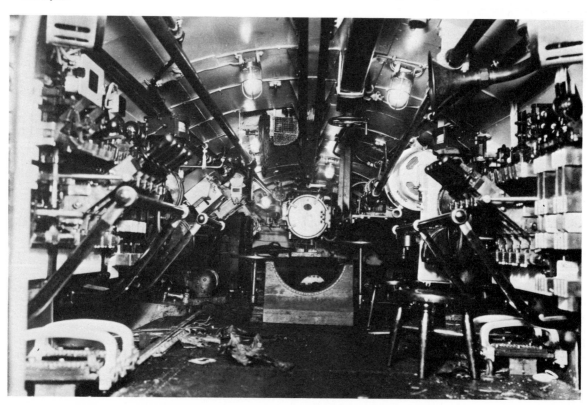

broadcast every three hours commencing at 0500, and every endeavour was to be made to keep this routine as well.

The South Dogger Bank was on what was known as the 'Kingsway Beat' (55°3'N6°E) and two submarine patrol lines had been established to watch the northern exits from the Heligoland Bight. These X and Y patrols, as they were officially designated in Grand Fleet orders were on a line 24 miles, 230° from the Dogger Bank Noord Light Vessel (X patrol) and a similar distance and bearing from position 56°4'N5°39'E. Normally the primary duty of patrolling submarines was to report outward bound German surface vessels, thus giving Grand Fleet forces an opportunity to intercept. Inward bound vessels could be attacked by patrolling submarines as could single ships or submarines leaving the Bight.

Leaving Harwich at 1700 on 30 March, *E 31* proceeded on the surface until she was obliged to make a rapid dive at 2130 when encountering two destroyers. They were probably British but it was nevertheless prudent to take avoiding action. Destroyers, trawlers, and other anti-submarine vessels were inclined to treat all submarines as hostile. The engines gave a good deal of trouble of this trip. On 31 March repairs to the diesels were carried out whilst submerged at 60ft. On 2 April *E 31* spent most of the morning submerged and was lying on the bottom at 138ft when propeller noises were picked up on the hydrophones. Lt Blacklock brought his boat up to periscope depth but saw nothing in sight. At 1400 *E 31* surfaced but almost immediately dived again as a Zeppelin was sighted. She remained down until 1955 and then ran on the surface until the port engine was stopped at 2127 for repairs.

The next day at 1700, whilst on the surface a W/T signal was received instructing *E 31* to proceed to a new billet in the vicinity of 53°42'N3°36'E. 4 April passed without incident but the next day the starboard engine had to be stopped for repairs whilst charging the batteries when surfaced in the late evening. Nothing of any note occurred other than four explosions being recorded on 6 April. On 8 April *E 31* returned to the *Maidstone* and half the crew were given the usual four days leave on 9 April. The remainder of April was spent at Harwich while the engines were overhauled.

To be continued

book review

BATTLESHIPS IN TRANSITION
By Andrew Lambert.
160 pages (240 × 184mm). 120 illustrations. Published by Conway Maritime Press £11.95. (ISBN 0 85177 315 X)

Between 1846 and 1860 the Royal Navy commissioned 66 steam, wooden battleships. The French completed 37 such ships in the same period and some were built for other navies. Andrew Lambert is the first writer to produce a serious account of the design, building and operations of these ships and he has done it well. The book is carefully researched, very readable and the number and quality of the illustrations are outstanding.

The British ships fall into three categories, those designed from the start as steamships, those converted during building and existing ships fitted later with engines. The new ships show a clear and logical progression from the first such ship, *Agamemnon,* which was an exceedingly good first shot. The form of these ships differed considerably from their sailing predecessors with finer entrance and run and a much fuller midship section. The author's account of the design of *Agamemnon* is debatable. He leans heavily on evidence to the 1861 Parliamentary Commission where Edye claimed that *Agamemnon* was based on his earlier 1846 design. Isaac Watts' evidence to the same commission was that *Agamemnon* was a new design and this statement is confirmed by her recorded dimensions and shape.

The book brings out the major contribution of Admiral Sir Baldwin Walker to the steam fleet. It would seem that he was largely responsible for the 'staff requirements' as well as influencing the overall design concepts. He was a strong leader, an excellent administrator and well liked both in industry and by his own staff. The contribution of Isaac Watts who designed the great majority of the ship and of Thomas Lloyd, responsible for their machinery, seems somewhat undervalued.

Ships converted during building were brought as close as possible to standards of the new designs being lengthened and given finer ends. All these ships were generally satisfactory in service. The limited conversions of existing ships were less satisfactory but were seen as essential to increase the number of steam battleships in the Royal Navy in the light of the rapidly growing threat from France.

The engineering of the ships was fairly conventional, the majority having the well proven Maudslay or Penn engines, working at 10–15psi and driving a single propeller which could be hoisted out of the water for sailing. Lambert draws attention to a number of problems relating to the installation of machinery. Of these the most serious was leakage round the stern gland due to vibration excited by a two-bladed propeller working in the very non-uniform flow behind a bluff stern. This was aggravated by the flexibility of the wooden hull, only partially cured by the extensive use of iron reinforcement. In 1856 Penn introduced lignum vitae stern bearings which largely cured the problem.

Other problems included excess heat from the boilers affecting the magazines and coal bunkers. The space left over for the crew was much overcrowded, particularly in the conversion from existing ships. An ingenious invention, by Grant, used the galley range to distill fresh water for drinking; not for the engines as suggested, since the boilers still used salt water.

Andrew Lambert shows that the British ships were conceived as sailing ships with auxiliary power while the French, with less requirement for long distance cruising, put more emphasis on performance while steaming. Since the British engineering industry was well ahead of the French, there was little difference in practice between the two countries' ships either steaming or sailing.

The blend of strategic and tactical background, the choice of armament and the design of the ships makes this an excellent introduction to a neglected period of the Royal Navy.

D K Brown RCNC

NAVY AND EMPIRE
A short history of British Seapower from the Armada to the Falklands, by James L Stokesbury
Published by Robert Hale September 1984. 430pp (22cm × 14cm), index. ISBN 0 7090 1787 £11.95.

The greatest problem of this, or any other attempt to cover the last four hundred years of British naval history is the fact that the finished product will reflect the strengths and weaknesses of the existing literature. Consequently my first point of enquiry lay not in the text, but in the suggestions for further reading. Stokesbury lists some useful titles, but curiously ignores his fellow American, and one of the most highly regarded naval historians of the twentieth century, Arthur J Marder. To look at the Royal Navy between 1905 and 1919 without consulting Marder's epochal study, *'From the Dreadnought to Scapa Flow'* is to neglect a majestic work of original research.

In the well presented text some areas reflect this weakness. It is argued that the Crimean War was 'a small masterpiece of muddle and confusion'. In all fairness this description sits rather better on Stokesbury's account than on a war of which contemporary research is revising the negative opinions of fifty years ago. Stokesbury adopts a very cavalier attitude to the events and places of the war, transposing them to such an extent that his account makes little sense.

Warship readers will not be surprised that a general history has once again adopted a simplistic and inaccurate approach to the major developments in naval architecture. For example the *Warrior* is considered to be far less revolutionary than the primitive and unseaworthy batteries *Monitor* and *Virginia* that followed. Surely the coast defence ship has always been considered a false start in the development of the ironclad, or is the author merely reflecting a patriotic view?

In conclusion this book offers an American's view of Britain's sea empire. Unlike certain other American historians of the Royal Navy, Mahan and Marder especially, this account has nothing new for the British reader. Paul Kennedy's *'The Rise and Fall of British Naval Mastery'* is a far better synthesis and one that is constructed around a useful analytical framework.

Andrew Lambert

NAVAL BOOKS

Conway Maritime offer an unrivalled range of authoritative and well-illustrated titles on naval subjects. A free catalogue is available, but some of the leading titles are listed below:

* These titles are available in North America from the Naval Institute Press, Annapolis, MD 21402.

BATTLESHIPS IN TRANSITION
The Creation of the Steam Battlefleet 1815-1860
Andrew Lambert

The first book to cover the period between 1815 and 1860, the great neglected area of naval history – yet between these dates the construction, hull design, armament, propulsion and tactics of the battlefleet changed beyond recognition; the author sets out to study the influence of these advances on ship design and international politics.
240 x 184mm (9½" x 7¼"), 160 pages, 120 illustrations.
ISBN 0 85177 315 X. £11.95 (+ £1.50 p & p)

A CENTURY OF NAVAL CONSTRUCTION The History of the Royal Corps of Naval Constructors 1883-1983
D K Brown RCNC

This behind-the-scenes history of the Royal Navy's designers offers a new insight into the factors governing British warship design from the 19th century to the Falklands conflict.
240 x 156mm (9½" x 6"), 384 pages, 92 photographs, 20 line drawings.
ISBN 0 85177 282 X. £20.00 (+ £2.00 p & p)

US NAVAL WEAPONS*
Norman Friedman

This exhaustive study by an acknowledged expert on the subject discusses the development and function of every weapon system employed by the US Navy from the birth of the 'New Navy' in 1883 to the present day.
310 x 216mm (12¾" x 8½"), 288 pages, 200 photographs, 150 line drawings. ISBN 0 85177 240 4. £18.00 (+ £1.80 p & p)

NAVAL RADAR*
Norman Friedman

A layman's guide to the theory, functions and performance of seaborne radar systems, from their introduction just before the Second World War to the present day, including a catalogue of every major piece of radar equipment to have seen service in the world's navies.
250 x 216mm (11" x 8½"), 240 pages, 200 photographs, 100 line drawings. ISBN 0 85177 238 2. £18.00 (+ £1.80 p & p)

CONWAY'S ALL THE WORLD'S FIGHTING SHIPS

This four-volume series covers the history of iron and steel warships from the first ironclad until the present day. Each volume contains a complete listing of all warships from the period, illustrated with numerous photographs and line drawings. The introduction and class notes contain both a major revaluation of published information and the wide-scale use of unpublished sources recently made available for the first time.
The four volumes are:

CONWAY'S ALL THE WORLD'S FIGHTING SHIPS 1860-1905*
310 x 216mm (12¼" x 8½"), 440 pages, 471 photographs, 506 line drawings. ISBN 0 85177 133 5. £30.00 (+ £3.00 p & p)

CONWAY'S ALL THE WORLD'S FIGHTING SHIPS 1906-21*
310 x 216mm (12¼" x 8½"), 440 pages, 400 photographs, 600 line drawings. ISBN 0 85177 245 5. £35.00 (+ £3.50 p & p)

CONWAY'S ALL THE WORLD'S FIGHTING SHIPS 1922-1946*
310 x 216mm (12¼" x 8½"), 464 pages, 506 photographs, 530 line drawings. ISBN 0 85177 146 7. £30.00 (+ £3.00 p & p)

CONWAY'S ALL THE WORLD'S FIGHTING SHIPS 1947-1982*
Part I: The Western Powers
Part II: The Warsaw Pact and non-aligned nations
Each part: 310 x 216mm (12¼" x 8½"), 256 pages, 250 photographs, 240 line drawings.
Part I: ISBN 0 85177 225 0. £25.00 (+ £2.50 p & p)
Part II: ISBN 0 85177 278 1. £25.00 (+ £2.50 p & p)

ANATOMY OF THE SHIP SERIES

This new series is a radical departure from the usual monograph approach for each volume contains, as well as text and photographs, a complete set of superbly executed line drawings, both the conventional type of plan as well as explanatory perspective views; this, combined with a full design and service history for the vessel and a photographic section concentrating on close-ups and on-board shots, provides the enthusiast with a novel insight into the technicalities of each ship type covered.
Published so far:

THE BATTLECRUISER HOOD*
John Roberts
240 x 254mm (9½" x 10") landscape, 128 pages, 24 photographs, 320 line drawings. ISBN 0 85177 250 1. £8.50 (+ £1.25 p & p)

THE AIRCRAFT CARRIER INTREPID*
John Roberts
240 x 254mm (9½" x 10") landscape, 96 pages, 20 photographs, 300 line drawings. ISBN 0 85177 250 1. £8.50 (+ £1.25 p & p)

THE TYPE VII U-BOAT*
David Westwood
240 x 254mm (9½" x 10") landscape, 96 pages, 20 photographs, 300 line drawings. ISBN 0 85177 314 1. £9.50 (+ £1.25 p & p)

THE FAIRMILE 'D' TYPE MOTOR TORPEDO BOAT*
John Lambert
240 x 254mm (9½" x 10") landscape, 96 pages, 20 photographs, 300 line drawings. ISBN 0 85177 321 4. £11.95 (+ £1.50 p & p)

THE DESTROYER ESCORT ENGLAND*
Al Ross
240 x 254mm (9½" x 10") landscape, 96 pages, 20 photographs, 300 line drawings. ISBN 0 85177 325 7. £10.95 (+ £1.25 p & p)

THE CRUISER BELFAST*
Ross Watton
240 x 254mm (9½" x 10") landscape, 96 pages, 20 photographs, 300 line drawings. ISBN 0 85177 328 1. £11.95 (+ £1.50 p & p)

From your local bookseller or by post from **Conway Maritime Press Ltd,** 24 Bride Lane, Fleet Street, London EC4Y 8DR

When ordering direct please add the posting and packing charge noted after the price

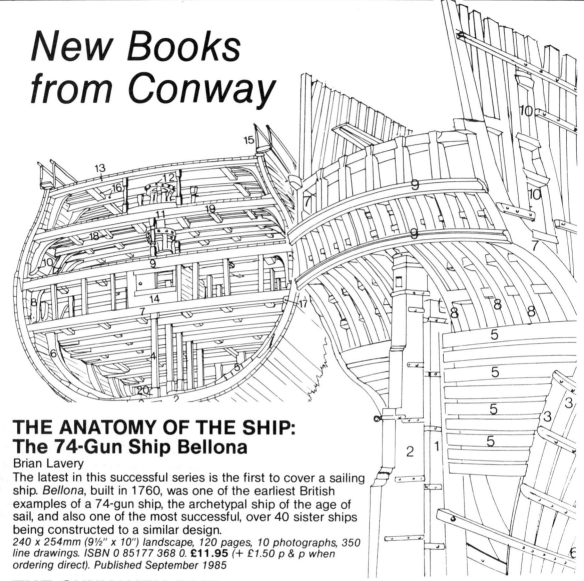

New Books from Conway

THE ANATOMY OF THE SHIP:
The 74-Gun Ship Bellona

Brian Lavery

The latest in this successful series is the first to cover a sailing ship. *Bellona*, built in 1760, was one of the earliest British examples of a 74-gun ship, the archetypal ship of the age of sail, and also one of the most successful, over 40 sister ships being constructed to a similar design.

240 x 254mm (9½" x 10") landscape, 120 pages, 10 photographs, 350 line drawings. ISBN 0 85177 368 0. **£11.95** *(+ £1.50 p & p when ordering direct). Published September 1985*

THE CUXHAVEN RAID
The World's First Naval Air Strike

R D Layman

On Christmas Day 1914 a small and very mixed force of British seaplanes was launched from their carriers to attack the German airship base near Cuxhaven. It was a highly significant event in the history of warfare:
the first attempt to exert sea power upon land from the air, and the cause of the first sea battle of a type that would become common in the Second World War; in addition the operation represented the birth of what was later known as the 'carrier task force' concept. The full fascinating story of the genesis of a new era in human conflict at sea is told for the first time in *The Cuxhaven Raid.*

241 x 156mm (9½" x 6"), 160 pages, 40 illustrations, ISBN 0 85177 327 3. **£10.50** *(+ £1.25 p & p). September 1985*

CONWAY
MARITIME

From your local bookseller or by post from
Conway Maritime Press Ltd
24 Bride Lane,
London EC4Y 8DR

editorial

The German battlecruiser *Seydlitz* on 5 June 1916. The defensive strength of this fast battleship design had been tested to the extreme at Jutland.

The central theme of this journal is the study of warships, their evolution, construction and operation. When considering the origins of any particular class or type we are often reminded of the technological advances that made them possible, but the higher policy decision to build a certain type of ship is largely ignored. Basically the question is : 'why are warships built?'. The answer might seem obvious, but in assuming that we make a fundamental mistake.

The most cursory examination of the development of the world's navies over the last 100 years will demonstrate the enormous variation in the size and composition of the world's fleets and the changing structure and balance of each nation's naval strength. This reflects the changing requirements of each nation for seapower; some can no longer afford as much as they did before, others no longer have a coast – Austria being an excellent example. The factors that determine the size of the fleet are primarily political. In the case of Great Britain it would be impossible to explain the construction of *Warrior* and *Dreadnought*, or the cancellation of the G3 Battlecruisers and CVA01 without considering the political background. These may be spectacular examples, but the hand of the politician can be seen in every ship; at the end of the process he is responsible for what has been produced and must ensure that the balance of factors has been struck in accordance with the policy of the Government of the day. As I suggested in Warship 33 political decisions do not always lead to the best ships.

However talented the designer he cannot escape control from above.

The different designs adopted for battlecruisers by Britain and Germany before 1914 illustrate this point. Fisher conceived the type as the ultimate capital ship, destroying other ships with accurate gunnery at extreme ranges. His ships therefore required little or no protection. Tirpitz, like everyone else, misunderstood the purpose of the battlecruiser and built high-speed battleships. Under the German Navy Laws he could build a number of large cruisers and realising that he could manipulate this to increase the number of ships fit to lay in the line of battle, Tirpitz reacted accordingly. He wanted to build a battlefleet, specifically to engage the Royal Navy between Heligoland and the Thames Estuary. This fact alone explains many of the design features of the Imperial German ships. The origins of the new fleet however, were primarily domestic and political, as historians of Wilhelmine Germany have recently demonstrated.

In the past main-line academic historians have usually ignored or misunderstood naval developments – a failure excused by their lack of technical knowledge. In so doing they have passed by much valuable material, notably political discussion of strategic and technical problems. This only serves to maintain an artificial barrier between elements of the historian's discipline. To understand naval policy and its influence on design it is necessary to combine a wide spectrum of research.

Andrew Lambert

Early Aircraft Carrier Projects

by D K Brown RCNC

From 1916 onwards all new configurations for aircraft carriers were tested in the wind tunnels of the National Physical Laboratory[1]. Photographs of some of the more interesting models provide the main feature of this article and are reproduced by permission of the National Maritime Institute Ltd who are the inheritors of NPL's wind tunnel activities.

In order to make the air flow parallel to the waterline, double models were used, symmetrical about the waterline giving the appearance of a reflection. *Argus* was the first one tested, in November 1916 (Fig. 1). At that time, she had a double island with a bridge between. There was found to be a low velocity and, combined with down wash just abaft the flight deck this would have made landing in the light aircraft of the day very difficult. It would have been essential to cross the aft end at a height of not less than 25 feet, flying fairly fast.

Buffeting from the twin islands was unacceptable. The clear space between the flight deck and the hangar roof

was intended to supply air to fill in the void abaft the ship but this space was so full of exhausts and structure that there was no effective air flow.

In January 1918 a series of tests was carried out to try to improve the conditions on the aft landing on deck of *Furious*. Various fairings were tried round the funnel and mast but none was effective. Later that year some

1 Original concept for *Argus*. Note the goal post bridge and guns forward. These port and starboard bridges were fitted and removed before completion.
NMI Ltd

2 An attempt to improve the airflow over the landing deck of *Furious* by streamlining the funnel and reducing the size of the bridge.
NMI Ltd

3 A study of *Furious* with two islands.
NMI Ltd

1

2

3

1

2

3

1 A study of *Furious* with a single, port, island.
NMI Ltd

2 *Furious* with a large starboard island. Probably the basis for
Courageous.
NMI Ltd

3 *Vindictive* with a starboard island, the 7.5in guns have been
retained (most probably five out of the original complement of
seven).
NMI Ltd

more radical ideas were tried for *Furious*.
(a) Flush deck
(b) A streamlined funnel
(c) A streamlined funnel and a light cruiser mast (Fig.
2)
(d) Two funnels and an island each side, joined by a
bridge
(e) Two funnels and an island each side (Fig. 3)
(f) Two funnels and an island on one side only, port
(Fig. 4)

A little later, the last configuration was developed into
a big starboard island with mast, funnel and guns which
seems to have been the basis for the *Courageous* layout
(Fig. 5). The single island was seen as the best but was
recommended to be kept as small as possible. Minor
changes to the shape of the after end of the flight deck
made little difference and the need to land high and fast

was noted again. The mast alone caused most of the
disturbance at heights above 26ft from the flight deck
and was recommended to be kept small. Two islands
were quite unacceptable as the turbulence merged leaving no calm air in which to land.

In July 1918, *Vindictive* was tested both in her as-built
arrangement and with a starboard island (Fig. 6). Landing on the original layout was expected to be very
dangerous (it was) while the starboard island gave an
acceptable air flow, though the deck was rather narrow.

In August 1918 experiments were carried out with
models of *Eagle* with an arrangement fairly similar to
that with which she completed and also with a flush deck
(Fig. 7). The island carried a 6in gun abaft the second
funnel and others forward and aft of the island on the
flight deck. It seems that the flush deck model was tested
to gain basic information and was not a serious project.
The island caused a good deal of turbulence and a reduction in size was advised. Tests were also carried out with
a 10° yaw which caused severe eddies off the deck edge.

Some of these worries were reduced in November
1918 when *Argus* was completed and carried out landing
trials with a dummy island on the starboard side (Fig. 8).
A Sopwith Pup and a 1½ Strutter landed without difficulty and a Camel and a torpedo bomber carried out
simulated landings. The air flow was better than predicted from the model.

A model test of *Hermes* in August 1919 called for
little comment other than a recommendation for a slight
round down. *Eagle* was tried while still incomplete in

1

2

1 *Eagle* without an island. Probably not intended to be a practical design.
NMI Ltd

2 *Argus* in November 1918, she is fitted with a dummy starboard island for landing trials.

June 1920. Only half her boilers were fitted, limiting her speed to 20 knots. She had a temporary bridge and mast and only one funnel. Landing with the wind fore and aft caused no problems but with the wind 11° from the port bow there was severe buffeting. The main objection to the island was seen as one of morale. It was thought that the island would pose problems in bad weather and a flush deck layout was preferred.

However, by this time the basic layout of the carrier, with a starboard island, was established. When these tests started, in 1916, wind tunnels were still fairly novel and considerable credit is due to J H Narbeth RCNC for perceiving the value of such work and to L W Bryant of NPL for developing the test methods.

My thanks are due to Mr B N Steele, Deputy Managing Director of NMI Ltd, for permission to use these photographs. This article is reprinted by courtesy of the magazine 'Flight-Deck'.

Reference
[1] D K Brown RCNC. 'The development of the aircraft carrier prior to World War II.' Flight-Deck No 2. 1983.

The French Dreadnoughts

The 23,500 ton Courbet Class Part 2

by Robert Dumas

	Builder	Laid down	Launched	Completed
COURBET	Arsenal de Lorient	01.09.10	03.09.11	19.11.13
JEAN BART	Arsenal de Brest	15.10.11	22.09.11	19.11.13
PARIS	Forges et chantiers de la Mediterranee (La Seyne)		28.09.12	01.08.14
FRANCE	Ateliers et chantiers de la Loire (Saint Nazaire)		07.11.12	10.10.14

Displacement (tons)

Normal Load	23,475;
Full Load	25,579.

Dimensions (metres)

Length Overall	166
Length between perpendiculars	165
Extreme Breadth	27
Draught at the bow, normal load	9.04
Draught at the stern, normal load	8.66
Centre of Gravity	1.47

Protection

Armoured belt of 270mm at the centre, reducing to 180mm at the extremities. The belt was 4m deep
Above this was a belt of 180mm armour, 4.50m deep covering the centre of the ship
Four armoured decks; 30mm, 30mm, 12mm and 40mm

Turret armour	320mm
Barbette armour	280mm
Conning tower	300mm

Courbet in 1925, after her reconstruction, note the stump mainmast.

Author's Collection

Propulsion

Jean Bart, Paris and *France* 24 Belleville boilers
Courbet 24 Niclausse boilers
Coal fired driving through four Parsons geared turbines. 28,000hp, 4 screws

Maximum speed	21 knots
Cruising speed	14 knots
Bunkerage	906/2700 tons

Cruising range 4200 miles at 10 knots, 1140 miles at 20 knots

Armament

12 305mm guns, 1910 pattern 45-calibre in six twin turrets. Maximum elevation 12°, giving a maximum range of 13,500m
22 138.6mm guns, 1910 pattern 55-calibre in casemates
4 47mm guns, 1902 pattern
4 450mm submerged torpedo tubes 1909 pattern

Rangefinders

The original rangefinding equipment of the *Courbets* was very weak. It was composed of two coincidence rangefinders with a base of 2.74m on top of the blockhouse.

1 *Courbet* viewed from the quarter deck in 1932, the increased tophamper can be clearly seen.
Author's Collection

2 *Courbet* in 1935–36, with the range clocks at the masthead.
Author's Collection

For independent fire each turret had a 1.37m rangefinder in an armoured cupola on the rear of the turret roof

Searchlights
2 750mm lamps
8 900mm lamps on rails on the second deck

Boats
On deck:
2 steamboats 10m
3 11m vedette boats, stowed between the broadside turrets
1 11.5m longboat
1 10.5m dinghy
On the second deck:
1 11m longboat
1 10.5m dinghy
2 5m dinghies
On the outboard davits:
2 Whaleboats 8.50m

Crew
Normal 1115 men; with an Admiral and staff 1187 men
Note: to distinguish the *Courbets* when first built it is necessary to examine the large cranes.
Courbet; the arm of the crane is pierced
Jean Bart; fitted with a swan-necked crane
Paris; the support post of the crane is pierced
France; the base of the crane is perforated

THE RECONSTRUCTION OF THE COURBETS
France did not receive a rebuild because she was lost by an error of navigation of 26 August, 1922.

In 1920 the state of the French Dreadnoughts was compared with that of the modern battleships of the era. They were defficient in several areas:
(a) No director control for the guns
(b) The angle of elevation of the 305mm guns was insufficient
(c) The protection against torpedoes was weak
(d) The horizontal protection against plunging shells from heavy guns at long range was defective. (This fault was common to all other navies)
(e) The anti-aircraft defence was negligible
(f) They were coal-fired
(g) The organisation of the crew, the lighting and the method of transmitting orders were old fashioned.
To remedy these failings the État-Major de la Marine Francais ordered that each of the ships should be rebuilt.

PARIS. First rebuild at Brest, 25 October, 1922 to 25 November, 1923
To improve the seaworthiness the bow was stripped of its armour. The heavily loaded bow had caused the ships to labour in head seas.
One set of oil fired boilers was installed. The other four sets remained coal fired.
The angle of elevation of the 305mm guns was increased from 12 to 23°.

A fire control director was installed on the new tripod foremast. The anti-aircraft guns were replaced by more modern pieces. The position of the searchlights and the boats was modified.

Second rebuild at Toulon, 16 August, 1927 to 15 January, 1929
Director control of the Saint Chamond Granat pattern was installed for both main and secondary armament.
The rangefinders were all replaced, except those on the roof of the 305mm turrets.
These consisted of one type C with a 4.57m base and one type S with a 3m base.
On top of the conning tower a pair of 4.57m rangefinders were installed in a double mounting.
Beside the mainmast a 4.57m type C was installed in an armoured hood.
The directors for the 138.6mm guns on the navigation bridge each received a 2m coincidence rangefinder.
The anti-aircraft guns had three directors, one on the double rangefinder on the conning tower, one on 'B' turret and one of the aft superstructure.
The arrangement of the optical equipment and the searchlights was again modified.
The arm of the port side crane was elongated to permit the hoisting in of seaplanes.
The mainmast was given a longer upper mast.

Third rebuild at Toulon, 1 July, 1934 to 21 May, 1935
This last rebuild of the *Paris* was mainly intended to repair the boilers and replace the heavy and anti-aircraft guns.
All the boilers were repaired.
The 305mm guns were replaced with new guns.
The new anti-aircraft guns comprised 7 75mm of the 1922 pattern. *Note:* in May 1940 the light anti-aircraft guns were augmented by six double Hotchkiss 13.2mm guns of the 1929 pattern and 2 13.2mm Browning machine guns on open mounts.

COURBET. First rebuild at Forges aux chantiers de la Meditérranée de La Seyne from 9 July, 1923 to 16 April, 1924
The work undertaken on the *Courbet* at this time was very similar to that done on the *Paris*:
Disarmouring the bow.
Installing one set of oil fired boilers.
Increasing the elevation of the 305mm guns to 23°.
On the tripod foremast a fire control was fitted, this had a 4.57m rangefinder. An experimental 7.60m rangefinder was placed on the conning tower.
The searchlights and boats were modified as in the *Paris*.

Second rebuild at Forges aux chantiers de la Mediterranée de La Seyne from 15 January, 1927 to 12 January 1931.
This very long rebuild was undertaken to renovate the machinery, improve the anti-aircraft guns and the fire control.
A second set of boilers were converted to oil firing.
The high and medium pressure turbines were replaced

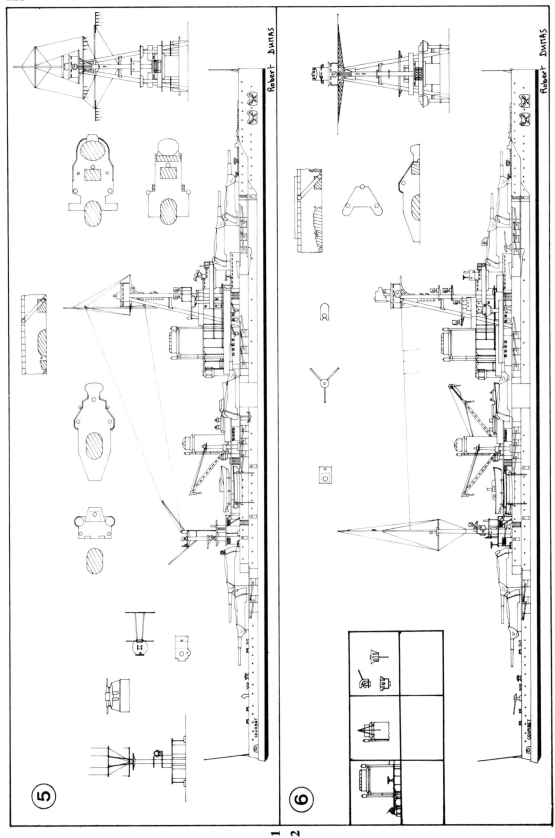

1/2 *Courbet* in 1924 and 1931.
Drawn by the Author

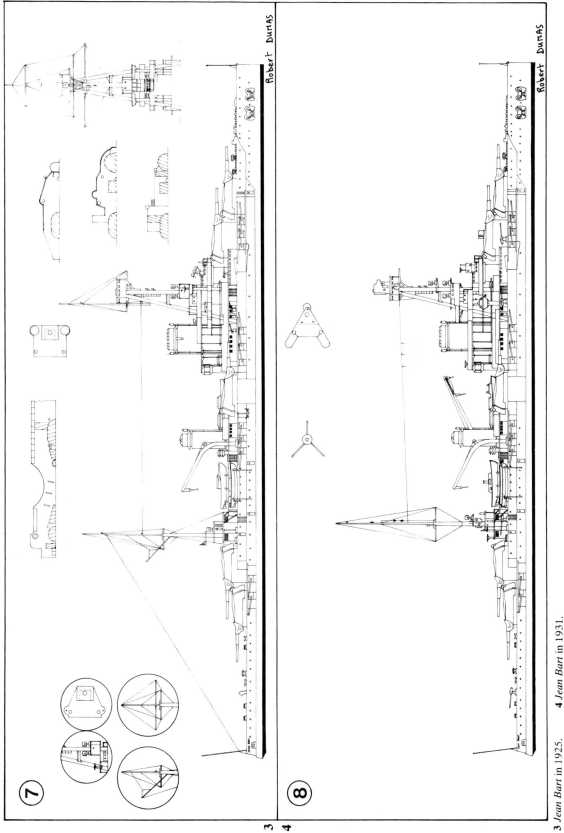

7

8

Robert Dumas

Robert Dumas

3 *Jean Bart* in 1925.   4 *Jean Bart* in 1931.
Drawn by the Author   *Drawn by the Author*

3
4

1

2

3

1 *Courbet* in 1939.
  Author's Collection

2 *Jean Bart* in 1925, she carries a mainmast, unlike *Courbet*.
  Author's Collection

3 *Jean Bart* in 1925–26 in a rather better state of decorative order than the previous photograph.
  Author's Collection

by geared turbines.

The 75mm guns of the 1918 pattern were replaced by 1922 models.

The fire control and rangefinders were modified in line with the work carried out during the second rebuild of the *Paris*, except that an 8.20m rangefinder was placed on the top of 'B' turret and the 7.60m rangefinder on 'X' turret was suppressed.

The searchlights and crane were modified as in *Paris*.

Third rebuild at Toulon 1 April, 1037 to 19 September, 1938

In the course of this final rebuild the following work was carried out:

The boilers, both oil and coal fired, were rebuilt.

The submerged torpedo tubes were taken out.

Note: in May 1940 the light anti-aircraft guns of *Courbet* were reinforced to the same extent as those of *Paris*.

JEAN BART. First rebuild at Toulon from 12 October, 1923 to 29 January, 1925

Work undertaken:

The bow was dearmoured as far back as the 155mm upper belt.

The boilers in the first group were converted to oil firing.

The elevation of the 305mm guns was increased to 23°.

The 75mm guns, 1897 pattern were replaced with four of the 1918 pattern. The 47mm 1902 guns were retained and 24 8mm machine guns were installed.

A tripod mainmast and firecontrol were installed, as in *Courbet*s first rebuild.

The forward pair of funnels were trunked into one, as in *Courbet*.

Second rebuild at Toulon from 7 August, 1929 to 28 September, 1931

The work undertaken was identical to that on the *Courbet* during her second rebuild.

Installation of a second set of oil-fired boilers.

Replacement of the cruising turbines with geared turbines.

Modifications to the fire control, rangefinders, searchlights and crane were identical to *Courbet*.

Note: *Jean Bart* had an enclosed bridge fitted on the foremast above the conning tower, which distinguished her from *Courbet*.

The poor general condition of the *Jean Bart* prevented her from receiving a third rebuild. She was reclassified as a schoolship in 1936.

1

3

1 *Jean Bart* in 1932, after her second refit.
Author's Collection

2 *Jean Bart* displaying a remarkable number of aerials, spreaders and awnings, in 1933.
Author's Collection

3 *Ocean*, ex *Jean Bart*, awaiting demolition in late 1945 at St Mardier.
Author's Collection

CONCLUSION

During the first part of World War I the four *Courbets* were the most modern units of the French Navy. For most of the war their role was obscure; it was limited to blockading the Austrian Fleet in the Adriatic. After the war *Courbet*, *Jean Bart* and *Paris* were rebuilt to take into account the many lessons learnt by the Royal Navy at the Battle of Jutland. These first French Dread-

noughts had been handicapped, and their dimensions limited by the size of the existing docks and basins of the period. Therefore their rebuilds were not as effective as they might have been. Therefore, by the ends of the 1930s the three surviving battleships had been relegated to the secondary, but important, role of schoolships.

FATE

Courbet	Scuttled on 9 June, at Oiustreham to form part of the breakwater for the D-Day landings. Broken up after the war.
Ocean (ex-*Jean Bart*)	Broken up at Toulon from 14 December, 1945.
Paris	Condemned 21 December, 1955, broken up at La Seyne from June, 1956.
France	Sunk in Quiberon Bay, 26 August, 1922 after striking an uncharted rock.

The Heavy Cruiser Admiral Hipper at War

by Pierre Hervieux

Hipper at sea.
DAM

The Germany heavy cruiser *Admiral Hipper* was built at the Blohm und Voss Shipyard in Hamburg. Laid down on 6 July 1935, launched on 6 February 1937 and commissioned on 29 April 1939. Right from the outbreak of World War II she was placed under the Commander-in-Chief West, together with the battlecruisers *Scharnhorst* and *Gneisenau,* the heavy cruiser *Admiral Scheer,* the light cruiser *Leipzig* and three divisions of destroyers.

On 18 February 1940 Admiral Forbes received a report from Bomber Command aircraft that major enemy warships appeared to be held in the ice off the entrances to their North Sea bases. This indicated the possibility of a foray being made against British shipping. The Commander-in-Chief's expectations were perfectly correct for, on the day when the bomber aircraft made their report Admiral Marschall had sailed

withe the *Gneisenau, Scharnhorst, Admiral Hipper* and two destroyers with the object of attacking British shipping between the Shetlands and Norway – Operation *Nordmark*. But the seas were found empty of traffic and the German squadron returned to Wilhelmshaven on 20 February where it encountered difficulties due to ice. Progress was only possible with the help of ice-breakers. Bomber Command carried out one operation which accomplished nothing. For Operation *Weserübung,* the invasion of Norway, the *Admiral Hipper* belonged to the Trondheim group under the command of Kommandant Kapitän zur See Heye and sailed on 6 April 1940 with four destroyers, at 2200, after having embarked 1700 troops at Cuxhaven. After meeting the *Scharnhorst* and *Gneisenau,* the *Admiral Hipper* and the 14 destroyers (Narvik and Trondheim groups) were unsuccessfully attacked by 12 Bomber Command Blenheims from 107 Squadron. At 0815, on 8 April, an unidentified destroyer was sighted by the German destroyer *H*

Glowworm on fire, as seen from *Hipper.* Note that the bows are already broken off and the torpedo tubes are trained to starboard.

Druppel

Lüdemann and then at 0910 another German destroyer *B Von Arnim,* signalled on the ultra short wave radio that she was exchanging gunfire with a British destroyer. She was the *Glowworm* (1935, 1350 tons) which had been detached from escorting the battlecruiser *Renown* to search for a man overboard. At 0922 the *Admiral Hipper* altered course to help her destroyer and opened fire at 0957. The *Glowworm* was making smoke and turning violently in the heavy seas; she fired her ten torpedoes without effect. She was hit by *Hipper*'s 8in shells but before sinking her courageous Captain, Lieutenant-Commander Roope decided to ram the *Hipper.* This happened at 1013, the destroyer being pushed underneath the water, her bows broken off and set on fire . . . 40 metres of the *Hipper*'s hull plating were pulled off. The *Glowworm* capsized and sank at 1024. More than 500 tons of water poured into the *Hipper*'s hull, she nevertheless kept sailing for Trondheim. Thirty eight British survivors were rescued by the Germans despite the heavy seas, but Roope was not among them.

The Royal Navy decided to attack Trondheim, where the *Hipper* was with four destroyers, with 18 Swordfish torpedo aircraft on the morning of 11 April. But the heavy cruiser and one destroyer had already set out undetected and sailed to the south, narrowly escaping running into Admiral Forbes' fleet during the night. There were only three destroyers in the harbour and two

of them were attacked with no results. British air reconnaissance located the *Scharnhorst* and *Gneisenau* with the *Hipper* on their return south west of Stavanger. By taking advantage of the bad weather and with the help of wireless telegraphy intelligence they avoided the forces of the Home Fleet. Ninety two bombers of Coastal and Bomber Command took off to attack but none found a target and the three German ships reached the Jade without incident on the evening of 12 April. The damage to the *Hipper,* caused by the *Glowworm* was not serious and she was repaired in time to take part in the next sortie, against British evacuation transports in the area west of Harstad.

This was Operation *Juno* under the command of Admiral Marschall aboard the battlecruiser *Gneisenau.* Also taking part were her sister ship *Scharnhorst* and four destroyers. They sailed from Kiel on the morning of 4 June. The *Hipper* and the four destroyers were refuelled from the fleet tanker *Dithmarschen,* disguised in Russian colours on 7 June. On the same day two groups of ships were reported by air reconnaissance. The first one comprised the British tanker *Oil Pioneer* (5666 tons) escorted by the brand new naval armed trawler HMS *Juniper* (530 tons), commissioned on 9 March 1940. The second group was made up of the empty troopship *Orama* (19840 tons) and the hospital ship *Atlantis,* both British. At 0555 on 8 June, the *Hipper* opened fire on the *Juniper,* soon joined by the destroyer *H Lody* who rescued 29 survivors. Then the *Hipper* set the tanker *Oil Pioneer* on fire, she was finished off by a torpedo from the destroyer *H Schoemann,* who rescued 11 survivors. Both ships were sunk in position

Hipper during Operation Nordmark, February 1940.
DAM

67°44N 03°52E. The big transport ship *Orama* was caught under the fire of the *Hipper* and the destroyer *H Lody* and then sunk by two torpedoes from the latter – 247 survivors were rescued by the heavy cruiser and two destroyers. The immunity of the hospital ship *Atlantis* was respected, her Captain having in return given his word not to attempt to transmit radio messages. The *Hipper* and the four destroyers were detached to Trondheim on 8 June and so took no part in the sinking of the aircraft carrier HMS *Glorious* and her two escorting destroyers, who were all sunk by the battlecruisers *Gneisenau* and *Scharnhorst* on the same day. During 10 and 11 June the *Hipper* and the *Gneisenau* and four destroyers made a sortie from Trondheim into the Arctic, but without any result. To divert British air reconnaissance away from the return of the damaged battlecruiser *Scharnhorst* the *Gneisenau* and *Hipper* left Trondheim on 20 June to make a sortie into the Iceland Faeroes passage. Forty nautical miles north west of Halton the British submarine HMS *Clyde* (Captain Ingram) obtained a torpedo hit on the *Gneisenau*'s bow, the operation was then abandoned.

Between 25 July and 9 August the *Hipper* undertook mercantile warfare operations in the Arctic between Tromsö and Spitzbergen. She only encountered neutral merchant ships. But on 1 August, off Vardö, the *Hipper*

stopped the Finnish steamer *Ester Thorden* (1940 tons) which was carrying cellulose, piece goods, post and gold (!) from Petsamo to New York. Being considered contraband cargo she was taken by a boarding party to Tromsö.

On 24 September the *Hipper*, now under the command of Kapitän zur See Meisel, left Kiel for Saint Nazaire from where she was to carry out mercantile warfare in the Atlantic. But on 27 September, west of Stavanger, she developed engine defects and had to return home, reaching Kiel on 30 September. The *Hipper* was detected by British photographic reconnaissance at Brunsbüttel on 29 November but its importance was not realised and she sailed next day, crept north up the Inner Leads and was not sighted by British air patrols. The *Hipper* then waited until bad weather had stopped all flying, and passed unobserved through the Denmark Strait into the North Atlantic on the night of 6/7 December. On Christmas eve, she encountered some 700 miles to the west of Cape Finisterre the British troop convoy WS/5A of 20 ships bound for the Middle East and proceeding southwards. This convoy was powerfully escorted by the heavy cruiser *Berwick,* the light cruisers *Bonaventure, Dunedin*, and the aircraft carriers *Argus* and *Furious* destined for Takoradi with cased aircraft, to be flown thence to Egypt. The *Hipper* shadowed the convoy by night and on the morning of 25 December there was a brief engagement between her and the *Berwick* which was damaged by two hits. Then in

Another view of the ship taken during the Operation in February 1940.

DAM

an attack on the convoy the transport *Empire Trooper* (13994 tons) was damaged on the same day, 43°58N24°15W, as well as another ship. Because of the strong escort, combined with her machinery defects, the *Hipper* broke off the engagement and headed for Brest. As she withdrew she met an independent cargo ship, the British *Jumna* (6078 tons) which was sunk, approximately 43°N20°W. It was expected that the *Hipper* would make for a French port, and the approaches to Brest were therefore patrolled by Coastal Command aircraft during the succeeding days. But British aircraft were prevented by enemy fighters from approaching close inshore and, as the *Hipper* made Brest unexpectedly from the south, she entered the port undetected on 27 December. She was not sighted there until 4 January 1941. Then she was heavily attacked in dock by both Coastal and Bomber Command aircraft. In spite of a total 175 sorties being flown for that purpose and 85 tons of bombs being aimed at her, she escaped damage.

On 1 February the *Hipper* left Brest for her second Atlantic operation, just after she had been reported still at her berth by British reconnaissance aircraft on the very same day. She steamed to a position some 1000 miles to the west of Finisterrre to fuel and await developments until the 9th. The *Hipper* was then directed to the attack of Convoy HG/53, with the eight

ships left out of 16, five having been sunk by FW200 bombers and three by the *U 37*, who had also provided bearings for the *Hipper* and the bombers. But on 11 February she only found one straggler from the convoy, which had been meanwhile dispersed, and sank her. She was the British cargo ship *Iceland* (1236 tons), 37°03N19°50W. In the night of 11/12 February the *Hipper* made contact with the convoy SLS/64, comprising 19 ships and still unescorted! On the morning of 12 February she sank the following seven ships with gunfire and torpedoes: British cargo ships *Warlaby* (1876 tons) 37°12N21°20W, *Westbury* (4712 tons) 37°10N21°20W, *Oswestry Grange* (4684 tons) 37°10N21°20W, *Shrewsbury* (4542 tons) 36°46N20°21W, *Derrynane* (4896 tons) 37°12N21°20W, the Greek cargo ship *Perseus* (5172 tons) and the Norwegian cargo ship *Boregestad* (3924 tons). Two more ships were severely damaged, one of them being the British cargo ship *Lornaston* (4934 tons) 37°12N21°20W. Kapitän zur See Meisel, in a sense of fair play left one of the ships undamaged and told her in morse: 'Save the crews'. Her presence had been reported and her fuel was again running low so her Captain decided to return at once to Brest, which he approached from the south and so again made port undetected on the 15th.

The *Hipper* had to go back to Germany to complete her refit and to remedy her constantly recurring defects. She had escaped damage in the numerous bombing attacks made during her previous five weeks' stay in

The *Hipper* engaging the *Orama*.
Druppel

Brest and she was indeed a lucky ship for she came through more attacks unscathed, although in a heavy raid on 24 February 15 bombs fell within 200 yards of her!

The *Hipper* sailed from Brest on 15 March to fuel at a

Gneisenau, Hipper and *Scharnhorst* with three destroyers and merchant ships at Trondheim in June, 1940 during Operation *JUNO*. In the foreground are three He115 floatplanes and one He59 ambulance plane.

rendezvous south of Greenland. On 23 March she passed through the narrow ice passage in the Denmark Strait, unnoticed thanks to bad weather and also because her movements being unknown to the British Admiralty, no special measures were taken in that area. She fuelled again at Bergen and reached Kiel on 28 March. Her refit and training lasted for almost a year, and on 19 March 1942 the *Hipper* left Brunsbüttel and, although British intelligence had once again detected what was afoot, neither British reconnaissance aircraft nor the torpedo striking force of Coastal Beauforts managed to find her, and she safely reached Trondheim on the 21st, being escorted on the way by the destroyers *Z 24, Z 26, Z 30* and three torpedo boats.

The *Hipper* was now based at Trondheim with the battleships *Tirpitz* and four destroyers. With the addition of two torpedo boats they all sailed on 2 July for the Altafjord where they arrived on the 3rd, for the purpose of attacking Convoy PQ17 together with another surface force comprising the heavy cruisers *Lützow, Admiral Scheer* and six destroyers. They all joined up being reinforced by two destroyers, but on 3 July the *Lützow* and three destroyers went aground near Narvik and took no further part in the operation. On 5 July, German air reconnaissance and U-boats reported the breaking up of the convoy and the departure of the cruisers westwards. Then the *Tirpitz, Admiral Scheer, Admiral Hipper*, seven destroyers and two torpedo boats put to sea from Altafjord between 1100 and 1130. When it became clear that the scattered convoy was

The *Orama,* 19,840 tons, listing. Note the shell hole in the fore funnel.
Druppel

suffering heavily at the hands of the U-boats and aircraft, Admiral Raeder cancelled the operation. At 0930 that evening Admiral Schniewind reversed his course. Though preparations were made to attack him with carrier aircraft and submarines, the *Hipper* and her consorts reached Narvik safely on 6 July. Because of the threat they had represented, the German surface ships were undoubtedly responsible for the departure of the escorting cruisers and destroyers, leaving the merchant ships almost defenceless against the German U-boats and aircraft. So, indirectly, they also were responsible for the PQ17 disaster, 23 transports being sunk out of 34! Among the ships was the British fleet tanker *Aldersdale* (1937, 8402 tons). A 24th vessel, a rescue ship, was also lost. The *Hipper,* with the *Tirpitz* and *Scheer* were now using Narvik instead of Trondheim as their main base. On 6 August they were joined by the light cruiser *Köln.*

On 10 September, the *Hipper* with the *Scheer, Köln* and some destroyers had moved from Narvik to Altafjord. They were sighted by British submarine patrols, but only the HMS *Tigris* got in an attack, but she missed. On the 13th the German Group Command North wished to sail the Altafjord Squadron to attack QP14. But Hitler warned Raeder that, because the ships were so important to the defence of Norway, he must not accept undue risks. Raeder thereupon cancelled the operation, and the surface ships remained idle throughout the convoy's passage and also for convoy PQ18. Under the command of Kauteradmiral Meisel who had been promoted, between 24/28 September the offensive mining operation *Zarin* was undertaken by the *Hipper* and the destroyers *Z 28, Z 29, Z 30* and *R Beitzen,* off the north west coast of Novaya Zemlya in the Arctic. On 5 November the *Hipper,* now under the command of Kapitän zur See Hartmann, with the Commander cruisers Generaladmiral Kummetz on board, and the destroyers *Z 27, Z 30, F Eckoldt* and *R Beitzen* sailed for operation *Hoffnung,* to attack the Soviet sea traffic in the Arctic. Their sweep was not fruitless for on 7 November, at 0515 a Soviet auxiliary submarine-chaser, the *BO 78,* was sighted and quickly sunk by destroyers. Most of her crew, seven officers and 36 men, being rescued. On the same day, at 1445, a much larger target was encountered, a tanker. She was the Soviet *Donbass* (1935, 7925 tons) which had escaped destruction in convoy PQ17 four months earlier. But this time her luck ran out and she was sunk by three torpedoes from the destroyer *Z 27.* Her Captain, one officer and 14 men were also rescued by the Germans.

On 22 December 1942 the convoy JW/51B left Loch Ewe for the Kola Inlet and Archangel, comprising 14 transports escorted by six destroyers, one minesweeping sloop, two corvettes and two armed trawlers. One of the destroyers lost contact with the convoy and sailed independently for the Kola Inlet. The close escort comprised the light cruisers *Sheffield* and *Jamaica* with two destroyers and the distant cover was made of the battleship *Anson,* the heavy cruiser *Cumberland* and three destroyers. There was also a flanking cover including four submarines. On 24 December the convoy was located by a German reconnaissance aircraft. On 30 December the German force put to sea from Altafjord, under the command of Generaladmiral Kummetz, consisting of the heavy cruiser *Admiral Hipper* and *Lützow* with six destroyers. On the same day the convoy was also sighted by the *U 354,* south of Bear Island, and thanks to her signals the German force was directed to the area where

Hipper sailing for Trondheim, 20 March, 1942.
Koehlers

Achates, the British destroyer sunk by *Hipper* 31 December, 1942.
IWM

the convoy was sailing. The weather was bad and the convoy well covered by a smoke screen. Though the German Generaladmiral has been criticised for dividing his force in two groups, it is to be remarked that events worked out almost exactly as he planned. The *Hipper* and three destroyers approached from the north west, the *Lützow* and the other three destroyers from the south. The *Lützow*'s group passed very close indeed, less than two miles to the south of the convoy while almost all its escorts were engaged with the *Hipper*'s group on the other flank. It seems that only the overcaution of the *Lützow*'s Captain then saved the convoy from utter destruction. The action began at 0942 when the *Hipper* opened fire with her four 8in turrets against the destroyer HMS *Achates* (1929, 1350 tons) who was screening the convoy with smoke, but she missed her. In a confused and rapid action the destroyer HMS *Onslow* was heavily damaged and set on fire by four 8in shells from the *Hipper* at 1019, 40 men being killed and wounded. At 1036, the *Hipper* opened fire on the minesweeping sloop HMS *Bramble* (1938, 875 tons) which was put out of action; she then ordered her three escorting destroyers (*F Eckoldt, R Beitzen* and *Z 29*) to finish her off. By 1108 that was done. In the meantime the *Hipper* steamed south and met the destroyer HMS *Achates,* which was still protecting the convoy with a smokescreen, at 1115. It was 1118 when the unfortunate destroyer was hit and quickly crippled by several 8in shells, 41 men, including her captain being killed. Many others were wounded, a total of 81 men being rescued by the armed trawler HMS *Northern Gem*, after the destroyer sank at 0115. Then, at 1136, the *Hipper* shifted fire to the destroyer HMS *Obedient* who was slightly damaged.

At 1130 the British light cruisers *Sheffield* and *Jamaica* sighted the *Hipper* and engaged her at about seven miles range, obtaining three hits with their 6in shells. The first of them was in No 3 boiler which reduced her maximum speed to 28 knots. The *Hipper* fired back without scoring any hits and the gunnery action ceased after a cautionary signal from SKL (German Navy Staff) convinved Kummetz to disengage at 1137. At 1143 two German destroyers suddenly appeared, mistaking the British cruisers for their own ships and one of them, the *F Eckoldt*, was soon sunk by overwhelming gunfire from the *Sheffield*. At about the same time, the *Lützow* opened fire on the convoy at about nine miles range, damaging the destroyer HMS *Obdurate* and the freighter *Calobre*. At 1203 Kummetz repeated his order to withdraw. After his action with the German destroyers Admiral Burnett sailed west again to pursue the *Hipper*, then at 12 miles, ahead on the port side. At 1223 he saw two German destroyers and was about to fire at them, when the *Lützow* was sighted. He fired at her, the German heavy cruiser replied, and the *Hipper*, being at only seven miles, joined her with a much more accurate fire. Burnett had to disengage to the north to avoid being caught between two fires. This action ceased at 1236, and the battle was over. It could have been a German victory, but it was not. Why? Because of the confused situation, the poor visibility and the restrictive German Navy Staff's message received at 1840 on 30 December: 'In spite of operational orders, exercise restraint if you contact enemy of comparable strength, since it is undesirable to run excessive risks to the cruisers'. It also must be recalled that it was the first operational sortie for *Lützow*'s Captain Stange. Another reason for his marked timidity in the fighting could have been that *Lützow* was under orders to break out into the Atlantic after the attack on the convoy. That project was of course abandoned. The German destroyers were also obliged to follow the order of staying close to the *Hipper* and *Lützow* to protect them, instead of attacking the convoy as they could have done. And nobody can forget how skillfully the convoy was defended by the destroyers

of Captain Sherbrooke. On New Year's day 1943 Kummetz was back again in Altafjord. The main body of convoy JW/51B entered the Kola Inlet on 3 January 1943 and the Archangel detachment reached port three days later.

Early in February the *Hipper* returned to Kiel for repair of her engine damage. She was immobilized until March 1944, priority being given to work on U-boats. At the end of May the *Hipper* was in dock and was then used to train sailors for a future battlefleet and as an accomodation ship in the Baltic. She also took part in the anti-aircraft defence of Kiel and other harbours with her 4.1in, 40mm, 37mm and 20mm guns. It was in the harbour of Gotenhafen (ex Gdynia) that the *Hipper* was based to escape the Anglo-American air raids. On 30 January 1945, after the German passenger ship *Wilhelm Gustloff* was torpedoed and sunk by a Soviet submarine, the *Hipper* at first came up, but was unable to participate in the rescue operations because of the submarine danger and had to withdraw to the west for Kiel with 1500 wounded on board. Due to her untrained crew she was unable to fire on Soviet land targets unlike other heavy cruisers. On 9 April the *Hipper* arrived again at Kiel. During the following night RAF Bomber Command dropped 2634 tons of bombs on the harbour installations, the *Hipper* was badly damaged. She was then moved into dry dock. Loaded with U-boat parts she was scuttled and sunk by her crew, on 3 May 1945, before the port was captured by British forces. In 1948/1949 the wreck was broken up.

The *Hipper* had the unique distinction, for a German surface warship, to have sunk two British destroyers, who also were the first and the last victims among the 16 ships that she sank and captured between April 1940 and December 1942.

TABLE 1: Ships sunk directly or shared* (and captured) by the *Admiral Hipper*

Date	Ship	Tons
8 April 1940	British destroyer HMS *Glowworm*	1350 tons
8 June 1940	British passenger ship *Orama**	19840 tons
8 June 1940	British tanker ship *OilPioneer**	5666 tons
8 June 1940	British armed trawler HMS *Juniper**	530 tons
1 August 1940	Finnish cargo ship *Ester Thorden*	1940 tons
25 December 1940	British cargo ship *Junma*	6078 tons
11 February 1941	British cargo ship *Iceland*	1236 tons
12 February 1941	British cargo ship *Warlaby*	4876 tons
12 February 1941	British cargo ship *Westbury*	4712 tons
12 February 1941	British cargo ship *Oswestry Grange*	4684 tons
12 February 1941	British cargo ship *Shrewsbury*	4542 tons
12 February 1941	British cargo ship *Derrynane*	4896 tons
12 February 1941	Greek cargo ship *Perseus*	5172 tons
12 February 1941	Norwegian cargo ship *Borgestad*	3924 tons
31 December 1942	British minesweeping sloop HMS *Bramble**	875 tons
31 December 1942	British destroyer HMS *Achates*	1350 tons
		71,671 tons

16 ships — 4 warships / 12 merchant ships

US Aircraft Carriers:

Combat Systems and Catapults

by Stefan Terzibaschitsch

Following to the addition of the aft island structure *Midway* carried for a short time three main radar antennas: SPS-49, SPS-48, and SPS-43A. The ship has two BPDMS Mk 25 launchers. The photograph was taken on 17 May 1981 in the Indian Ocean

Collection van Ginderen

INTRODUCTION

Since World War II the US Navy has been based around aircraft carrier and their tactical aircraft. *Midway* and *Coral Sea*, two of the carriers delivered shortly after the end of World War II, as well as the World War II-built *Lexington* (now classified AVT-16) are still in the inventory of the US Navy. As far as possible, they have been regularly overhauled and renovated. So, for a couple of years they will still serve the Navy in accordance with the current aircraft technology and pilot training requirements, respectively.

In the post-World War II era the importance of Naval Aviation, and Aircraft Carriers has grown. Apart from the Strategic Submarines (SSBN), and the nuclear powered Attack Submarines (SSN), the carriers are still today the most important, and also the most expensive

ships in the Navy. Since World War II twelve of the huge 'Super Carriers' have been constructed, five of which are driven by nuclear-power. Another CVN is under construction, and it will be undocked before the end of 1984. Two others also of the *Nimitz* class are already ordered, with a final delivery date of 1991.

The oldest of the post-war Super Carriers, the *Forrestal*, has been in commission around 30 years, since 1955. Usually these huge ships are designed for a normal service life of 30 years, but the Navy is trying tō prolong this by half as much again. This can only be achieved by a variety of measures. For some carriers these measures are incorporated in the so-called SLEP program, being an abbreviation for 'Service Life Extension Program'. However, it is very difficult to outline exactly the extent of a SLEP program (some other ship types are also involved in SLEP!), because the amount of work varies from ship to ship. SLEP for one ship, has already been executed in another ship long before SLEP, ie during regular yard maintenance.

Some of these measures executed during the various yards periods are not evident to the casual observer.

Independence (CV-62), photographed in July 1984 in Norfolk. This photograph, obviously taken during heavy rain, shows the forward BPDMS Mk 29 launcher, as well as the collapsible signal light mast, further SPS-48 adar on the heightened island structure (similar to *Ranger*), URN-25 on the mast top, the full width of SPS-43A radar and the starboard antenna group for ECCM purpose. Unlike other carriers, the rectangular OE-82 antenna belonging to the WSC-1 system, was installed relatively low.

W Donko

These include:
- Installation of new or alterations of existing internal ship plants and other parts
- Modernisation of living and recreation spaces
- Installation or augmentation of air conditioning plants
- Addition of Kevlar armour plates over vital areas
- Enlargement of fuel tanks
- Increase of aircraft ordnance capacity
- Switch to a new aircraft type
- Overhaul of boilers and turbines
- 'Refueling' of nuclear propulsion plants
- Installation of improved command facilities, NTDS, computers etc

Other measures provide for the replacement of obsolete weapons and electronics. These external measures change the appearance of a ship again and again. The best evidence of this can be seen in the alterations to the 40 year-old *Midway*.

The task of this pictorial is to present a documentation of the appearance of several aircraft carriers by using a selection of photographs taken by the author and Willi Donko. Other pictures are to be credited to the photographers indicated. Only the ship's self-defence system are studied in this report, not the aircraft.

The table included in this presentation shows the inventory of self-defense weapons related to the particular aircraft carriers. This is based on information from *Combat Fleets of the World 1984/85* as well as evaluation of the photographs. However, it must be emphasized that the table is only accurate for Spring 1984. This especially concerns the three carriers at the time of writing in the yards. Some changes in the combat systems will have occurred in the meantime.

BPDMS

Under this all-embracing term ('Basic Point Defense Missile System') all seaborne systems are assembled, being connected with the use of the Sea Sparrow missile RIM-7.

From 1967 several aircraft carriers embarked 8-cell launchers Mk 25, similar in appearance to the ASROC-launchers on ASW-oriented Surface Combatants. From the Mk 25, RIM-7E could be launched against hostile SSM or low flying aircraft. Apart from the 5in 54 Mk 42 guns embarked in the first service years on the four *Forrestals,* and the Terrier launchers Mk 10 on the *Kitty Hawk/America* class, the Mk 25 was the first effective missile weapon system designed for defense against ship-to-ship missiles. The Mk 25 launcher was linked with the fire control system Mk 115, and the Mk 76

COMBAT SYSTEMS ON US AIRCRAFT CARRIERS: SPRING 1984

PN	Name	LANT PAC	Self-defense weapons	Electronic systems	Catapults
CVN-70	*Carl Vinson*	P	3 BPDMS Mk 29 4 Phalanx Mk 15	SPS-49, SPS-48B, SPS-10F, LN-66 SPN-41, 2 SPN-42, SPN-43A, SPN-44 6 Mk 91, 2 WLR-1H, 4 SRBOC Mk 36, URN-25, WSC-3	4 C13 Mod 1
CVN-69	*Dwight D Eisenhower*	A	3 BPDMS Mk 25	SPS-43A, SPS-48B, SPS-10F, LN-66 SPN-41, SPN-42, SPN-43A, SPN-44 3 Mk 115, WLR-1H, 4 SRBOC Mk 36, URN-25, WSC-3	4 C13 Mod 1
CVN-68	*Nimitz*	A	2 BPDMS Mk 29 3 Phalanx Mk 15	SPS-49, SPS-48B, SPS-10F, LN-66 SPN-41, 2 SPN-42, SPN-43A, SPN-44 4 Mk 91, SLQ-17, 4 SRBOC Mk 36, URN-25, WSC-1	4 C13 Mod 1
CV-67	*John F Kennedy*	A	3 BPDMS Mk 29 Phalanx Mk 15	SPS-49, SPS-48C, SPS-10F, LN-66 SPN-35, SPN-41, 2 SPN-42, SPN-43A, SPN-44 6 Mk 91, 3 Mk 28 Chaff r., WLR-1, WLR-11, SLQ-26, URN-25, WSC-3	3 C13 1 C13 Mod 1
CVN-66	*America*	A	3 BPDMS Mk 29 3 Phalanx Mk 15	SPS-49, SPS-48C, SPS-10F, LN-66 SPN-35, SPN-41, 2 SPN-42, SPN-43A 6 Mk 91, SLQ-29, 4 SRBOC Mk 39, URN 25, Sonar SQS-23, WSC-3	3 C13 1 C13 Mod 1
CVN-65	*Enterprise*	P	3 BPDMS Mk 29 3 Phalanx Mk 15 3-20mm Mk 68	SPS-49, SPS-48C, SPS-65, LN-66 SPN-41, SPN-35A, SPN-44 WLR-1, WLR-8, WLR-11, 4 SRBOC Mk 36, URN-25, WSC-1, SLQ-17	4 C13 Mod 1
CV-64	*Constellation*	P	3 BPDMS Mk 29 3 Phalanx Mk 15	SPS-49, SPS-48C, SPS-10F, LN-66 SPN-35, SPN-41, 2 SPN-42, SPN-43A 6 Mk 91, WLR-1, WLR-11, SLQ-26, 4 SRBOC Mk 36, URN-25, WSC-3	4 C13
CV-63	*Kitty Hawk*	P	2 BPDMS Mk 29 3 Phalanx Mk 15	SPS-49, SPS-48C, SPS-10F, LN-66 SPN-35, SPN-41, 2 SPN-42, SPN-43A 4 Mk 91, WLR-1, WLR-11, SLQ-26, 4 SRBOC Mk 36, URN-25	4 C13
CV-62	*Independence*	A	2 BPDMS Mk 29	SPS-43A, SPS-48C, SPS-10, LN-66 SPN-35, SPN-41, 2 SPN-42, SPN-43A 4 Mk 91, WLR-1, WLR-3, WLR-11, SLQ-26, 3 Chaff r., SRBOC Mk 28, URN-25, WSC-1	4 C7
CV-61	*Ranger**	P	2 BPDMS Mk 29	SPS-43A, SPS-48C, SPS-10, LN-66 SPN-35, SPN-41, 2 SPN-42, SPN-43A 4 Mk 91, WLR-1, WLR-3, WLR-11, SLQ-26, 4 SRBOC Mk 36, URN-25, WSC-3	4 C7
CV-60	*Saratoga*	A	3 BPDMS Mk 29 3 Phalanx Mk 15	SPS-49, SPS-48C, SPS-10, LN-66 SPN-35, SPN-41, 2 SPN-42, SPN-43A 6 Mk 91, WLR-1, WLR-3, WLR-11, SLQ-26, 4 SRBOC Mk 36, URN-25	4 C13
CV-59	*Forrestal**	A	3 BPDMS Mk 29 3 Phalanx Mk 15	SPS-49, SPS-48C, SPS-10, LN-66 SPN-35, SPN-41, 2 SPN-42, SPN-43 6 Mk 91, WLR-1, WLR-3, WLR-11, SLQ-26, 4 SRBOC Mk 36, URN-25	4 C13
CV-43	*Coral Sea**	A	3 Phalanx Mk 15	SPS-43C, SPS-30, SPS-10, LN-66 SPN-41, 2 SPN-42, SPN-43A WLR-1, WLR-10, WLR-11, ULQ-6, 4 SRBOC Mk 36, URN-25	3 C11 Mod 1
CV-41	*Midway*	P	2 BPDMS Mk 25	SPS-49, SPS-48C, SPS-65, LN-66 SPN-35A, 2 SPN-42, SPN-44 2 Mk 115, WLR-1, WLR-10, WLR-11, ULQ-6, 4 SRBOC Mk 36, URN-25	2 C13

Mod. O fire control gear. Meanwhile, most of the Mk 25 were landed from the aircraft carriers, and replaced by the lighter launcher Mk 29, used also in other types in the US Navy as well as in several NATO navies. *Midway* and *Dwight D Eisenhower* are still to receive Mk 29. This launcher is linked with a new version of the Sea Sparrow missile, designated RIM-7F, which itself later will be replaced by RIM-7M. Each launcher is linked

Constellation (CV-64), photographed 19 April 1984 in North Island. Recognizable are: the starboard-Phalanx beneath the bridge, SPN-43A radar on the aft mast platform, the ECCM antenna group belonging to the SLQ-17 system, one of two aircraft approaching antennas SPN-42, as well as the meteorological satellite antenna SMQ-10 along the flight deck edge.

Terzibaschitsch

with a pair of Mk 91 fire control. The Mk 29 launchers onboard *Spruance*-destroyers include only one Mk 91.

Two as yet un-named aircraft carriers are destined to receive the recently introduced radar system TAS Mk 23 ('Target Acquisition System') developed to be used with the MK 29 launching system. (The new carriers will be named *George Washington, Abraham Lincoln* and *Theodore Roosevelt.*)

PHALANX

The full designation is here 'Phalanx CIWS Mk 15' (CIWS = 'Close-in Weapon System'). Phalanx itself represents the self-working twin radar system beneath the white radome. Phalanx radar is linked with a six-barreled 20mm Vulkan gun assembly, using hard core shells. The shooting sequence is 3000 rounds per minute. The Mk 15 is a 'last ditch' weapon destined to protect the ship against low flying aircraft and missiles in the final stage of their flight, whereby the missile's warhead should be detonated by a curtain of shells. Phalanx is now in the delivery phase. Many ships of all types are already equipped with Phalanx.

For self-defense purpose each aircraft carrier will receive three or four Phalanx. In the first half of 1984 *Ranger, Independence, Dwight D Eisenhower*, and *Midway* were still without this weapon system.

20mm GUN Mk 68

As far as is known only *Enterprise* disposes of three of these small guns, the range of which does not exceed 3000m. They are normally intended to engage small torpedo boats or to eliminate surfaced mines. The Mk 68 can also be found in other types of ship, including amphibious ships and auxiliaries.

ELECTRONIC SYSTEMS

A large collection of electronic systems for various purposes is assembled on board each aircraft carrier. The Navy is trying hard to install the latest electronic gear during SLEP, or during regular overhauls.

SPS-

This is the prefix for full radar systems used onboard ships. Usually the related radar antenna is designated like the full system, but to be correct it must be emphasized that each radar antenna bears its own designation, belonging to the AS- series.

For the time being the most important air surveillance radar sets are SPS-49 and SPS-48, the last using a 3-D antenna, of which at this time the versions B and C are in use. Most of the carriers are already equipped with these sets. In the first half of 1984 only *Dwight D Eisenhower, Independence,* and *Ranger* were still equipped with the 20 year-old, obsolete radar antenna SPS-43 with its length of nearly 13m. The last set of the 20 year-old 'Highfinder' radar SPS-30 was landed in 1983 from *Coral Sea.*

Almost all aircraft carriers have in addition one set of the SPS-10F surface search system on board. Instead, *Enterprise* and *Midway* meanwhile received SPS-65, a

1

3

2

4

1 *Enterprise* (CVN-65), photographed on 16 April 1984 in Alameda. This is the best known view of the starboard side of the rebuilt island. Phalanx Mk 15 is placed on its own platform, here extremely elevated. Abaft the bridge pulpit one antenna group of the ECCM system SLQ-17 can be observed, and on the aft mast platform the approaching radar SPN-43A. The ship's identification number on the island is illuminated at night to facilitate the night landing procedure of the aircraft.

Terzibaschitsch

2 The island of *America* (CV-66), pictured on 5 April 1984 in Norfolk. Atop the island are the radar antenna SPS-49, as well as the drum-shaped antenna OE-82B belonging to the satellite communication systems WSC-3. The Phalanx controls Mk 91.

W Donko

3 The aft port side Sea Sparrow launcher Mk 25, as shown in July 1984 on *Dwight D Eisenhower* (CVN-69). The base structure as well as the 8-cell launcher itself are considerably higher than the Mk 29.

W Donko

4 A rear view of the island belonging to *Dwight D Eisenhower* (CVN-69), pictured in July 1984 in Norfolk. The both approach antennas SPN-42 can easily be recognized on the left edge of the island, as can also the casing with (probably) SPN-41 radar on the electronic mast. It gives the impression that an SPN-44 antenna is located on the island's roof, just left of the electronic mast.

W Donko

new system which, however, uses the same radar screen as SPS-10. A light navigational set is fitted, the commercial LN-66, which does not belong to the SPS- series. It can be found on almost all carriers.

SQS-

One of the prefixes used for sonar detection systems, destined to discover submerged submarines. Only *America* carries an active/passive sonar system SQS-23, which can be found on some old cruisers and destroyers

SPN-

The prefix for aircraft approach radar systems on board carriers. They also can be found on Amphibious Assault Ships (LHA), as well as on Amphibious Helicopter Carriers (LPH). The aircraft carriers always dispose of several SPN-systems assembled in various combinations. In the current inventory there are the old systems like SPN-35, -41 and -42 (the last one always used in pairs!), -43A, as well as the modern SPN-44. SPN-45 is just in development for use by CVN-72 and -73. All these antennas 'look' aft to the area, where the aircraft are approaching for landing. One can discover the SPN-antennas on mast platforms, along the aft vertical surface of the ship's island, on the separate electronic mast behind the island, and – recently SPN-35, separated from other sets, placed on a radar support platform along the flight deck edge.

URN-

This is the prefix for TACAN air navigation terminals. Only few carriers still mount the older antenna URN-20 covered by the distinctive radome. In recent years URN-25 is preferred, having a much lighter, flat antenna, which again can be observed on the mast.

OE-, WSC-

Almost all US warships, including many auxiliaries, are equipped with satellite terminals for navigation and communication purposes. They mostly belong to the WSC- series. WSC-1 and WSC-3 are well distributed, and the related antenna is the rectangular drum-shaped OE-82. Almost all of the carriers are equippped with a pair of these antenna. For this reason the attached table does not include OE-82.

WLR-, SLQ-, ULQ-, AND SRBOC

These are all together prefixes and abbreviations for the important ECCM-systems, destined to suppress the enemy's ECM activities. The most modern ECCM gear, SLQ-32 is already installed on many ship types, excluding aircraft carriers. This probably also applies for the torpedo decoy system SLQ-25 NIXIE. With the assumption that all escorting surface combatants are equipped with SLQ-32, the carriers use somewhat older sets, the antenna groups of which are of course heavier than those of SLQ-32. *America* seems to be the sole carrier utilizing the combined set SLQ-29, itself composed of the both sets WLR-8 and SLQ-17. The other carriers use in various combinations the WLR-1, -2, -8, -10, -11, SLQ-26, and ULQ-6 systems.

Closely linked with all of the ECCM-systems are the so-called Chaff Rocket Throwers. The cartridges blown up by the throwers include tinfoil strips destined to confuse the enemy's radar. Each cartridge can spread as much tinfoil as is necessary to create a full radar target. This applies also for hostile missiles, which can be diverted from their target. Only *John F Kennedy* carries some two-barreled Mk 28 throwers, utilizing Zuni rockets as tinfoil cartridges. All other carriers already are equipped with four six-barreled SRBOC Mk 36 throwers (the reactivated battleships have eight such throwers).

CATAPULTS AND ARRESTING GEAR

Although catapults installed on aircraft carriers are closely related to the embarked aircraft, which are not mentioned in this article, the opportunity is given to present a short survey of the types used.

The standard catapult model is C13. With this the heaviest aircraft – up to 35 tons – can be launched, but only when the ship is directed against the wind to support the launching procedure. The latest C13 Mod 1 is able to launch all aircraft without wind support, practically from the anchored ship. This model is installed with four catapults on each carrier of the *Nimitz* class. *America* and *John F Kennedy* are the two ships having only one C13 Mod 1 and three C13. The four carriers of the *Forrestal* class by the end of the 50s had been equipped with four C7 catapults. As reported, *Saratoga* and *Forrestal*, during their SLEP refits, will have been re-

equipped with four C13. It can be assumed, that *Independence* will receive C13 during the SLEP refit in Philadelphia (1985/87), and *Ranger* during the regular overhaul in Puget Sound (1984/85). *Coral Sea* has long possessed three C11 Mod 1 catapults, which, as reported, will be brought up to the capacity of C13. This will have happened during the recent year period at Portsmouth, Va in 1983/84. *Midway* has been equipped with two C13 catapults since 1970.

Since World War II the spellout number of arresting wires on board carriers has been constantly reduced. During World War II many wires were spread over the entire flight deck, to facilitate the landing procedure of aircraft over the stern, or – as practised only occasionally – over the bows. The development of sophisticated landing approach gear favoured the drastic reduction of arresting wires, as did the introduction of the angled landing deck. So the first postwar carriers of the *Forrestal* class were completed with six arresting wires. In the following years the number of wires was reduced, and the *Nimitz* class ships were completed with only four wires. As reported in 1984, the new arresting system, Mk 7, will be delivered with only three arresting wires.

Apart from the changes described afore each carrier still carries the well-known 'crash barrier', made of nylon strips. Normally this barrier is lowered under the flight deck surface, from where it can be erected within minutes, if necessary, ie when an aircraft is approaching the deck either with loss of power, a broken hook, with wounded or disabled pilot, with landing gear failure etc.

1 A detailed view on *Carl Vinson*'s island shows one of the 'swallow's nests', as well as the upper antenna SPN-42.

Terzibaschitsch

2 Rear view of the island and the electronic mast of the *Carl Vinson*, pictured 16 April 1984 in Alameda. Note the radar antenna SPS-49 on top of the lattice mast, and both the 'swallow's nests', destined to support Mk 19 controls. The main mast supports TACAN URN-25 and the both satellite antennas OE-82.

Terzibaschitsch

3 The island of *Carl Vinson* (CVN-70), photographed 16 April 1984 in Alameda.

Terzibaschitsch

4 The fantail of *Enterprise* (CVN-65), photographed 16 April 1984 in Alameda, resembles that of *Constellation* (CV-64).

Terzibaschitsch

The Royal Sovereign Class Battleships 1913-1948

Part 3 by R A Burt

Ramillies at Devonport in the early 1930s, before her refit.
CPL

RAMILLIES

Laid down and built by Messrs Beardmore on the Clyde. She was launched on 12 September 1916, but whilst sliding down the slipway, her bottom hit the underneath of the runway which resulted in serious damage to her keel plating and rudders. On inspection, it was agreed that she would have to be docked and repaired, but there was no dock available to take the length of *Ramillies* in the area. Arrangements were made for her to proceed to Gladstone Dock in Liverpool, and be repaired by Cammell Lairds. Temporary repairs were carried out for the journey and *Ramillies* left her builders on 7 May 1917. Unfortunately, however, she managed, to run aground again, even though managed by eight tugs, and was not freed until the 23 May. Arriving at Cammell Lairds on 24 May, she was repaired and completed with her small fittings.

In September 1917, she joined the Grand Fleet, and in doing so was the last major unit to join the Fleet in World War I. An enquiry into her grounding on two occasions proved that there might have been a little neglect on the part of her original builders, but it was never proved, or taken any further. Her weight at launch was recorded at 18,750 tons, whilst the sister ships were 9407 tons for *Resolution*, 11,954 *Revenge*, 9635 tons *Royal Oak* and 10,225 tons for *Royal Sovereign*. The

officials of the enquiry checked the supports of the launching runway, took into account the increased weight of the bulges (1403 tons) and even took recordings of the tides, but they came up with no concrete evidence of neglect on behalf of the builders, and so the case was dropped. *Ramillies* was serving with the Grand Fleet from September 1917 until April 1919, when the Grand Fleet was dispersed.

On postwar reorganization, the Fleet was broken up into the new Atlantic, Mediterranean and Home Fleets. With the Atlantic Fleet from April 1919 to August 1927.

She was with the 1st BS when it was attached to the Mediterranean Fleet during operations against the Turkish Nationalists at Constantinople, and also the Fleet was seen in duties in the Black Sea from March to July 1920.

Ramillies rejoined the Atlantic Fleet in August 1920. In May 1921, the 1st BS and 2nd BS merged as one, with the *Royal Sovereign* class forming the 1st Division, and the *Queen Elizabeth* class the 2nd.

Ramillies was again detached to the Mediterranean, along with all her sisters except *Royal Oak*, in September 1922 to reinforce the Mediterranean Fleet during more troubles in the area. She was employed mainly in the Dardanelles, and Sea of Marmora. Rejoined the Atlantic Fleet in November 1922.

Underwent refit at Rosyth from June to September

Resolution leaving Devonport in Mediterranean Fleet colours in the early 1930s.
CPL

1924. On 1 November 1924, the *Queen Elizabeth* class transferred to the Mediterranean as the 1st BS whilst the *Royal Sovereign* class remained as the Atlantic Fleet until 1926.

Ramillies underwent extensive refit at Devonport from September 1926 until March 1926. Recommisioned on 1st March 1927. Transferred to the Mediterranean in August 1927. Mediterranean Fleet from August 1927 until June 1932. She was stationed at Jaffa in October 1929, during troubles in Palestine.

Paid off into Reserve at Devonport for refit in June 1932. In Reserve until August 1934. Extensive refit from February 1933 until August 1934, completing on 31 August, and then recommissioned for the Mediter-

Resolution August 1939, on the eve of war. Note the catapult on 'X' Turret.
Author's Collection

ranean Fleet on 17 September. Mediterranean Fleet from September 1934 until July 1935.

Early in 1935, it was decided to revert to the distribution of the *Royal Sovereign* class and *Queen Elizabeths* which had been adopted back in 1924. The *Royal Sovereigns* would now become the Home Fleet, and the *Queen Elizabeths* would all join the Mediterranean Fleet. *Ramillies* exchanged positions with *Barham* in August 1935. Home Fleet: 2nd BS July 1935 until February 1939. Present at the Jubilee Fleet Review at Spithead on 16 July 1935. *Ramillies* was in collison with German steamer *Eisennach* in a gale off Dover on 31 August 1935, sustaining some slight damage to her bows. Present at the Coronation Fleet Review in May 1937. Employed as a sea-going training ship from February 1936 until December 1937. (Boys and RNR officers.) Refitted at Devonport in July 1938 until February 1939. Recommissioned at Devonport 22 Feburary 1939 and transferred to the Mediterranean Fleet in February 1939. Again transferred back to the Home Fleet in July 1939. Home Fleet: July 1939 until October 1939.

1

2

3

Employed as training ship during this period.

Present at Portland Review of the Reserve Fleet by the King, on 9 August 1939. She left the Clyde for Alexandria, via Gibraltar and served at this post until October.

Ordered to join the North Atlantic Escort Force (Halifax) on 5 October, but was recalled on the 6th to replace *Malaya* in the Mediterranean Fleet. Later, ordered to the Indian Ocean to take part in the search for the raider *Graf Spee*. Served with the Mediterranean Fleet until November 1939. November 1939 to May 1940 East Indies. 3rd BS Aden.

WARTIME PERIOD

Transferred to the Mediterranean Fleet in May 1940, via Suez Canal, owing to the threat of war with Italy. Mediterranean Fleet: 1st BS May to November 1940. With *Malaya, Warspite,* and the cruiser *Kent,* bombarded Bardia on 15 August 1940.

Ramillies was a unit of the supporting force for the attack on the Italian Navy in Taranto by aircraft from *Illustrious* on 11 November 1940. She was then transferred to the North Atlantic Escort Force in November 1940, following the reduction of Italian battleship strength as a result of the Taranto raid.

Attached to Force 'H' on 27 November while on passage through the Mediterranean to Gibraltar, and was with this force during the convoy action with Italian warships at Cape Spartivento, although *Ramillies* herself was not engaged.

At Devonport for refit from December 1940 until January 1941 when she left Devonport on the 12th for Halifax via the Clyde to escort a Middle East convoy on its initial stage. Arrived in Halifax late in January 1941. North Atlantic Escort Force: Flagship RA. 3rd BS Halifax. January to August 1941, employed as escort ship on Bermuda-Halifax-UK convoy duty. Sighted by the German Battlecruiser *Scharnhorst* and *Gneisenau* when they had planned to attack the convoy, but the sight of those eight 15in guns of the old *Ramillies* caused them to abandon the attack.

Ramillies was detached from convoy duties and sent off to take part in the *Bismarck* operations on 23 May 1941.

Owing to a greater threat of war with Japan; it was proposed to send the four *Royal Sovereigns* to the Indian Ocean by the end of the year, as the first part of the newly formed Indian Ocean Fleet. This force was to be based at Colombo in the first instance, and later removed to Singapore, after it had been brought up to full strength possibly by March 1942. The First Sea Lord had proposed to send the battleships *Nelson* and *Rod-*

1 *Ramillies* off Gibraltar, November, 1940.
Author's Collection

2 *Royal Sovereign*, also in November 1940.
Author's Collection

3 *Resolution* off Bermuda, September 1941.
Author's Collection

ney, along with the battlecruiser *Renown* in December 1941, but unfortunately this was never carried out.

In December, however, as a concession to this idea, the *Prince of Wales* and *Repulse* were sent down to Singapore, arriving on the 2nd. The result being, that both ships were sunk by Japanese aircraft on the 10th, only two days after the outbreak of war with Japan. The vital third ship, the carrier *Indomitable,* never joined the force.

Following this great loss, the *Royal Sovereigns*, which had arrived at Colombo between October 1941 and March 1942, were kept in the Indian Ocean, until the summer of 1943, constituting the 3rd BS with *Warspite* as Flagship, from March 1942 until March 1943. *Ramillies* refitted at Liverpool from August to November 1941. Eastern Fleet: 3rd BS December 1941 to December 1943. She was attached to Force F at Colombo until April 1942 for the occupation of Madagascar.

She took part in the bombardment and occupation of Diego Suarez on 7 May 1942, and remained there until the surrender. During her stay, an attack by midget submarines was sent from parent Japanese submarines 1-16 and 1-20.

ATTACK ON RAMILLIES AT DIEGO SUAREZ 30 MAY, 1942.

The torpedo struck just forward of 'A' turret on the port bulge, and damaged the ship from frame 27 through to 58. Extensive flooding took place from frames 27 to 42 below the middle deck, with the exception of certain wing compartments. Frames 42 to 58 below the main deck inboard of the incline were also flooded, and many seams in the hull plating were seen to be leaking.

Although she had been badly damaged, the old vessel took the blow quite well, and staff were soon able to bring the ship under control, and out of immediate danger. The explosion had penetrated well inboard, she had been hit in a highly dangerous area, near to the shell and magazine rooms. The explosive equipment in these compartments was removed to a safer position, the anchor was removed, and the cable laid on the quarterdeck.

On inspection of the damage by divers, it was recorded that the hit was just before number 42 bulkhead, and the explosion had opened the bulge completely, from frame 27 to 42 at the bottom of the underneath compartment, down to the bilge. The damage extended inboard, in the shape of a cone, sloping forward with its apex at the middle line in which the bulkhead on the platform deck had a hole of four feet in diameter blown out of it. The bulge plating, which was ½in thick, was well corregated abaft from 42, and curved well inboard. The 6in armour forward, was displaced a little and some of the support channels were damaged, otherwise no harm done.

The *Ramillies*, although taking on tons of water had managed to right herself (actual tonnage of water unknown) but had a corresponding draught as follows: Port, forward: 39ft 3in, Starboard, forward: 39ft 1in, Port aft: 31st 3in, and Port Starboard: 29ft 11in. The freeboard forward was approximately 14 feet! The

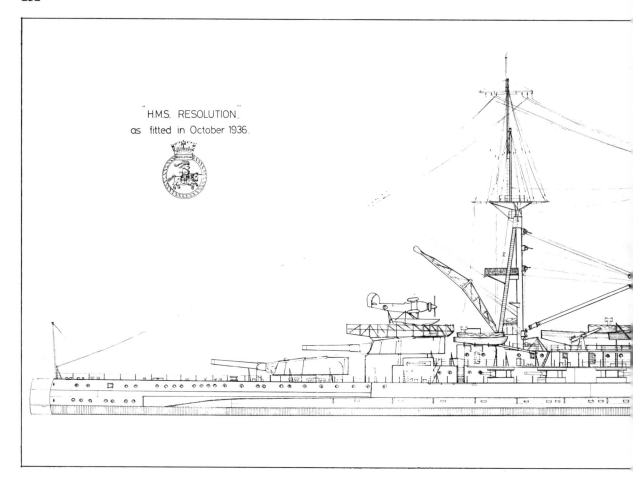

"H.M.S. RESOLUTION."
as fitted in October 1936.

bulkheads in the area were quickly shored up, and local damage was brought under control. The ship was able to proceed to Durban for repairs at a speed of 9 to 10 knots.

Whilst at Durban, the constructor H S Pengelley had flown over to inspect the damage, and commented on the vessel very favourably: 'although the vessel is now 26 years old, and felt by most to be of little value owing to reduced size and slow speeds, the *Ramillies* is in exceptionally good shape, and I should wonder whether or not the modern capital ships of today (1943) with their lighter scantlings would survive a blow as well as this old girl, some 26 years after they were built (1966!)'.

Ramillies was temporarily repaired at Durban from June to August and then sailed for Devonport to complete there. She was under refit until June 1943.

She rejoined the Eastern Fleet at Kilindini (East Africa) in July 1943 and was the only battleship remaining at that station. She left Colombo on 28 December 1943 for home, to transfer to the Home Fleet. Joined Home Fleet in January 1944.

Ramillies was refitted for duties as a unit of the bombardment force, during the Normandy invasion in June 1944. She bombarded batteries at Villerville, Benerville and Houlgate on 6 and 7 June, and again attacked Houlgate on 17 June, putting this shore battery out of action.

She became a unit of the force which bombarded southern France for the invasion in August 1944, and bombarded batteries at Toulon on the 25th and 28th.

Finally, she was reduced to Reserve at Portsmouth on 31 January 1945. Reserve Fleet, Portsmouth: January 1945 until December 1947. Attached to the Vernon Establishment as accommodation ship, and was known as Vernon 111. Placed on the disposal list in December 1947.

Sold to British Iron and Steel Co on 20 February 1948, and allocated to Arnott Young Ltd for scrapping. She arrived at Cairnryan on 23 April 1948.

RESOLUTION

Laid down and built by Palmers of Jarrow: launched on 14 January 1915. She was commissioned for service with the Grand Fleet on 7 December 1916, and actually met with the fleet on the 30th at Rosyth.

With a few alterations, her early life was much the same as *Ramillies,* as the class usually served together as a group. See appearance changes and alterations for refit dates.

WARTIME HISTORY

Assigned to the Channel Force at Portland, under the

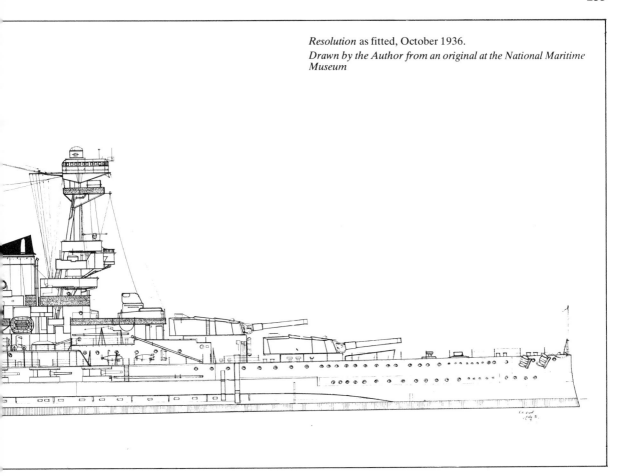

Resolution as fitted, October 1936.

Drawn by the Author from an original at the National Maritime Museum

war organization in August 1939. Channel Force: August to October 1939.

Ordered to join the South Atlantic Command (Freetown) on 1 October following the sinking of SS *Clement* by the German Panzerschiffe *Graf Spee*. These orders, however, were cancelled on 5 October, and she was transferred to the North Atlantic Escort Force (Halifax) with her sister *Revenge*. *Resolution* left England on 5 October, carrying bullion for Canada. North Atlantic Escort Force: October 1939 to April 1940. *Resolution* helped on escort duties whilst convoys of Canadian troops came to England, throughout December of that year.

Rejoined Home Fleet in April 1940 for the Norwegian campaign. Home Fleet: April to June 1940.

Took part in the capture of Bjerkvik on 12 May, during operations against Narvik, and carried tanks and motor craft for this landing. She was attacked by aircraft, and damaged by a bomb later in the month: two were killed, and 27 were injured. She transferred to the Mediterranean in June 1940. Leaving Scapa on 4 June, she joined Force 'H' (Gibraltar) on 28 June 1940. Force 'H' June to September 1940. Took part with *Hood, Valiant, Ark Royal, Arethusa, Enterprise* and a destroyer force in the attack on the French Fleet at Mers-el-Kebir

(Oran) on 3 July.

Along with *Barham, Devonshire, Cornwall, Cumberland, Australia,* and the carrier *Ark Royal*, bombarded Dakar from 23 to 25 September. *Resolution* was engaged by *Richelieu* (battleship) and shore batteries and received four hits as a result.

She was torpedoed by a French submarine on 25 September 1940, and considerably damaged. The port engine room was flooded, and she developed a serious list: the draught forward of the ship was as much as 40ft. Her speed dropped to 12 knots, and later as little as 5 and 3 knots. She was, with great difficulty, towed by *Barham* to Freetown, and arrived there on the 29th. Temporary repairs were carried out there, and later moved to Gibraltar until March 1941.

She left Gibraltar in March 1941, and was attacked by enemy aircraft, but, luckily not hit, reaching Portsmouth safely. Left Portsmouth for the USA as it was not safe for big ships to lay in dock due to frequent air attacks on that dock during this period. She was completely repaired at Philadelphia Naval Dockyard from April to September 1941.

Selected for the new Eastern Fleet in August while still under refit (see *Ramillies*). Hoisted flag of VA 3rd BS Eastern Fleet in December 1941. Arrived at Colombo 26 March 1942. Eastern Fleet: December 1941 to September 1943. She was a unit of the escort force, whilst conveying Australian troops from the Suez to Australia, in February 1943.

Returned home in September 1943. Under refit as Rosyth from September to October 1943. Reduced to Reserve for subsidiary service on completion of this refit.

Reserve: October 1943 to February 1948. She lay at Southampton until June 1944, and then transferred to Devonport as part of the training establishment *Imperieuse*. However, in a memo, from the Prime Minister, W Churchill, to the First Sea Lord, he reflected that the ship might be put to better use. Many uses for this class had been proposed, but the most interesting was an idea to convert *Resolution*, and possibly one or two others of the class into 'super shore batteries'.

The method, was to give the ships flame-cut armour plates of 5in thickness over vital positions on the decks, and 4in over all openings such as ventilation and pipe ducts over 17in in diameter. Exceptionally large bulges were to be provided, much like those of the old big-gunned monitors, so as to make them completely secure against mine and torpedoes.

To compensate for this additional weight, however, it was necessary to remove part of the machinery (10,000shp) and reduce them to 30,000shp: the ships would still be able to make 18 knots, which was accepted as adequate for the purpose in mind. The 5in and 4in armour would amount to 1990 tons, and the displacement would rise to 36,420 tons, with a corresponding draught of 32ft; the GM would approximately by 8.69ft. This idea, was not a new one, and had been placed before the Board as early as February 1940, but, unfortunately, in 1944, as in 1940, it was seen as a long project, taking up too much time and money. From October 1943 to February 1948, *Resolution* was employed as a stoker's ship.

Her main armament was removed for spares in the *Warspite* and *Ramillies* whilst those ships were bombarding the coast of Normandy. She was finally paid off on to the disposal list in February 1948. Sold to the British and Iron Steel Co, and allocated to Metal Industries Ltd, Faslane.

Arriving at Faslane for scrapping on 13 May 1948.

ROYAL OAK

Laid down and constructed at Devonport Royal Dockyard from 1913 until 196.

Commissioned at Devonport for service with the Grand Fleet, 4th BS on 1 May 1916. She was only with the Fleet for a few weeks, when she went into action at Jutland, on 31 May 1916. Engaged the German battlecruiser *Derfflinger* at a distance of 14,000 yards, and obtained several hits. Her total expenditure of 15in shells throughout this whole action was 38.

Again, with few modifications, her history was very like that of the *Ramillies*. Refit dates in appearance notes.

WARTIME HISTORY

Home Fleet: 2nd BS August 1936 until October 1939.

Conveyed the body of Queen Maud of Norway, from UK to Norway after her death in November 1938.

Commissioned at Portsmouth on 7 June 1939 for service with the Mediterranean Fleet, but never actually joined, staying with the Home Fleet on the reorganization of Fleets in August 1939. Based at Rosyth and Scapa Flow throughout the early months of the war.

Whilst *Royal Oak* lay at anchor, on the night of 14 October 1939, she was attacked and sunk by the German submarine U47. The vessel was taken completely by surprise, as it was thought to be quite safe in the surrounding waters: the submarine had managed to squeeze through the underwater defences at Hoxa Sound entrance. A torpedo was fired at *Royal Oak* at approximately 1 am but failed to do any damage, and went relatively unnoticed by those on board; the torpedo had hit an area near the anchor, and it is thought that it probably struck the anchor chain itself.

U 47 was able to reload her torpedo tubes and fire at least two more into the underneath of the battleship, tearing out her bottom. The ship turned turtle and sank within 13 minutes of being struck, and took with her 24 officers, and 809 men of the crew.

She is still in this position, underwater in Scapa Flow to this day (1985) and remains a war grave to the memory of all who perished in her, despite the frequent demand to have her raised and sold for scrap.

REVENGE

Laid down and built by Vickers, from 22 December 1913, until February 1916. Commissioned at Barrow on 1 February 1916, and joined the Grand Fleet 1st BS on 29 March 1916.

Present at the Battle of Jutland on May 31 1916, and engaged the battlecruisers, *Von-der-Tann*, and *Derfflinger* at 11,000 yards. She fired a total of 102 15in shells, and was not herself hit. She relieved *Marlborough* as flagship of 1st BS after that ship was hit by a torpedo in this action.

See *Ramillies* for inter-war periods.

WARTIME HISTORY

Present at the Portland Fleet Review (Reserve) on 9 August 1939. Channel Force: August to October 1939. Ordered to join South Atlantic Escort command. (See *Resolution*.

Transferred to Plymouth Command in August 1940, over the anticipated German invasion of England. North Atlantic Escort Force: October 1939 to August 1940. Plymouth Command: (Base ship) August to November 1940. *Revenge* bombarded Cherbourg coastline at 15,700 yards. Rejoined the Atlantic escort force in November 1940, remaining so, until August 1941.

Took part in the search for the German battleship *Bismarck* from 23 to 27 May 1941, leaving Halifax for this operation. Selected for the newly formed Eastern Fleet, and was based at Colombo from April 1942.

She was employed mainly on convoy duties in the Indian Ocean. Part of the convoys for carrying Australian troops from UK to Australia, in February 1943.

Returned home in September 1943, arriving in the

Royal Sovereign, 14 September, 1943. This overhead view demonstrates the crowded state of the upper deck between the funnel and the mainmast.

Author's Collection

Clyde on the 31st, where she was reduced to the Reserve for subsidiary service. Reserve: September 1943 until March 1948. This early retirement was partly due to the poor condition of the vessel, which had been reported as early as 1936. Her electrical layout was in very poor condition, with many of her main cables being more than due for replacement. Moreover, her hull was showing signs of strain, and was in need of an extensive refit. This problem was partly alleviated during her refit of 1939, but from that date, she still remained the worst ship of the whole class.

She was employed as a stoker's training ship at Devonport, but was later detached to convey Churchill to the Cairo-Teheran Conference. Transferred to Portsmouth Command at Southampton in January 1944.

Attached to the Training school at Devonport from 17 December 1944.

In March 1948, she was put on the disposal list.

Sold to British Iron and Steel Co, in July 1948, and was allocated to Messers T W Ward Shipbreaking Co. *Revenge* finally arrived at Inverkeithing on 5 September 1948 to be scrapped.

ROYAL SOVEREIGN

Laid down and constructed at the Portsmouth Royal Dockyard from 1913 until 1916. Commissioned on 18 April 1916, and joined the Grand Fleet on 25 May 1916.

Unfortunately, she was not present at the Battle of Jutland on 31 May, owing to troubles with machinery, and saw this day through with civilian personnel on board, who were completing her for service. Grand Fleet: April 1916 until April 1919.

See *Ramillies* for inter-war period, and see alterations for refit times.

WARTIME HISTORY

Home Fleet: From April 1935 until October 1939.

Transferred to North Atlantic Escort duties in October 1939. Refit at Devonport in December 1939.

Royal Sovereign was then transferred to the Mediterranean Fleet with the pending threat of war with Italy. Mediterranean Fleet: 1st BS May to August 1940.

With *Warspite* and *Malaya* in action off Calabria, with Italian battle squadron, whilst on convoy duty from Malta to Alexandria, but only *Warspite* was able to get within range to fire on the enemy vessels.

Royal Sovereign left the Mediterranean in August, to rejoin the North Atlantic Escort Fleet, proceeding via Suez, Aden, Durban, Capetown and Gibraltar. Under

Royal Sovereign, 7 February 1949 at Rosyth, still under the
Soviet flag and bearing the name *Arkhangelsk* on her quarter.
This view was taken before the ship was handed back to the
Royal Navy.
CPL

Ramillies at Portsmouth, January 1947, serving as a training ship.
L&L Van Ginderen.

Royal Sovereign, 10 February, 1949. The handing over.

CPL

Resolution in Eastern waters, 1942. She is still carrying the distinguishing catapult, unlike her sisters.
IWM

refit at Durban from September to October 1940. Arrived in Halifax in December 1940. North Atlantic Escort Fleet: December 1940 until August 1941. Escorted Canadian troops to England in February 1941.

Under refit at Norfolk Navy Yard USA from May to June 1941. Selected for East Indies Fleet (see *Ramillies)*. Refit in Glasgow from August to October 1941. Eastern Fleet: October 1941 until November 1943. Detached September 1942 for refit in the USA, and proceeded via Capetown and Freetown. Under refit at Philadelphia Naval Yard, USA from October 1942 until October 1943.

Withdrawn from Eastern Ocean duties on finish of refit, and returned home. On reaching home, she was paid off into care and maintenance at Rosyth on 5 November 1943. In Reserve at Rosyth from November 1943 until May 1944.

She was then earmarked for loan to the USSR, which had been carried out under the agreement concluded in lieu of the handing over of a large proportion of the surrendered Italian Fleet. The cruiser USS *Milwaukee,* six destroyers, and four British submarines were also loaned to Russia. The *Royal Sovereign* was renamed *Arkangelsk* and left for Murmansk on 17 August 1944.

Little is known of the activity with the Russian Fleet, even when the vessel was finally handed back some five years later. It was noted by the Royal Navy personnel that they were not allowed to mix with any of the Russian crew.

The *Royal Sovereign* was still in Russian hands well after the war had finished, and they, at one point, hinted that they might keep her, along with any of the other vessels on loan. The Admiralty realized, that short of military force, nothing could be done to stop this happening, and it was decided to wait for a suitable occasion to get the vessel back in British waters. Sir Winston Churchill asked the Prime Minister in January 1948, 'Whether or not, the ship was in fact to be returned to this country'. The question was raised during a debate on foreign affairs whilst in the House of Commons, but the answer given was one that might have been expected, especially when there was much interest being shown in public circles concerning the affair. The PM stated 'I can see no reason why we, in return for such help to Russia throughout the war, should leave our ships in their hands. We are entitled to get those ships back; and the scrap would be extremely useful to us at this present moment'. Moreover, it was generally considered by the Admiralty, that the effectiveness of the *Royal Sovereign* would diminish in Russian hands, because they had no spares for the vessel.

After much discussion, the *Royal Sovereign* was handed back to the Royal Navy, and left Murmansk on 15 January 1949, arriving at Rosyth on 4 February 1949. She was immediately placed on the disposal list.

Sold to British Iron and Steel Co, being allocated to TW Ward. Arrived at Inverkeithing on 18 May 1949, the last unit of the class to reach the scrapyard, after all but one of them had served for over 30 years.

Surcouf

Part 2 **by John Jordan**

Maille Brézé, 31 September 1983.
L&L Van Ginderen

LA GALISSONNIÈRE

The last ship of the T47/53 series was built to a completely revised design, which was designated Type 56. *La Galissonnière* was authorised under the 1956 programme, laid down at Lorient in November 1958, launched 12 March 1960, and finally completed in July 1962. The last two units of the T53 class, *Tartu* and *Duperré,* has been laid down in November 1954, and the long delay in beginning construction of *La Galissonnière* was the result of design changes which were to continue even after the ship had been laid down.

The original T56 proposal appears to have stemmed from a desire to produce the definitive gun-armed air defence escort. The long-barrelled twin 127mm Model 1948 adopted for the T47 and T53 classes almost cer-

tainly proved to be on the heavy side for effective anti-aircraft fire, as its somewhat conservative design was dictated in part by a continuing requirement for anti-surface performance (hence the S-Band DRBC-11 fire control radar of the earlier vessels). In the early 1950s the French therefore began development on a new fully-automatic single mounting with a high rate of traverse and elevation. The 100mm calibre selected was considered to be the minimum acceptable for effectiveness against surface and shore targets, and a 55-calibre barrel was adopted to give the weapon the required accuracy and penetration at longer ranges. The theoretical rate of fire (60rpm) was double that of the two-gun 127mm mounting, providing some compensation for the reduction in range and weight of shell against surface targets, and yielding a significant increase in effectiveness against aircraft.

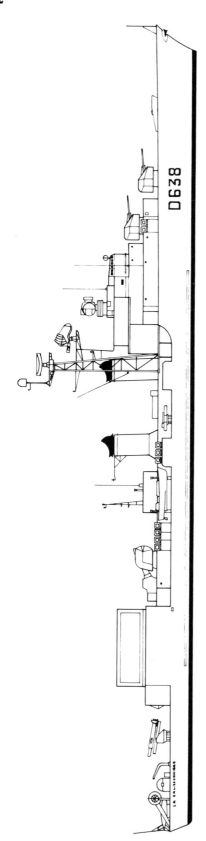

La Galissonnère, the only ship of the T56 type, in 1963.
Drawn by the Author

2

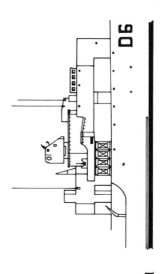

1

1 The bridge structure of *Surcouf* following her conversion to a command ship. Her two sisters had similar bridge arrangements when first converted, but photos of *Chevalier Paul* taken in the late 1960s show a much-modified bridge structure with the 20mm Oerlikon guns moved from the bridge wings to a position atop the superstructure (see full profile drawing).

Drawn by the Author.

2 A Malafon anti-submarine missile on the launch platform of the *Duguay-Trouin*, seen in August 1980.

Author's Collection

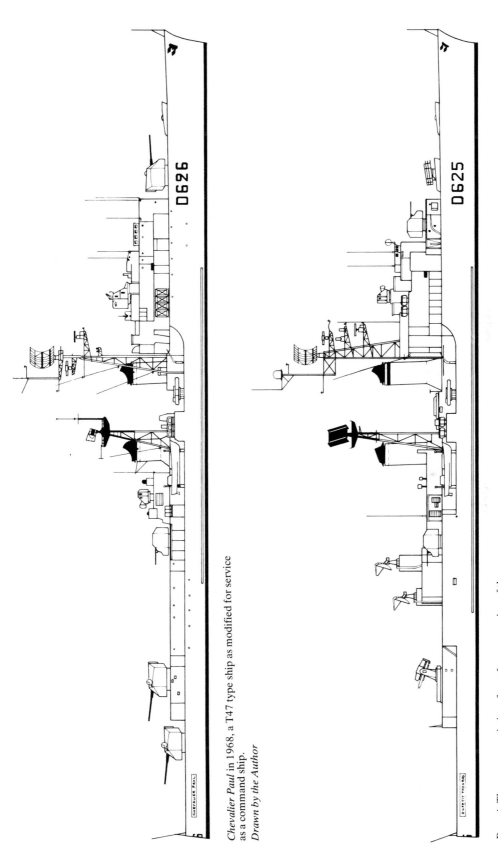

Chevalier Paul in 1968, a T47 type ship as modified for service as a command ship.
Drawn by the Author

Dupetit Thouars, an anti-aircraft warfare conversion of the T47 type, as seen in 1970 after her radar had been updated.
Drawn by the Author.

1

2

TABLE B: 100mm Mod 1953 and 1968

length:	55 cal
elevation:	−15°/+80°
muzzle velocity:	870m/sec
range:	17,000 (9nm) max,
	6–8000m practical (air targets)
projectile:	13.5kg
mounting:	22t
rpm:	60rpm

The original drawings apparently allowed for four of the new mountings, distributed evenly fore and aft and controlled by two X-Band fire control radars. This version was superseded by a revised design with only three single 100mm mountings, plus two 30mm guns of a new model. However, the most dramatic revision was yet to come.

Air defence had been the primary mission of both the T47 and the T53 types, and would have been the primary mission of *La Galissonnière* had she been completed to the original designs. In the mid-1950s, however, the French naval staff were becoming increasingly aware of the growing threat to surface forces posed by the submarine. The lessons of World War II had been that submarines were most effective when employed against slow mercantile convoys, and posed less of a threat to naval task forces operating at speeds of 20–25kt. In the immediate postwar period the Marine Nationale had therefore followed the major naval powers in making a clear division between surface escorts for naval task forces, with a primary AAW mission, and surface escorts for convoy work, with a primary ASW mission; the T47/53 series was designed for fleet work, and the E50/52 series of escorts for the protection of convoys in mid-Atlantic.

The advent of the nuclear-powered submarine, which could make 25–30kt underwater and had no need to surface to recharge its batteries, changed all this. The naval task force could no longer count on high speed alone for protection against the underwater threat. There was therefore an urgent need for fast surface escorts with a primary anti-submarine mission to accompany the carriers. *La Galissonnière* was to become the prototype for this new type of ASW escort, and the design was completely recast.

When the ship finally entered service in 1962 it was with a completely new outfit of weapons and sensors. Two of the new 100mm Model 1953 single mountings were placed forward of the bridge as in the original air defence design, and these were controlled by the new DRBC 32A radar director, located atop a bridge structure which was one deck higher than that of the T47/53 classes. A single lattice tripod was fitted, carrying the DRBV 22A air search radar and a new S-Band radar, the

1 *Du Chayla* another T47 AAW conversion, seen at Lisbon in 1983.
L&L Van Ginderen

2 *Du Chayla*, June 1984.
Author's Collection

DRBV50, for surface and low-altitude aerial contacts. It was topped, as in the T53 Type, by a TACAN aerial for aircraft control.

The arrangements of the after part of the ship were completely revised. In place of the former 127mm deck-house for 'X' mounting a new, larger deckhouse was constructed out to the ship's sides. This housed the magazine for Malafon anti-submarine missiles, the trainable single-ramp launcher being located on the quarterdeck, immediately abaft the magazine doors.

MALAFON
Malafon was the French Navy's first operational guided missile, and was designed for the prosecution of long-range submarine contacts. Like the US Navy's ASROC missile, which entered service shortly before Malafon, and the later Australian Ikara missile, Malafon is built around a homing torpedo which is dropped by parachute in the vicinity of the last known contact of the submarine. Once it enters the water the torpedo follows a circular search pattern until its acoustic detection head locates the target. The missile, which has a conventional aeroplane configuration with short, stubby wings and a twin-boom tail, has a maximum range of about 12km and, like Ikara, is radio-controlled during flight, enabling course-corrections to be made on the basis of the latest target data. The standard above-decks magazine, in which the missiles are laid out horizontally on racks, contains 13 missiles.

TABLE C: Malafon A/S missile

length:	6.15m
wing span:	3.3m
diameter:	650mm
weight:	1500kg
propulsion:	2 solid-fuel boosters
speed:	230m/sec
range:	12,000m
guidance:	radio command

A MANNED ASW HELICOPTER
Other European powers, notably the UK and Italy, had adopted the small manned helicopter as an anti-submarine torpedo delivery system for their latest ASW-frigates while *La Galissonniere* was still under construction. It was therefore decided to install handing facilities for the Aèrospatiale Alouette helicopter aboard the ship. This proved problematical because the Malafon installation occupied most of the after part of the ship, and an ingenious solution was devised. The roof of the Malafon magazine became the centre part of a landing pad for the helicopter. A collapsible hangar was constructed atop the magazine roof, the hangar sides and ends folding down to form an extension of the helicopter flight deck during flying operations. In the event the collapsible hangar proved less successful than the fixed installations adopted by other European Navies, and was not repeated either on new construction or on the later T47 ASW conversions. The provision of a helicopter did, however, provide valuable experience in rotary-wing ASW operations, and the manned helicopter was later to supplant the Malafon missile in French anti-submarine construction.

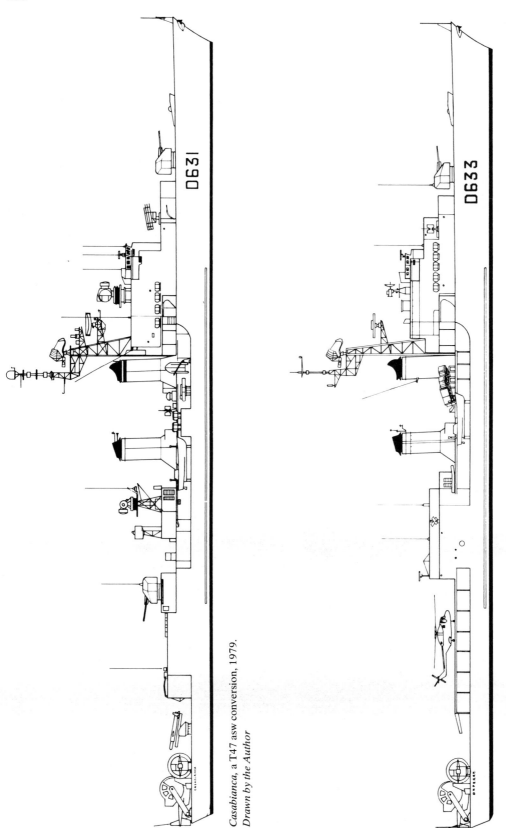

Casabianca, a T47 asw conversion, 1979.
Drawn by the Author

Duperre, a T53 conversion and the last word on modifying this class. This drawing makes an interesting comparision with the original outline (see part one of this article in Warship 35).
Drawn by the Author

CLOSE-RANGE ASW

The third new anti-submarine weapon system was the Bofors 305mm four-barrelled A/S mortar, which was located between the helicopter hangar and the second funnel. The 305mm mortar was designed by Bofors for use as a shore bombardment mortar, firing a smaller bomb at longer ranges than a conventional mortar. An unusual feature of the weapon is that it is turret-mounted, and reloads automatically by depressing its four-barrel muzzle to mate with a hoist located forward of the turret. The weapon was first installed in the four escorts of the E52B type, and was also adopted for the *avisos escorteurs* of the *Commandant Rivière* class.

Finally, the two triple banks of 'short' ASW torpedo tubes of the earlier T47 type were reinstated, but were placed farther aft, apparently with a view to locating a second reload locker (aft-facing) forward of the tubes.

The ASW weapons outfit of *La Galissonnière* was therefore exceptionally complete, with two long-range systems (Malafon and the Alouette 11 helicopter) and two shorter-range systems (the 305mm mortar and the L3 torpedo).

SONARS

To complement this extensive array of new anti-submarine equipment a new generation of sonars was developed.

Sound conditions in the Mediterranean are unusual in a number of respects. Because it is shallower than the Atlantic and the Pacific much stronger signals are possible (albeit over shorter distances) in the bottom bounce mode. Moreover, from April until December there is generally a very shallow surface layer of water that cannot be penetrated by conventional hull-mounted sonars which are restricted to a range of only 2000m in these conditions.

The French solution to these problems was to develop a matching pair of hull-mounted and towed sonars, operating on the same frequency, to cater for every possible tactical situation. The production model of the hull sonar, which is bow-mounted, is designated DUBV 23; the matching variable depth sonat is the DUBV 43.

La Galissonnière was engaged in testing the prototypes for these two sonars throughout the 1960s. Photographs of the ship as completed in 1962 show her with the handling apparatus for the variable depth sonar installed, but not the VDS 'fish' itself. The same photographs reveal a conventional T47/53 bow, suggesting either that the prototype hull sonar had not as yet been installed, or that it had been installed in a conventional hull dome beneath the fore part of the ship.

By the following year the towed sonar was in place, and the stem had been modified to the exaggerated 'clipper' form generally associated with bow-mounted sonars. Modifications to the bow and to the stern associated with the installation of the new sonars increased overall length by 4.2m to 132.8m. *La Galissonnière* did not receive the definitive version of the DUBV 43 towed sonar until the end of the decade, when she underwent an extensive refit to prepare her for active service. In the same refit the 305mm mortar and its magazine were

removed, and a number of minor modifications made. She served as a squadron and divisional flagship in the Mediterranean throughout the 1970s, transferring to the Atlantic in 1981.

COMMAND SHIP CONVERSIONS

In the late 1950s the two former cruisers of the *Attilio Regolo* class, *Chàteaurenault and Guichen*, had been fitted out as command ships for the Mediterranean and Atlantic squadrons. These ships were now nearing the end of their useful lives, and it was decided to replace them by conversions of some of the earlier T47s. From 1960 to 1961 *Surcouf, Cassard* and *Chevalier Paul* were duly taken in hand and refitted for the command mission. The refit involved the rebuilding of the bridge structure, which was extended outwards and forwards to create the additional internal volume necessary to accommodate an admiral's staff. The forward 57mm mounting was removed. Additional accommodation was provided by the construction of a large deckhouse between the after 127mm and 57mm mountings, which extended to the ships' sides and replaced the 'long' anti-ship torpedo tubes. *Cassard* was initially fitted with a flight deck above the stern as an experimental measure, but this was subsequently removed.

These three ships received no further modifications during their service lives, and were the first of the type to be disposed of during the 1970s. *Surcouf,* which was severely damaged in a collision, was broken up in 1971, and *Cassard* and *Chevalier Paul* were stricken 1975–6.

AAW MISSILE CONVERSIONS

The T47s had been designed primarily for the air defence mission, and with the advent of surface-to-air missiles it was natural that they should be prime candidates for conversion. Four units (*Dupetit-Thouars, Kersaint, Bouvet* and *Du Chayla*) were duly taken in hand and were refitted 1961–5 with the American Tartar medium-range missile system.

The conversion involved the removal of all three 127mm mountings, plus the main fire control director and the 'long' anti-ship torpedo tubes. The Tartar system was fitted in place of the after 127mm mountings. The single-arm MK 13 launcher atop its cylindrical magazine replaced 'X' mounting and its associated magazine and hoist. Twin SPG-51 tracker illuminators were mounted on pedestals between the original 57mm mountings, atop a new deckhouse which extended to the sides of the ship. The forward 127mm position was now occupied by a sextuple 375mm Bofors A/S rocket launcher, similar to that fitted in the T53. The bridge was heightened, and the DRBC 31 fire control radar for the 57mm guns was relocated above it. The funnels were also heightened in order to keep the exhaust gases clear of the bridge and the SPG-51 trackers.

New, taller lattice tripod masts were fitted. The foremast continued to carry the DRBV 20A air search antenna, MK 10 AFF and the navigation radar, but there was a new platform for ECM, and a TACAN aerial was fitted on a tall topmast. The mainmast carried a US SPS-39 three-dimensional radar to provide height-finding data for the SPG-51 tracker-illuminators.

From 1968 onwards the Tartar systems installed in these ships received a major update. The SPS-39A 3-D radar was replaced by the SPS-39B model,which incorporated the planar SPA-72 antenna, and a SENIT-2 action information centre was installed in the after end of the bridge structure. The ships could now fire the Standard SM-1 MR missile, which steadily replaced Tartar.

The ships subsequently remained unmodified until the late 1970s, when it was decided that they would be replaced by an air defence version of the C70 type *corvette*. The Tartar system aboard the T47 conversions had been updated and was still in production for the US Navy, thereby guaranteeing the provision of spares and missiles for some time to come. The Marine Nationale therefore took the opportunity to economise on the construction of the C70s by removing the launchers and radars of the T47s and installing them in the new vessels. *Bouvet* duly decommissioned in January 1982, shortly before the first of the C70 AA type was laid down at Lorient, and *Kersaint* followed in December 1983. The other two ships of the sub-group were further modernised in 1979, when the elderly DRBV 20A air search radar was replaced by a DRBV 22A, and the Tartar deckhouse was extended aft to provide additional internal volume. *Dupetit-Thouars* is due to pay off in 1985 and *Du Chayla* in 1987, the dates again corresponding to the projected starting-dates for the third and fourth units of the C70 AA type.

T47 ASW CONVERSIONS

Within ten years of the completion of the first of the T47s, three had undergone conversion to command ships, and four had received the Tartar missile system. This left five ships unmodified, and from 1966 onwards these vessels were taken in hand for an extensive ASW conversion based on experience with the T56 trials ship *La Galissonnière*.

The ships emerged from refit between January 1968 and January 1971 with a much-changed profile. They were completely stripped of their original gun armament and the associated fire control directors, and only the forward (ASW) banks of torpedo tubes were retained. The bridge structure was rebuilt on the modern 'block' pattern, and the funnels were heightened accordingly. The arrangement of the after part of the ship was similar to that of *La Galissonnière*. A large deckhouse containing a Malafon A/S missile magazine was constructed in place of the former 127mm deckhouse and the 'long' anti-ship torpedo tubes, and the Malafon launcher was on the quarterdeck, together with the massive handling gear for the DUBV 43 towed sonar. However, helicopter-handling facilities were not installed, and although this inevitably reduced flexibility in ASW opreations, there can be little doubt that it resulted in a more balanced, less cramped layout for the other weapons systems installed. Whereas the two single 100mm mountings of *La Galissonnière* were concentrated forward of the bridge, in the T47 conversions they were distributed fore and aft, the latter mounting being located atop the deckhouse containing the Malafon

magazine. A second DRBC 32A fire control radar was mounted on a short lattice tower abaft the second funnel, thereby covering the stern arcs and providing a second fire control channel. The revised gun arrangements freed 'B' position for a Bofors 375mm A/S rocket launcher of the same model fitted in the T53s and the T47 Tartar conversions.

DRBV 22A air search and DRBV 50 surface/low-altitude search radars were carried, as in *La Galissonniére*, on a new lattice foremast, the former tripod mainmast being suppressed. A DUBV 23 bow sonar was fitted to complement the DUBV 43 towed sonar. The rebuilt clipper stem associated with this installation was largely responsible for an increase in overall length to 132.5m.

No SENIT action information system was installed and only *Maille Brézé* and *Casabianca* were fitted with TACAN. In 1977 *D'Estrées* had British SCOT satellite communications terminals fitted experimentally atop the bridge structure, and similar systems of French design and manufacture (designated Syracuse) are now being installed on major surface units, but it is unlikely that their installation will extend to the remaining vessels of the T47 type in view of their age.

Of the five T47 ASW conversions *Casabianca* paid off in September 1984.The other units will decommission over the next few years as more ships of the C70 ASW type enter service.

THE T53s

By the end of the 1960s the five ships of the T53 type were in need of a half-life update. *Duperré* had been disarmed in 1967 and was operating as a trials ship (pennant no. A 633) for a large variable depth sonar of a new model which occupied her entire quarterdeck; the other four units had remained essentially unmodified since completion. The construction of new surface vessels for the Marine Nationale had been reduced to a trickle because of expenditure on the SSBN programme, and there were insufficient funds available for a radical AAW or ASW modernisation such as the T47s had received. Updating was therefore limited to the installation of a computer-based SENIT-2 action information system housed in an enlarged bridge structure. *Duperré*, which was still conducting sonar trials, was excluded from this modernisation.

In 1973 *Forbin* was refitted as a training ship to serve alongside the helicopter cruiser *Jeanne d'Arc*. The forward 57mm mounting and the after 127mm mounting were removed and she was fitted with a helicopter flight deck above the stern to enable her to participate in interchanges of personnel and stores with her larger companion. Forbin served in this guise until 1981, when she was stricken and her place taken by one or other of the *avisos escorteurs* of the *Commandant Rivière* class.

Because of the failure to give these ships a thorough modernisation they remained in service only until the late 1970s. *La Bourdonnais* and *Jauréguiberry* were stricken in 1977, and *Tartu* in 1980. Only *Duperré*, which was given an extensive modernisation in 1972–4 following the completion of her sonar trials, survives.

Maille Brézé, an anti-submarine warfare conversion, August 1983.

L&L Van Ginderen

DUPERRÉ

Duperré was the last of the T47/53/56 series to receive a radical modernisation, and whilst her refit was once again for the ASW mission there are fundamental differences between this configuration and that of the T47 conversions which provide a valuable insight into the development of French tactical thinking during this period. The provision of Malafon plus a manned helicopter had not proved successful in *La Galissonniére* because of lack of space. In the T47 conversions the helicopter had been dispensed with in favour of Malafon, but in *Duperré* this decision was reversed. Freeboard aft was considered inadequate for helicopter operations, so a flight deck was constructed at 01 deck level, with a fixed hanger forward of it. The helicopter installation therefore occupies the entire after part of the ship, from just abaft the second funnel to the handling gear for the DUBV 43 variable depth sonar above the stern. The helicopter is the Anglo-French WG 13 Lynx, larger and more effective than the Alouette.

Only a single 100mm mounting is fitted. It occupies 'A' position, forward of a completely rebuilt bridge structure. Single 20mm Oerlikons are mounted on either side of a deckhouse which projects from the forward end of the bridge structure.

Between the funnels a broad shelter deck has been constructed, on which are located four launchers for MM38 Exocet missiles, which are angled out in pairs abreast the fore-funnel. Passive defence against hostile surface-to-surface missiles is provided by two Syllex chaff-dispensers, located on either side of the hangar structure.

As originally completed *Duperré* and her sisters had no 'short' ASW torpedo tubes. Close-range anti-submarine defence is therefore in the form of two catapults for L5 homing torpedoes, each with four reloads. The L5 catapult systems are located in the sides of the hangar structure beneath the hangar floor. The L5 torpedo has a diameter of 533mm, ans is faster than the early L3 with a more sophisticated active/passive homing head. It first entered service in 1967 aboard the AAW *frégates* of the *Suffren* class.

The electronic equipment of *Duperré* is more advanced than that of the T47 conversions, and not all of it had been installed when the ship emerged from refit in 1974. The air search radar was still the DRBV 22A, but the ship was to have received a new surface/low altitude search radar, the DRBV 51. The latter was not available when *Duperré* was refitted, and she received a DRBV 50 as a temporary measure. The 100mm Model 1968 mounting installed is a newer, lighter version of the Model 1953 and it was intended that it should be paired with a new all-digital fire control radar, the DRBC 32C. This radar was not available when *Duperré* completed her refit, and it appears to have been installed only since the ship underwent repairs following damage sustained when she ran aground in 1978.

Duperré's conversion was designed to fit her as a flagship. She therefore has a SENIT-2 action information system incorporated into her enlarged bridge structure. She served as flagship of the Atlantic Fleet from the completion of her refit in 1974 until her grounding in 1978, when she was replaced in that role by the new ASW *frégate De Grasse*. In spite of the modernity of her equipment, it now appears that *Duperré* will decommission at the end of 1985.

HM SUBMARINE E31

Log of her War Service Part 4

by Brian Head

An aerial view of Parkeston Quay, Harwich in 1918. The depot ships *Forth,* in the foreground, *Maidstone* and *Pandora* are moored alongside. *E 31* lies at the bow of *Maidstone.*
HMS Dolphin

MORE MECHANICAL PROBLEMS

On 2 May *E 31* sailed from Harwich at 0800. Two hours later a floating mine was sunk, but she arrived on billet without further incident apart from sighting and challenging three British TBDs. On 3 May a Zeppelin was sighted steering west north west at 0930. Half an hour later she had disappeared from view and *E 31* was able to surface for a W/T broadcast. She remained on surface patrol until 1110 when the steering broke down. Lt Blacklock decided it would be a lot safer to carry out

repairs whilst submerged, so *E 31* dived to rest on the bed of the North Sea. Repairs were reported as completed at 1252 and *E 31* returned to the surface where she remained just long enough to receive a W/T signal and then dive on sighting a Zeppelin. At 1400 a buoy was sighted through the periscope and 45 minutes later a similar buoy was sighted abeam. The probability was that they had been laid by German minesweepers but before investigations could proceed further a German seaplane was sighted and Lt Blacklock deemed it prudcent to remain unseen. This patrol was dogged with equipment problems – a sure sign that *E 31* was in need on a major overhaul after two years at war.

At 0940 on 4 May she was resting on the bottom again at 115ft to effect further repairs to the steering gear. It took until 1818 before she was reported ready again and Lt Blacklock brought *E 31* to the surface at 1900 for a W/T routine. She had been dived since 0725 that day. 5 May passed without incident apart from finding that *E 31* was bottoming in 12 fathoms where the chart showed a depth of 15–16 fathoms. 6 May was notable only for another 2¾ hours spent repairing the hydroplane motor. On 8 May the starboard engine failed and three hours were spent rectifying the fault. Later that evening a British submarine mine was found drifting so that was duly despatched. Another British mine was sunk the following day. Two days later Lt Blacklock was able to return to the buoys sighted on 3 May and he accurately charted their positions as 53°31′N4°3′30″E and 53°31′45″N4°3′30″E. The patrol ended when *E 31* returned to *Maidstone* on 11 May, and half the crew were given four days leave.

INFLUENZA APPEARS
No further patrols were undertaken in May. An experiment was conducted with a smoke sprayer outside the

A closer view of *Maidstone* and her flotilla.
HMS Dolphin

harbour on 18 May and an exercise due to take place on 21 May had to be abandoned because of fog. An exercise with *Melampus* took place on 22 May including a gun action.

That afternoon five hands reported sick with influenza and the next day six more cases were sent ashore. The boat was closed down at 2300 and thoroughly disinfected. The next day a further 11 members of the crew were sick, including ERA Mullins who had to be sent to the depotship sick bay.

It was not until 28 May that there were sufficient fit members of the crew for Lt Blacklock to take *E 31* to sea for an exercise attack with *C 21*. On 29 May there was another exercise with *Melampus*.

HARRASSMENT BY AIRCRAFT AND MINES
On 3 June *E 31* left Harwich at 0945 for her 38th War patrol. The intention was to observe whether enemy minesweepers were working in *E 31*'s patrol area. There was a warning that German aircraft could be expected in positions 53°39′N4°20′E and 53°48′N4°20′E. This warning was to prove amply justified, one attack being made in almost exactly the first position given. It was perhaps symptomatic of how warfare was developing that on this

patrol *E 31* was frequently harrassed by German aircraft. There also seemed to be an ever increasing number of floating mines swept from their moorings and a danger to either side not to mention non-combatants.

On the second day out *E 31* was put down twice – by a Zeppelin and then by two seaplanes. On 5 June a German mine was sunk at 0510, a British submarine mine at noon followed shortly after by a German mine and then at 1432 an old-type Bar-top British mine. In between times *E 31* was forced to make a hurried dive by a German seaplane.

The next morning, at 0500, again an old British Bar-top mine had to be sunk. Shortly afterwards three seaplanes were sighted and a rapid dive executed. Another British mine was sunk that afternoon and two more seaplanes caused a rapid descent to 60ft at 1925. On 7 June a Zeppelin was sighted at 0530 resulting in *E 31* returning to periscope depth but at 2130 Lt Blacklock decided to surface whilst a defect in the steering gear was repaired. This took until 0245 next morning and *E 31* remained stopped on the surface until the repair was completed.

Whilst on the surface the next day three seaplanes nearly caught *E 31* by a classic attack out of the sun. A rapid dive to 90ft was made whilst three bombs exploded close by. Luckily they were small bombs as *E 31* was 'bracketed' – one astern, one on the port bow and one on the starboard quarter, at 30 second intervals – in position 53°32′N4°8′E.

On 9 June *E 31* was under constant harrassment by seaplanes. Twice during the forenoon Lt Blacklock was obliged to avoid attacks by diving to 60ft and there were two further attacks in the afternoon. In between times, a German mine was sunk. These attacks took place in the vicinity of 53°32′N4°8′E.

The rest of the patrol was uneventful and *E 31* returned to Harwich at noon on 12 June. No mention is made of the German minesweepers which had been thought to be operating in the area.

UNDERWATER HUNT

Whilst half the crew were given leave, the suspect steering gear was refitted and other repairs made to the engines. Torpedo exercises with destroyers and another submarine took place on 19, 24 and 26 June. On 1 July *E 31* sailed again for another patrol with the intention of trying to catch a German minelayer. At 1855 that evening, whilst on the surface for a W/T routine, the conning tower of a hostile submarine was sighted. A British convoy with a destroyer escort was in the vicinity but Blacklock quickly dived his boat and prepared to attack.

In May 1980 Captain Blacklock CBE, BSC, RN (Rtd) told the writer how he sent Ordinary Telegraphist Head and Lt Stephen King-Hall to the hydrophone cabinet to try and pick up the sound of the U-boat's motors and get a directional bearing. It was his intention to ram the enemy underwater if he could get close enough.

King-Hall was later to become better known as an MP, writer and BBC broadcaster but in 1918 he was a torpedo specialist at Harwich and was taking a trip in a submarine 'for experience'. He described this particular experience in his autobiography 'My Naval Life' (but refers to *E 29* instead of *E 31*) and freely admits that the thought of *E 31*'s fate if the ramming took place was never very far from his mind! Ronnie Blacklock, on the other hand, said his only thought was to close with the enemy. Months of boring, frustrating patrols with little chance of positive enagement with the enemy had made him determined to try by whatever means he could. However, although the enemy was heard on the hydrophones physical contact was not made.

At 1945, Blacklock brought *E 31* to the surface – and immediately a destroyer was sighted approaching at high speed. Whilst *E 31* was answering the challenge signal, the U-boat also surfaced, about five miles away. The destroyer identified herself as HMS *Teazer* and *E 31* reported the U-boat's presence.

The U-boat dived about three minutes later and was obviously making for the convoy. *E 31* closed the convoy and gave warning of the enemy submarine's presence. About an hour later approximately 25 depth charge explosions were heard, so the U-boat had obviously been detected. There had been an escort of five anti-submarine motor launches and destroyers.

The next evening *E 31* surfaced at 2145 and immediately sighted a U-boat on the surface. Both submarines dived but, again, contact was lost. Whether this was the same enemy submarine as *E 31* had tried to sink the previous day, is not know, but it is possible *E 31* and the U-boat were sharing the same billet as it lay near the East Coast convoy routes. No U-boat sinking was claimed by the convoy escort.

The depth charge was not allied to a sophisticated sonar detection system such as was developed between the Wars, so it was very much a matter of the surface vessels listening on a primitive hydrophone and releasing depth charges if underwater noises were identified as being made by a submarine. This was a new hazard for a submarine and it was 1917 before the depth charge became widely used. The effect on those subjected to a depth charge attack was recorded in a report by Lt Cdr V J Cooper, then CO of *J 2*, after having been depth charged by our own forces on 6 August 1917. Ships of the 2nd Light cruiser squadron under Commodore Walter Cowan in HMS *Caledon* mistook *J 2* for a U-boat. Only three charges were dropped, the last of which put out all the lights in the boat. Men in the steering flat aft, were lifted off their feet by the first explosion. *J 2* bottomed in 125ft and stayed there for seven hours.

Lt Cdr Cooper reported 'There is no doubt that an experience of this nature is most trying as one can only wait and listen in silence and darkness without being able to strike back. I do not think that in the majority of cases there is any permanent moral effect, although it might perhaps affect highly-strung individuals. It was noticed that for a day or two afterwards some men started on being wakened from sleep or on being touched suddenly and unexpectedly by other persons. In my own case I felt at the time I would much rather remain on the surface and engage the enemy, however large, and at all costs, than endure the strain of a further similar experience. I think to to some extent one's

An overhead view of the submarine minelayer *E 34*, showing the minelaying tubes.

Author's Collection

judgement is most likely to be adversely affected for several days after an occurrence of this kind and that overcautiousness or rashness might result. . . The behaviour of the men was admirable. Having been assured by their officers all was well, they settled down to read and otherwise occupy themselves'. A very perceptive report.

Submariners, however, would have to learn new tactics to evade such attacks and endure far more testing experiences than *J 2*, although no doubt the first time for everyone was no different from that felt by Lt Cdr Cooper's crew.

The increase in anti-submarine air patrols by the Germans almost brought them a success on 6 July when Lt Blacklock's former command *C 25* was caught on the surface in the English Channel, off Harwich, by five German seaplanes. Lt Bell, the commanding officer, and two other men, were killed in the initial machine-gun attack on the bridge and Leading Seaman Barge was severely wounded. As he lay dying he told the second-in-command to dive the boat and not to worry about him. However, Barge was brought down into the control room – where he died. Unfortunately, another body jammed the conning tower hatch and the only solution was to remove the leg of this body (literally) which was jammed in the lower hatch. It was inviting death by machine-gun bullets to venture into the conning tower to heave the body out of the hatch. Two men were killed by bullets penetrating the conning tower whilst trying to do this. The leg was duly amputated by Chief E R A Crawford with a hacksay and knife and the hatch closed, but by now *C 25* was full of holes and the main motors were

out of action, so the boat could not be dived. Being an old type of boat the bullets had easily pierced the pressure hull. Rescue was at hand, however, when *E 51* arrived on the scene and drove off the attackers with her 12 pounder gun. *C 25* was then taken in tow and brought in to Harwich. The interior was in a shocking state after Crawford's surgery and the hail of machine gun bullets. Had the German seaplanes been armed with bombs, as when they attacked *E 31*, the story might have had a different ending. They had been on the return journey, however, from a bombing raid on Lowestoft.

LIEUTENANT BLACKLOCK LEAVES E 31

E 31 returned to Harwich on 3 July and this proved to be Lt Blacklock's last patrol as her commanding officer. *E 31* was now to have a refit in Sheerness Dockyard and Lt Blacklock was offered command of *E 45*, a minelayer.

Minelayers were thought to be a high-risk venture although their patrols were often of short duration since their employment required them to go in, lay their mines, and return to base ready for the next trip. Six E-class boats were built as minelayers and two were lost in action – possibly as a result of accidents with their own mines.

E 31 went into dock on 5 July and Lt Dudley Peyton-Ward took over command on 16 July when Lt Blacklock left the boat. This was Lt Peyton-Ward's second command as a submariner. He had been Mentioned in Despatches in 1917 following 145 days on patrol during 17 cruises totalling 19,000 miles. He had been 1st Lt of *G 2* at Blyth and CO of *C 8*. Lt Chapman was relieved as navigator by Lt Andrew Christie RNR. *E 31* remained in dock at Sheerness until 22 September. Her engines were taken out and a major overhaul carried out on all her equipment including the suspect steering gear.

Diesel engines fitted in British submarines in World War I were often unreliable. As a slow speed motive power for factories, the Diesel engine was very effective. However, there were numerous engineering difficulties when converting it to a high speed marine-type engine. Stresses in material were greatly increased and cracked cylinders, pistons and cylinder heads were the main problem.

The Diesel engine had first been introduced into British submarines in 1910. Its fuel consumption per horse-power was about half as much as that of the petrol engine and since it used crude oil it was both cheaper and safer than petrol, which was used to drive the A, B, and C class submarines. What was ideally required was a lightweight engine with high rotative speed developing maximum power within a minimum space. This ideal did not materialise in marine Diesel engines. World War II submarines were not very different in terms of motive power, from their predecessors of the E class, although their Diesel engines were more reliable.

On 24 September, *E 31* left Queenborough Pier at Sheerness and returned to Harwich with TB114 as escort. The next week was occupied with further maintenance work and preparing the boat for active service again, with its complete new team of officers.

THE LAST LAP

1 October saw four boats from the Harwich Flotilla – *L 10*, *E 56* (Lt C P Satow), *E 29* (Lt A M Carrie) and *E 31* – sailed for Heligoland Bight. Naval Intelligence believe there was a chance of five or six U-boats assembling during the afternoon and evening of 2 October in position 55°5′N4°15′E in readiness to be escorted through the minefields into the Bight during the night. There was also the possibility of a Fleet action in the Bight and constant W/T watch was to be maintained whilst on the surface.

In the event, no U-boats were sighted and *L 10*, one of our latest boats, under the command of Lt Alfred Whitehouse, failed to return. *E 31* returned to the *Maidstone* on 4 October. Torpedo and gun exercises were carried out on 8 October and experiments with grendades on 10 October.

The war was now rapidly drawing to a close but *E 31* still had two more operations to go. Starting on 11 October, she had an uneventful eight-day patrol, sighting, but not sinking, two mines, and returned to *Pandora* on 18 October. Half the crew were given four days leave on 19 October. Repairs were required to the Diesels but she went to sea again for torpedo exercises on 31 October.

On 5 November, *E 31* sailed from Harwich on her 42nd and last War patrol. The only incidents recorded on this patrol largely concerned the ceaseless struggle with the elements. After calm seas for the first part of the patrol, strong winds were blowing by 7 November. A strong gale with high seas was recorded at 2000 on 10 November, and 11 November, that memorable day of 1918, began with *E 31* on the surface trying to keep a W/T watch in the gale. At 0100 her auxiliary aerial was carried away. Raising the big 30ft masts carried fore and

aft for the main aerial was not thought desirable in the prevailing conditions, so a second auxiliary aerial was rigged. At 0230, that too, was carried away, so the main aerial was now raised. Twenty minutes later that had gone too. Another temporary aerial was rigged. Heavy spray was breaking over the boat and one can just imagine the appalling conditions in which the men were working in the confined space of the bridge and below, with the boat rolling and plunging and drenching spray breaking over those on the bridge and showering down on those in the control room below.

In his patrol report Lt Peyton-Ward noted at 0540 that no W/T signal had been received. Not very surprising in the circumstances. The auxiliary aerial was finally repaired at 1115 that morning when *E 31* surfaced for the all-important W/T routine, but it wasn't until 1757 that evening that the long-awaited final recall signal was received.

At 1400 on 12 November *E 31* was reported as all fast alongside *Maidstone*. The War was over.

RETURN TO THE PEACE TIME NAVY

The next few months must have felt slightly unreal to men who had spent much of the previous four years living from day to day and experiencing periods of nerve-biting tension. The Harwich submarines had suffered many casualties – nearly one third of their boats lost including most of the crews.

Now the German U-boats began to come in to surrender and the River Stour became lined with U-boats moored in rows. Some were to be turned over to the Allied powers for trials and evaluation purposes. The others would be scrapped.

Until decisions were made concerning disposal, the U-boats were put on a 'care and maintenance' basis. Their crews were returned to Germany. One of *E 31*'s tasks was to charge the batteries of various U-boats from time to time, so on 28 November, for example, she was alongside *U 155* with her Diesels running and delivering a charge to *U 155*'s batteries. On 3 December she was alongside *U 90* for the same purpose. However, on 12 December, *E 31* went into dock at Ipswich for engine repairs and replacement of cracked propellor shafts. She left the dock on 21 December but was back again the following month on 14 January 1919 with more engine trouble. *E 31* returned to Harwich on 25 January and continued in her role of 'mothering' U-boats. *U 130*, *UB 97*, *UB 84*, *UB 138*, *U 3*, *UB 121*, *UB 51*, *UB 76* all appear in the Log. The ex-German repair ship *Cyklops* was also at Harwich and so was a German Pressure Dock used for testing a submarine's capacity to withstand pressure at depth.

On 23 February *E 31* escorted in *U 25*, one of the oldest boats sent across from Germany.

Lt Christie left the boat in February as all RNR officers were being released to return to their normal peacetime occupations. The only incident noted over the next few months was a four day visit to the Floating Dock to repair leaking rivets. In June 1919 Lt Cdr David W Fell relieved Lt Peyton-Ward and suddenly things reverted to the previous year's routine. On 10 June *E 31* prepared to go to war again. The hands were employed preparing torpedoes and the next day six torpedoes were hoisted in.

On 17 June a gun and diving exercise was carried out. The *Maidstone* flotilla was being brought to readiness because of Allied intervention in Russia. A number of boats were sent to the Baltic and Commander Max Horton (later Admiral SiR Max Horton KCB, DSO, C-in-C Western Approaches in World War II) took command of the flotilla.

In the event, *E 31* did not go to war. Instead, on 30 June the *Maidstone* and her submarines took passage to Plymouth for the official Peace celebrations. At 2015 on 1 July, *E 31* secured alongside *Arrogant* at Devonport, thus renewing an association of 1917 when *Arrogant* had been depot ship for *E 31* and *E 52* when they were operating against U-boats slipping through the Dover Barrage.

19 July 1919 was recorded in the log as the Official Peace Day. On 27 July *E 31* arrived back at Harwich.

Life continued very much in a quiet routine enlivened only by a major railway strike on 27 September when the torpedo gunner's mate was landed to work on the power station at Parkeston. On 30 September a petty officer and four hands, constituting a volunteer party, were landed to unload a ship at Parkeston Quay which was being delayed by the rail strike.

EPILOGUE

Lt Leathes was relieved as 1st Lt in September by Sub-Lt Ewart G Roberton. To all intents and purposes *E 31*'s active career was now at an end and in November 1919 she joined many other boats in Reserve. They were moored in Haslar Creek and other 'trots' in Portsmouth Harbour before finally being disposed of to the breakers. *E 31* was sold in September 1922 to Youngs at Sunderland for breaking.

Many of the crews joined the new H and L class submarines now coming into service, some of which would see active service in World War II. Having twice been Mentioned in Dispatches Lt Blacklock received the Distinquished Service Cross in October 1918 and went back to the Baltic in 1919 as C O of *L 12*. He was on patrol with Lt Cdr C M S Chapman DSC commanding *L 55* when the latter was sunk by Bolshevik forces in June 1919. Chapman was also a veteran of the Baltic having been 1st Lt of *E 9* under Max Horton.

Ronnie Blacklock later became Captain of the Submarine flotilla at Devonport and Captain of HMS *Dolphin*, the home of the Submarine Service. Unfortunately he was invalided out of the Navy just prior to World War II, before he could achieve Flag rank, as he was clearly destined to do. He returned to duty during World War II, being put in charge of the Navy's welfare services – a post for which his personality and energy undoubtedly fitted him. His efforts were recognised by the CBE at the end of hostilities, when he retired for a second time. Still very interested in all things connected with Submarines, he contributed to a BBC interview when the old *Holland 1* was found by divers off the Eddystone Light in 1981. As a Sub-Lt he had actually been to sea in Holland

boats and *Holland 1* in particular.

He recorded the story of his naval life for the Royal Navy's Submarine Museum archives on his 90th birthday.

Dudley Peyton-Ward retired as a Captain at the end of World War II, also with the CBE, having served on the staff of Flag Officer Submarines. After leaving *E 31*, he commanded *L 7* on the China station and was invalided home with suspected TB. Happily it was not a serious illness and he actually fought a duel (contrary to KR & AIs) when in Hungary with the Danube flotilla of River gunboats in 1923. Captain Peyton-Ward died in July 1976.

'Ferdie' Feilman had an unfortunate ending to his career, due to a weakness for drink. He was relieved of his command of *K 14* four months after his appointment and returned to General Services to command a flotilla of motor launches. When Ronnie Blacklock took over *E 31* in February 1917 he found that the boat was in a poor state of discipline and general cleanliness. Too gentlemanly to say so, he plainly felt this had been the responsibility of his predecessor.

Morice Blood went on to achieve a command – *H 52* – in 1922 but he retired from the Navy at his own request in January 1927 at the age of 29. Captain Blacklock thought very highly of Morice Blood.

In an unpublished memoir of his Naval career, Ronnie Blacklock described an incident where he was on the bridge one night in the Heligoland Bight. As *E 31* surfaced for a battery charge, Lt Blacklock sighted a small patrol vessel nearby, so quickly dived again. A game of hide and seek ensued and on one of the spells when *E 31* was on the surface, Ronnie Blacklock suddenly became aware that he was the only one on the bridge and that *E 31* was submerging without any orders from him. The sea was almost level with the bridge before he had got into the conning tower and not been swept overboard. The lower lid had been clipped shut and with the sea pouring into the conning tower, Blacklock, by a superhuman effort just managed to get the upper hatch closed and clipped down. He then fell unconscious to the bottom of the conning tower.

The noise of his fall made Morice Blood realise his CO was still on board. He quickly drained down the conning tower, opened the lower hatch and dragged Lt Blacklock into the Control Room. What had happened was that one of the crew coming down from the bridge pressed the klaxon alarm by mistake and Morice Blood, in accordance with his Captain's standing orders, immediately dived the boat. With the water coming down the conning tower he assumed that Lt Blacklock had been washed overboard so closed the lower lid and continued to dive.

The sequel to this incident occurred when Ronnie Blacklock went on leave on return from his patrol. Staying at his London club, a passing car sounded its horn in the early hours of the morning and he awoke to find himself rushing downstairs in his pyjamas.

Lt Nicholas Manley joined Submarines in April 1915. After leaving *E 31* in July 1917 he joined the 2nd Flotilla based in the Tyne with the *Bonaventure,* where

1

2

3

4

1 Bow tubes of *E 48*.
Author's Collection

2 Fore ends of *E 48*.
Author's Collection

3 The beam torpedo space on *E 31*, looking forward. The tubes are clearly visible.
Author's Collection

4 Members of the crew of *E 31*. The author's father, Ordinary Telegraphist Charles E Head, is standing on the left of the group.
Author's Collection

The crews of *E 31*, *E 53* and *E 56* watch the surrender of U-boats at Harwich in November 1918. *E 31* is nearest the camera.

From the collection of the late Cdr K M Fardell RN

he commanded *C 12*. Lt Manley was only the second Royal Navy submarine commanding officer to have been promoted from the lower deck. It is a fascinating commentary on the importance then attached to social accomplishment to note that in the periodic reports made on submarine officers it was felt necessary to observe that Lt Manley's conversation and table manners were good and he was well self-educated. No such observations were thought necessary on his colleagues who had reached their present station in life by a more conventional path.

He was regarded as a very sound officer with a thorough knowledge of his job, keen and efficient. In October 1918, *C 12* was sunk in an accidental collison in the Humber estuary. *C 12* was proceeding on the surface when her main motors failed. Out of control, she was swept broadside on, by a strong ebb tide, against a destroyer's bows. As a consequence, *C 12* was badly holed. Lt Manley ordered all hands on deck as he could see the submarine was sinking. When the last man was out of the boat, he and his 1st Lt (Lt GHS Sullivan) went below, clipping the conning tower hatch over their heads. They then investigated the damage, despite most of the lights having gone out and chlorine fumes filling the boat. By now, *C 12* was on the bottom and it was obvious the two officers would not be able to bring the

submarine to the surface. Climbing into the conning tower, they shut the lower hatch and flooded the tower. When the pressure exceeded that of the sea, they opened the upper conning-tower hatch and swam to the surface. As a result of the information they were able to give the salvage experts, *C 12* was later raised. As an example of cool courage and professional competence, this incident was outstanding.

Apart from receiving the 'appreciation' of The Lords Commissioners of the Admiralty, both officers were also recommended for accelerated promotion. Unfortunately, Lt Manley had to retire from the Navy in 1920 at the age of 34, for health reasons. It seems likely that the after-effects of the somewhat harrowing experience in the *C 12* must have taken their toll.

The Submarine Service which had been an untried weapon in August 1914 had come of age by 1918. The East Coast flotillas had replaced the inshore squadrons of Nelson and Collingwood in the watch across the North Sea. It was essential that close observation be kept on the movements of the German High Seas Fleet and this was done by the Submarine Service. In the early days of the War, they worked close inshore but prudence later dicated a safer distance be maintained. Aided by the other twentieth century infant – wireless – the submarine could report and be directed in a way that those earlier admirals would have envied. It was a long and monotonous waiting and watching in all weathers in boats that prior to 1914 had never been subjected to such stresses – or indeed thought capable of withstanding them, except by a few visionaries. Neither was the endurance of the human element a known quantity in August 1914.

Nor must those other flotillas be forgotten, who kept their patrols in the North Atlantic waiting for the chance to sink a U-boat engaged in commerce-raiding – or those who endured the Northern Winters and continued to deny the Germans unrestricted use of the Baltic despite the troubles of the Russian Revolution. Or patrolled the Adriatic off the coast of Yugoslavia and penetrated the Turkish defences into the Sea of Marmara and the harbour of Constantinople itself.

Their glimpses of the enemy were few, their losses by mine and anti-submarine forces were many. The Submarine Service suffered a higher rate of casualties than any other branch of the three Services in World War I.

It is often forgotten that the submarine of 1914–18 was not an ideal craft from the navigator's point of view –

yet more accurate navigation was required in these craft than in any other type of ship. The part played by those highly professional seamen, the Merchant Seamen officers in the Royal Naval Reserve, cannot be too highly praised – yet today, save for a few, they are but names in official records and rare indeed were their rewards except of a job well done.

The officers and men were all volunteers and, certainly in the case of the latter, the pick of the Royal Navy. Despite the hardships and dangers, one can rarely find an instance of an individual returning to General Service for reasons other than health.

The standard had been set for a later conflict and some of the ratings would be at sea again 21 years later off those same North Sea coastlines in submarines, some of which had been almost as long in the service as the men themselves. Therein lies a theme for another 'biography'.

As & As

GRAF ZEPPELIN (*Warship* 33) from M J Whitley, Wolverhampton.

Following part 1, I have received some correspondence which could usefully be put in the A's and A's column.

1 Gerd-Dietrich Schneider of Bremerhaven, former commander of the 8th Artillerie Landings Flotilla tells me that wartime talk was that the main armament intended for *Graf Zeppelin* eventually ended up in coastal batteries, possibly in the Ostend area. Also a high ramp was built on the quayside at Bremerhaven in order that aircraft could be loaded directly onto the flight deck and avoid crane use. Whilst his flotilla was evacuating Swinemunde, he suggested that his landing craft(gun) be used to tow the incomplete carrier west but this was not agreed to by the local naval commander.

2 Erwin Sieche has sent details of a book about *Graf Zeppelin* written by her designer about which I was previously unaware. Fortunately it does not disagree with my work, but some extra points are interesting:

(A) The internal longitudinal water-tight subdivision in the machinery spaces was deficient since the wing auxiliary machinery spaces outside the longitudinal bulkheads could not be fully sealed off from their adjacent boiler rooms inboard. The reason for this lay in the fact that the boiler rooms had been made too small and vital connected machinery had to be installed outside them. This could well account for her loss, if as surmised, she was mined postwar.

(B) The 15cm armament was doubled because prewar destroyers could successfully attack capital ships. This stemmed from 12.7cm armed destroyer attacks on the

radio-controlled target ship *Hessen,* an old pre-dreadnought battleship.

(C) Restrictions in the overall size of the island caused severe cramping of its installations and cabins. When the decision was made to carry a flag officer, provision of cabins for the staff officers was very difficult. Ship's company spaces were also cramped.

(D) To provide fire control for the 15cm guns on after arcs the aftermost flak director carried a 5cm range finder.

M J Whiteley

NORDENFELT SUBMARINES (Warship 32) from C de Saint Hubert, Kenya

Referring to Mr John Maber's very interesting article on the Nordenfelt submarines, recently published in Warship, may I be allowed to point out that d'Equevilley was not French but Spanish (albeit of French origin) and that the submarines he designed and built were not of the Nordenfelt type (*).

Raimundo Lorenzo d'Equevilley-Montjustin studied naval engineering in Paris and was one of Maxime Laubeuf's collaborators when the latter built the *Narval,* a submarine far in advance of its time.

A few years later d'Equevilley designed a submarine of his own but the French Admiralty did not to have the boat built.

D'Equevilley then submitted the plan to Germaniawerft, Kiel (established in 1865 as Norddeutsche

Schiffbau, AG and recently – 1896 – acquired by Krupp) which decided to have a submarine built on spec. This boat was acquired by Russia in 1904 and served in the Imperial Russian Navy as the *Forelle*.

In 1905, three larger d'Equevilley submarines were delivered to Russia by Germaniawerft. These were the *Karp, Karas* and *Kambala* of 205 tons.

The German Navy then also became interested in submarines and their first submarine, the U-1, delivered in 1906 was designed by d'Equevilley and built by Germaniawerft.

The first submarines of the Russian and the German Navies were thus designed by a Spanish naval engineer, while the first boats of the Royal Navy were designed by John P Holland, an American of Irish origin!

I hope this information may prove of interest to you.

(*) Enrique Dupy de Lome, a Spanish dipolmat of French origin was Minister in Washington from 1896 to 1898, a crucial time in Spanish-American relations. Another member of the family, Stanislas Dupuy de Lome, was the French Navy's DNC from 1857 to 1869 and the designer of the world's first screw ship-of-the-line (*Napoleon*, 1850) and of the world's first sea-going armoured ship, the armoured frigate *Gloire*, launched in 1859.

A NAVAL CURIOSITY OF WORLD WAR ONE

The SS *Liemba* must have been one of the most unlikely warships never to have sailed the seven seas, for her war and peace was entirely on Lake Tanganika.

Built in Berlin just before the Great War she was shipped in pieces to Dar-es-Salaam and railed up to Kigama on the eastern shore of Lake Tanganika. There she was re-assembled and launched not for cargo/passenger service, but to take control of the Lake, which bordered on the Belgian Congo and part of British Northern Rhodesia.

Renamed the *Graf von Gotzen* she was a 1500 ton vessel capable of carrying one battalion the length of the lake, 400 miles, in two days. In 1915 she was equipped with a 102mm gun from the German cruiser *Konigsberg*, then bottled up in the Rufiji river delta and was joined by two smaller vessels, the 150 ton *Hedwig von Wissmann* armed with two 6 pounder Hotchkiss guns, and the 53 tons tug *Kingami*, which had one 6 pounder.

The smaller vessels were sunk in late 1915 and early 1916 by Belgian and British vessels under Lt-Cmdr Spicer-Simpson. However, Spicer-Simpson's flotilla allowed the *Gotzen* to cover the rescue of the German garrison of the fort of Bismarcksburg and threaten the allied forces, then advancing into German East Africa.

Though the *Gotzen* appears to have taken no further part in hostilities her mere existence agitated the allies sufficiently for Belgian aircraft to bomb her at Kigama in mid 1916. The vessel was claimed to be sunk, and although this was not true her active service came to an end soon after, when the German General Lettow-Vorbeck relieved her of the 102mm gun.

Weeks later, in July 1916, Belgian troops entered Kigama to find the *Gotzen* scuttled. Her machinery had been carefully greased, in anticipation of raising her after the war, which the Germans expected to win.

In fact she was raised by the British, in I believe, 1922, refurbished and put into service in the role originally conceived for her, plying the Lake between Kigama and Zambia until her retirement in 1970. Her other appearance on the world stage was as the victim of Humphrey Bogart and Katherine Hepburn in the film of C S Forester's '*African Queen*'.

Brian Blancharde, Bristol

JUNYO and HIYO
by Hans Lengerer

MODIFICATIONS AND ALTERATIONS DURING THE WAR

The following is a brief summary of the modifications and alterations that took place during the war. In order to save space, modifications with regard to aircraft complement are dealt with in table 3, whilst table 4 gives a summary of the radar installations, and table 5 lists the reinforcement of light AA weapons and the installation of rocket launchers.[11]

Alterations to ventilation of machinery spaces, emergency ways for machinery personnel, fire preventing measures, etc, are summarised as follows. When the ships received the second type 21 radar on the flight deck and additional 25mm triple mounts the ventilation of the machinery spaces was altered and reinforced. Before the Battle for Midway ventilation was only on one side of the ship; the side opposite the funnel. During this battle four Japanese CVs were bombed and at least two of them heavily damaged on the side on which the ventilation system was installed. Hot fumes and fire vented into the machinery spaces and were responsible for the deaths of the engine room crews. In order to take air from ventilation ducts on the undamaged side a ventilation system was installed on the funnel side. Moreoever a number of openings were cut as an emergency outlet for the crew in the top part of the longitudinal middle bulkhead. This measure allowed them to escape on the side not yet damaged. Of course, the watertight integrity of the bulkhead had to be sacrificed. The emergency way built through the ventilation ducts to the uppermost deck also assisted the engine room crews to escape. All these modifications were based on the lessons of the Battle for Midway.

On *Junyo* until June 1944 all bulkheads built from wood and other wooden articles were removed as a fire

SS *Liemba* in 1970.
Author's Collection

precaution. On this ship fire prevention measures to safeguard the crew were carried to extremities. To mention only a few examples:

- painting and linoleum was removed
- in the mess rooms only a few tables and sofas were left
- the sanitary facilities were stripped to the bare essentials
- the crew berthed and messed in the same compartments, mats were placed on the deck to provide living accommodation (the hooks formerly provided for swinging hammocks were removed together with the hammocks).

During repair work, July to August 1944, (in the Battle for the Marianas *Hiyo* was sunk, *Junyo* received bomb damage) the support of the funnel was altered and the superstructure near the signal-mast located on the after part of the funnel/island bridge, was heightened by one step.

Before the sinking of CV *Taiho*, ventilation was provided for the cofferdam surrounding the gasoline tanks. Both supply and exhaust ventilation were installed, the system serving the cofferdam, serving no other spaces except the gasoline system pump room. After the loss of *Taiho* during the A-go operation from a gasoline explosion some hours after torpedoing, the spaces around the gasoline tanks were filled with concrete to provide more protection, as already mentioned. With the installation of concrete, the ventilation for these spaces was removed. The reinforcement of the ventilation of the hangars was most probably carried out at the same time.

Camouflage against submarine attacks was painted on the sides of the *Junyo* until October 1944. After this time, it is unlikely that further modifications and alterations were carried out.

Junyo with the cruiser *Chikuma*.
Jurgen Peters

TABLE 6 GENERAL DESCRIPTION OF THE HIYO AT THE TIME OF COMPLETION

1 PRINCIPAL DIMENSIONS

Length above all	219.32m
Length at trial waterline	about 215.30m
Length between perpendiculars	206.00m
Maximum beam	26.70m
Maximum beam at trial waterline	26.70m
Depth – from base line to flight deck at side midship section	21.79m
Depth – from trial waterline to flight deck	13.64m
Displacement, trial condition	27,500 metric ts
Draft, trial condition, fore	8.15m
aft	8.15m
middle	8.15m
Full load displacement	29,471br ts
Mean draft – full load condition	8.60m
Standard displacement	24,140br ts
Length of the flight deck	210.30m
Beam of the flight deck – fore	16.00m
– maximum	27.30m
– aft	25.00m
Fuel oil capacity full load condition	41,00br ts
Cruising radius	10,000sq m at 18kn
Designed speed	25.50kts
Shaft Horsepower	56,250shp

2 ORDNANCE EQUIPMENT

12.7cm L/40 type 89 HA twin mounts	6 (12 barrels)
25mm mL/100 type 96 MG triple mounts	8 (24 barrels)
Bullet elevators for HA, vertical	6
horizontal	2
Bullet elevators for MG, vertical	4
Number of rounds for HA (each barrel)	12/250[1]
Number of rounds for MG (each barrel)	10/2600[1]
HA fire directors type 94	2
MG fire directors type 95	4
Training gear (gun) for HA	1
Antigas system (gasoline gas detectors)	1set
Rifles, pistols, etc.	1 set

[1]first numeral = exercise rounds, second numeral = action rounds

3 AIRCRAFT

Fighter type rei no 1	(Zero)	12 + (3)
Bomber type 99	(Val)	18 + (2)
Torpedo bomber type 97	(Kanko)	18 + (0)
Total		48 + (5)

Arrester wires
Type Kure × 9
Arresting motors
Type 3 model 10 × 3
Type 3 model 11 × 1
Crash barriers
Type 3 model 10 (fixed) × 2
?
(transportable) × 2
Bomb capacity
No 80 (800kg) × 54
No 25 (250kg) × 198
No 6 (60kg) × 348
No 3 (39kg) × 240

4 TORPEDOES AND TORPEDO EQUIPMENT

Kampon type air compressor model 3 modific.1	3
Oxygen generator type 94	1
Air compressor type 94	1
Air pressure flasks model 2	17
Oxygen flasks model 2	2
Minesweeping gear composed of	
– small minesweeping gear model1 (modific. 1)	
– Underwater disposal gear model 1	
– No 2 bomb disposal chain (modific. 1)	1 set
Middle paravane model 1 modification 1	2
Torpedoes type 91 modification 2	27

5 NAVIGATING EQUIPMENT

Type Armstrong no 3 gyro compass (double)	1
Type 90 no 3 magnetic compass	1
Type 90 no 3 modification 1 magnetic compass	2
Depth meter – type 99	1
electrical	1
Type 6 no 2 model 1 modification 1 dead reckoning tracer	1
Type 96 modification 1 pitometer log	
Type 91 modification 2 wind intensity transmitter	1
Type 97 modification 1 balloon probe	1
Type 92 modification 1 wind direction transmitter	1

6 OPTICAL EQUIPMENT

Binoculars
12cm High angle binocular	2
12cm binocular	2
12cm High angle binocular (search)	2
8cm High angle binocular (search) (prov)	2
18cm binocular type 13 (surface search)	2
18cm binocular on pedestal (surface sarch)	2
12cm binocular (surface search)	2
12cm binocular (modification)	1
12cm high angle binocular model 13 (for future enemy course)	3
12cm binocular (air search)	
12cm high angle binocular model 5 (air search)	8
Aiming device	
Type 13 No 1 modification 1	4
Type 15 high angle (prov)	4

7 ELECTRICAL EQUIPMENT

Primary Power Plant
AC 230V 6395KVA at 75% power factor
2000KVA turbo generator	3
250KVA turbo generator	1
145KVA diesel generator	1

Secondary power plant
Batteries and MG sets
320 AH – 112 cells no 3 model 1	1 bank
M–G DC 225V 3kW	1
power for Selsyn motors	
Step down transformers	
Power for telephone, motor generators, and batteries	
M–G DC 22V 2.5kW	1
320 AH – 11 cells	2 banks
Searchlight motor generators	
17.6kW at 88V DC	4
15.0kW at 105V DC	

Searchlight
Type 96 110cm searchlight model 1	4

Searchlight director
Type 96 model 2 searchlight director	4

Signal/searchlight
60cm signal searchlight model 2	2

Signal/light
2kW signal lamp	2
Other electrical equipment	1 set

8 RADIO EQUIPMENT

Transmitters
Long wave	2
Short wave	2

Receivers
Long wave	3
Long and short wave	16
Short wave	2

Voice radio
a) Transmitters
Medium wave	2
Short wave	2
Ultra short wave	3

b) Receivers
Medium Wave	2
Short wave	1
Ultra short wave	3

Direction finder
Long wave	4

Wave meter (consisting of Long, Medium, Short, Short, Ultra short wave meters) 1 set
Testing apparatus (Wireless controller) 3

Decoder

Typewriter	4
Underwater phone (suichi choonki)	
(?) Most probable	nil
Radar (dempa tanshingi)	
See table 4	

9 MACHINERY

Main Turbines	2 sets
Shaft horsepower, ahead	56,250
astern	27,000
RPM	170
Number of shafts	2
Diameter of propeller	5.5m
Boiler (3 drum Mitsubishi water tube boiler)	6
Steam pressure	40kg/cm²
Steam temperature	420°C
Auxiliary boilers (Scotch)	2
Steam pressure	10.5kg/cm²
Steam temperature	saturated
Capstan (forward only electric operated)	1
Steering engine (electric-hydraulic operated)	1
Funnel	1

10 PROTECTION

Magazines, deck	25mm DS
sides	25mm DS
Machinery spaces, deck	
side	20 + 25mm DS
Gasoline tank, deck	25mm DS
sides	

11 COMPLEMENT (with flag aboard)

Commissioned officers	54 (7)
Special service officers	36
Cadets	47
Enlisted men	1043
Civil servants	7 (1)
Total	1189 (1214)*
(* if flagship of a squadron)	

12 FITTINGS AND EQUIPMENT

Anchor

Main anchor (bower anchor)	10t × 2
Stream anchor	2.6t × 1 (stern)
Cable for main anchor (80mm, 19 shackles)	× 2
(one shackle = 25m, 19 shackles = 475m)	

System of command steering engine

Telemotor, transmitter and receiver	1 each

Boats

12m motor boat	2
12m motor launch	2
8m motor launch	1
9m cutter	2
6m motor	
13m special service ship (landing craft)	2

Cooling equipment

50,000BTU CO_2 Refrigerator	2

Crane

4ts aircraft crane (tiltable)	1
Boat hoist	2
2.5t motor winch	2

Elevators

14m × 14m	2

book reviews

KREUZER DER US NAVY
Von der Omaha klasse bis zur Long Beach by Stefan Terzibaschitsch.
Published by Koehler 1984. 280mm × 220mm, 348pp, heavily illustrated, index. ISBN 3 7822 0348 8.

Already well known for his work on the United States Navy, Dr Terzibaschitsch has produced a major work on the American cruiser from the 1922 *Omaha* to the first of the nuclear-powered guided missile ships, the startling *Long Beach*, some 118 ships in all. The main element of the book is a superb collection of photographs and plans with a detailed career guide for each ship, details of modifications and tables of weapons and sensor fits. The non-German reader would find few obstacles in the text, once a few points of grammar and the odd technical term were understood. The encouragement offered by the superb illustrations would encourage anyone to attempt the exercise.

This book serves to emphasise the sheer scale of American war production during the Second World War by pointing up the number of 8in and 6in cruisers that were built between 1941 and 1945. This was at a time when other types – aircraft carriers, destroyers and escorts and landing craft – all had a much higher priority. Production power on this scale was the decisive factor in the Pacific war.

Perhaps the most surprising thing about this book is that there should be a sufficient market in Germany for such a luxury production on American Warships.

Andrew Lambert

THE FUTURE OF BRITISH SEAPOWER
Edited by Geoffrey Till
Published by MacMillan December 1984

220mm × 140mm, 265pp, index
ISBN 0 333 37976 4 (£25.00)

In the aftermath of the 1981 Defence Review and the 1982 Falklands Campaign the War Studies Department at King's College, London assembled a conference on the future of British Seapower. This admirable book comprises 36 papers by a variety of well qualified naval and academic authorities. Michael Heseltine opens the book with a defence of Government policy; thereafter almost every aspect of the present and future of Britain as a maritime power is examined.

This is a book that should be read by everyone interested in the Royal Navy in the twentieth century, or in the wider issues of defence. The editor and his contributors are to be congratulated.

Andrew Lambert

CONWAY'S ALL THE WORLD'S FIGHTING SHIPS 1906–1921
Published by Conway Maritime Press
310mm × 216mm, 416pp, 400 photographs, 600 line drawings
ISBN 0 85177 245 5 (£35.00)

This fourth volume in the series of reference works completes one of the publishing events of the decade. No one interested in the First World War will want to be without this book. It combines all the latest research with a cornucopia of illustrations and the highest standards of presentation.

The introduction hints at further volumes for the earlier periods; they will be eagerly awaited.

WINGS AT SEA
A Fleet Air Arm Observer's War 1940–45
by Gerald A Wood
Published by Conway Maritime Press 1985
234mm × 156mm, 272pp, 30 photographs, 5 drawings
ISBN 0 85177 319 2 (£9.50)

This book is justified by the section on the vital strike that crippled the *Bismarck*, in which the author took part. However there is much more here; service in *Ark Royal* being followed by spells in *Victorious* and *Formidable*, along with shore service in North Africa, Scotland and India. A stimulating and enjoyable book.

THE FIRST TEAM
Pacific Air Combat from Pearl Harbour to Midway
by John B Lundstrom
Published by United States Naval Institute Press 1984
260mm × 180mm, 547pp, heavily illustrated, appendices, index, bibliography
ISBN 0 87021 189 7 (£24.50)

Author Lundstrom concentrates on the fighter squadrons of the USN as he builds up the most detailed picture yet of the sea-air war. Despite a welter of detail, personalities and the intricacies of individual dogfights his narrative flow is excellent. Furthermore the theme of

explaining American success by reference to better tactics and certain vital items of equipment is the key to any understanding of the battles. This is a superb book and an encouragement to other authors. Another volume is in preparation.

YANGTZE PATROL
The US Navy in China
by Rear Admiral Kemp Tolley
Published by United States Naval Institute Press 1984
235mm × 155mm, 342pp
ISBN 0 87021 798 4 (£17.95)

Real gunboat diplomacy this. Already a classic, Tolley's book first published in 1971, has been reprinted. It provides a detailed and well researched account of the activities of one of the Great Powers in China before the revolution.

FLAGSHIP HOOD
The fate of Britain's mightiest warship
by Alan Coles and Ted Briggs
Published by Alan Hale 14 February, 1985
269pp 220mm × 140mm, 35 photographs, 4 diagrams, index, bibliography
ISBN 0 70902 024 4 (£10.95)

This book combines an interesting anecdotal study of

the *Hood*'s peacetime career, written by Alan Coles, with Ted Briggs' eyewitness account of her war career. The latter half of the book is of great interest, for the author was a signals rating on the bridge during the bombardment of Mers-el-Kebir and the *Bismarck* action. His version of the final moments of the ship conveys an impression of the stoic qualities of both officers and men. Even though the ship was sinking rapidly there was not a hint of panic; not a word was spoken. There was no loud explosion, but the ship broke in two, and just like the *Invincible* before her the bow section stood up in the water before sinking.

As one of only three survivors, 1400 men were lost and not one of their bodies came to the surface, Ted Briggs clears up several points of debate concerning the conduct of the action. He concludes with a brief and provoking resumé of the tactics used. Admirals Holland and Tovey are both criticised.

Elsewhere his co-author, Alan Coles contends that the reconstruction of the *Hood* was delayed because she was constantly in use as a diplomatic frightener. He argues that this 'gunboat' role was so important from 1935 on that she could not be spared for two years. This ensured that in her final action she was outdated and in poor repair. Thus the great symbol of British maritime power was lost because her value in preserving the peace was more important than her ability to fight.

Andrew Lambert

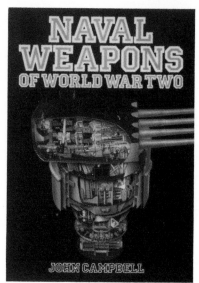